Harvard Studies in Business History

XXVI

Edited by Ralph W. Hidy

Isidor Straus Professor of Business History
Graduate School of Business Administration
George F. Baker Foundation
Harvard University

T. H. Perkins, by Thomas Sully, 1832

# Merchant Prince of Boston

*Colonel T. H. Perkins*, 1764–1854

CARL SEABURG AND STANLEY PATERSON

HARVARD UNIVERSITY PRESS
Cambridge, Massachusetts / 1971

Distributed in Great Britain by Oxford University Press, London
Library of Congress Catalog Card Number 71-165419
SBN 674-56910-5
Printed in the United States of America

To Walter Muir Whitehill

Dean of Boston Historians

# Editor's Foreword

In this biography of Thomas Handasyd Perkins, Carl Seaburg and Stanley Paterson have produced a rarity in recent business history. In vivid, swift-moving prose they have written a pen portrait of a many faceted man, the whole man and not merely the man of business. In the ensuing pages the reader can follow the "merchant prince of Boston" from his antecedents to his descendants, from his early consciousness of the Boston Massacre to events in the administration of Franklin Pierce. With him the reader lives through four conflicts with foreign nation-states, not to mention fires and conflagrations, hurricanes and typhoons, the formation and decline of political parties, successes and failures in business and family ambitions.

To be sure, the authors emphasize the business activities of Colonel Perkins. After all, he was the businessman par excellence of his time. From a beginning of two small legacies and a position as an apprentice clerk in a retail establishment he amassed a fortune of more than a million dollars, largely in the China trade but also through investments in mining, iron-making, quarrying, hotels, and theaters, to mention a few. Before the mind's eye of the reader pass unfortunate and unwise ventures as well as successful ones. Wherever profit beckoned the merchant followed, whether to slaves and sugar in Santo Domingo or opium, sea otters, and tea in Batavia and Canton. The market dictated business behavior in foreign trade, seemingly without any serious questions of morality as interpreted in domestic affairs.

In Boston the colonel is portrayed as the civic leader, patron of the arts, and philanthropist that he was. An active Federalist, he was one of the three men who carried the views of the Hartford Convention to Washington in 1815. An early participant in local militia organizations, he also won elective office on occasion. Numerous projects won his public support, often financial as well; among them were the initial move to fill in Back Bay, the Bunker Hill Monument, the Museum of Fine Arts, and the Massachusetts General Hospital. Of all the Perkins philanthropies undoubtedly the best known remains the Perkins Institute for the Blind. While recording the problems and trials associated with launching and completing both profit and nonprofit ventures, the authors evoke a lively sense of participating in the "passing scene" in Boston, the United States, and the world. The merchant prince lives, as few businessmen have, in print.

June 1971 — Ralph W. Hidy

# Contents

# Illustrations

Money is, in its effects and laws, as beautiful as roses. Property keeps the accounts of the world, and is always moral.

Ralph Waldo Emerson

---

# Merchant Prince of Boston

# Young Tom I 1764–1785

Many of their arses will be laid low before morning.

Mrs. Hugh Montgomery,
March 5, 1770

# I

# Death on the Doorstep

A first-quarter moon was rising. It sparkled in bright cold on the foot or more of snow that had fallen. The tide was high and washed ice chunks round the wharf pilings. Headed home to Bull's Wharf in the South End of Boston, some time after six, James Crawford saw people carrying sticks. They were going, he judged, toward the Town House in King Street. Very great sticks they were, not common walking canes, but pretty large cudgels.

Somewhat later, an out-of-town merchant left the North End to visit Crawford. Crossing the swing bridge over the town dock into the marketplace, he noticed people running every which way. It seemed as if they all had sticks. Uncommon sticks, he thought, like those pulled out of hedges. Alarmed, he was afraid to continue. But outside Faneuil Hall he met a young man who said he would see him safely across town. Going down Green's Lane, where part of the British Twenty-ninth Regiment had barracks, he saw twenty or thirty townspeople together, and the streets as full of commotion as ever he saw in his life.[1]

That Monday night, with the Sunday evening snow storm over and the weather warming, all sorts of people were roaming the streets. There were red-coated soldiers. There were what John Adams was to disparagingly term "saucy boys, negroes and molattoes, Irish teagues and out landish jack tarrs." Even John Adams had walked over to the South End to attend a meeting of his "Clubb."[2]

Yet not all Bostonians went out this Monday evening. Some, like the respectable hat maker Thomas Handasyd Peck, were in the respectable quiet of their homes. Peck lived just a few doors down from the Custom House on King Street, and at the moment all was peaceful there. Peck's five-year-old grandson Thomas Handasyd Perkins, named after him and living with him, was getting ready for bed.* While history happened almost on his doorstep, he would be sound asleep.[3]

The soldiers and townspeople had weathered a year and a half of grievances and frustrations. Since the fall of 1768, when the regiments had first been quartered in Boston, there had been parties and suppers among the officers and gentry of the town, and scuffles and blows between the soldiers and townsfolk. This March weekend had brought matters to a head. The previous Friday a soldier of the Twenty-ninth, sauntering by a ropewalk near his barracks, had been hailed by William Green, one of the ropeman.

"Do you want work?"

Poorly paid as the soldiers were, they were always seizing whatever odd jobs came their way.

"Yes I do, faith."

"Well," laughed Green, "go clean my shithouse."

"Damn you," exploded the soldier, and the two men started to scuffle. A couple of ropemakers came to their mate's aid, and the soldier went off bruised, bleeding, and swearing to get even.[4]

Back he came with half a dozen of his fellows, but twice that many ropemakers turned out. With their large, heavy "wouldering sticks," they "beat them off directly." Shortly, with more recruits, the soldiers returned, rushed into the ropewalk, and a general melee began near

* The odd middle name was once thought to have come from a general of Oliver Cromwell's, but seems to be after Thomas Handasyd who was Lieutenant Governor of Jamaica early in the 18th century and apparently a good enough friend of Thomas H. Peck's father John, that he stood god-father to young Peck. Thus the name was perpetuated in the family and continues down to the present time. If the phonetic spellings of it met with in records are sufficient evidence, it should be pronounced as would the two words "handy side."

the tar-kettle. But the reinforcements proved no match for the murderous swipes of the wouldering sticks in the expert hands of the ropemakers. The soldiers were driven off, and a local constable stepped in and persuaded the ropemakers not to follow them. Here, for the moment, it ended.

But Saturday afternoon, a day of "smart cold," things boiled over again. Three stout grenadiers passing by another ropewalk, taunted some of the apprentices spinning rope. "You damned dogs, don't you deserve to be killed? Are you fit to die?" At first, the youths prudently kept their mouths shut, not being armed. But finally one muttered, "Damn it, I know what a soldier is."

Over came one of the grenadiers and swung at the apprentice, who fended off the blow with his arm. Then the soldier struck at another of the ropemakers and missed. One of the apprentices dashed into a nearby tan-house and came back with two bats. He gave one to a bystander and wickedly flailing the other, soon cleared off the soldiers.

Similar altercations occurred elsewhere. A chimney sweep who knew the soldiers well reported that they had vowed to have revenge on the ropewalk workers. A maid of John Gray's, one of the ropewalk owners, carried this tale to him. Off he bustled to complain to Lieutenant-Colonel Dalrymple, commander of the Fourteenth Regiment.

"Your man," pointed out Dalrymple, "was the agressor."

Gray agreed to fire the offender, and Dalrymple said he would order the soldiers to stay away from the ropewalk. So the matter was settled at the top, but it was straightaway unsettled at the bottom. On Monday morning John Gray fired William Green.

That Monday night, the fifth of March, all was still quiet in King Street when young Tom Perkins went to bed. The first serious encounter took place a few blocks away in Boylston's Alley. A long, narrow alley—"wheelbarrow wide"—it ran from Cornhill to Brattle Street. Almost opposite where it came out on Brattle stood the barracks used by the Fourteenth Regiment, the old Sugar House buildings called Murray's Barracks in derision of the loyalist owner.

Opposite Murray's Barracks lived Dr. Richard Hyrons. He had been listening uneasily that evening to the muffled shouts outside. The sound of people running by, rattling their sticks on fenceposts, alarmed him. Disturbed, he stepped out and heard of the wrangling between soldiers and inhabitants in various parts of the town. Soldiers were going by with bayonets and clubs. As near as he could guess, the main uproar was coming from Dock Square.

Now after eight, it was too dark to make anything out clearly. The moon, its reflections on the snow, and the faint yellow-orange candle glow from the houses were the only light. Jagged shadows stood out suddenly against the snow, shifting, disappearing. Worried, Hyrons went in and shut his door. Perhaps ten minutes later he heard someone run violently through Boylston's Alley. The person ran directly to the barrack gate, shouting, "Town born, turn out! Town born, turn out!" Prudently, Dr. Hyrons locked his front door, and blew out the lights.

Four young fellows came down Cornhill to see where the action was. They went up Boylston's Alley, and encountered a soldier in the alley swinging a cutlass, and another chap armed with a thick cudgel.

"Damn you, ye Yankee buggers, what's your business?" snarled the soldier.

They started to push and haul in the constricted space. One lad came running out of the alley into Cornhill shouting he had been slashed by the soldier. The other three, armed only with sticks, retreated before the slashing sword. John Hicks and some companions standing nearby, leaped into the fray and pushed the soldiers back into the alley. More soldiers came out of the barracks to help their comrades. These new recruits were armed with whatever was handiest to grab, firetongs, shovels, swords, or cutlasses. They came out swinging.[5]

One soldier slashed with his tongs at John Hicks, missed, and got knocked down by him. When the soldier tried to get up, another lad knocked him back down again, breaking the soldier's wrist. Hicks and his friends had good hefty sticks and whacked away lustily with them. They were slowly driving the soldiers back to the barracks, when more redcoats appeared yelling, "Where are the sons of bitches?" The newcomers piled happily into the bash and pushed the youths back into Cornhill where they scattered in several directions, soldiers in hot pursuit.

In the midst of all this hubbub, a good many of the 15,000 inhabitants of Boston were asleep on their cord beds. Tom Perkins and his younger brother Sam were two of these slumberers. Even their nine-year-old brother James was a bit too young to be abroad in the nighttime harassing the king's troops.[6]

Whom should those troops meet at this moment in their pursuit but Captain Goldfinch of the Fourteenth. He was heading for the alley and the barracks when he came upon the scufflers. Several townspeople who recognized him begged him to order the soldiers back to the barracks or there'd be murder done. With difficulty, he made them hear his orders, and started them, muttering and unhappy, back up the alley to the barracks. With the help of some officers who appeared, he got them inside.

But by now some youths had gotten into Dr. Samuel Cooper's unpainted wooden Meeting House just up the street, and were ringing its bell. This alarm of the bell at 9:20 P.M. was the signal that drew these random incidents together and gave them a new pattern. In colonial Boston, the ringing of a church bell usually meant fire. Other church bells picked up the alarm, and soon the whole town was ringing with danger. When he heard the alarm, the keeper of the Custom House cautiously locked its door. After all, the king's money was kept there. Best be careful.

John Adams and his "clubb" were startled. "Supposing it to be the Signal of fire, We snatched our hats and cloaks, broke up the Clubb, and went out to assist in quenching the fire or aiding our friends who might be in danger."[7]

Young Samuel Maverick, seventeen and apprentice to Mr. Greenwood the ivory-turner, was at Jonathan Cary's house, with another lad and the four Cary boys. They were eating a late supper in the kitchen when the bells rang. Mr. Cary told them there was a fire. They said they'd eat a few mouthfuls more and go.

Nicholas Ferriter met Samuel Gray, a fellow ropemaker both of whom had taken part in Friday's fracas. They walked up Quaker Lane to King Street. Ferriter asked him where he was going. "To the fire," replied Gray. When they got to King Street they saw nobody there. Only the sentry at the Custom House walking his pace as usual. They decided to go home.

Patrick Carr, a thirty-year old Irishman worked for and lived with Field, the leather-breeches maker in Prison Lane. When the bells rang he ran upstairs to put his surtout on. "He got a hanger," said Mrs. Field later, "and put it betwixt his coat and surtout. My husband coming at that time, gave him a push and felt the sword." Field and another man there tried to persuade him to leave the sword home. A neighboring woman in the house, by much coaxing finally got him to take it off. But, sword or no sword, out he would go and out he went. In other parts of the town as well, men had rushed outside with buckets, bed-keys, and canvas bags, prepared for a fire. Members of the fire companies had gone to drag their engines to the blaze. It was only the yells in the half-dark that told them something else was happening. "Damn your bloods," came the voices from running figures, "don't bring buckets, bring clubs."

By one corner of the town hall, which was just opposite the main guard, a group of people clustered, talking and arguing.

"Let's go and attack the main guard."

"For God's sake, do not meddle with them."

Boys were shouting to the sentinels at the main guard: "Lobsters! Bloody backs!" and the taunt of "Who buys lobsters?"

Another group of boys had gathered about the sentry outside the Custom House, down the street and on the opposite side—perhaps half a city block away from the main guard, and just a few doors from where young Perkins was sleeping. The sentry was Grenadier Hugh White of the Twenty-ninth. Earlier he had had a set-to with some barber's apprentices. Now these youngsters, and some not so young, spoiling for some excitement, had focused their taunts on him. An occasional snowball smacked the ground near him. One of the barber's apprentices had gone up to the people at the Town House and complained that the sentry had knocked down one of the boys from his shop. The people started to drift down to the growing group around Sentry White.

Captain Thomas Preston of the Twenty-ninth, a forty-year-old Irishman, was in his lodging near the main guard. He supposed the alarm bells were for fire too, "but was soon undeceived." A message came from the guard to inform him that the town inhabitants were assembling to attack the troops and that the bell ringing was a signal to summon in people from the countryside. Since he was Captain of the Day, he immediately went to the main guard.[8]

Down in Dock Square, part of the mob that had come down from Murray's Barracks were grabbing sticks from butcher's stalls, pulling off legs of the stalls, helping themselves to thick solid chunks from the firewood piled there for sale. Some people later claimed they saw them gather about a tall gentleman in a red cloak, who seemed to be giving them instructions. Then they shouted for the main guard and headed off up Cornhill again. There were twenty or thirty of them, mostly sailors, under the leadership of a tall, stout mulatto Indian named

Michael Johnson, also known as Crispus Attucks. Patrick Kenton had followed this part of the mob from the barracks down to Dock Square. He noticed Attucks had two clubs in his hands. "Here," said Attucks stopping for a moment, "take one of them." Kenton did. It was a cord-wood stick.

Attucks ran on, cursing the soldiers as he ran. They made for the town pump by Jackson's Corner at the head of King Street. As they went by Colonel Jackson's, someone shouted, "Damn it, here lives an importer," and four of his windows were smashed in. No doubt about it now, this was going to be an ugly mob. When they came to the corner they saw a small crowd gathering around Sentry White at the Custom House and they headed down there.

Samuel Gray, who had started home to his wife and children, met Benjamin Davis, Jr., standing by his gate in Green's Lane. As Gray came by he asked Davis where the fire was. No fire, replied Davis, it was the soldiers fighting. "Damn it," said Gray, "I am glad of it. I will knock some of them on the head." He turned on his heels and started to run back towards the noise. Davis shouted after him, "Take heed you do not get killed in the affray yourself." Gray's answer was flung back, "Do not you fear, damn their bloods."

Captain Preston had reached the main guard just before Attucks and his mob, which Preston judged to be about a hundred people, ran down towards the Custom House. Preston thought, suppose they should attack it, that's where the king's money is kept. A nervous twenty-year-old officer was in charge at the guardhouse. What should he do, he asked Preston. With fifteen years of service behind him and a reputation as a "cool and distinct officer," Preston replied, "Take out 6 or 7 of the men and let them go down to the assistance of the sentry." A person in the group around the main guard yelled out, "Will you stand there and see the sentinel murdered at the Customs House?" Somebody else hollered to Preston, "They are killing the sentinel." "Damn you," shouted Preston to the guards, "why do you not turn out?"

When Attucks arrived with his mob, he began harassing the sentry, poking him rather severely with his stick, calling him "lobster" and swearing he would have off one of his claws. What could be heard clearly above all the yelling and confusion was Attucks's peculiar and frightening war-whoop.[9]

Coming down now to the relief of the sentry was a little procession of eight British soldiers. Corporal William Wemms led the group and Captain Thomas Preston in his gold-laced hat and red coat brought up the rear. They moved swiftly and authoritatively through the crowd, pushing aside anyone slow to move out of their way, calling out, "Make way, make way there," and if they still didn't move fast enough, "Damn you, make way you buggers!" When they got to White they formed a loose half-circle around him, about a man apart, and by charging their bayonets kept the crowd at a little distance.

The mob stood beating their clubs and bludgeons together, making mob noises, hollering the stale insults and taunts—"Bloody backs! Lobster scoundrels!" Others yelled, "Fire if you dare, God damn you, fire and be damned." And still others, "Fire, fire you lobsters, fire, you dare not fire." Over all came the piercing cry of the boys, "Who buys lobsters?" Some had suggestions for action—"Let's burn the sentry box"—"Let's heave it overboard." But nobody made a move to do anything, except to press closer and closer.

The crowd gathered about the soldiers and forced James Bailey who was in the forefront towards Grenadier Carrol. Carrol pushed his bayonet up to Bailey's chest to keep him back. Sentry White, who knew Bailey, said to Carrol, "Do not hurt him." Grenadier Montgomery, on the upper end of the semicircle, reached over and pushed Bailey behind him. Bailey stood there with his arm atop the post near the corner of the Custom House.

Running around in the crowd was Samuel Gray, whom some suspected had been at the liquor. Back and forth he ran clapping people on the shoulder, saying to one, "do not run, my lad. They dare not fire"; to another, "What's here to pay, Langford?"

Preston was standing in front of the soldiers endeavoring to persuade the people to depart peaceably. Richard Palmes came up to Preston, and in all the racket of shouting, the plup of the snowballs, the banging of the sticks, leaned close, putting his left hand on the captain's right shoulder to speak to him.

"Are their guns loaded, Captain?"

"They are sir. With powder and ball."

"I hope you do not intend they shall fire upon the inhabitants."

"By no means."

Boys started throwing missiles up onto the roof of the Custom House so that they would roll down onto the heads of the soldiers. The shouts continued, "Fire! fire!"—"They dare not"—"Who buys lobsters?" Some people were jumping up on the backs of others trying to get a better view.

Then Attucks, so some say, struck a blow at Preston, which he warded off. Attucks turned and lunged for Montgomery's gun, grabbing the bayonet with one hand and pushing it aside while he reached by and swiped Montgomery's head. The soldier twitched his gun out of Attucks's grasp, stepped back, and "with a certain hand gun of the value of twenty shillings . . . held in both his hands, charged with gun powder and two leaden bullets" fired directly at the mulatto. Preston angrily turned to ask Montgomery why he fired. At the same moment, he was struck by a club on the arm which made it useless for some time. Some people did not yet realize they had been fired on with live bullets. They thought it only gunpowder used to frighten them.[10]

More snowballs piled in upon the soldiers and somebody with a loud voice yelled, "Damn your bloods, why don't you fire?" As if triggered by the cry, three guns went off, almost together, then a brief interval, and another three guns went off, in the same confusion and hurry. Reflections from the firing in the second-story windows of the Custom House made it look to some as if guns had been fired from there too. People now realized what had happened and started running away. Someone, even in his hurry, saw what he took to be greatcoats lying in the street. He supposed that they had been shucked off as the crowd scattered.

One of these "greatcoats" was Michael Johnson alias Crispus Attucks. He had been hit "in and upon the right breast a little below the right pap of him" and "in and upon the left breast a little below the left pap of him." He wasn't quite dead yet. He lay, head in the gutter, gasping, all six feet two inches of him stretched out on the trodden snow of King Street.[11]

Samuel Gray had seen Attucks fall and turned toward him just as a gun pointed directly at Gray's head went off. Gray struggled a moment, "turned himself right round upon his heel" and fell. Langford was standing near to Gray and Gray fell on Langford's left foot. John Hickling ran over to Gray and seeing the blood gush out of his head, "felt for the wound and found a hole as big as my hand."

James Caldwell, second mate of a vessel commanded by Captain

Morton, was killed in the middle of the street. He was standing beside George Hewes, who caught him in his arms as he fell. Patrick Carr, who lived for ten days after the shooting, had been standing by the old stocks. He was hit as he crossed the street to Warden & Vernon's shop, almost directly opposite the soldiers.[12]

Seventeen-year-old Samuel Maverick had come out of Quaker Lane and started up towards the Town House, when he was shot. Dr. Hyrons, who was called to tend Maverick, thought it strange by the direction of the ball, how Maverick could have been killed by the shooting at the Custom House. Hyrons decided "the ball must have struck some wall or something else, before it struck him."

Two doctors came to look at Attucks. As they stooped to pick him up, the soldiers presented their weapons as if going to fire. Preston pushed up their guns. Attucks was carried into the Royal Exchange Tavern on the other corner of the lane from the Custom House. Samuel Gray was taken down to his brother's house on the south side of Exchange Lane. A bystander picked up Gray's round hat, which had fallen off when he fell, and followed them. Several people helped carry James Caldwell's body up to the jail on Queen Street. Friends picked up Patrick Carr, mortally wounded but still alive, and took him back to Mr. Field's in Prison Lane which he had left so impetuously such a short time before. Young Maverick was borne to a house in Cornhill where he died early the next morning.

A townsman came and told Captain Preston that four or five thousand people were assembled in the surrounding streets, with more gathering all the time. Preston ordered his little group back to the main guard, and there ordered the entire force into what the manuals called the Street Firing Maneuver. They could hear the almost constant cry of the inhabitants, "To arms, to arms, turn out with your guns." The town drum was beating the alarm. Preston ordered the guard drum to beat arms, and sent a party to inform Colonel Dalrymple of the emergency.[13]

Thomas Peck, hatter, was still in his house, law-abiding man that he was, when the guns went off. "I heard 'em distinct," he later told a jury. But now he put on his coat and came out to see what had happened. He marched resolutely up to the main guard and asked Preston, "What have you done?" "Sir," said Preston to the fifty-eight-year-old respectable citizen, "it was none of my doing. The soldiers fired of their own accord. I was in the street and might have been shot." Peck went across to the Council Chamber in the Town House where the civil authorities were gathering to see what could be done to prevent further disturbances.[14]

When John Adams finally arrived on the scene of combat, he saw some small field pieces placed by the south door of the Town House and some engineers and grenadiers drawn up to protect them. He immediately thought of his wife, who was six months pregnant and mourning a young daughter buried just a month before. Knowing she was alone except for her maids and a boy in the house, and seeing that all seemed quiet here, he decided his place was at home and he went there.[15]

But the quiet was deceptive. Joseph Belknap had come on the massacre scene shortly after the bodies had been removed. He had heard people crying out that men had been killed, but now he believed it, for he deposed that he saw "half a pale full" of blood in one place. He turned back to Dock Square, met one of the selectmen and one of the overseers and joined them in fetching Lieutenant-Governor Hutchinson.

They met him part way, for he had already started for the Town House. When they came to King Street, Belknap indicated, "Here, Sir, is the blood that has been spilt tonight." When Hutchinson reached the Town House he was surrounded by the people there telling him what they knew of the night's happenings. Peck was among them, and as soon as he got a chance he reported what Preston had told him, that "it was none of my doing. The soldiers fired of their own accord." Peck thought that Preston, both as an officer and a gentleman, bore a good character, exceeding any in the corps. That fall he would so testify in the captain's behalf, even though politically he was not a British sympathizer, and to speak up for the British "murderers" at that moment was a most unpopular thing to do.[16]

The people had now returned in great numbers to King Street, and Hutchinson went to the balcony at the east window and spoke calmingly to them. Promising the people that justice would be done, he ordered the soldiers returned to their barracks. A town meeting was set for the next day, Tuesday, at Faneuil Hall. Captain Preston was arrested about 2 A.M. and examined until 3:00. The soldiers involved in the affair were arrested the next morning.

Early that Tuesday, King Street was crowded with curiosity seekers.

When five-year-old Tom Perkins woke up, Richard Salter, "an indiscreet family servant," carried him on his shoulders up street to see the sights. He was taken to view the several corpses "who lay in the adjacent houses to where they were shot," so of course he would have seen the stiff six feet, two inches of Crispus Attucks. Perhaps Maverick was not too newly dead to receive visitors, and for Carr they had to wait some days yet. Caldwell was way off in Cold Lane, but Gray was just down the street from Attucks. Certainly the boy would have seen these two, the ropemaker and the sea-going mulatto Indian.

Perkins would carry the memory of this day with him up to the edge of the Civil War. "The impression made on my mind by the death scene, and the frozen blood in the street, was of course indelible and I now well remember the location of each body, although the houses where the bodies laid have long since been replaced by new stone edifices."[17]

It is not every town where a boy can see the beginnings of a revolution almost on his doorstep. Who could have foreseen that day that this child, born when King George III had been four years on his throne, would live to see fourteen presidents preside over a United States of America?

Come swallow your bumpers, ye Tories and roar
That the sons of fair Freedom are hamper'd
once more;
But know that no Cut-throats our spirits can
tame,
Nor a host of Oppressors shall smother the
flame.

Massachusetts Song of Liberty

# 2

# There Is Two Iron Guns in My Store

By the ship the town of Boston hired to send its version of the "massacre" to England, Grandfather Peck sent letters to his two main London buyers. The troops, he wrote on the Sixteenth of March, had been removed from town and were presently stationed on Castle Island in the harbor. "We are now all peace and quietness." He enclosed a copy of the March 12 *Gazette* with its account of the massacre, adding, "if I can gett a Pamphlett that setts fourth the whole affair will send it." Death and disaster disposed of, he turned to business. "Please to send me the following . . ."

His business was furs and hats and "lately imported." The furs came from New England and Newfoundland and went mostly to England. Throughout the year the people "down east" hunted and trapped. Red, grey, and "mungral" foxes snared in the woods; wolves and wildcats; bears surprised in a blackberry patch; mink, fisher, otter, and muskrat caught in the brooks and streams of the North.

By coasting vessel and farm cart, the skinned slaughter came to Grandfather Peck. "I think myself a good judge of furrs," he had written one of his buyers the year before. "I have been in the business more than Twenty-five years and have done a great deal at it and purchase all my furrs myself and allways note what they are when I pack them."

The difficult problem for a local merchant was to find something in the colonies that would sell in England and earn enough credit to finance a return cargo. Fur skins were just about ideal. The northern forests supplied them in abundance. Grandfather Peck provided "the eastern people" with the powder and shot. The furs sold at a good profit. Then the merchant made a second profit on the sale of the imports. It was a steady business too. In one nine-year period (1767–1775) Peck shipped 120,000 skins to England, averaging more than 13,000 skins a year.[1]

As a young emigrant from Scotland, Peck had joined the Scot's Charitable Society in 1735, founded to furnish relief to "any of the Scottish nation." It was a canny thing for a young man with a growing family to do. A dozen years later, however, this hat and felt maker was affluent enough to buy land on Mackerel Lane, off King Street. Down the street from him lived the Edmund Perkins family with their fourteen-year-old son James. In the late 1740's, young James went to work for Peck as an apprentice and stayed on to marry the boss's daughter, Elizabeth.

By 1751 Peck was able to afford a house and land on Merchants Row, off the other side of King Street. He moved his growing business there and started buying land and houses in Corn Court, just off Merchants Row, for rental income. With a church friend, he began investing in property in the North End. He even took a flyer in Maine Lands, buying 2,250 acres on the Penobscot River. Finally, he got together £700 lawful money and bought a fine brick house on King Street, half a block from the Custom House. After sixteen years on Merchants Row, he moved in 1767 to the prestige of a King Street address. The young ambitious emigrant from Scotland had come a long way, and he was now a solid citizen of his adopted town.

Business was not his only interest. In 1748 he was one of five trustees who bought the property of the French Huguenot church on School Street. This was to provide a preaching station for the Reverend Andrew Croswell. Some people called this Congregational minister "Merry Andrew" and others thought him a "madman." The *Ballad of Boston Ministers* jibed:

> the man means well, but none can tell,
> With what his noodle's stored.

It was not for want of Andrew Croswell shouting his message in their ears. In his "Narrative of the Founding" of his church, he came out strongly against "disregarding Promises and not fulfilling . . . Engagements, Tattling, and Back-biting, spending Time idly at Taverns, Tipling-houses or elsewhere, and vain and unnecessary worldly Conversation on Lord's day."[2]

Such appeals to strict morality had a strong attraction for the Scottish Peck and his wife, Elizabeth. She was a Spurrier and two of her sisters had displayed that frailty men find so interesting in women. One had a bastard by a ship's captain, although the court denied her claim for support on the fascinating ground that conception required exactly nine months to the day, by which odd timetable the captain had been a few days out to sea and thus could not possibly have been the father. The other sister never had a chance to bear her bastard. Once the relatives she was living with learned she was with child, they beat her so severely, in the presence of the Pecks, that her death a few months later is probably attributable to their rough treatment. Some of her relatives said as much, and a series of squalid lawsuits resulted in which murder and thievery charges were bandied about and nothing conclusive came of it all.

The Pecks attended Reverend Croswell's service faithfully, and when their daughter, Elizabeth, and former apprentice James Perkins were married on December 29, 1754, it was he who performed the ceremony.

The Perkins family had arrived in New England several generations before the Pecks. The bridegroom's grandfather, Edmund Perkins, was said to have come to Massachusetts with his widowed mother in the 1650's when Boston was only two decades old. He must have had some pretensions to gentility, for about a century ago a tombstone for a young son of his was unearthed, and it bore a heraldic device.

Edmund Perkins married Susanna Hudson, the widow of John Howlett. They had four children including an Edmund born in 1683. Perkins supported his small family as a shipwright, building vessels at Bendall's Cove in the Dock Square area. He was fairly successful, for when he died in 1693 he left an estate worth nearly £450, which included two clocks, sterling plate, three swords, two guns, three pistols, a wife, three children, and two Negroes each worth £30.

His son, the second generation Edmund Perkins, was the black sheep of the family. He was ten years old when his father died. Three years later Mrs. Perkins remarried, and if the fashion of the day was followed, young Edmund was put out as an apprentice. He became a joiner or what would now be called a carpenter. The tax collector in 1707 listed him as boarding with his mother, once again a widow. By the next year, in addition to his carpentry, he was speculating in several small merchandizing ventures, sending "oyl" to London, mackerel and gunpowder to South Carolina, shipping a horse to Antigua, and buying a few Indian slaves in the south to sell in Boston.

He had already made the friends who were to get him into trouble with the law. These were Richard Hughes and Thomas Odell, one a thief, the other a forger. Of Odell, Samuel Sewall said he was "a very dangerous person," calling him "hostis humani generis"—an enemy of the human race. Margaret Barton, a convicted fence, testified she had seen Perkins standing on a ladder at Boston jail talking to Odell through the grates. Occasionally she had seen him in the prison yard playing at nine-pins with Odell. When Odell escaped from jail, Margaret Barton was sure it was Perkins who had dropped the knives or chisels through the bars.

The year 1709 was a tempestuous one for Perkins. In August he married Mary Farris, and in November a grand jury brought in two indictments against him: one that in July 1707 he had broken into Thomas Palmer's warehouse with Richard Hughes and robbed it; the second, that in the summer of 1709, he had "willfully and knowingly" passed "a parcel of base Counterfeit money" as genuine. Perkins was immediately clapped into jail, and when he heard his trial was to be postponed, he petitioned to be tried right away as he had "an aged mother to maintain and a family." Delay could mean his "utter ruin." He got his wish and was tried in December. The jury freed him of the breaking and entering charges—all that could be proved here was that Hughes, who was now dead, had gone into the warehouse while Perkins stayed outside—but found him guilty of the counterfeiting charge and fined him thirty pounds. This was a mild enough sentence for an offense for which he could have been branded on the right cheek with the letter "F," had an ear cut off, been given a year in prison, or even the death penalty, depending on the court's judgment of the seriousness of the act. Apparently the court felt there were extenuating circumstances.

Two years later in 1711, evidently thinking it legal, he and his wife claimed a legacy left to her by a Captain Scott, thought to be dead.

In 1716, however, Scott turned up very much alive and demanded his estate back. Perhaps it was the Scott money that helped Perkins buy a piece of land on Mackerel Lane in 1713. Here he lived and had a shop for making furniture, particularly chairs.

Mary died in 1721, leaving him with three children to care for. Within four months he had married Esther Frothingham of Charlestown, daughter of a shipwright. By her he had eight children, the sixth of whom was the James who was to marry Elizabeth Peck.

The need to sit down in Boston was so great that this second generation Edmund was able by 1738 to buy the property adjoining his and expand his operations. In 1760 he was living in a "Brick House Hansomly finished and winscoted." By then, his son James and Elizabeth Perkins were married and with their family of two girls, Elizabeth and Nancy, were living on Mackerel Lane too. Here "the Great Fire of 1760" burned them all out of the brick house, along with three or four hundred other houses in the heart of Boston. The fire was seen as far away as Portsmouth, New Hampshire. An explosion of gunpowder stored near Fort Hill, not far from Mackerel Lane, was heard up the coast at Hampton Beach and thought by many to be an earthquake. Ten percent of the center of the town was wiped out. Charity poured in from everywhere. Christopher Kilby, hearing in London of the fire, sent the town £200 sterling for the sufferers. Some years later the name Mackerel Lane was changed to Kilby Street as a mark of the town's gratitude. The sufferers of the fire made out lists of their losses and the town gave such compensation as was available.

Despite the fire, the James Perkins family continued to grow and prosper. On a cold windy Saturday, Dec. 15, 1764, their second son to live, Thomas Handasyd, was born. For a time James worked as a bookkeeper to the wealthy merchant John Rowe. Then he branched out on his own. In a letter of May 1766, Peck mentions his son-in-law shipping a cask of furs to England and getting two shillings more per skin for the good otter than Peck did for "the same sort." From time to time he joined in speculations with George Erving, one of the town's principal merchants. On August 13, 1767, the town selectmen gave Perkins permission to sell wine in his shop in the King Street house. By then both his father and mother were dead.

Perkins and his father-in-law attended the Sons of Liberty celebration on August 14, 1769. It was the anniversary of a triumph over the Stamp

Act. More than three hundred men sat down to dine at a Dorchester tavern, cheered by the recent recall of the province's governor. Numerous toasts were downed, cannon touched off, and the company voices raised in song. To the tune "Hearts of Oak," they sang the American Song of Liberty, concluding:

> In freedom we're born and in Freedom we'll live
> Our purses are ready
> Steady Friends steady
> Not as slaves but as Freeman our money we'll give.[3]

It is not all feasting and toasting that makes a revolution. There is roasting too, and Grandfather Peck was soon to be one of those on the grill. To break the Townshend Acts imposed by the British Parliament on a rebellious Boston, the local merchants had agreed to boycott British goods—what was called the Non-Importation Agreement. Most of the merchants signed it, including Peck. Some of the government supporters did not. One of these was another member of the Scots Charitable Society, John Mein. Hailing from Edinburgh, Mein had come to Boston and joined the society in 1765. He ran the London Bookstore a few doors up King Street from Peck. There he operated the first circulating library in Boston, and with another Scot published the *Boston Chronicle,* a paper that passionately supported the government policies.

Mein, said the antigovernment people, was as mean as his name. He refused to support the boycott, and continued, as did a few others, to import goods. This gave him a decided commercial advantage in an artificially baren market. Much pressure was exerted to bring him and the others into line lest they tempt their weaker brethern into breaking the boycott.[4]

Mean he might be, stubborn he certainly was. He retaliated by publishing in his newspaper the names of all the signers of the boycott whom he said were importing contrary to the agreement. He got his information from friends in the Custom House who were in a position to know. On Thursday, September 7, 1769, little more than three weeks after "Hearts of Oak" had been wafted on the Dorchester air, Mein published the name of Thomas Handasyd Peck as a breaker of the agreement by importing "Forty Dozen of Hatts . . . in the Ship *Thomas,* William Davis, Master."

Peck acted fast. The next day—a "heavy morning"—a box marked "THP No. 5" was hanging from Peck's shop window with an inscription reading, "This is the case that John Mein in his paper of yesterday says contained Forty Dozen of Hatts." Measurement of the box was given which showed it to be 23″ long, 14½″ wide, 16″ deep. At the bottom of the notice, Peck added this comment: "There was not one Hatt in the box. Query, Does he lie or not?"

But Grandfather Peck did not leave it there. At noon the same day, he staged a little parade. Attended by his servant bearing the box on his head, and the town bellman, Peck marched out into King Street. First he led his little group to the middle of the street between the British Coffee House and the Bunch of Grapes Tavern. Here he had the bellman make proclamation for all persons to come and view the box. Then he marched up to where the merchants met, and repeated the performance. Again the three moved on to the west door of the Town Hall in Cornhill. Once more the bellman rang his bell and made his proclamation. They did the same in front of John Mein's. Finally, the closing performance was given in Market Square, all "to the very great diversion of a large number of spectators."[5]

With March came dances for Captain Preston and the other officers, and street fights for teenage apprentices, idle youths, and bored soldiers. Then came the Massacre on King Street, the removal of the soldiers, and "peace and quietness."

The trials of Preston and the soldiers had been put off until the fall of 1770 in hopes that the town would cool off. Preston was acquitted after a six-day trial. The soldiers were tried for nine days, and all but Kilroy and Montgomery were freed. Those two were found guilty of manslaughter and given benefit of clergy, a curious legal device of Catholic origins intended to protect clerics from secular justice. By extension, the ability to read was considered sufficient evidence of clerical character. So Private Kilroy, who couldn't write his name, and that bald benedict, Hugh Montgomery, nine months after that violent March evening, were burnt on the thumb and discharged.

But revolutions do not thrive on "peace and quietness," and Samuel Adams had hard work, after the removal of the soldiers, to spur his drive against the British. At the end of January 1771 he persuaded seventy-five citizens, including James Perkins and Paul Revere, to petition the town meeting for the removal of the powderhouse in Boston on the basis that it might accidentally explode. Although it was an anti-British move, perhaps James Perkins was also thinking of the terrible fire in 1760.

Then on a cloudy Saturday, May 8, 1773, when he was forty years old, James Perkins died, leaving a large family to be provided for. On Monday, Peck wrote his London agents to ship him "by the first opportunity 2 chests good Bohea tea pray see that it is good one bag pepper and about 1500 pounds Single Refined Loafe Sugar the Loafes about 8–10 pounds each. Lett goods be markt E. P. as my daughter is going to keep a Grossary shop what goods she send for you may charge to my account."

When James' estate was appraised, it came to less than his grandfather's the first Edmund. It amounted to about £350, of which more than £200 was merchandise in the store, which the widow intended to continue. It included a Negro woman valued at less than £27. Elizabeth Perkins was to increase this estate a hundredfold before her own death thirty-four years later.

In a couple of months, all was ready. A large advertisement appeared in the Massachusetts *Gazette* of July 12. "Elizabeth Perkins at her shop two doors below the British Coffee House in King Street. Has for sale a very large and genteel assortment of . . ." The ad went on to list a variety of special dishes, glasses, and household articles of interest to the discriminating housewife. From Mrs. Perkins could be had anchovies by keg, bottle, or pound. She offered choice Cheshire cheese. The tea and sugar ordered in Peck's letter was available for the tea drinkers of Boston, although there was hardly time for a vessel to have gotten back from England with Peck's order. For those who wanted something stronger, she listed a few barrels of good cider, wine, and brandy. Later advertisements expanded the list of items she offered, although it was a most miscellaneous lot, from pickled walnuts to "Best Velvet," and from corks to "Turlington's Balsam of Life."

It was not unusual in that age abounding in widows and orphans for women to open stores. The Boston papers of the period list more than a dozen others advertising from time to time. A great many of them seemed to specialize in garden seeds, as if that somehow were suitable trade for females. Peck—who had lost three other children and only had Elizabeth left—would and did provide for Widow Perkins.

But she had the energy and determination to do what she could for herself and her children.*

She had need of all the energy she possessed. James had given her ten children in the eighteen years of their marriage. When he died in May 1773, his youngest, little Margaret, was just six weeks old. His oldest, Elizabeth, was just over seventeen years and to be married that November to Russell Sturgis. Two of his boys died before him, leaving Elizabeth with five girls and three boys to raise. After young Elizabeth's marriage, Mrs. Perkins would have the care of only seven, and the next oldest, Nancy (reaching fourteen a few weeks after her father died), undoubtedly helped with the younger children.

One of the items Elizabeth Perkins sold was tea. Being a woman, she didn't take part in the meetings of the merchants to discuss the attitude they should adopt on the sale of this item, now one of controversy between the London government and the Boston patriots. Instead, her father went in her place. The question was, should Boston continue to drink tea and pay the British government a small tax for the right to do so? The patriots decided for the town that the answer was no. When the tea ships arrived in the harbor, and negotiations got nowhere, the patriots turned into "Indians," who settled matters with a *fait accompli*. The tea was put to soak in cold salt water on December 10, 1773.

The London government responded by shutting the Boston harbor and moving troops back into the town. Bostonians were to be hit square in their pocketbooks. The merchants reminded their English dealers, as did Peck, "we have had vast quantitys of goods this spring and your Parliament are taking all methods they can that they should never be paid for." Nor would they be able to order more. These acts, supposedly to punish Boston, would actually, the Bostonians hastened to point out, hurt their English creditors much more.

By the end of May 1774, Peck was writing England that "I must be obliged to look out for a new market for my furs." Over sixty years old now, he did not anticipate starting anew with much relish. "However, as you have forced us to be adventurers, you can't blame us for doing the best we can."

* Descendants joked that she made her grocery store successful by inserting a large thumb into all her measures as she served her customers.

His "best" was to ship from nearby ports, since Boston Harbor was blocked in June by British men-of-war. "We are not allowed to carry any goods over a ferry that is but half a mile over." Then Peck's irritation with the government broke out angrily. "I believe such a Cruel Cursed act Could not have been Contrived but in Hell and believe the Promoters of it are Sons thereof. We have some thousands of poor Widows and Orphans that are turned out to starve or beg which before could have got a comfortable living, although it is certain they could not have been the destroyers of the Tea." Then Peck turned prophet: "I believe this will cause such an allienation as will never be forgot. It is Pity it ever should."[6]

Six weeks before the outbreak of the insurrection at Lexington, Peck was writing to Sam Holman, a hatter in Salem, in an effort to supply some gunpowder to "a young Gentleman . . . who says that there is no powder to be gott in Salem and urges me very much to spare him sum." Peck had a little powder for his "eastward men" who supplied him with furs. "I gave him some encouragement that I would spare him a quarter cask" though doing so might leave Peck short. "However," he told Holman, "if you think it not best I leave it wholly to you." That spring many people wanted powder, and not to shoot at foxes or bears. Some people were planning to shoot, strangely enough, at "lobsters."[7]

By Wednesday, April 19, they were doing it. The troops General Gage had sent out to get the gunpowder stored at Concord had attacked or been attacked in Lexington. They brushed that group aside, went on to Concord, and frustrated in their search for powder and those two arch revolutionaries, Hancock and Adams, endured a stinging counterattack all the way back to Charlestown. It was Friday before Gage had all his troops inside Boston.

What so many dreaded, so many thought impossible, was now upon them. Angry country people swarmed into what became the American camp, shutting the British up in Boston. Most communication between town and country ceased. No fresh provisions were brought to Boston market. It was apparent that it would not be long before Boston would be in serious want of food. On Friday afternoon, the selectman met with Gage to see what could be done. After bargaining back and forth, the townspeople agreed at a meeting on Sunday the twenty-third to turn in their weapons and "such of the inhabitants as had a mind to leave the town might go out with their effects."

On Monday the arms were surrendered at Faneuil Hall. John Rowe wrote in his diary that 2,674 were given up, others said more. On this same Monday, Grandfather Peck sat down and wrote General Gage a letter. It is a straightforward letter on the surface. One could think it was by a man who was most anxious not to give the least offense to the British general. Then, remembering the man who had publicly refuted Mein, one might suspect that Peck's tongue was somewhere in the vicinity of his cheek.

> To His Excellency Governor Gage.
>
> Sir as the Inhabitants of this town are this day delivering up their arms I thought it my duty to inform your Excellency that their is two Iron guns in my store. I think about four Pounders if your Excellency thinks best that the guns should be removed if you Sir will Order to what Place I will take care and have it done.

Peck was never much of a man for punctuation or spelling and even writing to a general didn't bring out the grammar in him. He closed the letter in the customary style and then added this: "P.S. Those guns have no carrages and have Laid Ever Since Last War."[8]

There were other decisions to be made by the Peck-Perkins family. You didn't try to bring up children in a town where food was scarce and every day getting more so. Nor was it wise to linger on what might at any moment become a battlefield. People were already leaving the town by vessels. That same Monday when Peck was writing Gage, Rowe had seen six friends off for Salem. Those departing had to obtain passes signed by the town major. Saturday, the twenty-ninth, an officer was ordered to Charlestown ferry to examine and receive the passes. Rowe tried to get one himself, but even with his connections "could not prevail."

By May 5 the inhabitants were pouring out of the town. Mrs. Perkins left shortly before the battle of Bunker Hill on June 17. That was the decision that she and her father had reached in those first anxious days. He and her mother would stay in town and protect their property and interests. She and the seven children would go to Barnstable on Cape Cod. The young Sturgis family of three went with her. Just in time too. Early in June an inhabitant of the town wrote to a friend that "could you see Boston it would break your heart."[9]

By the waters of Watertown
We sat down and wept
When we remember'd thee
O Boston.

William Billings

# 3

# The Drums Beat and Away

Mrs. Perkins and her brood came to Barnstable as refugees of war. For several generations the Sturgis family had lived in this town. Presumably Russell Sturgis and his family moved in with his relatives. Mrs. Perkins stayed with Squire Edward Bacon in his one-story, gambrel-roofed, double house that stood on the easterly part of the Lothrop lot.

Squire Bacon was not an inconsiderable man. Sixty years old, he was living with his second wife, Rachel, having buried his first. The squire had been town selectman, town clerk, judge, representative, and church deacon. But some question of his loyalty to the Revolutionary cause has persisted through the years. When he was elected to the General Court in 1778, James Otis and twenty-eight other Barnstable citizens petitioned to have his election revoked, declaring he was "an avowed Opposer of Congresses Colonial & Continental & a professed Enemy to the Independency of America." Partisans of Bacon replied that these attacks sprang from an old family quarrel and that "the good squire" was "as forward in raising men and money as anyone" to help the revolt.[1]

Though the Perkins family had fled the war in Boston, it was still with them. The Barnstable militia were constantly on the alert after the battle of Bunker Hill on June 17. Alarms were frequent. British cruisers were often seen off Sandy Neck. Rumors came in of warships off Hyannis. The fear was always present that the British would do more than threaten; that they would actually land, plunder, burn, and kill. But these were adult worries. As much of a normal existence as possible was provided for the youngsters: they went to school.

Ten-year-old Tom's schoolteacher was the Reverend Timothy Hilliard of the East Parish Congregational Church. Hilliard was a thirty-year-old New Hampshire man of courteous, affable manners, who had graduated from Harvard in 1764, the year Tom was born. He had been in Barnstable for five years and needed all his tact in those trying times, for Squire Bacon, one of his deacons as well as a neighbor, refused to attend church on account of political disagreements with some of the brethren. Hilliard's diplomacy eventually reconciled all factions. Monday through Saturday was the school week. Sunday was meeting day, when Hilliard mounted his pulpit and preached in a "singularly plaintive voice" which for many "rendered his devotional services striking."[2]

A number of Boston families had fled to Barnstable with their children, and here at Hilliard's school, Tom met Harrison Gray Otis, who became a lifelong friend. Saturday afternoons during the fishing season, Tom, brother Jim, and Harry would go trout fishing in the plentiful streams and ponds of the Cape.

Young as they were, Mrs. Perkins allowed them the use of guns, saying she didn't know but that they might have to fight for their country some day, and she wanted them to know how. Perhaps they tried for the head bounty of two shillings then paid on foxes. Sometimes they joined the deer-hunts on the hills, or during the autumn of 1775 shot flight-birds on the Barnstable Great Marshes.

Jim was the bookish one of the two older brothers. Tom was always more of a sport than a scholar, though his schooling had not been neglected. Hilliard was his fourth teacher. In the fall of 1771, Tom had been sent thirty miles south of Boston to the town of Middleborough to be taught by the Reverend Sylvanus Conant. A "New Light" clergyman, Conant probably appealed to followers of the Reverend Andrew Croswell for that reason. He was fifty-one when Tom went to school to him, of a mild and inoffensive disposition, and had just buried the second of his three wives. Reputed to be a good scholar, he had, however, in his junior year at Harvard had to make public confession "for drinking Rum at the public worship of God."[3]

Tom probably had little time to explore the Middleborough neighborhood with its ponds with lovely sounding Indian names: Assawompsett and Great Quittacas. He was not allowed to miss Sunday preaching in the Meeting House on the "Upper Green." This was an elegant building for its time and place, with pillars painted in rough imitation of marble sculpture by a local artist, Cephas Thompson. Its most notable feature was a peculiar sounding-board suspended over the high pulpit. Circular in shape, it hung from the roof by a rod that was difficult to see. Youngsters used to marvel what held it up; to them it seemed to float in space. One day a boy decided that "God holds it up just as he does the world, and that is why it does not fall down and break the master's head." In Conant's three-story gabled house with its big chimney, seven-year-old Tom lived until his mother brought him back to Boston. Probably this was in the spring of 1773 when his father died.[4]

For his second teacher he went to Master John Griffith, who ran a private school on Hanover Street in Boston, "a little to the Northward of the Orange-Tree Tavern." Here Griffith taught "spelling, reading, writing, and arithemtic." When Griffith died Tom was sent to Master James Carter. This was his first public school. Carter taught in Scollay's building, where Queen Street (now Court) ran into Tremont Street, two blocks west of the Town House.[5]

Though Perkins was only there a short time, he probably used the same books Harry Otis worked with: Cheever's *Accidence,* Corderius's *Colloquies,* Ward's *Grammar,* Eutropius for history, and Clark's *Introduction to Latin.* For "making Latin," they studied Caesar, Tully, and Virgil. The school day was long, beginning at seven o'clock in the summer (eight o'clock in the winter) and running to eleven, then resuming at one and closing at five, with Saturday afternoons free.[6]

History gave them an unexpected holiday. Walking to school early on April 19, 1775, Harry Otis found Percy's brigade drawn up along Tremont street from Scollay's buildings nearly to the bottom of the mall. They were preparing to march to the assistance of the troops sent out to Lexington and Concord. When Otis finally reached school by a roundabout route, the teacher announced "deponite libros," and the scholars fled home cheering. All was confusion after this date, and Perkins and his family soon left Boston, ending his few months under Master Carter's tutelage.

While Perkins spent the first winter of the war schooling on the Cape, a young Boston bookseller turned soldier, Henry Knox, was superintending the hauling of the artillery captured at Fort Ticonderoga to Boston. Once they had arrived, and the Americans had secretly in one night fortified Dorchester Heights, the British realized their military situation was untenable. There was "great Disorder, Confusion & much Distress," Rowe, who had remained in Boston like Peck, wrote in his diary. By March 7, 1776, the troops and Loyalists were hastily loading their goods onto ships. Vessels were seized and "pressed into the service" of the fleeing army. The troops began plundering stores and warehouses. They behaved with great insolence to the inhabitants, particularly those with rebel inclinations, as the moment of their humiliation neared.[7]

Sunday morning, March 17, 1776, the British left Boston, nevermore to return as rulers. About eleven o'clock a small group of Americans entered the town "without the least shadow of opposition," and that evening several more regiments marched in. The inhabitants, one observer noted, looked like "sceletons."[8]

In Barnstable, three or four days before they learned that the British were about to leave Boston, Tom had gone for a Saturday afternoon excursion into the woods with Squire Bacon. Tom was after birds' eggs, Bacon after a load of wood. Coming back, Tom was tired from the long walk, and Bacon suggested he ride on the tongue of the cart. Coming down a hill, Tom fell off the tongue and the wheels of the cart with its heavy burden of logs, passed over both his legs and broke them "in the gristle." Being young, the legs soon healed without crippling him. Yet even in old age, in damp weather he felt twinges reminding him of that accident. His recuperation kept him in Barnstable a few weeks after the rest of his family had returned to Boston.[9]

When the British withdrew, the Boston selectmen advised General Washington that smallpox was everywhere in the town and he had better send in only troops that had already had the disease. It was not until September 19 that the town was finally declared free of infection. Only six houses still had cases and they were marked with red flags to warn people away. Apparently Tom Perkins and his family were back in Boston by mid-July 1776, before it was completely cleared of the pox, because in old age he spoke of hearing the Declaration of Independence read out to Boston's citizens from the east balcony of the old State House. The reading took place on July 19, when the copy had arrived from Philadelphia. In his old age, Perkins thought that Sheriff Henderson had read the Declaration to the crowd, but it was actually William Greenleaf. Colonel Crafts stood at his side and "deaconed out" the phrases line by line after Greenleaf.

That same Thursday evening, mobs of excited people surged through the town and pulled down all the signs bearing replicas of the King's Arms. These, and signs belonging to suspected Tory sympathizers, were brought into King Street and thrown into a huge bonfire blazing Boston's assent to the Declaration of Independence.

King Street, and the neighborhood around it, were the playground of Tom, his brothers and their friends. He would later remember spinning tops and playing marbles in the Town House. Near here were the stocks and pillory and whipping post. Often they must have seen culprits—male or female—fastened to the post and whipped on their bare backs. This busy street was also where the town's principal business was transacted. Merchants met here to exchange news and plan new ventures. Captains of ships, arriving or departing, stopped to report to their owners or visit the insurance offices, or gossip in the taverns and coffee houses.

Truckmen pushed their barrels and their barrows through the crowded street. Coachmen carefully guided their conveyances in the throngs; fashionable ladies and gentlemen shopped; oyster sellers sat on chairs on the flagstone sidings and yelled the virtues of their sea-fresh delicacies. And through them all raced the children pursuing their quicksilver phantoms.

But twelve-year-old Tom was not to be left to the delights of King Street for long. That fall of 1776, he was sent to Hingham to be prepared for college by the Reverend Daniel Shute. For three years Tom studied with this man, then in his middle fifties, whom John Adams described as a "jolly, merry, droll, social Christian." Shute was paid a meager salary by his church, the Third (later the Second) Parish in Hingham, but he supplemented his income by teaching. So good a teacher was he, that many families sent their sons the twenty miles to Hingham to have the advantage of Shute's skill.

The extra income enabled Shute to build a handsome mansion on the corner of Main and South Pleasant streets that is still standing today. Here he lived with his second wife and his pupils. In the neighborhood the pupils could explore the huge rock on Glad Tidings Plain, the fulling mill down the street, and perhaps swim or fish in Cushing Pond. Harry Otis and John Welles, among others, shared this sylvan schooling with Tom.

When Tom went to Hingham, his grandfather Peck was not well. After a "lingering Indisposition," he died on June 21, 1777, "a worthy Citizen and well respected," said the *Continental Journal*. By his will made three years before, this "Hatt-Maker," as he called himself, left his estate to his widow and to his daughter Elizabeth Perkins, with certain specified gifts of land in Maine to Jim, Tom, and Sam, among other bequests. Each of the Perkins children was to receive £66. 13s. 4d. when he reached the age of 21. Within a year, Peck's widow followed him to the grave, and Elizabeth Perkins was left alone to bring up her children.

After three years at Hingham, his longest period with one teacher, his fifth and last, Tom did not register for Harvard, but instead entered a countinghouse. Whether from choice or necessity, it was to William Dall's countinghouse he went that fall of 1779.* But before he did, and before young Harry Otis could be examined for Harvard, Tom became a hero.

The millpond in Boston was in the north end of town, a natural cove that nature had nearly dammed in with a strip of land across the entrance. The first settlers finished the job and by a simple utilization of tidal flow had provided enough water power to keep several small mills operating. On a hot day it was a favored spot for Boston lads to plunge in and cool off.

One such day in that heroic summer, Tom and Harry Otis went to the pond for a swim. As they were splashing about, Harry suddenly cried out. Since Harry was a good swimmer, Tom paid no attention, thinking it done in sport. Then paddling towards where he had seen him last—no Harry! "I dove, and found him under water and dragged him to the surface as soon as possible. Fortunately, there was a large spar floating near us, to which I bore him and on which I placed him,

* Sixty-seven years later, in 1846, Perkins stated he was "disinclined to entering college." A few years after that he told a grandson it was because his mother could not afford to send him "owing to her losses during the war."

for he was quite unable to help himself." Pushing the spar to shore, some men heard the youth's cries and came to his assistance. Years later, telling the story to a grandson, Perkins added, "Harry always said he had enjoyed many good times in this world owing to me getting him out of that pond."[10]

Harry's good times were just beginning that fall when he entered Harvard. Tom, on the other hand, buckled down to work. His brother Jim was working for W. & J. Shattuck, a large mercantile enterprise, but they had sufficient apprentices. So Tom went to work for William Dall, a retail store owned by the Shattucks. After he had "suffered this purgatory" for a year, a position opened up in the Shattuck establishment. Jim was foreman of the apprentices, the others being Stephen Gray and William Crafts. Gray made Tom's stay with Shattuck memorable. He was an amiable chap, "well qualified for business," owned considerable property, was a favorite with the Shattucks, and was to be taken into partnership with them when he reached twenty-one.

In the classic pattern, Gray announced several times that he intended to commit suicide. His fellow apprentices did not believe him. On Thursday, February 7, 1782, he provided himself with a pistol and showed it to the others. He went about the countinghouse that day, firing the pistol from the window into the water several times in order to "prove its fire."

A short while before closing, he told them how he had been standing before the mirror holding the pistol up to his head to see if it would go off or not. But Jim, Tom, and Bill got busy shutting up the shop and paid no attention to him. Stephen left them and went upstairs to the counting room. In a few moments they heard the discharge of the pistol and something fell on the floor. So far were they from suspecting the truth that they joked that Gray had fired the pistol out the window again and then tipped a chair over to alarm them. Would they be such fools as to run up in fright, only to find him sitting there laughing at them? One of them went to the stairs and called up that if he did not come down they would lock the store and leave him in there all night. Getting no answer, they did just that. Giving him time to see how his joke had fallen flat, they went back to let him out. But not seeing him, and getting no answer when they shouted to him, they were too frightened to go upstairs and see what had happened. They called in a neighbor, and only then went up to the counting room.

There was Gray, stretched out dead. The coroner's inquest subsequently brought in a verdict of lunacy, and the remains of the young aprentice were "decently attended to the place appointed for all the living."[11]

Jim finished his time with Shattuck's shortly after Tom joined the firm. Reaching twenty-one at the end of March, and having received his grandfather's legacy, he booked passage on a Shattuck ship sailing to Virginia to pick up a cargo of tobacco for Europe. Off he went to make his fortune. But the war was still on, and the vessel was captured by a British frigate and taken into New York. Here he was released and made his way back to Boston. That autumn he tried again in the *Beaver,* a ship owned jointly by the Shattucks and Mrs. Perkins. Under charter to France, it was carrying cavalry horses to Cape Francis in the French colony of Santo Domingo. The *Beaver's* captain was Robert Cushing, who had married Tom's older sister Nancy. It was a short trip to Cape Francis on the north part of the island, in the country now called Haiti. This was a major port, an enterprising place where fortunes could be made and lost quickly. Jim went to work for the firm of Wall & Tardy, commission agents for many North American merchants.[12]

Tom was nineteen years old now, six feet tall, weighing 184 pounds, and a striking lad. Above his hawklike nose, his blue eyes under his brown hair looked out quizzically at the world. But more than his athletic, supple body, a stranger's eyes would have been drawn to the birthmark on his right cheek. Technically called a *haemangioma,* or popularly a "port-wine stain," this was a group of dilated capillary blood vessels, neither dangerous nor important except psychologically.*

Perkins did not let this blemish inhibit him, and showed an active interest in the female of the species. One of these nights, while still at Shattuck's, he came home late, as young men will, to find his mother waiting up for him. She was perfectly calm and silent, with no words of reproach, no cross-examination. Perkins told his daughter years later that he wished she had scolded him, for the silent admonition was too hard to bear.[13]

By now, Tom was getting impatient for his own majority to arrive

* The birthmark does not show in any portraits of THP because painters were careful to show his left side foremost. Gilbert Stuart alone dared a nearly frontal pose, very cleverly suggesting ruddy "English" cheeks.

and free him from the confines of Shattuck's store. The letters from Jim at the Cape sounded much more exciting and worldly than selling ship's bread or wines or books or what-have-you at Shattuck's.

The end of the war in 1783 brought a sense of euphoria, of stimulation, of galvanic energy that uplifted the spirits of the whole country as well as those of a twenty-one-year-old apprentice. Suddenly everything seemed possible to these new Americans, at last masters in their own country. Young Tom Perkins shared that sense of possibility. When he came into his prime and in his turn received his grandfather's bequest, he was ready to strike out. Being unwell, the family physician, Dr. Thomas Bulfinch, father of the architect, advised him to spend the winter of 1785–86 in a warmer climate. What more encouragement did he need to visit Jim. He embarked for the Cape on the ship *Cato,* with Captain Stevens, sailing under Dutch colors.[14]

So he left his native town on his first extended journey by the sea road. That road, which took Boston out to the world and brought the wealth of the world back to the hustling town, was soon to favor so kindly the ships and ventures of the Perkins brothers.

# T. Handasyd Perkins II 1786–1799

As winter comes, I take my way
Where other suns prompt other dreams.

Philip Freneau,
November 26, 1785

# 4

# Puritan in Paradise

Cape Francis was two weeks away from Puritan Boston by ship if the wind and weather were right. It was much further than that in its lighthearted attitude toward life, its carefree enjoyment of the senses, its singleminded preoccupation with pampering the tastes and lusts of the body. The most elegant city in the West Indies, it was built at the foot of a mountain, Morne du Cap, that nearly pushed it into the harbor. Sugar plantations and refineries were crowded into the great plain that stretched a level fifty miles north from the city. These supplied Europe with half the sugar it stirred into its coffee. The coffee too, likely enough, came from the Cape.

From some distance at sea, Perkins could see the high mountain looming over the Cape. His ship tacked in by Fort Picolet, which showed its cannons threateningly to strangers. A pilot came aboard and took the vessel through the narrows. Disembarking, Perkins found himself in a large, pleasant, busy metropolis. The stores fronting the wharf were immense. The houses, generally of stone and mostly one story, were ornamented with balconies, and often had gardens where thick trellises provided not only shade from the sun but also excellent muscat grapes.

Workmen on the wharves were lowering hogsheads of sugar or kegs of indigo aboard the vessels. Others were boiling cotton or filling sacks with coconuts. Spread out and still wet were heaps of coffee beans and piles of wood pulp to make dye. Carts and horses and men were coming and going through the melee. Other men were laboriously rolling heavy logs of mahogany aboard the ships. Over it all the workers sang songs like no Puritan hymn; the rhythm jumped the pulse, and pushed the heavy work along.

People of all countries and all colors flocked through the streets of this city of twenty thousand. It was a port town, with three or four thousand soldiers and sailors always in evidence. The idleness, the luxuries, the dissipation of the Cape were well known. It was famous through the whole Carribean for its women: the languid, pale Creoles; the chattering crowds of Negresses with their vivid turbans; the mulatto courtesans gorgeous in towering headdresses and flaming scarves. The skills and tricks of these mulatto prostitutes were advertised far and wide by sailors who had been to the Cape. Back in cold colonial Boston, they had heated the fantasies of many a New England lad, and helped to hurry him aboard a vessel to know their enticements himself.

It seemed as if everybody came to the Cape, among them a vicious rabble of adventurers out to make money in a hurry and not particularly caring how they made it or who sweated for it as long as it was not they themselves. Underneath the surface gaiety festered this mass of crooks, criminals, and fortune hunters. The whole voluptuous, shimmering pyramid was carried on the bent backs of the black slaves. Forty thousand of them were shipped into Santo Domingo every year. Two thirds of the half-million slaves in the country were African-born, and unlike the domesticated, tame Creole slaves. This fact was soon to have fearful significance.

Tom arrived in winter, a good season. The hot months, April through September, were the most unhealthy, when malaria and yellow fever ravaged black and white alike. Even the cooler, rainy months were hard on white men fresh from chill New England. Intestinal troubles particularly plagued the white man in these tropics. Tom found his poor health not at all improved by the Cape. The pleasures of this country, someone said, were "a blue sky and no cold weather. I can name no others." So despite the attractions of life at the Cape, the playhouse, the botanical gardens, the delightful tree-shaded promenades, the beautiful public square with flowing fountains, despite the good hospital, perhaps even despite the art of its mulatto women, Tom decided after a short time to go back to the States.[1]

He may well have missed his brother. That same winter James had returned to Massachusetts to be married on January 11, 1786. With his sister Mary, James rode in a small open sleigh the fifty miles to Worcester where his bride Sally Paine lived. In her old age, Mary could still remember that ride, for the sleigh had overturned and they had been dumped into a snow bank. This was hardly sufficient to cool the ardor of the twenty-three-year-old bridegroom and on they went.

Tom sailed for Charleston, South Carolina, about that time, where he had letters of introduction from General Lincoln and General Knox to some of the town's most distinguished citizens. Since Lincoln had been the defender of Charleston during the Revolution and a great favorite of the local gentry, his introductions gave Perkins quick entrée into the best society. He experienced in full that warm Southern hospitality that became both a tradition and a cliché. He visited about, receiving and accepting invitations to many of the neighboring plantations, particularly in the section called Pon-Pon on the Edisto River, and was a frequent guest of Mr. Thomas Ferguson. A fellow apprentice from Shattuck's, William Crafts, was in the city and when there Perkins stayed with him. He even went on a short visit to Savannah during that winter.

This round of partying appealed to young Perkins. There was fine sport with the gun: geese, duck, teal—all shot in great abundance. Every Saturday morning, the Pon-Pon gentlemen gathered to hunt deer; then the slaves set up tables for a woods dinner. Ham, chicken, and other "comforts" were handed round, plus whatever had been shot. Tom's health improved, and by the middle of April he was ready to sail home to Boston with Captain Tilden on the brig *Fame*.[2]

On June 7, 1786, readers of the *Massachusetts Centinel* saw in an advertisement that Wall, Tardy and Co. of Cape Francis "having by mutual consent been dissolved the first of May last, James Perkins, jun. and Walter Burling, late partners in said House in company with Thomas H. Perkins have established themselves at said Cape Francis with every possible advantage for the transaction of Commission Business, under the firm of Perkins, Burling & Perkins." They begged leave to offer their best services to their friends on the continent. The announced arrangement was that Jim would be the Boston agent, while Tom and Burling would reside at the Cape.

If Tom had not already gone back to the Cape by June, he was certainly there by the end of July, right in the middle of the worst Cape weather. Such are the necessities of making a fortune. Circulars about the new partnership went out to more than seventy-five firms, most of them in the Boston–Newburyport area. A few went to New York, Philadelphia, and the West Indian connections of Wall, Tardy and Co. By the end of July, Jim was at the Cape too, and the new partners were hard at work.

At times it would seem as if Tom were in two places at once. Probably the brothers shuttled back and forth fairly often between Boston and the Cape. For how could Tom write a letter from the Cape on July 27, as he did, when at the same time he was supposed to be joining the Independent Corps of Cadets being reorganized in Boston on July 20? The fastest winds that blew could not get him from one place to the other in time to do that himself. Yet the records of the Cadet Company, lost in a fire so only copies exist, show "T. Handasyd Perkins" was one of the original subscribers at that July 20 meeting. Obviously some friend subscribed for him. Perhaps the new cadet when in Boston spent some time at the Green Dragon Tavern with his military companions, where they met Thursday evenings "to acquire experience in the Art Military," but most of this year Perkins was at the Cape.[3]

"We have taken a very convenient store," a correspondent was advised on July 24, "and are fixed to our wishes." A few days later Tom was informing an account in Boston that "agreeable to your desire we have already made some advances in establishing such a place for the disposition of Slaves in this quarter as will be attended with safety and advantage to the proprietor."[4]

There was a great deal of money to be made in slaves. Everybody but the "commodity" benefited; the kings and traders in Africa who sold them to the ships, the captains and crews who brought them to the West Indies, the commission merchants like Perkins, Burling, & Perkins who sold them, the planters who worked them into their graves. Africa had an inexhaustible supply of them, seemingly, despite the thousands who died each year on the horrible crossings.

Commission merchants did not get their hands too greatly soiled in the business. Their job was to visit the "Guinea" ships coming to the Cape, select the prime slaves whom they would purchase either on customers' orders or their own speculation, holding them briefly until they could be sold. They were middlemen and their share of the obvious brutality could be minimal, indeed almost nonexistant. Their transactions were strictly businesslike: getting unsold goods off the shelf ("Your negroes are unsold, we have signified the necessity of finishing this business, and will see it done"); getting all the traffic would bear ("Your negroes were sold at Auction, our W. B. attended and trumped Bob up to 2300 and odd livres, the other went for 1600, he was lame"); coping with special problems ("Almost impossible to get rid of an infant negro").[5]

Slaves were only a small part of the commission business. Flour, horses, and dried fish were a big part of it. Like all the other foreign merchants, these transactions often involved the Perkinses in smuggling. The regulations of all these colonies were framed for the benefit of the Mother Country, not the colony. Americans well knew this from their own colonial experience. The wants and needs of the colonists were ignored or taxed or hamstrung or denied in many arbitrary and vexatious ways. Interpretation of the regulations was often capricious. Smuggling became the understood and accepted method to make the system "work." But merchants who smuggled had to be careful that bribes were large enough to keep the bribe takers content.

A Baltimore client was advised by the Perkins firm that if any more flour arrived in hogshead, "the searchers must know it and be brib'd at a considerable expense." Some things could not be mentioned in letters for fear that they might fall into the wrong hands. "Our J. P. will be in Boston last of September and will communicate to you the means of Introducing Flour to this Port and taking away Contraband Goods." It was risky. "Indeed in a government like ours smuggling is a heart-rending business." Yet the profits tempted many a merchant to chance it.[6]

During 1787 Tom had been in Boston long enough to sell a most important product—himself. The dark brown eyes of a neighbor's daughter had caught his attention. Around the corner from what Revolutionary fervor had renamed State Street (formerly King Street), was the tobacco shop of Simon Elliot. The tobacconist had a daughter Sally with dark brown hair and a charming figure. Perkins, who was fond of tobacco, found himself even fonder of the tobacconist's daughter.

He proposed, and on Sunday, March 23, 1788, Abraham Hayward, clerk of the Federal Street Church, certified that "Mr. Thomas Handasyd Perkins and Miss Sally Elliot have been three times publicly cried out in open Church."[7]

Two days later, on "a fine, clear" Tuesday, March 25, Thomas and Sarah became husband and wife. The Reverend Jeremy Belknap performed the rites uniting them. Standing in front of the couple, the short, thick clergyman whose face was much pitted with smallpox scars, scarcely moved his lips, as was his habit, as he recited the traditional words. And the bridegroom was never to want for choice "segars" again.[8]

He did need something else. On Thursday, the twenty-seventh, he dashed off a short note to M. M. Hays, enclosing some letters of exchange, and asking him to "please make as quick Sale of them as you can, as I am in want of the ready." So soon he had found that two, even a girl of Scottish descent, cannot live as cheaply as when parents are paying the bills.[9]

The newlyweds set up housekeeping in a small, ordinary house on the south side of Summer Street. Here eight months and eleven days later a young daughter was born to them on the sixth of December. When she was baptized on January 11, 1789 by Dr. Belknap, she was called Sarah after her mother. The marriage was happy even though the temperaments of the two partners were different. "Father," a daughter was to say years later, "was very social and almost always had some-one to dine with and went out a good deal into company from the first. Mother was not fond of company."[10]

Tom had decided to establish himself in Boston and not go back to the Cape. His younger brother Samuel, now twenty-one years old finished with his apprenticeship, agreed to take Tom's place in the Cape firm. They reorganized on August 15, 1788 under the name, "Perkins, Burling & Company."

Tom formed a company in Boston with his uncle by marriage, Captain James Magee, which they called T. H. Perkins & James Magee. Their letterbook begins on October 14, 1788 and tells of selling wines, spirits, and rice on commission for Charleston and Newburyport merchants. Their store was on the lower part of Butler's Row, near father-in-law Elliot's shop. On November 26 Perkins advertised "Excellent Sherry wine in quarter casks, Madeira wine," as well as iron, flour, and oil.[11] But already the two men were planning a bigger speculation than mere shopkeeping.

Soon after the end of the Revolution, merchants in New York had sent the *Empress of China* to Canton on a voyage that marked the start of American trading with that country. By 1785, Elias Hasket Derby, known as "King" Derby of Salem, became interested in the possibilities of this trade. He sent one of his best ships out to Canton, where it was loaded with tea, china, and cinnamon. It made excellent profits for him and he sent out others. By the early summer of 1788 Derby had arranged with James Magee to make a second trip to the East for him.

Magee was then a thirty-eight-year-old "convivial Irishman," who had been captaining ships since he was at least twenty-six. Exactly when he arrived in America from Ireland is not known, but it was in time to harass the British all through the war as captain of various privateer expeditions. After the war, lately married to an aunt of Sally Elliot Perkins, he continued at sea, with stops at home long enough to sire three children with a fourth on the way when he agreed with Derby to go to China again.

Derby was sending two ships to the East that season. Benjamin Webb was to captain the other, the *Three Sisters*. Magee was to be master of the ship *Astrea,* and he picked his partner and nephew, Tom Perkins, to be his supercargo for the voyage. The duties of a supercargo were varied, but as the name indicated, he supervised the cargo, handling all matters pertaining to its care, its sale, and the purchase of return goods.

Magee put an advertisement in the *Centinel* on December 17, asking for freight or passengers. The plan then was to sail in late January. All three were busy now rounding up shippers to venture cargo on the trip. Derby himself was shipping ginseng, English iron, Philadelphia beer, and other items which he expected would net $94,000 in Canton. Perkins was to take this money and invest it in nankeens, tea, coffee, silks, and cups and saucers for Derby to sell at home.

Magee and Perkins eventually rounded up a good dozen and a half shippers. Their cargo included 32,000 pounds of butter, 1,729 gallons of rum, 6,300 pounds of codfish, 8,933 pounds of spermaceti candles, 100 tons of bar iron from Russia, and many other small items. Simon

Elliot, since it was so much in the family, risked some of his snuff and tobacco to see if the Chinese would acquire the habit.[12]

Governor James Bowdoin himself was induced to ship 4,000 milled Spanish dollars to be laid out at Canton in good hyson tea. Bowdoin did not know Perkins personally, but he wrote to a friend that "the letters I have seen recommending him to Mr. Derby from gentlemen of distinction speak of him in terms of the fullest confidence in his integrity, capacity for business, sobriety, and good sense." By his own inquiry, Bowdoin discovered that "he justly merits that character."[13]

Magee and Perkins had freight of their own aboard. They were to receive 5 percent commission on sales of the cargo out and 2½ percent on sales of the cargo home. In addition they were given 5 percent profit on goods taken from Batavia to Canton and half the passage money. It was a generous agreement, but they had to do a lot of work for it.[14]

By the middle of February 1789 they were ready to sail. On the fifteenth, saying goodby to his wife of less than a year and his month-old baby, Tom and the *Astrea* put to sea, trusting themselves and their future to the winds of trade and chance. They were bound for Canton in China, half a world away, if luck and skill working together could bring it to pass.

It was a long month's passage down the Atlantic before they arrived at Saint Jago (Sao Thiago) on Sunday, March 16, 1789. The ship proved a slow sailer for her bottom was not coppered and tropical marine growth soon covered the hull of the vessel, greatly cutting her speed.[15]

At Cape Verde it was decided to transfer part of the iron from the *Astrea* to another vessel bound for Bombay, for they heard reports that iron was selling too cheaply in Batavia. Six days later, in company with the *Atlantic,* an English whaler with a Nantucket skipper, Captain Bassett, they headed south once again. The weather was fair and pleasant. Sailors worked on deck, the carpenter was busy securing the bowsprit, and the goats carried on board for milk gave birth to young kids. One of the sailors who had formerly been a whalemen "struck a large porpoise" which served as a fine dish for the crew. "I eat a part of the heart and a piece of the steak," wrote Perkins in the diary he kept on the trip, "both of which I thought excellent."

Visits went back and forth between the two ships as they inched their way along. Friday, March 28, Bassett with his mate Mr. Hayward "hoisted out his boat and came on board . . . they passed the evening with us." The next day Bassett came on board again, "tarried until evening and partook of a piece of shark with us." Nearing the meridian on the thirty-first, Perkins found the sun "so directly overhead that the figure of a pen knife stuck in the deck perpendicularly made no shade obliquely." The ship was approaching the equator and the crew got set for the ceremony of "crossing the line," which Perkins described for his wife.

"As soon as the Captain has declared that the ship is on the line . . . one of the people is dressed by the others like an old man.—His appearance is really to one prepared for the business, frightful. He addresses the Captain—demands from whence he came and whither he is bound—to which question he is answered by the Captain. He then inquires if all hands are upon deck, and when answered in the affirmative, he looks round to see if he knows them all, when he discovers those he has not seen over the line before and asks them a number of questions . . . He then tells them 'tis customary for all new comers to be shaved on passing his territories or pay a heavy toll—and then goes on to inquire if any one prefers paying the toll to being ducked. He pays according to his abilities; the passengers a gallon and the foremast hands a bottle of rum . . . From our ships company twelve were selected who were not known by the old gentleman and the toll exacted. The two mates, the Doctor, and myself were excused by paying our toll or rather giving security for it on the word of the Captain."

The ones who refused, or couldn't pay the toll, were sent below and brought up separately, blindfolded. "The subject is placed over a large tub filled with water and obliged to sit down on a hand spike which is set across it. He is then lathered with a large tar brush, dipped into a composition of Slush, lampblack and oil. While under this operation he takes an oath which is administered by Neptune 'to never kiss the maid when he can kiss the Mistress, unless the maid be the handsomer, never to eat brown bread when he can get white' and very much more." Since Perkins was writing this journal for his wife to see, he decided that all of the oath had better not be included.

When the poor victim agrees to the oath "the brush is thrust between his lips. After there is sufficient lather on, a couple of barbers step up with rasors made of a piece of iron hoop, ground saw fashion, which they exercise with much dexterity about the face of the operatee. When finished, the hand spike on which he sits is knocked out from under him which emerges [immerses] him in water and two trusty hands stand ready to shower oceans of water down upon his head from the long boat which is filled for the purpose." The shaving operation finished, a mock war commenced from which no one was exempt. "This rages until the Captain sends word upon deck for it to have an end, which was done by Capt. Magee at 6 P.M."

At 6:30, Magee, Bassett, and Perkins went out on deck. To all appearances, the disorder was done away with. "I was of course unconcerned about getting a wet jacket when Capt. Magee observed two hands in the Mizen Tops with a tub of water prepared for any unsuspecting head. He asked them if they had not heard his orders to desist and ordered them to have done with all pranks. A few minutes after they spattered some water on my umbrella. When the Captain spoke severely to them and told them to throw the water clear of the ship, when in direct opposition to his commands, they threw the whole upon Capt. Bassett, Capt. Magee, and myself."

It was a serious matter for the captain of a ship to be disobeyed. Magee ordered them down and seized Crandell—one of the two—by the collar as soon as he touched deck. Crandell started to grapple with Magee who swung on him. Jacobs, the other sailor, swore he would not see his messmate abused and seized Magee. "This made the mutiny rage. The exertions of the mates, Mr. Russell, Capt. Bassett, myself and some of the people who had been *used to obeying orders,* put them below, though not without some difficulty, as Jacobs swore he would not be confined. A centinel was put over them with a cutlass and ordered to keep them below until further orders." By the next day the two mutineers had sobered up and realized their mistake; one for which they could have been hung. They asked for and were given a hearing by Magee. Upon promising all kinds of reformation and begging forgiveness, they were let off.

A squall came up and separated the *Astrea* from the *Atlantic* and it was several days before the ships rejoined company. The squall drove them forward, and by April 12 they passed Saint Helena to the west. Flying fish were caught in the rigging of the ship and fell on deck. Bonitos and dolphins played round the ship. Perkins now saw albatross for the first time. Magee told him that on his last voyage this way he had killed one measuring sixteen feet tip to tip. A couple of days later Magee shot an albatross and hoisted out the jolly boat to bring him on board. Perkins loaded his gun and went out in the boat "and of four at which I shoot on the wing I brought on board three—the largest of which measured 10 feet nine inches." Eating them the next day, he found them "more than tolerable."

By May they were running on a long sea and coming abreast of Madagascar. The sailors were complaining they were not getting enough beef. When a twenty-eight pound piece was weighed before and after boiling, it was found that fifteen pounds had boiled away. The pork was equally bad.

On May 28 they passed the Indian Ocean island of Saint Paul, and Perkins made a sketch of it in his journal. The next day he checked the main hold and found it dry and in good order. Two days later, at 10 P.M. in a squall, Perkins saw a rainbow "which I thought, not a little *uncommon in the night* but found by inquiring they are frequent in the Southern latitudes. It was seen untill towards the close of the Squall." On June 5 "Capt. Magee and myself were weighed this day to convince him that he was the heavier man; his weight 204 lbs. mine 184 lbs. which is to a pound what I weighed at the age of 19."

As the ship neared Christmas Island, in the Indian Ocean, Magee began to worry about pirates. His men hauled out the carriage guns, mounted them, and prepared cartridges. But now a serious problem arose. Their drinking water had been stored in some casks previously used for coffee. Although they had been rinsed out before being filled with water for the trip, it hadn't been done properly. Later they were to find that even a "fourth rinsing" of these casks would leave the rinse water "as black as puddle water." By June 18 there was only this "very bad water" left to drink. When they sighted land on the twenty-fourth all were happy. Their wood supply, too, was nearly gone, and it was feared they would be able to cook only once in every three or four days.

By the twenty-eighth the ship was still beating about in the wind and could not get nearer to land, wood, or fresh water. Perkins had taken an emetic since he was feeling poorly "and was severely operated upon by it." He reasoned he could have used the drinking water for an emetic it was so foul. The next day brought a new alarm. Only 530 gallons of water were left. All hands were put on an allowance of one quart, and that horribly stinking, for the next twenty four hours.

The day after, Magee reduced the allowance again. "Mine will more than serve me, as the last twenty-four hours, so much do my stomach loath it that I did not expend a pint—in addition to the very bad flavour, it is so sour that it turns milk as soon as if it was put into vinegar."

The men were complaining bitterly now about the water. The exclusively salt diet only made matters worse. It was little pleasure on the Fourth of July to be granted an extra allowance of the brackish water. What *was* cause for celebration was that the stores of wine, rum, and beer were opened. "The Gentlemen of the Cabbin partook of the best the Ship afforded." Morris the barber spent the next day confined below "from entering too deeply into the *Spirit* of Independence."

Anxiously they scanned the horizon for land. The state of suspense kept Perkins from sleeping. At 6 A.M. of the sixth they saw Java Head. Guns were swung out to be loaded. Then they found "not a shott will fitt our guns." With true Bostonian restraint, Perkins found this only "most astonishing." Added to the blunder on the water casks, it must have caused Captain Magee to be astonished in less Bostonian fashion.

But all such troubles were quickly forgotten, for now they were anchored less than a mile off the shore of Java. Boats went ashore and the whole day was spent watering and wooding. Sixteen tons of wonderfül water were brought on board and all spirits soared.

Shortly, the ship headed for Batavia, and on the thirteenth they anchored in the harbor of that Dutch city. Here they found Webb with the *Three Sisters*. He was soon aboard the *Astrea,* giving Magee and Perkins the bad news "of the prohibition and restrictions on trade, and everything else which could serve to give us the dumps." Perkins had had great hopes for this trip. He was venturing much on it, including more than a year of his life. He not only expected a good profit from it, but anticipated that success for the merchants he represented would redound to his future benefit. Now, after the tedium and troubles of the trip, he found that all American trade was prohibited.

When once your bark is launch'd boys,
On Fortune's fickle seas,
May Patience be your Pilot then,
And gently blow each breeze.

Charles S. Powell

---

# 5

# Into the Bosome of the Ocean

When Perkins and Magee landed in Batavia they immediately visited the governor-general of the colony, who confirmed Webb's bad news: American trade was indeed prohibited. At the hotel where all foreigners were obliged to stay, Perkins met a compatriot, a Mr. Blanchard, who "had been here a week, and done nothing but petition." Perkins drew one up too and went to the governor-general to present it. "His house a palace. He received us, Dutchman-like, in his shirt-sleeves, and his stockings half down his legs." A nephew of this man had given Perkins a letter of recommendation before the *Astrea* left Boston. With the faint hope that this, and his knowledge of French, might turn the trick, Perkins went to his audience in the council chamber the next day to hear the results of his petition.[1]

He accompanied the captain of a newly arrived British ship. After cooling their heels for a long time in the reception hall "and being witness to a great deal of pompous parade" they were admitted to the council, presented their petitions and withdrew. Then further waiting. Finally the Britisher was given liberty to land his goods, "but we, poor, despised devils, were absolutely denied the liberty of selling a farthing's worth. Whatever I thought of the partiality, I very respectfully took my leave, but determined to persevere; and, after much difficulty, got leave to renew our petitions."[2]

While waiting the outcome of this, Perkins cultivated the local gentry, dining to the accompaniment of music in their elegant homes, washing his hands in rosewater before and after he ate, playing cards and putting in a discreet word now and then with people who could help his cause. During the day he explored the beautiful city with its canals of dirty water bordered by sycamore trees and crowded with boats. The unpaved streets were sprinkled morning and evening with water from the canals to lay the dust. Perkins thought this a great convenience, but "it took away the pleasure of it when I saw at what an expense of human feelings it is effected." Slaves, chained two by two, did the work.[3]

He met the sixty-eight-year-old governor-general at his home outside the city, and found him to be a genial, hard-working man, addicted to good wine, novels, and his fish ponds. Finally on the twenty-first the *Astrea* was given permission to sell part of its cargo, and by the next day the ban on trade was completely lifted.

It was one thing to be permitted to sell one's goods; it was another thing to sell them. On July 22 Perkins started the rounds of merchants who had been suggested to him as possible purchasers of his goods. There was not the least rush to buy. Prices offered him were well below the original cost of the goods. He began to realize that the merchants were in league to force the Americans to sell low. On the twenty-fourth a British ship arrived with a large stock of goods—and depressed prices even further. On the twenty-eighth he made his first sale, and the next day the goods were shipped ashore in proas, the "most despicable boats I ever saw," but which nevertheless cost a large sum to hire.[4]

The hot climate and the deadly malaria of the islands began to affect the crew of the *Astrea*. One died on the thirteenth, another on the fourteenth, and both were buried in the Malay cemetery. All were eager now to leave feverish Batavia and get to Canton. Coffee, sugar, rice, and hides were loaded onto the ship for sale in China. By bringing in a cargo of rice, foreign vessels could avoid paying duties at Canton. As a personal investment, Perkins purchased two birds of paradise. He made a last-minute sightseeing trip up to the Dutch fort to see the bones of a 136 foot sea monster that had been cast up on the Java coast, and he completed the very extensive notes he had made in his diary about Batavia and the people, the customs, and the food.

Finally, the last water casks were put on board, and at 4 A.M. on August 18, they hove up and stood out of the harbor of Batavia, "which I left with more pleasure than any place I ever was at in my life. Our crew very much fatigued and tired out with the amazing heavy work." The deaths of two of their shipmates had made all the crew "conceive they are unwell." Eleven days later at sea found the boatswain and James Dwyer on the sick list. Dwyer was dangerously ill with fever, made worse by his fear of dying, and his conviction that his time had come. Two days later, after making a verbal will in Perkins's presence leaving all he possessed to his aged father, Dwyer did die. The flag flew at half mast as the body was dropped into the sea.

On Sept. 10 they saw land again, "to our very great delight." The *Astrea* anchored off the Portugese town of Macao, a village built on a peninsula at the entrance of the great bay leading to Canton. Quickly the ship was surrounded by little boats full of chattering girls calling out in high-pitched voices, "Hy yaw Massa, you come again. I washy washy for you last voyage; washy washy three piece, one man, one catty. I washy washy your three piece." The sailors made the most of the suggestive overtones of this banter, but the girls for all their smiles and giggles were really washerwomen for the ships passing through Macao.[5]

Later a Chinese pilot came aboard and the ship moved with the tide and wind up the bay, passing Lintin Island, and much further on coming to the Tiger's Mouth, the *Bocca Tigris* of the Portugese sailors, a mountainous gap opening into the Pearl River. They sailed passed the Bogue forts which guarded either side of this entrance to the river. Changing pilots, the ship now moved through a barren countryside, uncultivated and uninteresting. Gradually this changed to rice paddies stretching flatly away on either side. They were but half-a-day's sail from Wang-Po, or "Yellow Anchorage," as the Chinese called the town the American knew as Whampoa. In 1745, Emperor Yung Ching had decreed that this was as near to Canton as foreign vessels could go. The decree was still in effect.

The Pearl River was crowded with boats. Huge, unwieldy junks passed with great loads of freight, gigantic staring eyes painted on each bow—"no have eyes, how can see?"—their bamboo sails tight in the breeze. Sampans, bursting with families, sculled by, their one oar being worked vigorously. Usually the children on these boats had gourds fastened to their shoulders to keep them afloat should they tumble overboard. Occasionally, one of the emperor's man-of-war boats sailed past, jammed with soldiers, colors flapping, great brass gongs beating out strange rhythms. Of a different world were the "flower boats." Neatly dressed women walked the decks of these, their jet black hair pulled back to the crown and skewered into a knot. But these delicacies were forbidden foreigners; their charms were only for domestic consumption.

Along the river, men, women, and children could be seen in little boats fishing with nets. Carefully the *Astrea* eased by fish weirs staked out in the stream. Those stakes, of the largest bamboo, had been known to damage smaller vessels that had carelessly blundered upon them.

It was September 18, 1789 when the *Astrea* arrived at Whampoa Reach or Anchorage, and moored in a road filled with foreign vessels, including quite a few American. A noisome little town was Whampoa, with two islands in its anchorage. One called "Danes" was where ships could be beached and scraped before the long homeward voyage; the other was "French" where sailors could walk and exercise and where Europeans were buried. The ship stayed at Whampoa, but business was transacted in Canton, some dozen miles further up the Pearl River. All the trade of the great Chinese Empire with the outside world was funneled, by imperial decree, through this one city of Canton.

It took a good two hours to row from Whampoa to Canton. The ship's boat would pull away with flags flying and the crew slicked up for the trip. All boats had to stop at customhouses on the way and be examined for contraband. An exemption was made for a captain's boat in deference to his flag.

About halfway to Canton, the boat would pass by famous Lob-Lob creek. Sampans with prostitutes aboard would sail out of this small inlet and accost the boats passing up or down with some such invitation as "Master caree Lob-Lob?" If master caree, the women would quickly climb aboard and provide service. Like the sea traffic, the sex traffic was carefully regulated by the Chinese mandarins who made it almost impossible for the foreign sailors to express their sexual inclinations anywhere else but here. For "overlooking" this breach of the law which they had made, the mandarins got their "cut" of the fees of the prostitutes.[6]

Canton was a surprising city, large and flat and white and squarish—square streets, square houses. A few tall round towers broke into the square geometry. Walled in, the city stood amid green fields that stretched out to merge in distant bluish hills, looking like so many ant heaps and often topped with brightly decorated pagodas. Many of the inhabitants did not live in the city at all, but on boats anchored in the streams and inlets. The villas of the wealthy were scattered along the river banks, and the river itself was busy with water traffic.

Perkins had too much to do, however, to spend his first days sightseeing. He had goods to sell at the best prices he could get and merchandise to buy. Not only was he determined to do a good job for the shippers—with all the advantages that would accrue to him as a result—but he had his own fortune to begin. After all, he was twenty-five years old, on his own for four years, a family man, and still not provided with a regular income. The West Indies business was uncertain and what little profit it had brought, had been risked on further adventures. This trip, if he survived it, could prove a turning point.

The Chinese government had not only limited trade with the Empire to this one port, it also restricted the number of people who could handle that trade. These were the famous Hong merchants, about a dozen in number, who purchased their licenses to engage in business with the foreigners at a great price from the government. Every foreigner was obliged to employ them in all transactions and naturally paid heavily for the privilege. The *Astrea* was bonded by the Hong merchant called Equa (the "qua" was the equivalent of "mister"), while two others, Skykenqua and Pankequa, were responsible to the government for the *Astrea's* duties.[7]

Perkins's first problem was to get rid of 75,000 pounds of ginseng that the *Astrea* carried. This root, dug out of New England soil was greatly desired by the Chinese who thought it an aphrodisiac that could restore or increase sexual potency. But in the fall of 1789 there were too many other American vessels at Whampoa with ginseng. Perkins had been warned he would have trouble selling the root, but he planned to combine it with "the two coming with Cotton."[8]

The *Atlantic* and the *Light Horse,* both Derby ships, were "the two coming with Cotton." On October 5 they anchored in Whampoa Reach. Two days later a fourth Derby ship, the *Three Sisters,* arrived. Now there were four ships and cargoes to sell where only one had been sent.

The other three had been destined originally for the Isle de France (now Reunion) in the Indian Ocean. Young Derby's son, stationed there, had sent them on to Canton in search of a better market.

With more than a dozen American ships in port, prices of all American products fell, and the price of tea accordingly went up. The Derby men got together and decided to sell two of their four vessels, and load the other two with teas. This was not an unusual thing to do as American ships usually brought a good price in that part of the world, and it meant getting rid of a ship that might not have withstood the long, rough voyage home. The *Atlantic* and the *Three Sisters* were sold. Their cargoes were first taken out by lighters and brought up to Canton together with the cargoes of the other two ships. There the Hong merchants finally arranged the disposal of all four cargoes. With the proceeds from all their sales, they bought Chinese goods for the home market.

Nearly 730,000 pounds of black and green teas were bought and loaded onto the *Astrea* and the *Light Horse,* plus other Chinese products such as a cotton cloth called nankeen. In exchange for his own little adventure of cheese, lard, and wine, Perkins took home cotton shirtings and flasks of mercury. The officers and supercargoes of each ship were allowed a specified proportion of space in the hold in which to bring home their own speculation without paying freight on it.[9]

Perkins watched the loading of some of the 2,000 chests filled with tea. Each chest held between 350 and 400 pounds and were packed by barefoot coolies tramping down the tea leaves. Fat coolies of 300 pounds or so were best for this job as their weight meant much more tea could be jammed into each chest. The purchaser had to insist though that they work barefoot for shoes or sandals would cut and spoil the leaves. The finer teas, however, were carefully packed by hand. Some of the unscrupulous Hong merchants were adept at mixing teas for an unsuspecting customer. In the packing places they had trap doors above the chests, and when the dust from the packing grew thick and obscuring, these traps would be opened and old inferior teas would be dumped down into the chests.

Perkins attempted to get a look at the main part of Canton, which was forbidden to foreigners. He was unceremoniously turned back, but not until he had gotten a brief glimpse of an elaborate marriage procession with its glittering retinue and richly caparisoned horses. He had better luck on his next venture. Having sold some wine to a native up river from Canton, he was given special permission to go and settle his accounts. He went by boat, but came back by land. His white skin made him a great curiosity to the peasants who crowded around him, pulling open his clothing to see if the skin underneath was as white as his face and hands. The village dogs growled on seeing such a strange bleached creature.

An English ship, the *Iphigenia,* had come into Whampoa on the fifth of October, the same day as the two Derby ships. This ship had been on the northwest coast of America trading with the Indians, and had brought sea otter skins to sell to the Chinese. These skins, if smuggled in, could bring as much as seventy dollars each. They had been bought on the coast for trinkets. Here was an opportunity for a fantastic profit. On November 17 the American ship *Columbia* arrived from the same place with the same story. She had sailed from Boston a year and a half before the *Astrea.* She had gone around the Horn to the Oregon coast and had been either cruising the coast or at the Sandwich Islands (Hawaii) ever since, with a sister sloop, the *Washington.* Captain Gray, presently commanding the *Columbia,* wrote his owners in Boston from Canton in mid-December observing, "Our expedition, Gentlemen, will not be equal to your expectations nor is there any American Ships here but will make bad voyages."[10]

First mate on the *Columbia* was young Joseph Ingraham. Perkins and Magee talked with him about the possibilities opened up by this pioneering voyage of the *Columbia.* Apparently they made an agreement at that time with Ingraham to send him out as captain of a ship to the Northwest Coast as soon as they all got back safely to Boston.

Excited by this opportunity for the future and eager to get his present venture home profitably, Perkins was now more than ever anxious to get started back. But first a splendid banquet was given by the Hong merchants for the American officers and supercargoes. A rich profusion of English and Chinese dishes were served, but Perkins thought the bird's-nest soup insipid. Nor did he fancy the shark fins.

Their vessels loaded, the Derby men got set for the long trip home. The crew of the *Atlantic* sailed on the *Light Horse,* while the men from the *Three Sisters* joined the crew on the *Astrea.* On January 22, 1790, the two crammed vessels left Whampoa for Boston. One hundred and twenty nine days later, the Ship News column of the Columbian *Centinel* for June 2 announced that "On Monday [May 31] arrived here the ship *Astrea,* James Magee, Esq., Commander; in 125 days from Canton in China with a valuable cargo."

Dr. William Paine, James Perkins's brother-in-law, wrote to him from Salem saying Tom appeared "very well but much altered in his looks; but from the air and good *Beef* of his return sail, he will soon recover his former good appearance." This would hardly be calculated to cheer up a concerned brother. Paine added, "he's a pleasant, well-informed man, and has picked up a great deal of useful knowledge and many anecdotes, with which I hope you will one Day be amused."[11]

The cargo of the *Astrea* had to be sold, and with the arrival of the *Light Horse* and the rest of the cargo, the problem was compounded. While the Derby ships had been away the country had organized under a new government and constitution. Import duties had risen sharply from the 5 percent ad valorem of the Massachusetts tariff of 1786 to between six and twelve cents per pound of tea, depending on its quality, in the new national tariff. This was more than the tea cost in Canton. The duties went into effect immediately and made no allowance for cargoes already on the way home at the time of the passage of the act.

Moreover, there had been an unusually large importation of teas into America in the year 1790. Total for the year was some 2,600,000 pounds of which the two Derby ships alone had brought in nearly 730,000. The yearly demand for tea in America was about a million pounds, so the bottom dropped out of the tea market. Derby had figured to store the tea until the price went back up, but there was then no system of bonded warehouses where products could be stored until taken out for sale, so the duties had to be paid upon the tea immediately. For the two ships these amounted to $27,109.18. It was a real problem for the merchant to find this much cash. Derby petitioned Congress for relief, and thanks to good connections, this was immediately granted.

All the shippers in the venture soon had advertisements in the paper informing the public of the fresh merchandise "just received." In the same paper announcing the death of Tom Doubleday, his sister Esther's husband, Perkins inserted this notice:

> Imported in the ship *Astrea,* from China, and to be disposed of at the store of
> THOMAS H. PERKINS
> at the lower end of Butler's Row

> Fresh Bohea, Souchong and Hyson teas, long and short Nankins, of an excellent quality, a small invoice of satins, lutestrings, and other silks and a few best coloured and black Canton Silk Handkerchiefs, etc. etc.

Derby himself, was offering both ships, the *Astrea,* "about 360 tons," and the *Light Horse,* "about 250 tons with all their materials as they arrived from Canton" for sale.[12]

Brother Jim came from Cape Francis to welcome Tom back, hear all about the trip, and make plans for the future. Captain Magee sent some tea as a gift to Mrs. Ingraham. The town began to anticipate the arrival of the *Columbia,* which, when it touched Boston, would have completed a trip around the world, the first American vessel to accomplish this feat.

With the knowledge they had gained in China of the new trade opportunities opened on the northwest Coast by the *Columbia,* Perkins and Magee were making every effort to be the first to get a ship out to exploit these new possibilities. The owners of the *Columbia* knew what was going on, and waited impatiently for the arrival of their own vessel so they could rush it back to the coast.

Bits of news began to leak out into the press. At the end of July there was a squib about the beauty of the sea otter skin, how it was an article of luxury to the Chinese mandarins, and that the natives on the coast wanted woolens. Five days later another article appeared telling the history of the early trade on the coast at Nootka Sound. Skins had sold for as much as $91 each, though the average of other vessels was anywhere between $20 and $50. Perhaps these were planted as subtle inducements to help raise the cash to finance the Perkins-Magee venture, or the forthcoming *Columbia* trip.[13]

Then Monday, August 9, after nearly three years and 49,000 miles, the *Columbia* sailed into Boston harbor. People quoted William Tudor's effusion from his oration to the Society of Cincinnati: "What shores have our ships not coasted?" Patriotic bosoms bulged with pride. The *Centinel* named the owners of the *Columbia* and trumpeted that "their country is indebted" to their enterprise. "We are told," said the *Centinel,* "that one of the natives of the island of Owhyhee arrived in the *Columbia.*"

On Friday, this native, "in the war-dress of his native country" marched through the streets of Boston, bringing an exotic touch of an unbelievable Eden to the narrow bricked-in streets and minds of Boston. The papers had great difficulty deciding how to spell the name of this island in the Pacific, and the native was now described as coming from the island of "Atowa." Bostonians would never have believed that his remote island would one day be the fiftieth state of the Union.

This native was Opie, a friend of Joseph Ingraham, mate on the *Columbia.* Both Magee and Ingraham had gifts for the museum at Cambridge. "Their donations consisted of a great number of natural and artificial curiosities—the Bird of Paradise from Moluccas, sea otter skins from Nootka—several manufactures of China, a small shoe worn by ladies, an abacus, a variety of cloths made from mulberry bark, military weapons, domestic utensils, fishing tackle, musical instruments, dresses, ornaments, and idols from the Sandwich islands and the North West coast."

Now that Ingraham was back in town, planning for the voyage to the coast accelerated. The partners had purchased the *Hope,* a brigantine built in Kittery the year before. The owners of the *Columbia,* even though the first voyage had not made a profit, had the faith of pioneers and, with a couple of changes of partners, immediately began to refit the *Columbia* for a second trip. The competition between the owners of the *Hope* and the *Columbia* to be first out was keen.

The *Hope* was a two-masted, square-rigged brigantine. Seventy-one tons was given as the size which made it only one fifth as big as the *Astrea,* and much less than half the size of the *Mayflower.* On September 13, 1790 it was registered at the Custom House and the owners were listed as Thomas H. Perkins, James Magee, and Russell Sturgis.

For twenty-eight-year-old Ingraham this was to be his first voyage as captain. Now, at last, he had his own ship, and had risen to the top of his trade. His supercargo on this voyage was Ebenezer Dorr, Jr., son of a well-known Boston merchant. The Dorrs had ideas of their own about getting in on the newly developing China trade, and young Dorr was to prospect the possibilities in Canton for his family.

On the fourteenth the owners gave Ingraham and Dorr their letter of instructions. They were to get fur seal skins at the Falkland Islands and Juan Fernandez if possible, but to waste no time there. They could touch at the Sandwich Isles for vegetables but were forbidden to stop there, perhaps for fear they might succumb to the blandishments of that idyllic place and not get about their business. They were to range the coast trading with the Indians for skins, but not to touch at Nootka Sound, as there had been fighting there between the Spanish and British. The owners had little doubt but that Ingraham and his crew would be able to kill two or three thousand seals on the coast when their trading should have abated. If they were fortunate the first season they were to sail to China with their furs, but otherwise should winter on the coast and not at Hawaii.

Now came an important comment that was to be productive of later difficulties. "Trade for furred seal. We have been informed their value is but $\frac{1}{4}$ Dollar each . . . As much as $70 pr. skin has been obtained last year at Macao." The owners were anticipating an enormous profit. They were giving the captain and supercargo 4 percent each of the proceeds of the sales in China to encourage them to be assiduous in business, yet not as much as Derby had allowed Magee and Perkins. The first mate got 2 percent and the second mate 1$\frac{1}{2}$ percent. They were to have an allowance of freight, but were not to trade on the coast on their own account. "Look out for base money, and keep the number of skins secret." Then came an important caution, "On arrival in China best sell the furs down the River, to avoid charges." This was a way of saying, smuggle the furs in—the highest prices being obtained this way because no duties had to be paid.[14]

Finally the day came, the last feverish preparations were over. At nine o'clock on Thursday morning the sixteenth of September "with a light breeze we weighed our anchors and turned down the harbor." Ingraham describes the scene in his journal of the voyage. "Several Gentlemen of the Company who fitted my vessel and others of my acquaintance accompanied me on board in order to sail out in the bay with us and to return in the pilot boat. Opie, the native of Atsai, one of the Sandwich Islands, which I brought from there on my last voyage likewise embarked to return to his country."

Down the harbor sailed the ship's company of fourteen men, a boy, a dog, and the guests and owners. "At 11 the flood tide making obliged us to anchor abreast of the Castle. Shortly after the Gentlemen took their leave with three huzzas which we returned. As there seemed little possibility of a chance to put to sea, I went up to town again leaving orders to proceed with the vessel to Nantasket roads on the following ebb tide and that I would be on board early the next morning."[15]

"On the seventeenth," Ingraham's journal continues, "I joined my vessel again. At 9 the same morning we weighed anchor with a light breeze at ENE and ebb tide and proceeded further towards the entrance of the Harbour. At 10 being calm we anchor'd in the Narrows. Here we hoisted our boats and secur'd them, like wise made every necessary preparation to put to sea the first fair wind. At 2 in the afternoon a breeze sprung up at SW which we improv'd. Soon after discharged the pilot abreast of the lighthouse—I took a parting view of my native shore which sunk deep into my heart but making all sail I launch'd my little Bark"—and the fortunes and hopes of Tom Perkins too—"into the bosome of the ocean."

Farewell, France, in past days so beautiful,
Antique abode of Honor;
Today the cruel retreat
Of Crime and Sorrow.

A Creole of Saint-Domingue, 1793

# 6

# Hence I Hauled My Wind to the North

By the first of November, the *Hope* had reached Saint Jago, midway down the Atlantic. There they had to rearrange the cargo because in the hurry to leave Boston, supplies had been badly packed in the hold and necessities were hard to get at.

A Liverpool ship was in the harbor and its captain invited Ingraham over for dinner. The Liverpudlians were bound for Africa, planning to buy five hundred slaves for the West Indies markets. The first toast at the meal was to "the land of liberty," which struck Ingraham as most ironic: "I could scarce conceal my feelings at hearing such a toast given on board a ship bound to enslave five hundred poor wretches. However, perhaps they possess'd ideas convenient to their business, which I have often witnessed in the West Indies, namely that Negroes were a lower order of Human beings, born to be slaves."[1]

Convenient as these ideas might be for the whites, and for the Perkins brothers, they did not prove quite so convenient for the Negroes. Or to those people who lived in the twilight zone between being one or the other—the mulattoes. Scarcely had the *Hope* left Saint Jago, when

Jim at the Cape was writing Tom in Boston, "We are again embroiled in a War with the Mulattoes, who have taken arms in this neighborhood, and menaced the Capital." This was bad in itself, but even worse—"Our Collections suffer inconceivably by it."[2]

On the eve of the French Revolution, Santo Domingo had, by the best estimate, 37,000 whites and 27,000 mulattoes living amid 425,000 Negro slaves. What was most dangerous for the whites was that two thirds, or nearly 300,000 of these slaves were not born into slavery (always the most tractable), but were African-born, recently arrived, and had known what it was to have been free men and women. Even in this climate which was favorable for them, there was a continual dying-out of the slave population. Over 40,000 new slaves were brought in each year. By 1789 more than one hundred ships were supplying the French colonies in the West Indies with slaves.

Such a high death rate was due partly to improper and insufficient food, partly to the severe labor exacted from pregnant women, causing a large infant mortality, partly to the nervous strain imposed by the change from African freedom to a life of constant, back-breaking labor, and also to the fact that many white masters deliberately worked their slaves to death, considering it cheaper to buy new slaves than to breed or care for the ones they already owned. Slaves were highly expendable.

The more determined and aggressive among the slaves were constantly escaping and living a free, wild life in the mountainous country near the Spanish border of the colony. From these hideouts they waged an irregular guerilla warfare upon the whites. Frequent expeditions were sent out to put down these outlaws. But the war with the mulattoes that brother James was writing about was not the usual kind. It was something with more fatal implications for the future of the French colony.

The turmoil in France was having repercussions in its colonies abroad, and especially in Santo Domingo, the jewel in the French crown of colonies. From the moment in 1787 when Louis XVI promised to call a meeting of the Estates-General, there had been agitation in Santo Domingo for representation. But who would be represented? Those discontented with the arrogance and waste of the colonial system? Supporters of the king? The absentee lords and planters and landholders, living sumptuously in France on their slave-gotten riches?

Some colonists thought it the best part of wisdom not to send representatives at all, but to appoint an agent instead. They feared what this unprecedented assembly might have to say about slavery in the colonies. A society calling itself the Friends of the Blacks had been formed in Paris in 1788, attracting people like Lafayette as members. Thus, many planters thought it a safer policy to keep their affairs out of the assembly and work behind the scenes with an agent. Nevertheless, an election on the island in late December 1788 selected thirty-seven delegates.

The winter of 1788–89 was a hard one for the colony. The French grain crop had been very short and a ban was put on export of foodstuffs. Since Santo Domingo was required to import its food from France, famine quickly set in. In March the governor opened the ports to trade with other countries for food. By May he went even further, giving the island virtually free trade. The Perkins firm wrote to customers that "all kinds of American produce, not excepting flour" could now be sent to Santo Domingo.[3]

This sensible decree, however, caused the governor's dismissal, although the news didn't arrive until autumn after exciting reports of revolt in Paris. The fall of the Bastille, that symbol of the king's power, on the fourteenth of July, the Declaration of the Rights of Man some five weeks later—grounding the Revolution on principles opposite to those of colonial life—spread consternation among the planters. By October 1789 the Perkins firm was telling clients, "We are all in confusion here." In February of 1790 they were advising, "The disturbances here, in consequence of those in France, have put a stop to business. We see little prospect of matters mending shortly."[4]

During the summer of 1790, as Tom Perkins and Jim Magee were rushing to outfit the *Hope* for its China trip, the assembly in Paris voted to allow six deputies from Santo Domingo to sit in on their deliberations. Now the fat was in the fire. Political rights for mulattoes had already been mentioned, and there was even talk of the abolition of slavery. The presence of the deputies from Santo Domingo meant that these matters would be openly discussed in the assembly rather than behind closed doors.

On the island, white groups were fighting among themselves for power. An uneasy truce was reached as both sides waited for news from France. Jim Perkins reported, "The two parties have begun their career by firing at each other; five men on each side have been killed, and every hostile preparation is carrying on. You may judge of the difficulty in the transaction of business . . . We sincerely lament the issue of the expected War . . . We have almost wept at the disappointment."[5]

Weeping was soon to be general. What came from France was more than a word—it was a young "person of color," a mulatto named James Ogé. Stirred by the revolutionary doctrines he had heard preached in Paris, resentful of the injustices done his class, he was determined to lead a revolt against the whites and secure rights for the mulattoes. On October 28, 1790, he and a small force of about three hundred men started their campaign in the mountainous areas to the northeast of the Cape. For several days they successfully kept the revolt going, arousing an emotional response all through the colony. But on the seventh of November they were defeated by troops from the Cape. Ogé and a few leaders fled east across the border into the Spanish part of the island. Here they were imprisoned, and the governor at the Cape demanded their return.

The Spanish agreed to hand Ogé and the others back, and on the morning of December 8, they landed at the Cape. Ogé had a large ring round his neck. A long chain circled his body and thighs and was fastened to his legs. Another chain was bound round his chest and arms and fastened to his wrist. In that condition he was driven through the streets to prison. Guarding this one fettered, hobbling wretch were four hundred regular troops and six thousand militia.

Ogé and his followers were brought to trial, and at the beginning of March, twenty of them were condemned to hang. Execution was prompt, but Ogé himself and his principal aide were saved for a more terrible punishment. For the skill of these things is not to give a man a quick extinction. That would be too merciful. Rather the trick is to stretch out the dying as long as possible, to prolong the agony as much as the body will stand, without that final collapse that takes it forever beyond the torturer's reach.

For this, breaking on the wheel is an ideal method. The victim is placed on a cartwheel, his arms and legs stretched out on the spokes. As the wheel is slowly revolved, his bones are broken with an iron bar, and thus is "justice" achieved. When Ogé heard himself sentenced to the wheel he collapsed and begged for mercy, promising to reveal important secrets. He was reprieved for twenty-four hours, then killed with great brutality, his secrets thought to have perished with him. Nine months later it was discovered that he had revealed the whole plan of the coming explosion. Why nothing was done about his information was never known. It was simply ignored until too late.

Ogé's terrible death contributed to the momentous decision reached by the French assembly in May. When news of the execution reached Paris, Ogé became a hero of the Paris mob, and his brutal death was re-enacted again and again on the stage. After prolonged and bitter debate the National Assembly passed the Decree of May 15, 1791, which granted political equality to "people of color born of a free father and mother." Although granting only a token four hundred mulattoes the right to vote, it was symbolic of the attitude of the assembly. It would take seven weeks for news of the Decree to reach Cape Francis.

On the South Atlantic, the turbulence of Paris and Santo Domingo were unknown; it was the turbulence of nature that engaged the *Hope* and its crew. On November 9 the ship *Hope* went through one of the worst lightning storms that Ingraham ever remembered in his sea career. It led him to remark rather tartly in his journal that merchants should provide their ships with "conductors and chains" as warships were protected. "Many ships and lives have been saved by this valuable contrivance."

On the eighteenth they crossed the "sixty-ninth line," the equator, with the thermometer in the 80°s. The twenty-seventh they spoke a Portugese brig. This vessel seemed to be manned entirely by blacks with no captain or pilot visible. Ingraham suspected that they were no better than pirates, but had neither time nor inclination to find out. On the morning of December 5, though they were then one hundred leagues from any land, they caught a large gray butterfly. "At noon the same day, the wind shifted suddenly from NW to SW in a kind of whirlwind which drove the sea before it like a Torrent. Fortunately before it struck us we got all our sails handed out and the vessel before the wind. In about an hour it abated."

The *Hope* was now far enough south for the men to see albatross and spouting whales. On the afternoon of the nineteenth "we saw a ball or meteor in the air resembling fire descend suddenly into the sea." The thermometer started dropping, "rather pinching to us who had so lately pass'd a warm climate."

Six o'clock in the morning on Christmas Day, Ingraham "was alarmed by a great noise on deck. I sprung from my Cabbin and was on deck in an instant when I observ'd one of our men in the sea. I immediately order'd the sails thrown aback, at the same time I threw several boards which lay on the quarterdeck into the water, which he soon reach'd and these buoy'd him up til we could get the boat out which was some time as we had many additional lashings to prevent" it being washed overboard in a sudden gale. By now the lad was "near a mile distant ere we got the boat in the water." They soon had him on board "to our great joy," for "to have lost one of our small number so early in the voyage would have occasion'd a melancholy Christmas. The weather being cool the lad was [too] and had boots on which got down about his heels [and] was near sinking him before he could reach the boards but with an admirable presence of mind he took his knife from his pockett and cut his boots on each side so that he shook them clear and what was very singular in such a situation [was] that he should be carefull to return his knife to his pockett again."

Ingraham had decided to go round the Horn. On January 22 they saw another ship on their weather bow, the whaling ship *Necker* going Dunkirk to Peru. "Agreeable sight. Most welcome at this vast extremity of the Globe where we least expected company to alleviate the tedious and anxious moments well-known to those who have experienced long voyages where every object even the most trivial is eagerly caught at to divert the attention and vary the Uniform dull scenes which at times become almost insupportable." Ingraham invited the captain of the *Necker* on board to dine; but since the *Necker* crew had just killed a fresh pig Ingraham did not require much persuasion to dine with them instead. "Hence I would recommend a piece of fresh pork as a very alluring bait to catch a man off Cape Horn for unless they are of a Jewish extraction there is absolutely no resisting it." Since the vessels sailed "as near alike as any two could," they agreed to keep each other company as they doubled the Horn.

Although the *Necker* sailed under French papers and colors it was an American-built ship, and the captain, officers, and most of the men were Americans. "The great encouragement given by the French government to Americans to settle in France and fit out ships in the whaling service has induced many of our countrymen to emigrate, yet I believe the major part of them have no idea of remaining among the French longer than they by their industry obtain a sufficiency to enable them to live comfortably in their own country."

While Ingraham was fraternizing with these first of a long line of postwar Americans to head for Paris, his employer in Boston was writing him a letter of advice. The *Columbia* and the *Hancock* were the only other Boston vessels Ingraham would find on the coast, wrote Perkins. And though Ingraham had not yet left the Atlantic ocean, Perkins was advising him to put much reliance on his making two cruises and not one between the coast and China, believing that the second cruise would make more money than the first.[6]

By the fifteenth of April Ingraham reached the Marquesas Islands. That afternoon at five o'clock a canoe came out to the ship from the island. Ingraham had a white flag displayed to show his peaceful intentions. When they got within a hundred yards of the vessel, the canoes stopped. They shouted back and forth, but even Opie couldn't understand their language. Ingraham threw a handkerchief into the sea making signs that they should pick it up. They waited until it had drifted a little way from the *Hope* before one of them bravely paddled over and retrieved it, holding it up proudly, then putting it on his head. Another canoe, getting up its courage, came close under the stern and Ingraham threw them some trifling gifts. An old man in a third canoe kept chattering away in his language as if they should understand him. When Ingraham gave the boys a knife, they pushed rapidly for land with their treasure and the old man's canoe took after them. That was the last seen of the natives that evening.

The next morning when the ship had moved nearer land, more canoes came out, with men holding fish in their hands and shouting "ee'ah," which now both Opie and Ingraham recognized as the Sandwich Island word for "fish." The men were quite naked. Ingraham noted in his journal that he "observed among them a very singular custom which no doubt was by them esteemed a mark of modesty, but due attendance to my female friends whom I expect will peruse these pages forbids an explanation."

Ingraham exchanged some nails for fish and breadfruit. Then the *Hope* sailed along the coast looking for a likely landing spot, the natives running along the shore. More canoes came out with breadfruit, coconuts, and fish to trade. One old man with hair and beard perfectly white even dared come on board the vessel. He trembled all the time and was anxious to leave, but when Ingraham gave him a knife for some fish and fruit, he was so delighted that he hurried to shore and rushed back with some baked fish wrapped up in plantain leaves. Ingraham anchored, fired off a gun to warn the natives they should clear away from the vessel, put up his boarding nets, and set a watch for the night.

The next day, April 17, they began trading again, the canoes increasing about the boat and the natives more daring than before. About ten o'clock women appeared in the crowd. "Most of them had beautiful and engaging features with fine teeth and hair, the latter hung loose in long ringlets, their limbs proportionable and delicate seemed turn'd to please by the hand of elegance. Like all the rest of the South Sea ladies, they seem'd not to esteem chastity as a virtue, many of them were naked without even a fig leaf."

On Tuesday the eighteenth the first serious accident occurred. Just before weighing anchor, the first officer, Mr. Cruft, was badly wounded by reloading a cannon and neglecting to sponge it. It went off while he was ramming down the charge, but he escaped better than could be expected from such an accident. Yet his face was so badly burnt that he was unconscious for thirty-six hours.

The next day, leaving the Marquesas and sailing north northwest, the *Hope* spied two islands off the leeward side. Since the ship had passed all the Marquesas then on the maps, Ingraham concluded they must be the first discoverers of these new islands. He immediately set about naming them, christening one Washington's Island and the other Adam's Island after the president and vice-president. By 5 o'clock he saw two more islands and named one Federal and the second Lincoln, after General Lincoln of Massachusetts. Unable to find a place to land so as to proclaim these islands in proper fashion, Ingraham called his officers and men to witness while he claimed them as a new discovery and belonging to the United States "on which we all gave three cheers." Ingraham would have liked to stay and explore his new discoveries but "to have remained for no other purpose might perhaps be deemed inconsistent by the gentlemen of the concern. Hence I haul'd my wind to the North."

Moving north he passed another island which he named Franklin in honor of old Ben; then two more islands, one of which he called

Hancock after the governor of Massachusetts, and the second Knox after the general and former bookseller. Knox Island had many fine bays and since Ingraham still had a few more names left, he called the best bay, Brattles Bay. Knox Island had a house on it but he saw no inhabitants, nor did he stop to find out what the people living there called their bay and their island.

He had intended to go straight north to the coast and start collecting skins, but he needed wood, and many of his crew had scurvy, or the beginning of it. He could not afford to use the blacksmith's forge coal for wood or spare the men or time to make charcoal, so on May 17 with only five casks of water on board, he headed for the Sandwich Islands.

Soon after the *Hope* sighted Hawaii, or "Owhyhee" as Ingraham spelled it, it was surrounded by one hundred canoes, and trading commenced at a furious clip. They heard all about the island wars. Ingraham decided to fire off a cannon to see if it would attract the attention of one of the principal chiefs, Tiana. "The seamen being all employed, Mr. Cruft, whom I mentioned was wounded in reloading a cannon at the Marquesas, touch'd it, and notwithstanding I saw him spunge and worm the gun yet by his neglecting to stop the vent he met with the same accident as before, the gun went off while he was ramming home the cartridge and wounded him in the most shocking manner . . . The wounds he had received at the Marquesas were not yet well having no surgeon."

The next day Opie met some chiefs he knew and embraced them "according to their custom by joining noses. At the same time he seem'd drown'd in tears." Opie warned Ingraham against Chief Tiana who had captured another vessel on the coast. "Take care. By and by you dead. Tiana too many men." Ingraham laughed, thinking it a trick to keep the *Hope* in the area trading. He told Opie that he had plenty of shot and powder. When Tiana sent out to know who was captain of the vessel Ingraham answered "Tietrum," the name he was known by in the islands. Now began some attempts to try and get Ingraham to land or anchor nearer the shore. Ingraham became suspicious and refused.

Opie left with affectionate goodbyes to all. He had been with Ingraham twenty months. "Although I took Opye as a servant I always treated him more like a friend. And being taken great notice of during his stay in America he was impressed with the most favorable ideas of our nation. I supplied him amply with cloaths, a musket, an American Jack, and many other things, but not so many as I should have done had I know of his intention to stay sooner."

The morning after Opie had gone ashore, a large double canoe came out to the *Hope*. Ingraham was surprised to see three white men in it, one of whom he recognized as having once served as the carpenter's mate on the *Columbia.* He hailed them and got for a reply, "By God, I'm glad you've come!" From them he learned that what Opie had said was true; that the natives had captured a small schooner, *The Fair American,* and murdered the captain and seamen. These three men had been in the area at the time, and escaped before they suffered the same fate.

Loading up with water, Ingraham was preparing to sail when he discovered that one of these new men had gone back to shore for his muskets and some clothes. When the man came back, there were about thirty canoes around the boat containing 250 to 300 men. Somebody fired a pistol and the natives made as if to attack the boat. One of the men Ingraham had rescued yelled to him, "They are for fighting, sir, you may depend on it!"

Ingraham ordered all his men under arms to fire. After a few volleys the canoes paddled toward the shore. Ingraham watched carefully but wasn't sure if any natives were killed or not. His men reported two had fallen as if dead, but Ingraham wasn't sure. "All this unhappy accident happened and was over in two minutes at furthest." Thinking about it afterwards, Ingraham wrote in his journal—very unlike most of the captains of the day—"I hope I think as much of the life of a savage as any man existing and God forbid my conscience should ever be charged with taking the life of any one wantonly however uncivilized."

The brief battle over, Ingraham sailed on, and spent the next few days watering and provisioning among some of the smaller islands. By June 4 he was ready to haul his wind to the north again, and make for the Northwest Coast of America, and the real business they had come upon, trading for skins to sell in China.

The *Hope* sighted Washington Island, off the Northwest Coast of America, by the end of June. Ingraham saw three openings, and sent an officer in a boat to see if a vessel could go in. About eleven o'clock the boat came out with a Jack flying, the signal for a good harbor. The *Hope* bore away and by four o'clock was moored in a snug cove in the eastern arm of the sound. "As I never had any information that there was a sound or harbour where we fortunately found so good a one, I thought it necessary it should have a name. I therefore named it Magee's Sound after Capt. Magee of Boston, and one of the company which owned the *Hope*." If there was one thing that bothered Ingraham it was to see places lying around without names. The lovely cove in which the *Hope* was anchored, for example. "The cove where we lay I named Crufts Cove after my chief officer whom I sent in the boat to examine the sound.

The *Hope* had been leaking considerably at sea, and the hull was fouled by sea growths that cut her speed considerably and made it hard to handle. Ingraham decided that he was in a good place to repair the ship before going further. There were no natives to worry about. There was a fine beach in the cove where the work could be done. There was plenty of wood and water with which to replenish their stock. So on the thirtieth of June they laid the vessel on the shore and started to clean and grave it. On this same day a ship from France sailed into Cape Francis, Santo Domingo, carrying the Decree of May 15, 1791.

When one realizes that thirty thousand whites are in the center of six hundred thousand semi-barbaric Africans, one should not hesitate to say that discipline is necessary.

A creole of Saint-Domingue, 1793

# 7

# On the Edge of Vesuvius

"No words," wrote an eyewitness, "can describe the rage and indignation" that greeted the decree. "In no place did the inhabitants breathe greater resentment than in the town of the Cape, which had hitherto been foremost in professions of attachment to the mother country." All the dissident white elements united in opposing the decree, which allowed four hundred mulattoes to vote. It was not the number, it was the principle.[1]

So angry were the citizens of the Cape that at first they proposed to seize all French ships in the harbor, confiscate the goods of French merchants, haul down the French flag, and raise the British one. Instant secession was a real possibility. The governor's power to enforce French decrees was virtually at an end. Threats were heard on all sides. "Do you think," snarled one white, "that we will take the law from the grandson of one of our slaves? No! Rather die than assent to this infamy!—that is the cry of all. If France sends troops for the execution of this decree, it is likely that we will decide to abandon France." Yet within two months these same colonists were pleading with France to send troops and more troops to the Cape.[2]

"Every kind of business," the Perkins firm reported to Boston, "is at a stand, owing to a late Edict of the National Assembly respecting the Coloured people of the Colonies." Another Perkins' adventure almost came "to a stand" too, at the same time.[3]

Up on the northwest coast Ingraham had discovered the leak in the *Hope*. It was serious, for it was between the lower part of the stern post and the keel. The latter had not been properly secured with dovetails or clamps, as was the usual practice. An opening of about half an inch had resulted. With nothing to hold the keel and stern post together, it would have grown wider and wider, until the end would have been, Ingraham wrote grimly, "nothing short of our destruction."[4]

This was fixed, and the vessel righted and floating by the time the anniversary of American independence arrived. "I caused," says Ingraham, "A Hog of 70 pounds weight to be roasted whole on which we all dined on shore. I with my officers and seamen drank the President's health and made the forest ring with three cheers." Then it was back to work, the men to caulking and painting the upper works, Ingraham to naming the unnamed.

He sent a boat to make a sketch of the sound and drew a map of the findings in his journal. "The southern entrance is Magee's Sound. The northern I called Port Perkins after a gentleman of the company and agent for the concern'd. The Island dividing the two I nam'd Dorr's Island" after the supercargo of the *Hope*. Not only did he name the new land, he colonized it. "I put three piggs on shore, two sows and a boar, which perhaps whoever may visit Magee's Sound at some future period will find the benefit of." To make certain they did he wrote a letter, put it in a bottle, and tied it to the bough of a tree on one of the heights above the sound. The letter told who had discovered the bay, what they had named it, and asked them not to molest the pigs until they had had time to increase and multiply in the land.

Then it was on to new worlds to discover and name. They sailed into another harbor looking for natives to trade with, but found none. This place, his officers named Port Ingraham and the island that split the entrance to the harbor into two was called "Young Frederick's Island—after my son."

Now Ingraham began to encounter the natives, and started trading for skins. But they were uninterested in the items Ingraham had brought for trade. They had gotten all these from other captains who had been on the coast before Ingraham. "Seem'd to indicate we were the day after the fair," Ingraham remarked ruefully.

On the twelfth of July an idea struck him. He had his blacksmith set up his forge "to make iron collars of three iron rods about the size of a man's finger." This was twisted and made according to a pattern Ingraham had seen on a woman's neck. When finish'd they weighed from five to seven pounds and would bring three of the Indians' best skins in preference to anything else Ingraham had on board. He also learned that heavy iron rings or bracelets for their wrists were wanted more than polished copper ones.

A new group of Indians came along and once they had seen the new iron collars they would have nothing but them. Ingraham had to keep the forge busy, since making the collars required much time and trouble. By the time he left this place on the nineteenth he had collected three hundred skins.

Several days later they met the *Columbia.* Ingraham had the French flag run up and fired two guns "which was the signal I informed Mr. Haswell I should make if I saw him on the coast." When the two vessels came alongside each other, the men gave three cheers "which was return'd." Captain Gray invited Ingraham on board and gave Ingraham his letters from Boston, dated September 26, 1790, ten days after he had left. For his letters he was indebted to Mr. Haswell "who brought them unknown to the owners of the *Columbia.* These gentlemen, filled with envy and malice against all who ment [sic] to share with them this valuable trade, gave orders that no letters should be borne out in their ship to any on board the *Hope.*"

The *Hope* continued trading up and down the coast, the smith busy making iron collars, and the seamen turned into seamstresses, making trading garments out of blue cloth with buttons sewed on in a curious manner. The end of July in the pitch black of night they returned to a harbor Ingraham had named Ucah's Harbor after the chief of the place. "There was something awfully solemn in entering this dreary port at this hour of the night. The surrounding high mountains threw an additional gloom over the face of the deep, whose vast silence was at time interrupted by the hollow surge of the sea on the surrounding rocky shores or the gamboling of immense whales."

Ucah visited them the next day wearing one of the iron collars scoured shiny bright. He wanted to trade for more collars. In vain did Ingraham show him the blue jackets which cost ten times as much as the collars to make. No sale. Collars were what they all wanted. Up went the forge and back to the bellows went the smith. Ingraham set the price of trade at three fine skins for one collar. Three skins could bring as much as $225 in China. The iron in the collar cost less than a dollar. The opportunity for such fantastic profits was what tempted merchants to finance these arduous, risky trips.

The *Hope* continued trading up and down the coast. The villagers wanted iron collars in preference to all else, and sometimes would not even begin to trade until they received some. So Sunday, August 7, "Making collars became so far the work of necessity that notwithstanding our respect for the day we kept the forge at work. It was ever my practice," wrote Ingraham, the conditioned New Englander, "to refrain from all work what ever on Sunday. If there was no religious motive for this I conceive it necessary, was it for no other purpose than for seamen to clean themselves which alone must be allowed a good custom as it is conducive to health. But to have stopped the forge here would have been putting an end to trade at once as the natives knew no difference in days. However, on this good day we bought 84 skins." Thus did the understanding New England God reward His own.

The natives were hard bargainers. Ingraham praised one tribe for its "truly mercantile spirit." They got the utmost for their skins. When his jackets were all gone, the natives, Ingraham found, would not take the trousers alone. Blue cloth only was saleable; green or white was of little value. All the blue cloth on the vessel was taken to sell, "likewise those of my officers and seamen, after which our only resource was working iron into the forms that pleased them. Collars still had the preference." The least flaw in chisels or daggers was sufficient for the natives to refuse them.

The trading was done in a curious manner. "When trading," Ingraham noticed, "they will not admit that they sell their skins, but after using every effort and persuasion to obtain the best price, finding you are determined to give no more, they will throw the skins toward you saying 'Ting leis tong' ('I'll give it you'). They likewise often brought skins on board making presents but these presents were sure to prove the dearest skins."

By August 11 they were trading the vessel bare. Ingraham even sold the feathered cap and two feathered cloaks which he had been given as presents at the Sandwich Islands. These were not to wind up in Harvard's collection, as had some of his previous keepsakes. He received five excellent sea otter skins for them. The chief who had bought the cloaks and cap at first was happy with the exchange. Then he repented and wanted to get his skins back. No, said Ingraham. The chief got mad, left the vessel and sat sulking in his canoe, until a small present from Ingraham mollified his feelings.

Dealing with the natives could be very tedious and called for "an uncommon share of patience." One had to let them take their time or the price demanded went up. But there were amusing events to break the monotony. One night a chief begged Ingraham to let him sleep on board the vessel. "One of his wives had beat him and he wish'd to keep his distance til her rage had subsid'd. Here, in direct opposition to most other parts of the world, the women maintain a precedency to the man in every point—insomuch as a man dare not trade without concurrance of his wife."

By the middle of August Ingraham had collected 850 skins, and he changed his plans of wintering on the coast and decided to sail for the Sandwich Islands and Canton. In so doing he was anticipating the instructions Perkins had sent him the preceding January, but which he probably had not yet received. It would also divide the risk of the voyage and mean that part of the profit of the trip would get back to Boston even if the *Hope* were wrecked or lost on the way home. It would also give them a chance to renew their provisions, and insure that they would be very early on the coast for the next trading season.

On the twenty-second of August the *Hope* met the *Columbia* again. Ingraham told Gray of his plans to go to Canton and that he would "with pleasure" take any messages they wanted sent to Boston. This was a proper Christian return for the refusal of the *Columbia* owners to permit messages to be sent out to the *Hope* from Boston. Gray told Ingraham of the killing of three of his men by the "savages," though Ingraham did not get all the details of the massacre. He learned too, that the *Hancock* would be following him to Canton in about ten days. This argued for a good collection of skins by the *Hancock* and *Columbia* and meant that there would be too many skins at once on the Canton market. So now the men of the *Hope* turned to packing furs for the trip, to wooding and watering for the long voyage ahead of them.

While Ingraham was learning about the massacre of the *Columbia* men there was renewed activity at Cape Francis. The new colonial assembly, which had met at Leogan early in August to plan a common strategy against the Decree of May 15, had adjourned to meet in the Cape on the twenty-fifth. There had been a small outbreak at one of the parishes on the plain in mid-August, but it had been quickly stamped out. The colonists continued to sleep, said Mirabeau afterwards, "on the edge of Vesuvius."

It was on the night of the twenty-second that Vesuvius errupted, with a fury and horror that stunned the whites. The uprising started only nine miles from the city. There, at a refinery, a group of slaves broke in, dragged out the young apprentice, and cut him to bits with their swords. His screams brought out the overseer, who was instantly shot. The slaves swarmed into the house and killed the owner. A young man sick in a nearby room was attacked and left for dead, but managed to crawl to the next plantation and give the alarm.

All over the plains the uprising took place with remarkable complicity. These slaves, who had been kidnapped out of their African homes by the whites, carried in great agony and brutality on a dreadful sea voyage, made to labor in heat and torment, whipped and brutalized, now acted like the beasts that the whites had made them. Mothers and daughters who had been pleased to have the slaves tickle their feet, or who had them viciously whipped for the slightest infractions, now found their husbands or brothers or sons being killed before their eyes, and themselves ravished by hordes of their slaves. Some of the young women were taken along to serve as prostitutes for the gangs. Others had their eyes scooped out with knives. At one place the slaves killed a white infant, stuck a stake through his body, and used this as their flag.

Reports and refugees from the plantations poured into the Cape. The governor and his staff had been in consultation since early morning of the twenty-third, but the stories coming in had been so contradictory and confused that they could decide upon nothing. Women and children were running from door to door in panic. There were ten thousand whites in the town, but also ten to twelve thousand blacks. Nor could the 1,400 mulattoes be relied upon. Indeed some of the criminal and alien white rabble were suspected of being willing to see the Cape destroyed, if only they were given a free hand to pillage.

And where were the James Perkinses on this night of the twenty-second? Out in the western part of the plains, where they had been spending a pleasant two weeks at the plantation of Comte d'Hautval. Returning to the Cape they stopped at the de Rouvry plantation for dinner. Arriving there with other guests, the Baurys, they found the mistress visiting at a neighboring plantation, but she soon came back with the frightening news of the insurrection. Her slaves did not know of it yet, but soon would as there was a general alarm and people were rushing everywhere. The Perkinses and their hostess decided to leave at midnight to reach Fort Dauphin. In the evening a slave came to the plantation and told the Negroes that everywhere in the country their fellow slaves were burning and destroying.

The whites tried to pretend nothing had happened. They sat down to dinner, eating from the usual rich service of plate, but the changed manners of the slaves—insolent, noisy, defiant—made them all nervous and they ate but little and in a gloomy silence. De Rouvry was in the mountains on business, and all preparations fell upon the lady of the house. She packed up her plate and ordered the carriages brought to the door, just before midnight. It looked as though the slaves might refuse to do it, but they did not, though the coachman had to be bribed to harness the horses and get ready to start.

They made a party of three carriages. The Marchioness de Rouvry, her daughter, and the governess in the first carriage, Mrs. Perkins, her child, Madame Baury and child, in the second, Mr. Perkins in the third with a lady who had escaped that afternoon from a neighboring plantation. Mr. Baury rode on horseback alongside them. He and Perkins were both armed. The coachmen were ordered to avoid a village on the route for fear the insurgents might attack them. Too late they discovered the coaches were already far along the road to the village. Perkins and Baury consulted and decided not to show their fears to the slaves by ordering them to turn back. But they agreed that if they refused to drive on, they would shoot them and drive the carriages themselves.

Through the night they went. As they came into the village the houses were lighted, the slaves and insurgents in them howling and dancing and beating their drums rejoicing over their freedom. In the center of the village the first carriage stopped. Now what? They didn't want to alert the insurgents in the houses. Madame de Rouvry ordered her coachman to proceed immediately or she would have him punished in the severest manner. He hesitated. But habit, and the sight of Mr.

Baury's sword, made him obey. Quietly through the village crept the three carriages. At four in the morning they arrived at Fort Dauphin, to the great surprise of the people there. So fearful were the regular troops that they would not venture into the countryside even a few miles. A boat was procured and took the party by sea the forty miles to the Cape.[5]

At the Cape, the women and children had been sent aboard the ships in the harbor for their protection. The known leaders of the Negroes in the town had also been seized and confined on the ships. On the plains, the rebels were setting buildings and fields of sugar cane afire. Soon the thick choking smoke was pouring upward everywhere one looked except seaward. An eyewitness wrote of "the whole horizon a wall of fire, from which continually rose thick vortices of smoke, whose huge black volumes could be likened only to those frightful storm-clouds which roll onwards charged with thunder and lightnings. The rifts in these clouds disclosed flames as great in volume which rose darting and flashing to the very sky. Such was their voracity that for nearly three weeks we could barely distinguish between day and night, for so long as the rebels found anything to feed the flames, they never ceased to burn, resolved as they were to leave not a cane nor house behind."[6]

The most striking feature of this terrible spectacle was a rain of fire composed of burning cane-straw which whirled thickly before the blast like flakes of snow, and which the wind carried, now toward the harbor and shipping, now over the houses of the city. This was the unpleasant prospect Perkins and his family came back to face.

Expeditions went out onto the plains to see if they could push the rebels back. On one of these went Perkins's partner, Walter Burling. They ran into a mob of insurgents. The whites were fifty mounted men. Facing them in the narrow road seemed to be eight or nine hundred blacks and mulattoes. Many of the insurgents were on horseback. In the middle of the highway, aimed directly at the whites, the insurgents had set up three cannon, one of them a large twelve pounder. Matches were lit and ready to touch off the cannon should the handful of white men dare charge them.

Some wanted to retreat until the infantry could come to their aid. Their leader, Colonel Touzard, would have none of this. He had lost his right arm in Rhode Island during the Revolution and was riding with the reins lightly held in his left. Halting them, he said that to retreat would be slaughter, that the only chance of escape would be a direct charge. Came his command: "Close your ranks firmly. Draw your swords and move forward on a quick trot. And when I give the word 'charge' give spur to your horses and dash into the cannon's mouth."

Burling, who had been riding behind, moved up near the head of the column. He was watching Touzard intently. He could hardly believe what happened next. He heard the colonel cry "Attention! Charge!" Then the colonel clapped his reins in his mouth and pulled out his sword with his one hand so rapidly, Burling could hardly see the motion of the hand doing it. But he had no time to think of this, only to grasp the image, for he was spurring his own horse and rushing with drawn sword on the group around the cannon.

The cannon had been filled with whatever the insurgents could lay their hands on. They had pillaged the copper boilers, in which the sugar cane was boiled down, of everything that could be crammed into the mouth of a cannon, particularly the vicious broad-headed copper spikes. All this came blasting out in a deadly cloud at the fifty men. Perhaps a dozen dropped from their horses. The rest swarmed past the cannon to where a thick group of insurgents were mounted. These were waiting for the smoke to clear away, fully expecting to see the whites fleeing in disorder. Instead, out of the smoke came a furiously charging force wildly swinging swords.

Burling rode straight for a mulatto whose head was covered with plumes. Evidently, he thought, a chief. Another mulatto came at Burling from behind to protect his chief. By chance Burling saw the swing of the sword and caught the blow on the back of his own broadsword, slid it off, then plunged his blade into the fellow's body, which slid off the horse. Burling looked for the chief again. But he had fled with the rest of the insurgents who had broken under the charge of the whites and were scattering in all directions. Burling pursued him but he lacked a good horse. Instead, he reined up, drew his pistol, and shot the chief's aide. The mulatto fell forward over the head of his horse, and Burling and horse then leaped over the falling body in pursuit of other game.

Touzard had the bugler sound retreat. He did not want his little group to get too far apart. Selles, an officer in the company, called to Burling to stop.

"Well, what do you want?" asked Burling impatiently.

"The men are recalled and you must go back."

"When I have knocked that fellow off his horse I'll go back."

"Why, man, you are wounded!"

"Not I," said Burling, but the moment of respite from the fury showed him one of his legs was stiff. Looking down he found his boot full of blood. Three pieces of shot had mangled his thigh. He went back with Selles.

The Cape had been an unfortified town but the hills between it and the plain offered natural defense advantages which the colonists were quick to exploit. A ring of forts had been built on all the heights around the plain by great gangs of slave labor and this effectively contained the revolt within that area alone, mostly isolating it from a mulatto insurrection in the western provinces.

Perhaps some groundswell sent the tremors of violence from Santo Domingo through the thousands of miles to the northwest coast of America, but Ingraham was definitely uneasy about the behavior of the Indians. His preparations were nearly finished for leaving for the Sandwich Islands and Canton, and he decided it was time to go while he was still on good terms with the Coast Indians. The nagging memory of the massacre of the three men of the *Columbia* bothered him too. After trying vainly to sail on the first of September, the wind keeping him back, he left on the second.

He had been two months on the coast, but not counting the time spent in repairing the *Hope,* he figured he had spent forty-nine days in actual trading time about the islands. In that time he had collected 1,400 sea otter skins and upwards of 300 sable skins, besides beaver, wolverines, and the like. It was grandfather Peck's business all over again—but under the changed "modern" conditions, and on a much larger scale.

Ingraham was pretty well satisfied with himself. This large number of skins had been collected in just twelve months. By contrast, the first trip of the *Columbia* had spent twenty-five months, and even with the assistance of a tender had only collected eight hundred skins. This season, as far as Ingraham could determine, the *Columbia* had collected about six hundred indifferent skins, and the *Hancock* perhaps five to six hundred. Anchoring, Ingraham decided, was far better for obtaining skins than cruising. He once spent an eight day period cruising about in search of Indians to trade with and found nothing. But there was not a day went by when he was anchored that he was not able to trade for skins. Besides, it was safer to stay anchored than risk the tides and unknown dangers of a strange coast. The Indians preferred it too.

He took along with him, to plant in Boston, the seeds of a red berry they were all unfamiliar with, "about the size of a huckelberry, the offspring of a beautiful tree which in general grows from 6 to 9 feet high," plus some other plants that he thought might be worth trying at home. He experimented with putting samphire (called chicken claws today) into vinegar, "which was a very fine pickel and kept good to China. There is a root at the Islands about the size of a walnut perfectly white and resembles in shape the paw of a cat nearer than any thing I could compare it to, it tastes when raw like wheat, but when boiled like new potatoes. It seems an excellent substitute for bread but was scarce."

He made a list of the language, the words of trade (wa'Tah) and the words a sailor needed to know (woman, "inna," sleep, "cud dee," yes, "ung a," make haste, "how yeat," I thank you, "kill sly"). Even the special invention, the iron collar, had a name, "Cun-sta-guh." Reflecting on these collars, which weighed five to eight pounds each, and the ones made for the wrist, which weighed a pound, Ingraham thought how peculiar people were. If the West Indian Negroes were forced to wear these, it would be thought a cruel and unusual punishment. And here were people buying these with valuable furs for pleasure! But perhaps it wasn't so strange, for he reported a conversation he overheard by chance on shipboard one day:

Sailor: "I wonder how these damned fellows came first to like these iron collars?"

Blacksmith: "I don't know. The fashion I suppose. And they are not half so bad as some things they wear in Boston."

Sailor: "In Boston? What?"

Blacksmith: "What? Why iron hoops under their petticoats which I have made many a one of, or sheeps wool on their heads."

The times are like an eight day clock
That runs without upwinding;
The man's a fool a useless tool,
That for money is not grinding.

Nathan Bowen's *Almanac*

# 8

# A Connection Between Brothers

When Captain Cutting collided with syphillis, being a sea-faring man, he described the encounter in nautical terms rather than medical. Confessing he had "sought for amusement in the Society of Sundry members of the Cyprian Corps"—the eighteenth-century way of saying prostitutes—he discovered their "Sweets, like the Bee's, are mingled with stings. This my intercourse with them verified. However I did not receive so much damage from *'the Fire Ship that fell foul of my house,'* but that *I was refitted* without being *hove down*—and was speedily returned 'fit for service.' "[1] It was the story of his life.

Born a stone's throw from heaven—that is to say, in Cambridge—Nathaniel Cutting remained always just shy of the mark. His book plate showed a side view of a rampant lion holding a seashell over his name. It would have been more appropriate if the lion had clutched a storm cloud with the rain pouring down, for the captain's fairest hopes were always being rained out.

His father died in the fall of 1760 when Nathaniel was only four years old and he was left to be brought up by his mother. She was a Brown, aunt to Peter Chardon Brooks, reputed to be New England's first millionaire. But none of the Brooks gold rubbed off on Nathaniel. He went to sea, learned the sailoring trade, and in time became a privateer captain for Nathaniel Tracy of Newburyport. But in 1779 he was captured and clapped into a British jail. Repatriated two years later, he made further cruises without much success, and after the war went to Spain as an agent for Tracy. By 1786 he was working for a French company in Le Havre, where he met Thomas Jefferson, then the American minister to France.[2]

In his years at Le Havre, Cutting had not found much trade developing between the United States and France, though he believed it to be inevitable and thought Le Havre the natural port to handle it. While waiting for the inevitable to happen, he decided on a long trip, as he wrote Jefferson on March 5, 1790, more for "observation than immediate emolument." A short time later, his ship touched in at Cape Mount on the windward coast of Africa. Captain Cutting had decided to take a flyer in slaves.

If any way was guaranteed to be a fast road to wealth, slaving seemed to be it. A vessel could reach the coast with a large cargo worth £400 sterling and exchange it for seventy slaves, who would bring £50 a head in the Indies. If they all reached the market alive this meant a gross profit of £3,500 sterling. "This," mused Cutting in his journal, "is almost incredible." He was hungry enough at the age of thirty-four to want a piece of the "incredible" for himself.[3]

By mid-April, Cutting was busy dickering for fifty slaves, intending to sell them in Santo Domingo. He found time one of those April afternoons to dash off a letter to his friend James Perkins at the Cape. James replied that he was "not surprised that a Gentleman of your known excentricity should have dated his letter from the Wilds of Africa; it would be singular to find you revolving in a Circumscribed Sphere while the World is your orbit."[4]

By the time Perkins sent his letter, Cutting was already on the island at Saint Marc, a few boat hours ride from the Cape. And a wiser man was he. He had learned that it was shrewder to trade West Indian rum for slaves than New England rum, for all rum was mixed 50 percent with water, and the harsher taste of the West Indian concealed the dilution better than the sweeter New England rum. He had learned that a few undersize (thus cheaper) slaves could be mixed in with a large lot of better slaves and the whole sold for the price of prime "pictures," as the best slaves were called. He had learned how difficult it was to get any of the slave traders to live up to their written agreements. And he had bought fifty slaves expecting to realize an enormous profit on their sale and set himself up for life. But he had not learned how to make money.

Cutting had sailed for Santo Domingo on one ship, his slaves on a second. To pay their freight, since he had no money, he agreed the ships would stick together on the dangerous crossing. If not, the captain of the other ship could sell his slaves to pay for their freight. No sooner had they left Africa than Cutting found his ship outsailing the other by eight leagues every hour. Frantic, he offered his captain, 100 Louis d'ors to slow down. Not for three times that, replied the captain. Cutting had hoped to make 1,000 guineas on this venture. Now, he wrote ruefully in his journal, it had "vanished into air." He resolved manfully to take it like a philosopher, even though, as he wrote later, "I was obliged to return home 'with my finger in my mouth' as the saying is, without having gained anything—except much information respecting a Trade which perhaps I may never pursue."[5]

That ended his 1790 attempt to make a fortune. In the fall he left Santo Domingo and returned to Le Havre, "until the Chapter of Chances may present some more eligible pursuit." By the end of the summer of 1791, he had decided that perhaps his fortune could be launched in Santo Domingo after all. With his usual run of luck, he left for that colony just after the Negro uprising broke out and drove all the planters into the security of the Cape.[6]

After a difficult passage, during which his ship became twice dismasted, he arrived at the Cape on November 3 to find the city enclosed on all sides except the harbor "by a pallisade having only two ports, one open at each end of the City." The next afternoon Cutting went ashore to call on James Perkins. "Found him in health, though much harrassed and fatigued by the military duties he has been obliged to perform." Perkins had been put in command of all the Americans at the port. There was no nonsense about "neutrals"; all whites were obliged to "mount guard for the security of the city."[7]

So threatening did the situation seem to Cutting at first, that he was undecided whether to land or remain on his ship. But he had brought a large consignment of muslins with him from France, hoping on the profit of their sale to finance a trip to the "Thirteen States." Saturday, dining with Perkins—"Mrs. Perkins did the honors of the table with graceful ease"—he received the bad news. James Perkins told him he had paid more for his muslins in France than they were currently selling for at the Cape. Once again—"my finger in my mouth."

The town was all confusion, crowded with refugees, prices soaring, single rooms hard to come by. Cutting and another traveler finally found a ground floor room, on a street "which is a thorofare for a little million of Negroes, mulattoes, etc." He went out to dine, listening to the varied stories of the refugees, of the terrible brutalities, recording many of them in his journal.

By day it was reasonably safe near the city. With a party, Cutting went out one November day to one of the hills looking down on the town. It was a superb picture, the harbor crowded with shipping, the town prosperous looking with its eight hundred or more brick and stone houses, fine squares with fountains, church, prison, playhouse, barracks, arsenal, and two good hospitals. The plain beyond, and the brooding mountains rising from it, were indisputably grand. Cutting commented in his Journal: "It was the most pleasant, the most productive and perhaps the richest spot in the universe. But now . . ."

But now by day the whites patrolled the countryside. At night they mounted guard throughout the town, everyone taking a turn on watch. Tubs of water were placed at the street corners to be ready in case of fire. At each intersection a sentinel stood through the night to keep order and to convince the blacks and the mulattoes that if the whites were not strong at least they were vigilant.

On the first of December came the full story of the destruction of the capital, Port au Prince, midway down the island, in the fighting between the whites and mulattoes. Cutting rushed over to Perkins with the news, and soon after 6 P.M. James walked back to Cutting's rooms for a drink with him. "While I was making a Bowl of Punch we were alarmed by fire having caught from a Candle in the room back of my apartment—It had caught a furniture check curtain which was inside the Jalousy, and had communicated to a piece of light stuff like Bunting which served for a ceiling of the room.—I tore down the curtains all in a flame, trampl'd upon and smother'd the blaze—I then leap'd upon the table and broke away that part of the Canopy which was blazing and by the assistance of a little water we soon extinguished the whole." Cutting injured his right hand in the process, but reflected gratefully that nothing worse had happened. So touchy were feelings in the town that a fire in a mulatto house with Negro domestics would not have been thought an accident. It might even, thought Cutting, have set off a general massacre of the colored people.

The news from the Port au Prince region that reached the Cape showed the furious nature of the fighting there. The race war was unrestrained. Cockades were made from the ears of dead enemies. Pregnant women had their bellies ripped open and their husbands were forced to eat the fetuses before they in turn were killed. Infants were thrown to hogs to be devoured. Grimly the Cape kept alert, determined this should not happen to them.

Cutting's days were varied. Perhaps he would go to the public baths with Sam. Perhaps it was to play billiards with Walter Burling. Or again, three days before Christmas: "Early this morning I accompanied Mr. James Perkins aboard a Guineaman and assisted him in picking sixteen prime slaves from among a cargo of 300. The sixteen all males." Cutting toyed with the idea of exchanging his muslins for slaves and sending them to the Havana market.

By January 1792, fires could be seen rising on the plain, "supposed to be sugar cane. Ripe cane burns very rapidly, the sugary sap being of a rich, oily nature." Coming home one Sunday morning from a refreshing bath with Sam Perkins, Cutting found "a disturbance among some Anglo-Americans, which made it necessary to conduct the principal author of it, who was a drunken Scotchman, first to the American Guard House, and afterwards to the Main Guard.—Soon after that Mr. James Perkins had by his interference restored a tollerable degree of tranquility among those who suffered themselves to be agitated by a temporary resentment."[8]

In spite of the siege, business went on as usual. Perkins had rented a new place for business "situated upon the Bay about the middle the length of the city." Cutting examined it one morning after breakfast with Jim. He spent several days assisting Perkins in moving his supplies and stores to the new building, and then he moved his own trunks of merchandise there too.

Jim could see, however, that new arrangements were going to have to be made at the Cape. As early as mid-December he had written to Tom suggesting the possibility of the "establishment of one of our House in Boston." A month later Cutting noted that 288 sugar plantations had been destroyed, plus 1,284 coffee plantations, 15 cotton, 72 indigo, the whole totaling 1,659. Such a loss not only disrupted the normal patterns of trade, but also the ability of the planters to pay, for most of their wealth had gone up in smoke.[9]

Tom replied to James's offer with the hope that Jim would "find it convenient" to leave the Cape "on the return of the Brig which I shall send you." He would await Jim's arrival "to determine some steady plan of business for the Cape." There was little to tempt Mrs. James Perkins in the prospect of another summer at the Cape. The memory of her escape from the de Rouvry plantation, the sickly, stifling summers, the constant danger from the plains—no, she would not persuade Jim to stay. So it was decided that in May the James Perkins family would go back to Boston.[10]

One evening in April Cutting met James in the street and walked with him "conversing respecting his Establishment in this city and the immense Profits his House reap'd, does and will reap from it. In these last five months which I have been necessitated to pass in expensive idleness, his House has gained at least $10,000 by one or two speculations already wound up and by its commissions." Small wonder James stayed on in the Cape until the last moment when such profits (enormous in terms of the purchasing power of the dollar then) could be made there.[11]

The thought of such wealth tantalizingly just out of his reach must have been bitter indeed to Cutting. He finally sold his muslins at a stiff loss. Borrowing some money from James he bought two hundred umbrellas to try his luck with in the States. For he too had decided to go north. He consigned the umbrellas to James's care, for it was time for the Perkins family to board the vessel for Boston. Sunday, May 6, "about 4 P.M., Mrs. Perkins with her two children embark'd aboard the ship *Providence,* Capt. Munro, for New York. Toward evening Messieurs Perkins, frères M. Sieman, and myself stroll'd up as far as the South Barrier but returned home early at Evening. It was between six and seven that Mr. James Perkins embark'd aboard the *Providence* to accompany his family to America." Early on the morning of the seventh, Sam, Mr. Sieman, and Cutting went aboard to say goodby. "Found much company abroad," Cutting wrote. "We went out as far as the White Flag—I then took leave of the amicable lady and her children—but came away so hastily as occasion'd my neglecting to shake

James Perkins by the friendly hand—however I'm sure he will excuse this want of ceremony—If they were the son and daughter of my blood mother I could not more sincerely wish them a pleasant passage and happy meeting with their friends in that happy country which gave them birth—adieu!—and I leap'd into Capt. Young's boat where that gentleman sat waiting for me."

Then it was Captain Cutting's turn to depart. He made arrangements to go in one vessel, but this fell through, inevitably. Then the gentleman who bought his muslins refused to pay him for them. Right to the very end of his stay his bad luck followed him. Sam and he killed the time of waiting by visiting the museum of M. Valentin, ci-devant Surgeon of the King's Own Regiment in France and Professor of Anatomy at Nancy. This gentleman had a curious collection of human skeletons, embryos, exhibits of the hearts, arteries, veins. "He showed us also an excellent pair of strong, well-made gloves, formed of the Human skin drest after the fashion of buff leather."[12]

Finally the waiting ended, and he had a last supper with Sam. "We took an exhilirating glass of delicious Claret which coming in aid of the good punch, etc., that I had previously drunk, in some measure obliterated the pain of parting with so good and hospitable a man as Mr. Samuel Perkins." Cutting was bound for Philadelphia. On Saturday, June 16, he wrote in his journal, "At daylight weighed and came to sail." Out beyond the White Flag. Out past the dangerous reef called the Square Handkerchief which had wrecked more than one vessel. Away from M. Valentin's museum which its gloves made of human skin. Away from the doomed city, Captain Cutting once again "revolved eastward," in a swelling breeze, his finger still firmly in his mouth.

If there was one place T. Handasyd Perkins did not intend to put *his* finger, it was in his mouth. He was not one to put all his bets on one venture, one brig. All his hopes were not on the *Hope*. During the fall of 1791, he had been busy with his partner James Magee preparing a second ship for the northwest coast. This was the *Margaret,* probably named after Magee's wife. The ship was a copper-bottomed beauty more than twice the size of the *Hope*. A member of the *Columbia's* crew, when he saw the *Margaret* on the coast called her "as fine a vessel as ever I saw of her size and exceedingly well fitted for this voyage, and I believe no expense was spared."[13]

The brothers James and Thomas Lamb had joined with Magee and

Perkins in this venture, as well as brother-in-law Russell Sturgis and Eleazer Johnson. The Lambs wrote to several important people in government for letters of "introduction and protection" from the Spaniards on the Northwest Coast. To General Knox, they described the ship as a "Credit to the builder Mr. Edmund Hartt of this place and to our Country." It had "every necessity for the preservation of our People's health and the probability of promoting the interest of her owners." Magee, they told Knox, was going in the ship himself, and his "ability" as a person "Competent to the undertaking" as well as his "Ambition" would insure that he would exert himself not only for his own and the owners' interests but also "for the Honor of his Country."[14]

So on Monday, October 24, 1791, a day when the *Hope* was twelve days out of Hawaii en route to Canton and before Cutting had reached the Cape, the *Margaret* sailed out of Boston Harbor. On board was the frame of a small vessel of thirty tons and several carpenters to set it up when they reached the coast. The plan was for his tender to cruise about gathering skins, the same scheme the *Columbia* had used previously.

Ingraham had arrived in China by December 1791, only to discover that his rich cargo of furs had dropped two thirds in value. The Chinese were at war with Russia and, under the mistaken notion that the fur trade was Russian-connected, had prohibited all vessels with furs from entering Canton. Prime skins worth $40 now sold from $15 when purchasers could be found. Ingraham and another captain wasted much time attempting to smuggle skins ashore. Eventually they were able to dispose of their skins but not very advantageously.[15]

Together the two captains charted a small vessel, the *Fairy,* invested their capital from the skins in teas, loaded the vessel, and sent it back to Boston with Ebenezer Dorr as supercargo. Ingraham headed back for the Northwest Coast on April 26, 1792. During May he spotted two low islands as the *Hope* sailed between Okinawa and Iwo Jima. True to habit, he named these the Otis Islands, after Tom's good friend.

Magee had reached Queen Charlotte Island on the same day Ingraham left China. He had been sick most of the voyage. The first thing he did was get himself ashore and eat a "mess of greens." Then he had his crew build a log house for him. He had had quite enough of the bounding main for awhile. One of the carpenters made a small carriage for him so he could ride along the shore. Gradually, his health improving, Magee came down with "Ingraham's Disease" and decided to name the place where he had regained health, calling it "Port Recovery." By early June he was able to stand on deck for half an hour at a time, and the *Margaret* began cruising about in search of trading Indians with furs.

Ingraham reached Queen Charlotte Island on the second of July, but did not drop anchor in Magee's area. He heard from the Indians of Magee's arrival. He also found that the fickle Indians had developed a new fad while he had been in China. "All my passage from Macao I had my smith at work making daggers in every form I had seen among these people . . . the smith who was a very ingenious man had executed vastly well indeed." But the Indians scarcely looked at them. Table spoons were what was wanted now, "an article," grumbled Ingraham, "they would scarcely except [sic] as a gift when I was here before." Copper, which they had not wanted the previous summer either, was now in demand. Ingraham had plenty except that his was too thin. "Leather for war garments was another article they wanted and a variegated shell green and white a species of pearl. For anything else they would not give near the value." The prospects for the season's trading looked to Ingraham to be "very indifferent."

The *Hancock,* another Boston ship that had been in China the past winter reached its anchorage on July 3 and moored twenty yards away from the *Hope*. They saluted each other with three cheers. The next day the men of the *Hope* and *Hancock* roasted a sixty-pound hog on the shore and had an Independence Day feast. At noon they fired a gun, hoisted the colors, and gave three cheers, which echoed strangely among the pines and wave-falls of that lonely shore. To the watching Indians it must have seemed very odd rituals that these palefaces performed. But to the men of Boston, so far from their homes and loved ones, it quickened their hearts and sped their thoughts some three thousand miles across the vast unsettled and empty continent to a bayside town that was banging its own cannons and ringing its bells too for that sixteenth Independence anniversary.

Ten days later, on Bastille Day, Handasyd Perkins in Boston was writing his brother James a letter that marked the union of the two brothers in business, and the pursuit of a fortune.

> Dear Jim . . .
>
> . . . The project of "clubbing our stocks" is a thing I have always looked forward to with great pleasure, and as an event which would certainly succeed your abandoning the W. Indies. The inducement to strangers to

> connect themselves in business ought to be great;—a want of Confidence, and of course a Jealousy in the parties, must be productive of great uneasiness to them, and make them appear unfavorable in the public eye . . . there are a thousand cases which give rise to the low suspicions which we so often see reigning between partners . . . on the other hand a connection between brothers is both natural and beneficial; they have fewer distrusts and are more communicative, which strengthens their confidence and makes their business but amusement.
>
> . . . For the present it would be idle to enter into any statement of what I cou'd throw into stock; suffice it to say that whenever you please we will declare our intended connection; nothing w'd make me so happy as to see you here with a prospect of permanency,—our good Mother renews her age upon the idea.[16]

An anonymous writer in the *Columbian Centinel* on August 1 stressed the encouraging business trends of the times. The Revolutionary War, in breaking England's control of American trade, had opened whole new areas for Yankee ships to trade with, such as China and India. Now they could get India piece goods first hand and eliminate middleman charges. The misfortunes of Santo Domingo increased American commerce in indigo and were to have some effect on the cotton and liquor traffic too. The disappearance of European forests opened up opportunities for ship building in the "Thirteen States."

To provide a firm base for expanding trade, the establishment of sound banks was needed, said the letter writer. The growth of cities, towns, and manufactories would help balance the fishing industry. The new laws banishing paper tenders, ex post facto laws, and improving contracts, could only serve to stimulate business. Wherever this sanguine correspondent looked, he only saw favorable signs; the mint, the laws regulating seamen and the fisheries, the rise of the public debt, the spirit of improvement leading to new roads and turnpikes, dredging rivers, building canals, the discovery of coal near navigable waters, the extension of the post office, the constant increase of lighthouses on the coast, the new trades, the progress of agriculture, everywhere things were on the upswing. There could not be a better time for a "connection between brothers," for a "clubbing of stocks."

Far from these enterprises, out on the Pacific coast and holidaying over, Ingraham began to cruise for skins, but soon found that the price was "beyond all reason." The *Margaret* was having as little luck as the *Hope*. Both ships were working their way to Nootka Sound on Vancouver Island, the principal settlement on that part of the coast, at the moment in the possession of Spain though soon to belong to the British.

On the last day of July, 1792, the Spanish pilot came out and worked their ship in. Salutes were exchanged and the men of the *Hope* found themselves staring at the little village of sixteen houses which included storehouses, a bakehouse, and a hospital. There were cattle, sheep, hogs, and poultry in abundance. Ingraham wooded and watered at Nootka Sound for a few days, then on the seventh of August the *Hope* set out to continue trading, returning on the tenth of September, having not acquired many furs.

The *Margaret,* under first mate David Lamb, was still out gathering skins. Ingraham had only collected about 450 on his present voyage, and at the Canton price of the previous year ($15 to $25) had made a poor voyage. So he welcomed Magee's decision to leave the *Margaret* in charge of Lamb on the coast, while Magee and his 1,200 skins went to China with Ingraham. At a freight of $3 per skin, it was a windfall of $3,600. Three weeks later, Magee changed his mind, and the two ships left for Hawaii and Canton together on the twelfth of October.

Two weeks before, an advertisement had appeared in the *Centinel* of September 29. "Thomas Handasyd Perkins Respectfully announces to the publick his connection in business with his Brother James Perkins, jun. under the firm name of James and Thos. H. Perkins, Who have for sale at their store, no. 64 Long Wharf Brown Sugars, and loaf sugars, cotton, Madeira wine in pipes, Sherry, and etcetera." The ad they ran in the *American Apollo* was similar except that it located the store at No. 11 Long Wharf. A minor mistake by a man whose oldest daughter had just died.

Cursed by he that crieth *oysters* in the evening in such a tone as to resemble the cry of *fire*. Amen.

*American Apollo,*
December 7, 1792

# 9

# The Gentlemen Drink Brandy Punch

"A farthing candle placed in a large candlestick" was how Captain Cutting described the obelisk on Beacon Hill. Beacon Hill, sixty feet higher than now, offered the best view of the town. Boston sat almost like an island in the blue bay that brought the wealth of the world to its wharves. Cutting enthused over the view here just as he had at the Cape. "The most variegated and luxuriant scenery that Nature and art united present through her extensive works."[1]

Reverend William Bentley up from Salem two weeks later—keeping, as Salem men do, a sharp eye on the doings in Boston—noted that "the plaster had fallen from the north side of the monument." It takes more than a view to impress a Salem man, and Boston has never quite satisfied Salem. But even Bentley had to be impressed that Boston had inoculated 8,000 peoople, almost half the town, against smallpox that September. This was more than the entire population of Salem.[2]

Boston was in the throes of a smallpox epidemic. A town meeting permitted a general inoculation to take place. This was not Dr. Jenner's cowpox vaccination, which was not used until 1799, but the injection of a serum from human patients who had had a mild infection of the disease. It was a primitive and dangerous treatment, but nevertheless had considerable success.

Dr. West of the Hollis Street Church was struck by the curious appearance of the town when inoculation first began. People "of all sexes, ages, and condition were continually flaunting about the streets in their calico loose gowns." "People seemed to think," wrote Dr. West, "that they were only engaged in a frolic which would amuse and divert them for a few days and weeks, and had no apprehension of the danger to which they were exposed." The party soon ended however. "It never before proved so distressing and fatal." The *Centinel,* ever looking on the cheerful side, wrote on September 26 to assure country readers that the smallpox was not "raging in Boston." Only eighty had died.[3]

One of these was Tom Perkins's first-born, the little Sarah born just before he sailed to China. She was almost four years old now. Cutting described how quickly it happened. On Saturday, September 22, 1792, he "brought my friend Perkins home with me from 'Change to dine, agreeably to previous appointment. Mr. Shaw has several gentleman to dine with him—so that we fill'd a long table—demolish'd much good cheer—and after dinner drank copiously of excellent wines. Mr. Shaw, besides excellent Claret, introduced some delicious Madeira, so that sober evening stole inperceptible upon us.—We rose from table time enough to visit a ship which Mr. Shaw is dispatching for India." This is hardly the portrait of a man worried that his child may die

But the next day, Sunday, at dusk, everything is changed. "I went to visit Tom Perkins. Found him and family much alarm'd respecting the dangerous state in which his eldest daughter is with smallpox. Two eminent Physicians have just been consulting on her case—their looks and prescriptions indicated but little hope, though their language was comforting." And on Monday: "About ten sallied out to distribute Circulars. Met Mr. R. Sturgis who informed me that the lovely daughter of his brother Tom Perkins is no more!—The Parents are excessively afflicted.—It is truly a damnably hard case." And Sally Perkins was seven months pregnant with her third.

Later that afternoon Cutting went by the Perkins house on Purchase Street "intending to visit him in his affliction, but when I came abreast of his house, I declined going in and passed on—for I think it best to let the first paroxisms of grief subside of themselves." He excused his cold feet by a long discourse on the subject of grief and the "common mode of condolence," arguing that he thinks it better not to refer to the subject when making a funeral call. Instead he recommends assuming "a cheerful and serene aspect and talk of indiferent matters in hope of diverting intense reflection." So he went over to see the Russell Sturgis family. "Found their children in a fair way. Mr. Sturgis inform'd me that my friend James Perkins had arrived in Town this evening and was at his mother's. I immediately repair'd thither to see him." It wasn't until Tuesday that he got up enough courage to call on Tom, "but did not remain there long."

The Perkinses nearly lost their other child, Eliza, a year and a half old. She had also been inoculated and broke out with the disease the same day. She was very sick and had been given up for lost. But Uncle James insisted on trying out a West Indian remedy on her. Thinking it hopeless anyway, Sally Perkins agreed. It was simple enough. It consisted of James carrying his niece into the air of the garden, keeping her there all day and giving her water in a spoon. Whatever the value of this method, Eliza recovered.[4]

Cutting had an apartment at Mrs. Eaton's boarding house, but he spent most of his spare time with the various members of the Perkins family. He thought Madam Perkins, Tom's mother, "one of the most worthy and agreeable old ladies existing." The "old" lady was then but fifty-seven and had fifteen more years left to her. She also had three unmarried daughters, or rather two unmarried and one—Esther Doubleday—recently widowed and so re-eligible. The fourth daughter, Nancy, married to Captain Cushing, was living in North Carolina, but her marriage, as the family had predicted, was beginning to fall apart.[5]

Any mother of three marriageable daughters would have cast an appraising eye on Captain Cutting. With so much undisposed merchandise on the shelf, even a thirty-six-year-old bachelor would begin to look quite attractive. The fact that he had not yet settled down to a steady trade was unimportant. He had many obvious virtues—the family could supply the rest. So by day, Cutting frequented the 'Change, that gathering of merchants on State Street where gossip was exchanged and deals made. Or he haunted the Counting House of the Perkins brothers who had moved up to 10 and 11 Long Wharf from 64. Since Long Wharf was an extension of State Street, he did not have far to go. The brothers were most obliging. They were his bank, his money lenders; they made small ventures for him (shipping 4,000 pounds of coffee to France plus a barrel of pickled peppers, speculating in potash and sugar), tried to sell his confounded umbrellas, gave him tips on the English market, and helped him with his circulars that he hoped would put some business in the way of his French firm. What would one not do for a possible future brother-in-law?

For decidedly, the captain had an eye for a pretty girl. He was hardly unpacked at Mrs. Eaton's, before he went to a rope dancing exhibition. He admired several girls there, but one stood out—Barbara Higginson. Cutting noted her effect on the men: "'Pon honour—she is a lovely girl!' vibrated on the lips of every male creature who was within ear-shot of me." In three years, this exquisite eighteen-year-old girl would become the wife of his friend Sam Perkins.

But what about the daughters of Madame Perkins? Cutting was tempted by the Perkins girls. One day he bet against Joseph Blake a complete outfit "from hat to shoes" that he would be married to an American lady within twelve months. Would it be Mary Perkins, whom they called Polly? She was twenty-three, gentle and amiable. Her niece Eliza remarked that Mary was "very stately as she sat, but when she got up she was not so tall as you would expect." Cutting realized she did not have a beautiful face, but thought that her mind and domestic virtues made up for that; a beautiful face, he consoled himself, was only "transitory."[6]

Would it be the twenty-one-year-old widow, Esther Doubleday, or would it be Margaret Perkins whom they all called Peggy? At nineteen she was "impulsive and vehement." Cutting observed that she had "most expressive eyes and a complexion that I am fond of—Brunette." So he took tea almost daily with their mother, escorted the girls home from the "exhibition rooms" where they had been seeing *Beaux Strategem, The Miser,* or *She Stoops to Conquer*. He squired them to brother Tom's or brother Jim's or around Fort Hill to the home of brother-in-law Russell Sturgis.

By late October he was feeling extremely fraternal towards this amiable family. The ladies "all seem like my sisters." This was progress but not quite in the right direction. A month later at Madame Perkins's, "Mrs. Doubleday and Miss Margaret Perkins appeared so amiable that my soul seem'd to expand toward them with—more than—fraternal affection!" What was the gentleman's trouble? Too much drink?

For in Boston they drank the fall afternoons into oblivion. Cutting drank with the Perkins brothers and their friends, and some he frankly envied. He dined with Tom's great chum, Harrison Gray Otis, at the end of October. "How infinitely happy must Mr. Otis be if he is fully conscious of the advantage he possesses!" One of the best lawyers in town, he was blessed with an ample income, a charming wife, a lovely daughter, and a "cherub-faced son." All this and good health too, for Otis was "in the prime and full vigour of thirty!" Cutting thought it best not to dwell on the enormous difference between Otis and himself, yet mournfully concluded that "no good seems to be written against my name in the Book of fate."

By the end of the year 1792 Captain Cutting had decided to see if his future lay in Philadelphia or New York. His relations with the Perkins family continued warm and cordial, but he was not to be linked to them by marriage. He spent Christmas Day in Boston fashion, calling at the brothers' countinghouse—the day was not then a holiday in that Puritan town. His Christmas dinner was at Vila's in a party of gentlemen that included Simon Elliot. On Saturday the twenty-ninth Tom Perkins gave a farewell dinner for him at his house. Sunday he called at James's for some letters of introduction to friends in Baltimore, then to Tom's "to take his commands for the Southward.—Then visited at Mrs. Perkins, *mère*—found only her blooming and agreeable daughter Margaret at home—past half an hour with her." The next day, he took the stage for the south, "for my part I do not like a formal leave of anyone." How could the genial captain revolve in such a circumscribed sphere as Boston? The world, as James had observed, was his orbit.

When Sam Perkins returned from the Cape in February 1793 to report on the situation there, he carried only bad news. He stayed in town awhile, perhaps courting the fair Barbara Higginson, then returned to the Indies in May. As much stock as possible had been removed from the island, but the Perkins firm was still owed large sums by the planters, who usually paid off in sugar and molasses. The revolution had put an end to such activities and the firm was in danger of losing much of their profit. When Sam arrived at the Cape he found it under siege.

Nightly, the town was attacked by the blacks. Added to the dispute with the former slaves, a bitter factional quarrel had broken out in the French ranks between the civil commissioners and the military. This degenerated into open battle. Seeing they were losing, the commissioners opened the gates of the city to the armed blacks outside, and then—chaos. Fights broke out in every quarter of the town.

After a night of terror, Friday, June 20, started with a strange calm. Burling and Sam Perkins found their section of the town apparently deserted. Pistols at the ready, they ate breakfast, growing more uneasy by the minute because of the unusual silence. They decided to get back to the safety of the ships. Once they had made up their minds, they left quickly, without a second shirt to their backs, not even taking their watches which they left ticking in their bedrooms. Hardly had they got on board the vessel nearest shore when, looking with a telescope toward their house, they saw it surrounded by a troop of black cavalry. All the houses on the bay were now given over to plunder. Money, plate, watches, and jewels—quick riches that could be easily carried—were seized first.

In an emergency men do strange things. They decided that night to go back the next day and get their clothes. To risk their lives for a linen shirt! Better to die than be naked. As soon after daylight as they had eaten, the little expedition set out. Three boats with four sailors in each, one commanded by Sam, the second by Burling, the third by Captain Clark. Together with a few volunteers they made a party of eighteen or nineteen armed men determined to bring back shirts or die in the attempt.

Seeing them rowing ashore, Captain Campbell from another vessel, eager for a fight, joined them with four sailors. The augmented unit moved down the quiet streets, slipping along the sides of the houses, and at the end of each street covering the approaches. Not a person was to be seen. The silence in the once busy town had an eerie quality to it. When they came to their house a dead Negro lay directly across the doorway with a bundle at his head. He had been shot in the back. One of the sailors caught up the bundle nonchalantly and tossed it to a friend. "Hello, Jack! Catch this and throw it into the boat, my boy; here is fine plunder for us!"

There were other dead Negroes scattered around inside the house, bodies stiffening and covered with flies. Carelessly they rushed into the bedrooms, found the watches gone, but the wardrobes untouched, the keys still in the door. They grabbed sheets and hastily filled them with whatever came to hand first. Then they dashed into the store room and filled other sheets.

Reinforcements were continually arriving from the back part of the town. Quickly they retreated to the boats, firing as they went. But just before they were ready to go, Burling, standing in the door of the store facing the bay, yelled, "Keep your guard, Campbell, while I run up and lock the goods-room door. We may have another chance at it yet." And up he ran, back the whole length of the building to lock the door. As soon as he returned they pushed the boats off and rowed rapidly back to the ships.

Here they had a hasty dinner and came up on deck to watch the shore. The insurgents had brought down long lines of mules and were now plundering the warehouses along the bay. This continued until darkness came. Then they set fire to the warehouses, the blaze spreading rapidly fed by the brandy, rum, spirits, the oil, tar, and pitch left in the warehouse. Up in flames went the property Sam had been unable to remove from the warehouse. Consumed also were the debts due the Perkins firm for goods sold to the inhabitants. Perhaps, however, they could yet save something from the holocaust, if the French government would pay for the damages.[7]

Now that the Cape, that "most pleasant," that "most productive and perhaps the richest spot in the universe" was but a heap of smouldering ashes, the ships with their refugees sailed. Sam went to Port au Prince to see what he could recover from the commissioners. Burling, who had charge of about fifteen thousand dollars, all the money they had saved from the flames, went in another ship, which was captured and carried to Jamaica.

The Santo Domingo trade of the Perkins firm was now gone. This was the main prop of the firm, and as it went up in flames the Perkins brothers became even more concerned about the outcome of their adventure to Canton.

Ingraham and Magee were in Macao by the first of the year 1793. Ingraham had collected perhaps as many as 550 skins, about a third of what he brought to market the previous year. The increased competition on the coast, the whimsical tastes of the Indians, and his flitting about from port to port in search of skins had contributed to his poor collection. Magee, on the other hand, was estimated to have amassed eleven or twelve thousand skins. Even if his were not of the same quality as Ingraham's, he could not fail to make more money on their sale.

The surviving records do not show how this sale went. Every Chinaman in Canton, complained William Fitz Paine, a Perkins agent there later, was an "unprincipled villain." The only safe rule, he concluded, was "to believe every Chinese a scoundrel till you are convinced of his integrity." For the firm's benefit he listed the principle Hong merchants with an assessment of each. After the name "Consequai" he wrote, "very lavish of promises, very shuffling but rich and doing much business. Very liberal credit." Sullivan Dorr, brother to Ebenezer and son of a Perkins competitor, was even more skeptical of Consequai. He is "a very good adept at mixing teas," he wrote his father. This was the merchant Ingraham had selected to handle his business.[8]

Ingraham was not the first captain to be taken, nor would he be the last. Another Perkins captain, James Rowan, later had trouble in Canton. Dorr wrote his father, "Rowan lost 500 tails and 24 skins, how is best known to himself. Some doubt his integrity." In the margin of his letter he cautioned, "Be secret." No good the old man gossiping about such matters on 'Change. "I have it from good authority he sold some to the Hoppoman, which he never rendered an account of. Perkins will hawl him over the coals; Ponqua made him great comeshaws."[9]

It would seem as if Magee must share some of the blame for Ingraham's troubles, since he was there with him. Much later Perkins ascribed the failure of the *Hope* to the incompetence of Ingraham, but he does not elaborate. John Howel, Jr., writing to the owners of the *Columbia* from Canton on May 11, 1795, gives a hint of what happened: "The owners of the *Hope* who will, I trust be obliged to pay Captain Ingraham's debts to Consequai, are now defaulters forty-three thousand eight hundred and twenty-one dollars. I have seen the bond in which Ingraham binds them; specifying also the names of Thomas H. Perkins, Frederick W. Geyer, and one of his brothers." Sullivan Dorr partly confirms Howel in a letter to his father of November 9, 1800. "Consequai holds Joseph Ingraham's note. Warn your Captains of putting themselves in his power." It is one thing to hold a note, it is another to collect it. Seven years having gone by, it would appear that the owners of the *Hope* at the very least disputed it.[10]

To the disaster of the Cape and the unhappy results of the *Hope* ("the voyage was defeated all together" wrote Perkins) were added troubles at home. The first of these were the French refugees arriving in vessel after vessel from both the homeland and the devastated French islands in the Indies. Many of them came to Boston, and the Perkins family were quick to provide help and friendship. A committee formed to aid the refugees included both Perkins and Russell Sturgis. Refugees in other towns were aided too. When news came that Gabriel Tardy was destitute in New York, money was sent with the promise of more for this member of the Cape firm for which Jim had first worked. Years later daughter Eliza would recall that quite a few refugees stayed at the Perkins house. "Beds had to be made up on the floor."[11]

Then disaster came to Boston itself. In an age of candles, dirty chimneys, closely packed wooden houses, and tar-covered ropewalks sitting like powder kegs in the midst of the town, fire was an imminent, daily threat. On Wednesday, July 30, 1794, the threat was realized. In the large section bounded on the east by Hutchinson Street and on the west by Atkinson Street (on which Russell Sturgis lived) were six long ropewalks, running from Milk Street on the north to Cow Lane (now High Street) on the south. Shortly after 4 A.M., Edward Howe, owner of one of the walks, had started a fire under one of the tar kettles. Through some "carelessness in kindling," a spark jumped to a large quantity of tarred rope yarn stretching six hundred feet down the walk, which had been made ready to be twisted into a cable that day.

The fire ran down the cable "like a train of Gunpowder" wrote Perkins's minister, Dr. Belknap. Howe himself was considerably burnt but gave instant alarm. Not that it did much good. Fed by the immense quantity of hemp, tar, and cordage, the fire enveloped the adjacent walks. It "spread with nearly the rapidity of electricity." The wind was blowing north northeast and drove roaring mountains of flames towards Purchase Street and the seaside docks. On threatened Purchase Street, in a house rented from Mrs. John Gray, lived James Perkins and family.[12]

Men swarmed to the inferno with their little buckets. The "fire departments," those semisocial clubs of volunteers, had hastily pulled on their clothes, made a dash for the firehouse, attached the long drag lines to their engines, and hauled them to the fire. Tom Perkins had rushed to the fire from the house he was now renting on Federal Street. He was not in an engine company but a fire company, whose job it was to help the occupant of a house get his goods to safety, storing away small articles in the canvas bags each man had.

The roof of Russell Sturgis's wooden house was continually catching from the heat and sparks of the nearby blaze. As often as it caught it was put out, but with the greatest difficulty. Even Belknap's Meeting House on Federal Street, near where Tom now lived, was threatened. James Perkins was not so fortunate. The full fury of the fire roared down on Purchase Street. Almost everything went. Mrs. Gray's large dwelling house, the outhouses, the garden itself trampled under the swarming crowds.

A town meeting held on the fourth of August elected Perkins as secretary of a committee to assist the "sufferers by the late Fire." He also served on a committee from the churches to help the fire victims. With Russell Sturgis and three others, he represented Federal Street. This committee "sat" at the Bunch of Grapes Tavern "from 3 to 7 o'clock P.M." on August 7 to receive estimates of the losses of the "sufferers." In the same issue of the *Apollo* with the committee's notice, Russell Sturgis had a notice thanking the people who had helped him save his house.[13]

James Perkins moved into one of the elegant new apartments just opening in Bulfinch's Tontine Crescent. But for the firm of James and Thomas H. Perkins, it must have seemed a dismal August after an equally depressing year. The Cape destroyed, with financial losses to the firm; the *Hope* a failure; plagues and fires.

Finally, on August 17 the *Margaret* arrived in Boston. It had made a slow journey from Canton around the Cape of Good Hope, taking six months for a trip that most ships did in five. Magee, apparently recovered from his illness, brought home a collection of articles in use among the Indians of the Northwest Coast and many artifacts used by the Hawaiian Islanders. In October, he gave these to the Massachusetts Historical Society.

And what for the owners of the *Margaret?* Reminiscing later about this voyage, Perkins said they collected "some 12,000 to 15,000 sea otter skins" which were worth about $30 to $40 each when Magee sold them in China. Here was a profit in the neighborhood of half a million dollars. A man, a firm, could stand the loss of a *Hope* or two for a profit of this dimension. Each share in the *Margaret* yielded $2,000 to the holder. If it was share and share alike, each holding a share apiece, this was the equivalent today of $100,000 for each of the five owners. Presumably the *Margaret* brought home teas, silks, chinaware, and nankeens. These would more than have paid all the expenses of the voyage and yielded an additional profit.

Here was a gold mine. Alongside this, the Cape was small change. Perkins had had a letter that May from a refugee who had returned to the Cape. It did not promise an early resumption of the profits from cane or molasses or slaves. "Our plain presents a horrid sight. Nothing but ruins and ashes. Our Negroes are out, all mules and cattle killed or scattered, the buildings burnt or demolished, and the plain is not yet safe; we dare not go on our plantations but with patrols."[14]

Well so be it. In Canton there might be a Consequai. Other captains like Ingraham might "ill requite" the confidence placed in them. But a Bostonian could be just as cunning as any Chinese, given such incentives as the *Margaret* had brought home. Indeed, with this kind of backing, a gentleman could drink brandy punch and the best Madeira forever.

I conceive many opportunities for speculation will present themselves during your stay in France.

James Perkins, February 7, 1795

# 10

# The Game Playing in Europe

Paris, that well-publicized city, was busy increasing its reputation as the capital of sin and vice. To such a city it was that Thomas Handasyd Perkins elected to go in the fall of 1794. It was not, however, to step into sin, but to step into speculation. The game playing in Europe was war. War brings shortages and scarcities. Shortage and scarcity bring merchants eager for the war-inflated profits.

France was fighting a group of powers who were determined to avenge the execution of Louis XVI and destroy the Revolution. The situation had been critical for the young republic in 1793, but by the following year France had been cleared of the invading armies and shifted to the offensive. Toward the belligerents President Washington pursued a policy of neutrality, though under strong pressure from friends of France or Great Britain to support the side they favored.

Because of its crucial help in America's own revolution, and because Americans saw the French Revolution as an extension of their own, France had obvious claims on the sympathy of Americans. When Perkins returned to Boston from Canton in 1790, the French tricolor cockade was being worn, and staid Bostonians were greeting each other as "Citizen." A writer to the *Centinel* justified it by saying that President Washington had addressed the members of congress as "Fellow Citizens."

Events in France were followed with extreme interest in the New World. Boston newspapers frequently issued extras when some ship arrived with news of late developments. In January 1793, Russell Sturgis placed a notice in the *Centinel* that a "CIVIC FEAST in commemoration of the glorious struggles and brilliant successes of the Citizen Soldiers of Liberty in France will be held at Faneuil Hall on Thursday the 24th inst." A roasted ox was carted through the town, and later, cut in pieces and thrown to the immense crowd packing State Street. Fireworks and a bonfire on Copps Hill ended the day.

The ghost of Louis XVI might have thought they were celebrating his execution, which took place three days before the great civic feast in Boston. When the news of this event arrived in America in late March, some of the more conservative people began to have second thoughts about revolutions. American politics was polarizing into two blocks: Federalist, including Washington and Hamilton, who were sympathetic toward the English; and the Democrat-Republicans who were sure, with Jefferson, that the French Revolution was "the most sacred cause which man was ever engaged in."*

Bostonians tore into politics with all the zeal they had shown for 150 years in hacking at religion. This partisanship generated great excitement, but Washington's policy of neutrality generated the profits. Since neutral American vessels were safer than belligerent vessels, the American carrying trade expanded enormously. Shipyards enjoyed the boom. Sailors' wages rose. The price of the farmer's produce and of the merchant's goods increased. American vessels now received the chance to move into the trade between France and its West Indian colonies, which had previously been monopolized by French ships.

As early as May 1793, the Perkins letterbooks report cargoes shipped to the West Indies and then transshipped to France. James Perkins went to superintend one of these voyages, for the partners preferred

* The Jeffersonian group were called variously "Republican," "Republican-Democrat," or "Democrat Republican." They yielded the "Republican" part of the hyphenation to the descendants of the Federalists much later when that party had passed through Whiggism and Free Soilism. To avoid confusion on the general reader's part, it should be understood that in the time span covered by this book, "Republican" will never mean the party formed in 1856, two years after THP's death. When used, it will always mean what is today the Democratic party.

to look the ground over personally if possible. "We conceive this business will be very great," the firm wrote a correspondent, "and we shall push it as far as our property and credit will allow." In June 1793, while the Cape was plunging to disaster, James left Boston for the Indies on the *Charlotte,* a ship owned jointly by the Perkins house and Stephen Higginson, Sam's future father-in-law. First he went to Martinique, then on to France. By the end of January, he was back in Boston.[1]

Even while James's trip was still being planned, Tom had written to a London agent, John Vaughan "at the fountain head of information" that they should rely on him furnishing them "with the earliest of importance . . . either as Merchants or Politicians. What think your wise heads of our being obliged to take a share in the game playing in Europe?"[2]

The profits of successful voyages there made the risks worth while. The greatest profits went to those who had the courage to trade directly with France. The turmoil of constant revolution and war had so disrupted French agriculture that there was danger of widespread famine. A single voyage to a French port could earn a 200 percent profit. The difficult part was not making the sale, but getting paid afterwards. It was decided that when the *Charlotte* went back to Europe in the fall of 1794 with a cargo of beef and pork (again a joint venture of the Higginson-Perkins group) that brother Tom should go along to manage the voyage.

In a letter written to Tom by James shortly after the former had reached France, James outlined the project. "I conceive many opportunities for speculation will present themselves during your stay in France." He pointed out the advantages of vessels "plying between Hamburg, Rotterdam, and France" and observed that neutral vessels "have been permitted a free trade *even from* England." So impressed was James with the advantages of carrying cargoes for both sides in the war, that he intended to send over as many ships as he could lay hands upon. He advised his brother that "if you can sell your different cargoes for cash, or sure bills on Hamburg or Amsterdam" to do that rather than to trust to paper. He suggested that Tom establish a fund in Holland, since he felt the best speculations were to be made on goods carried from the northern ports to France. "By having your specie at either of those places, or in London, you will not be detained to make your sales, but you can provide your cargoes for France with greater benefit and despatch." Speed counted. "The number of voyages made while the war lasts is certainly an important consideration."[3]

Tom sailed from Boston on Sunday, December 14, 1794, in the *Charlotte,* the same ship Jim had gone to Europe in a year and a half before. Walter Burling, up from the Cape, went with him. Pious Bostonians were preparing for church when the ship left at nine in the morning with a fresh northwest breeze filling her sails. The good breezes continued, and in two weeks they were halfway across the Atlantic. "This is not doing bad," wrote Tom in his journal. The wind continued northwards and a surprising number of rainbows were seen almost daily. The weather was as warm "as it generally is in Boston Bay in autumn." Back in New England, it was so unseasonably warm on Christmas Day that boys in Salem went swimming.

When the ship began steering south, they lost the time gained earlier. A large sea started running on January 10. It came on obscure and rainy. Contrary winds blew. By the twenty-fifth they saw nineteen sail directly ahead of them, an indication they were nearing port. Then just before dark, a heavy squall came up and the ship "was kept away before the wind to avoid falling in with any of those ships." Anxious lest they run into a straggler, it was not until midnight that Perkins went to bed. Hardly had he settled for sleep when "a number of voices from deck cried, 'She is close aboard of us' and, from all which could be heard below, the most fatal event was to be expected."

A light was hastily shown on the *Charlotte* and the other ship veered off. But it had been a very close call. It was estimated that the other ship was only a few rods away when it changed course. Perkins could see the rigging of it plainly even by the time he reached deck "which I did with the utmost haste, and but few clothes on, as there seemed every reason to expect the ship would run us down; and those who could escape by getting on board of her would alone save themselves." Perkins never remembered to have spent such a frightening night "and hope I never shall such another."

He hoped in vain. Heavy gales, even some snow, and then one final terrible night when they were very near to land but unable to get into the harbor, with a violent gale and heavy seas putting them in great danger. "The ocean appeared like one continued wave breaking over rocks." It was a storm as in the old sailor's tale printed in the *Centinel* that winter. It had been so furious that it took ten men to hold one man's hair on his head.

Finally the ordeal was over. The next morning, Tuesday, February 3, they sailed into Bordeaux. The harbor pilot told them they were lucky they had not made port sooner, since the ships already in had been so endangered by the ice that they had to cut cables and run on shore. "We know not," Perkins philosophized, "when we go too fast or too slow."

Here at last he was in France. And the Paris towards which he was now riding with all cautious haste had produced those edicts and laws that had brought the beautiful city of Cape Francis to burning destruction, had impoverished or caused the death of close friends of Perkins, and had consumed thousands of dollars worth of his firm's property. No longer was it something to read about in a Boston paper. It was to be seen out of the coach window.

In Paris Perkins had business to look after. Revolutions may come and go, but trade goes on forever. "My business has so much taken up my time since I arrived in Paris, that I neglected to keep a note of the time as it passed." After a month, however, things had quieted down and he had time to write in the journal that he kept for his wife and family to read, so that they could share, vicariously, his trip.

He did not unduly bother their heads with his business matters: organizing trading ventures, selling cargoes to the government, and dancing attendance on the various bureaus trying to secure payment for same. "This day confirmed my opinion of the perfidy of some of the agents of the government. Although the contract I made with them was signed, they now make difficulties, and wish to alter the tenor of the agreement." A week later he wasted another day "following up my business which is shamefully neglected by the members of the Committee of *Salut Public*. All is finished but their signature; which they pretend, at the offices, the members have not time to get." Since Perkins was trying to recover some of the losses of his firm from the destruction at the Cape—a letter of September 12, 1793 estimated that "the Government is indebted to this house fifteen or twenty thousand dollars"—his getting the run-around becomes understandable.

There were many Americans in Paris. Occasionally Perkins "dined with a decadi club of Americans who met on that day to the number of fifteen or twenty." Living with Perkins was Joseph Russell from Boston. They dined almost every Saturday with the American minister, Mr. James Monroe. Perkins thought him "a very gentleman-like, and to appearance, worthy man." He was less reserved about his wife: "Mrs.

Monroe is one of the finest women I ever knew; and she is said to combine the greatest worth with her personal accomplishments and beauty."

It was Monroe who put Perkins and Russell in touch with Madame Lafayette. Perhaps they could help a lady in distress? She breakfasted with them on March 27 and greatly impressed the sympathetic Perkins. "She is much worn down by her misfortunes, which she says, she fears will know no end but in the grave. Poor woman!"

This was exactly the impression the lady wanted to make for she had a plan and needed as much help as she could get. Her husband, one of the moderate leaders of the revolution, had been on the point of being arrested when the extremists took over. Attempting to flee to neutral territory he was captured by the coalition troops and, in spite of the efforts of President Washington to secure his release, was imprisoned by the Prussians and Austrians.

Madame wanted two things: to get her thirteen-year-old son, George Washington Lafayette, out of France and to the United States where she hoped President Washington would take care of him (and where the boy could work on Washington to secure his father's release), and to get herself out of France with her two daughters and into Austria where she intended to join her husband in prison.

Since Madame herself was only just out of jail the French government was not about to help her. All had to be done in great secrecy. Monroe issued the boy an American passport under the seldom-used and little-known family name of Motier. Perkins was to apply for the necessary French travel document, and to make the arrangements for the boy's passage to the United States. Russell and Perkins agreed to pay for the expense of the trip. They also lent Madame Lafayette 2,400 louis d'or for her own expenses. In good business fashion, Perkins collected a receipt for this which is still among his papers.

On the twentieth of April, Perkins wrote briefly in his diary, "This day I accompanied my friend J. Russel to the Croix de Berney, on his way to Havre. The day pleasant." No mention was made of the third passenger in the coach, young Mr. Motier whom Russell was to put aboard a vessel bound for America. The escape went without incident, and in a few months young Lafayette was in Boston.

There the boy stayed with Russell's family on Federal Street, and visited various members of the Perkins family. Later, he wrote Perkins,

"Remember me to your brothers, who overwhelmed me with kindness." As for Perkins himself, "be assured that I will remember all my life with deep gratitude the eagerness which you showed in Paris to help me and those dear to me." The gratitude took a solid form too apparently, for one of the Perkins descendents today wears a diamond ring said to have been given to Perkins by the Lafayettes. The marquis himself wrote a belated letter of thanks in May 1798 so effusive that one suspects complaints of ingratitude may have reached his ears.[4]

The time in Paris was not entirely spent in business and plotting. There was much of pleasure in the city that even a proper Bostonian could permit himself to enjoy. "The Opera House is the most beautiful I have yet seen; and the dancing is so far beyond what I had before seen that it appeared to me like magic." What kind of magic was a good question, for he immediately added, "The nymphs, upwards of forty in number, were dressed with all the wantonness imaginable: Their dancing, too, is, to us Americans, indecent in the extreme."

Because of his Federalist sentiments, his comments on the French Revolution are interesting, particularly in view of the unpalatable nature of that revolution to his fellow Federalists at that time. Writing of the vigorous young soldiers—a troop of cannoneers—to whom he was told the young republic was indebted for some of its finest victories, he exclaimed: "May every man be a cannoneer when opposed to tyrants, and every cannoneer an army in himself!" When he went to see the place where the Bastille stood, he commented that the blood ran cold in the veins when one thought of the misery that place once contained "and the soul is quickened with hatred against tyrants wherever they are found." He was not so moved that he could not immediately add "There have been, unfortunately, a great many Bastilles in France since that one was destroyed."

Visiting the Hôtel des Invalides (the Old Soldiers Home) he mused: "When one contemplates the causes which have produced the misfortunes of those people, or of most of them, and traces them to the ambition of kings, or tyrants under other names, he is led to wish that all the world would have the resolution to throw off the yoke, and enlist under a republican government, where all does not depend upon the caprice of a single villain, but upon the voice of the people."

None of this corresponds with what John Quincy Adams nearly a half century later listed as some of the elements of the Federalist mind—

"An utter detestation of the French Revolution and of France . . . A strong aversion to republics and republican government." The advent of Napoleon, however, was to change these sentiments of Perkins.

With some friends, Perkins visited Sèvres, where they went through the factory and watched the famous porcelain being made. "Codman and I bought a number of trifles." A few days later at a porcelain factory in the Rue du Temple, "Saw a great deal of china of most delightful fabric, which led me into some extravagances." In a memo of private expenses he kept, in addition to a large tailor's bill were such items as flower pots, prints, children's toys and books, watch and chain for Mrs. Perkins, watch and glasses for himself, botanical telescope, two profiles, and four prints.

The young republic staged one of the last demonstrations of the guillotine at work while Perkins was in Paris, and he and Russell went. They hired a window in a house strategically located. On May 7 the man was executed who, under Robespierre, had been prosecuting attorney for so many "of the innocent and helpless." "Fifty to sixty in a day were sacrificed to the malice of this monster," wrote Perkins, "who seemed to delight in the slaughter he was administering." This was Fouquier-Tinville. Along with him were executed the jury "who were partners in his guilt."

At 10 A.M. Russell and Perkins went to the Place de la Grève where several thousand people had already assembled in anticipation of the day's sport. People crammed the windows of all the nearby houses, and as much as fifty livres—a week's salary and more—were paid for rooms nearest to the guillotine. Perkins was disgusted with the number of women present, and noticed especially that "there was scarce a face that did not wear a smile." The crowd seemed to be anxious to "feast upon the sight of blood."

The wait was not long. At 10:45 the cavalry rode up and soon after them the three carts carrying the condemned. "They had their hair cut short, and their hands tied behind them, and were covered with loose greatcoats. They were seated with their backs to the horses; and I observed, that, as soon as the carts turned the corner to come into the square, they looked towards the instrument which was to deprive them of life."

Insults and invectives were shouted out by the crowd upon the prisoners. Some cried out "Give me back my father" others called for their mothers or sisters, or brothers or families or friends, whomever the public prosecutor had cruelly and senselessly taken from them and sent to death. Perkins began to lose heart and wish himself back in his lodgings.

Since he was only about twenty paces from the "fatal spot," or as it was popularly called "the theater of death," and also had an opera glass, "which gave me an opportunity to see every feature with great distinctness," he did not miss a thing. Fouquier was pale, the muscles of his face contracted, his eyes bloodshot. He had a chance, as his many victims before him, to think of his own wife and children whom he was leaving in destitution.

The first cart, emptied of its passengers, drove up beside the platform, and a basket about seven feet long was fastened to it. Up went the first victim. He attempted to speak but was shouted down. Quickly thrust under the knife, his head was severed "in the twinkling of an eye." One of the executioners picked up the bloody head, the other the mangled corpse "with as little ceremony as one would a beast at a slaughter-house. They are both thrown (not laid) into the large basket; the axe is again hoisted up and another victim brought forward."

Three of the executed would not let the executioners hold their heads down—which prevented the axe from mangling—but stared indignantly from side to side at the crowd. "They all walked up to the board against which they are tied with great firmness and looked round with great composure." With the aid of his opera glasses, Perkins could see how efficient a killing instrument the guillotine was. "The body does not move, not a spasm can be seen to contract it."

Finally it was Fouquier's turn. He had been saved for the last and made to watch his accomplices die before him. Up he went with an air of disdain. When his head fell there was a great burst of applause. The crowd called for the head to be shown. The executioner seized it and held it up with brutal indifference, showing it all around. The hair matted with blood, the eyes sightless, the tongue stilled. But the words that tongue used in its defense would find its echo down the centuries. "If it is a crime," wrote Fouquier-Tinville at his trial, "to have given effect to the resolutions of the Committees of Public Safety and of General Security, I confess that I am guilty; I should have been guilty if I did not execute them. What then ought I to have done?"

Timing the whole operation carefully, Perkins found it took only fourteen minutes to decapitate the group of seventeen. This included, he carefully noted, "at least two minutes lost in changing the basket" when it was full. He judged that if one basket could have held all the bodies, the group could have been killed in twelve minutes!

Perkins waited till the mob had gone and saw the machine washed down, "while gallons of blood were streaming from it." But he added thoughtfully, "it is dangerous to familiarize the public to exhibitions of this kind. I know this by my own feelings; for certain I am that my emotion decreased with every head that fell."

Following the advice of his brother James that he establish connections in Holland, Perkins left on May 11 for a tour through the Low Countries with Russell and Mr. Jeffrey, also of Boston. They were gone for a month, spending most of their time in the Dutch cities of Amsterdam and Rotterdam. This close-up view of the countryside gave Perkins a chance to compare the drab, dirty part of France with the "Dutch-neat" Low Countries.

At one of the post-stops on the way back to Paris, where they were held up waiting for fresh horses, he gave way to a bit of homesickness. "The reflection which cheers my spirit under every cross accident . . . is that I am on my way to meet those in the society of whom alone I am or can be happy. May the God of Heaven be propitious to my wishes, and land me safe in a country which has, in my opinion, the means of happiness much more within the reach of all classes of people than any I have yet seen!"

In Paris, he caught up with his correspondence. He was vexed "beyond means," he reported to James on June 21, with getting the *Charlotte* receipts. An American who had just arrived from England had told him of the daily depradations of the British on American commerce, and he burst out, "if this is the case, I hope we shall act with some degree of spirit and have nothing to do with a set of pirates and blood suckers as they are." So aroused was he, that he doubted if he would put foot "on that infernal island."[5]

There was also a long letter for his minister, Jeremy Belknap, about a notorious American currently to be seen in Paris. Thomas Paine was at that time about sixty-five. He had been released from a French prison the previous November and invited by Mr. Monroe to stay with him, where he was still living when Perkins met him. The impression he made on Perkins was of a man "very slovenly." He had a red and rugged face, much "hackneyed in the service of the world," said a friend. Perkins thought it "strongly denotes present or past intemperance—his health is very precarious, and I am told his *attachment to life very strong* . . . In Conversation, Mr. P is very agreeable, unless politics is the subject—upon which he an [sic] I seldom have anything to say, as he rails at every measure which I support—indeed I have very seldom had much conversation with him, but in mixed company—where the tone [of] the conversation was given by others, and I was a humble listener—he talks with great fluency and seems to be possessed of very general knowledge."

Then came a comment about Paine's famous book, the *Age of Reason*—"as he stiles it." This "was written while he was in the Luxembourg prison and I suspect was generated in an idea that it would please the men whose powers he was so much in, and support the system of infidelity which was the order of the day under Robespierre—He tells me he intends visiting America soon, and I have been told, he has the vanity to say he will effect great changes in the present government of that happy country." Perkins commented sharply, "IF bettering governments is his *taste*" (a Boston jibe at Paine's drinking) "he might be well employed where he now is—I suspect he will find as few advocates for his political, as for his religious tenets" in America.

His letter ended on a personal note. Apparently he was recovered from his Anglophobia. "I shall leave this in about three weeks for England from whence I shall embark for America by one of the Boston traders." He had seen enough of Europe, "and shall return to my native country blessing the good fortune which placed me there."[6]

Captain Cutting was also in Paris, and frequently at Monroe's, where he and Perkins both attended the celebration of the Fourth of July. In fact, the good captain had written a song for the occasion which was sung to the tune of "Anachreon In Heaven."

In Climes where fair FREEDOM, secure from her Foes,
Sees millions who bow at her shrine with devotion—
Where VETERAN PATRIOTS, in laurell'd repose,
Lament to see Arrogance crimson the ocean:—
Where ORDER pervades
The Mountains and Glades—
Where COLUMBIA reclines in her own, native Shades—
—Hark! millions of FREEMEN with joy hail the day
Which rescued the COUNTRY from Tyranny's sway!

Thus, poetically, Captain Cutting disappeared from Perkins's life, still with "his finger in his mouth."[7]

On July 26, Perkins left for London. After wasting a few days in Le Havre, waiting for the ship to sail, he landed at Margate on July 31 and the next day "jumped into a post-chaise for London." That night he was at the London Coffee House, "a large and superb mansion," so the guides say, "with a profusion of attendants, first rate cooks, the best of waiters, the smartest chambermaids, hair dressers, porters, and shoe blacks."[8]

London was mostly business: pressing the claims of the *Charlotte* and *Delight,* both Perkins ships that had been seized by the British; meeting the merchants and bankers and agents and so personalizing the contacts that until then existed only in letters. Perkins made a good impression on these shrewd financial men; he was one of their kind: responsible, cautious where called for, yet astute to see opportunities and press them hard. Writing to him from London a few months after he had returned home, a friend jokingly remarked, "I find a number of people here who in spite of all I can say pretend to think you were rather a clever fellow."

He arrived back in Boston early in December, too late by some months to see young Lafayette. The lad, with his tutor, had gone to New Jersey to live with a former aide-de-camp to Lafayette. Because of the delicacy of political relations with France, Washington had hesitated seeing the boy when he first arrived in Boston. Early in the spring of 1796 "his heart finally overcame his doubts" and Washington sent for his godson. By early summer the lad and his tutor were living at Mount Vernon.

It was here, by chance, that Perkins met the boy again. He had gone to the city of Washington, then building—for Congress still sat at Philadelphia. At a ball he was introduced to the President. Because of his part in getting Motier out of France, the president invited him to visit Mount Vernon. "This was not to be declined; and a few days later, I went, as invited, to pay my respects to the man I cherished in my mind beyond any earthly being." It was almost like visiting God.

Perkins hung on every word that "fell from the lips of this great man." A toad passed near where they sat talking on one occasion, and the President asked Perkins if he had ever seen it swallow a firefly. No, said Perkins, Well, he had, said the president, and from the thinness of the skin of the toad had been able to see the light of the firefly continue blinking after it had been swallowed.

"The day trenched far upon evening, and at seven or eight o'clock we were taking our tea; not long after which, the ladies retired." Knowing the President's habit of early-to-bed, Perkins made "a movement in my chair." Washington seized on this and asked him if he wanted to retire. Yes, said Perkins. As there was no servant in the room, Washington took one of the candles from the table and led the way to the great staircase, "then gave me the candle, and pointed out to me the door at the head of the stairs as my sleeping room. Think of this!"

Perkins was too excited to sleep. Here was T. Handasyd Perkins, mixing with history, house guest of Washington, helping heroes in distress, taking a modest but useful part in "the game playing in Europe."

Electioneering begins with all its frauds to prevail in America. Our gazettes are the vehicles of the several means of inflaming the public mind.

Reverend Dr. Bentley,
November 17, 1798

# II

## Firmly in Federal Paths

The 1790's were exciting times for Boston. New men with new ideas were running things. Perhaps the handsomest symbol of the change was the elegant theater on Federal Street. "The *primitive* Bostonians," wrote a young Englishman playing in the theater orchestra, "would as soon have admitted the plague as a company of players."[1]

An early attempt at drama had brought a law in 1750 strictly prohibiting theatrical performances. During the siege of Boston, British officers had a theater in Faneuil Hall, but when they went, their theater went with them. In the late 1780's, the younger, more liberal members of the community began agitating for the right to have theatrical entertainments like Philadelphia and New York. A mild effort to crack the frozen Boston attitude towards the theater went down to legislative defeat in 1791.

Discouraging as this event was, it did not prevent Bostonians from having a theater. They simply called it something else. A company of comedians came to town from London and set up shop in a remodeled stable in Board Alley (Hawley Street), which was named the Exhibition Room. They gave dramatic presentations of what they termed, in a sly dig at the stiff New England character, "Moral Lectures."

When Captain Cutting was in Boston in the fall of 1792, he attended several such "lectures" including *She Stoops To Conquer* and *The Beaux Strategem.* The Perkins family was also devoted to these "lectures." Stopping at Madame Perkins's house one afternoon to take tea with the lady and her daughters, the captain found that Esther and Mary had gone over to the Exhibition Room to hear that uplifting "lecture," *The School for Scandal.* They got more than their money's worth that night.

This open defiance of the law had angered many, and on that same night the attorney general secured a warrant for the arrest of one of the actors, Mr. Harper. As Esther and Mary Perkins, together with a respectable Boston audience, sat watching, or listening to, the moralities of *School For Scandal,* the lecture came to an unexpected halt. At the end of the second act, Mr. Harper informed the audience that the sheriff had a warrant for his arrest and would arrest the whole cast if the performance was not immediately stopped. As the *Centinel* delicately phrased it, "much agitation ensued." Judge William Tudor, one of those trying to secure a theater for Boston, arose and calmed the audience, asking them to leave peacefully, "which," said the *Centinel,* "took effect."[2]

Now the "Play House party" made an all-out effort to secure the repeal of the antitheater legislation. Enough support was mustered in the legislature so that by March 1793 a repeal of the old law was pushed through. Early in April a group met in Concert Hall and proposed building a theater. Their purpose, they stated, was "to encourage a cheap, elegant and rational amusement for the gratification of the Citizens." Before it was to be elegant and rational, it was to be cheap. It turned out anything but.[3]

The $20,000 theater they planned to build actually cost double that. They intended to sell 120 shares at £50 each, but the next day they had to cut the figure to 60 shares, not being exactly swamped with subscribers. T. H. Perkins bought a share. Simon Elliot and Russell Sturgis also became proprietors, along with John Adams and other prominent men. Bulfinch was chosen as architect. Within a month the cellar was dug. During the summer that Cape Francis fell and Bostonians were coping with the influx of refugees from that devastated island, the elegant but not cheap theater on Federal Street took form. It was a chaste example of the master's style.

Bulfinch was extraordinarily busy that December of 1793. The first part of his new Tontine Crescent on Franklin Place was being completed and the cellars of the second half were "in great forwardness." This handsome series of connected residences was immediately to become Boston's most fashionable address. The Perkins firm bought one of the houses, and brother Sam bought another in joint ownership with the Reverend John Murray. Just below and opposite the Crescent, the roof was going on the new theater.[4]

Finally the theater's inaugural night came. A brilliant audience, including most of the proprietors, crowded into the theater on February 3, 1794 to see *Gustavus Vasa,* described as a "truly Republican tragedy." The lead had to be prompted only once. Within three weeks, the musicians of the theater were requesting the public "not to throw apples and stones" into the orchestra. Someone had already thrown a piece of glass from the gallery and sliced the skin of the kettledrum.

It was several years before proprietor Perkins began to play a personal part in the affairs of the theater. Although a founder, his name does not appear at any of the business meetings before he went to Europe in 1795.* Elliot and Sturgis attended meetings with a fair amount of regularity and James Perkins, though not a proprietor, went once in October 1795, perhaps to represent his brother.

On his return from Europe, Perkins started attending proprietors' meetings frequently. In April 1796 he served on the committee to confer with John Williamson who wished to lease and manage the theater for the season of 1796–97. In June of 1796, Perkins and Sturgis were put on a committee to enlarge the theater. Perhaps his new interest came from his European theatergoing. More likely, it had something to do with the rising political spirit of the decade, which engulfed every activity, even the theater. For the Boston theater had taken on a Federalist tinge, and the Republicans had decided by 1796 that they had to have a theater of their own.

This new theater, the Haymarket, was a great barnlike building below the Hay Market on Common Street (now Tremont) near Boylston. Competition began in earnest between the two theaters. The Boston had to drop its prices; it opened a box office in State Street for the

* Except when he signed the articles on June 10, 1794. He could have signed them elsewhere.

convenience of the merchants on 'Change; it put on a wider variety of plays, some original; it lured two of the leading dancers away from the Haymarket and copied the dancing and pantomimic exhibitions of the "large theater," as the Haymarket was called.

Nothing helped. There simply wasn't enough of a theater audience to support two large theaters in the town. Political passions were not sufficient. Even before the new theater opened, Williamson had been running into financial difficulties. Perkins and the other proprietors had to dig down and come up with a $5,000 "loan" in exchange for the scenery, costumes, and properties, which the producer owned. In January 1797 the proprietors each paid another $200. In April they learned that the dead loss of the season was almost $8,000. This apparently was the last meeting Perkins ever attended. He was not present two days later when the proprietors, with Sturgis and Elliot in attendance, voted to raise $15,000 to continue the theater. Perkins had accepted a more exciting and less costly job.[5]

In the spring of 1797 there had been a rash of fires in crowded, wooden Boston. Incendiaries were suspected and nightly patrols marched the streets for additional protection. Harry Otis had charge of ten men in Ward 7. At town meeting, eight extra firewards were elected and one of these was Perkins. Busy as he was, in the following years he accepted re-election twelve more times.

The fireward, in whose district a fire occurred, acted somewhat as a local fire chief, directing the work of the enginemen and coordinating the efforts of the citizens. To identify himself he carried a heavy pole painted red with a bright brass blaze at its tip. Daughter Eliza remembered the big hat her father wore which came down over the nape of his neck. At the fire, the fireward would arrange the men and boys in double lines from each engine to the nearest water supply, usually a neighborhood well. Full buckets went quickly along one line up to the engine and were dumped into its tub, empty buckets going back down the other line. The enginemen pumped away trying to force a weak stream of water on the flames. Other citizens helped pull down nearby buildings in danger of catching fire, or rushed about rescuing, or damaging, furniture.

Reminiscing about his duties many years later, Perkins recalled how in pleasant weather there were plenty of volunteer operators to be found, but in bad weather it was otherwise. It was rough dirty work and could even be dangerous. At one fire he attended, Perkins ran a nail into his foot. Eliza helped a servant cut the boot off his foot. Perkins was lame for a long time after. He was fortunate in that preantiseptic, unsterilized age that it had not killed him.[6]

On Friday afternoon, February 2, 1798 Perkins had a chance to combine his interest in the theater and in firewarding, for the Boston Theater burnt to a shell. Since it was in his district presumably he was in charge of the fire-fighting operations. Nothing was saved. Some blamed the fire on special theatrical effects being prepared, others laid it to the stoves used to warm the building. The loss of this charming Bulfinch building did not make everyone unhappy. Some citizens had never become reconciled to the presence of a theater in their midst. One such, a spectator of the fire, offered to contribute money to help tear down the other theater and to keep any more theaters from being built.

He was due to be disappointed for, as Dr. Bentley pointed out, it was only a loss of property, it was not a change of manners. The proprietors voted to rebuild. Elliot was at the meeting but not Perkins or Sturgis. Instead of a great rallying-round of proprietors as might have been expected in this hour of need, only a minority of proprietors showed up at the meeting. Bulfinch revised his design, and on October 29, 1798 the new theater reopened. A year later Perkins transferred his share and ceased to be a proprietor. Perhaps he felt he had built the theater twice and did not care to build it a third time.

The theaters had solved their financial problem to some extent by an informal agreement in the summer of 1797 to split up the seasons and the available audience—the Boston took the winter and spring, and the Haymarket had the summer and fall. This did not mean political antagonisms were softening. Those were not so easily solved.

Early on, Perkins interested himself in public affairs. In those first years of the republic, there were no political parties as such. Towns, and even the state, were dominated by the "old families," and the "best people," just as in colonial times. The natural leaders of the country, observed a British traveler, were its "gentlemen of fortune, talent and education." As a young man making his way up, Perkins felt he qualified as one of these "natural leaders."[7]

But even "natural leaders" begin by following. Perkins's political activities first became visible in 1794 when the *Centinel* listed him as a "vote distributor" for the spring election. Early on the morning of April 7 he was at Faneuil Hall, along with such friends as Stephen Higginson, Harry Otis, Simon Elliot, and Paul Revere. As the voters lined up to go in and cast their ballot, they were handed previously prepared tickets by Perkins or the many other vote distributors, representing the two different candidates. Supposedly the voters took the names of the candidates they favored, but this open form of voting made it extremely difficult for a voter to resist the pressure from his employer to accept the "right" ticket.

During the elections of 1795, Perkins was in Europe, but he was active in those of 1796 when the Federalists thought they had a chance to unseat Samuel Adams, who had inherited the mantle and popularity of John Hancock. They nominated Judge Increase Sumner, and waged a vigorous campaign for him, but Adams came out on top. Though the Federalists had lost the April election for governor, the May election of representatives to the General Court gave them a chance to recover.

There being no structured parties then, nominations were made by an informal system of anonymous letters to the newspaper suggesting certain slates. A sort of fiction was preserved that the nominees were chosen by all and agreeable to all. Party, supposedly, did not enter into the business. But a definite disagreement surfaced in these spring nominations of 1796 and Perkins was in the thick of it. The nominees named in the anonymous letters to the *Centinel,* that flagrantly Federalist paper, were not exactly the same as the slate being proposed in letters to the editor of the *Chronicle,* that rabidly Republican paper.

A complicated minuet now ensued as each group jockeyed for political advantage, trying to persuade the other group, in the pious name of "union," to accept their candidates. Failing this, they at least hoped to convince the public that it was the "others" who had rejected "union" and nonpartisanship. Sunday night, May 8, 1796, twenty men, who happened to be all Federalists, met at Concert Hall. Perkins acted as secretary for the meeting, reporting on it later in the *Centinel.* This meeting nominated eleven persons, whom they claimed represented several "different sentiments" to run for office. They publicized the names the next day through handbills and called for a general meeting Monday night of "all friends to Union" to accept the slate.

"A numerous meeting was accordingly held," Perkins reported to the paper, "At which some of all parties were present." How many were Federalists and how many Republicans is not mentioned. This meeting drew up a new list of thirteen names, supposed to include "most of the known Candidates." Since Boston was only allowed seven representatives, the last six names on the list were dropped. What sentiments these represented is not reported, but the names left on the list were, strangely enough, all Federalist. A committee of five to confer "with any other gentlemen of different opinions" about additions to the list were chosen, and Perkins was one of this committee.[8]

Tuesday night, the tenth, the day before the election, *two* meetings were held. The gentlemen with Federalist views met at Concert Hall. Those with Republican views gathered at the Green Dragon Tavern. The Federalist group had not previously consulted with the Republicans, but now sent an emissary with a message of conciliation to the Green Dragon Tavern. At 9 P.M. word came back to the Concert Hall that their "conciliatory list" had been "immediately rejected," whereupon, blameless in their own eyes and they hoped, the public's too, they voted "unanimously to support their own list." Party politics in Massachusetts were now out in the open.

When the election was held the next day, 2,103 men voted at Faneuil Hall. Three candidates secured more than 2,000 votes each, indicating some natural harmonizing. Since these candidates had appeared on both lists, much of the shouting seems to have been for effect. The other four candidates elected, including Harry Otis, were all Federalists and polled about 1,300 votes each. So Boston went two to one Federalist, and throughout the state, the Federalists elected enough representatives to control the General Court.

When Adams, now seventy-four years old, announced his retirement from politics in January of 1797, the Federalists got the chance they were looking for. They renominated Judge Sumner and since the Republicans were split, Sumner was easily elected in the spring of 1797. The executive branch of government in Massachusetts fell to the Federalists as well.

Thus it was to a "friendly" state that President John Adams returned that summer to vacation at his Quincy farm. "Among the many great little events which agitate this puddle called Boston," Joseph Dennie wrote a New Hampshire friend on August 6, "the arrival of John Adams is one." Dennie was dining "with the king" as he styled Adams, the next day, and not looking forward to drinking the "some two dozen of such perplexed toasts as the bungling creatures here give." Later that month, the president was invited to a large dinner in Boston by a group that included many Federalist leaders. The dinner was planned for Wednesday, August 16, and Major T. H. Perkins of the Independent Cadet Corps had charge of the affair.[9]

Joseph Sewall of Marblehead stayed in town to see the reception for Adams since it promised to be "so much superior to any thing of the kind ever exhibited." He wished his wife could view the decorations in Faneuil Hall. They were said to be worth riding fifty miles to see. "The superb Tapestry Hangings own'd by Mr. Swan are to be used on this occasion, with some ornaments borrowed from the Theaters and the whole is said to be arranged with uncommon taste & elegance."[10]

The day began with a military parade, with both Perkins and his brother-in-law, Major-General Simon Elliot, prominent in the line of march. When the escort of the president reached the ancient fortifications on Boston neck, they were met by the cadets under Major Perkins. Because he wasn't feeling too well, Adams postponed visiting the ship *Constitution* until another time, although assuring the public that would be soon. He was able to attend the dinner at Faneuil Hall, however, where the company of three hundred dined on turtle soup, an elaborate assortment of meats, and washed their viands down with 317 bottles of the best Madeira and forty-five of excellent claret, not to mention abundant potions of punch, porter, and wine. For dessert they were served oranges, melons, cakes, tarts, ice cream, blanc mange, and four hundred macaroons. It all cost ten times the yearly income of an average New England farmer. Dennie wrote his friend sorrowfully that "the toasts were followed by clamorous hootings and applause quite in the French style. All this is suited to the taste of the Bostonians, who are unquestionably the merest boys at all kinds of play."[11]

In the fall, Adams headed back to Philadelphia, still the nation's capital, to wrestle with the growing hostility between America and France. By the spring of 1798 there seemed a serious possibility of war between the two former allies. In Massachusetts, Sumner was easily re-elected governor, having proved so popular that the Republicans did not bother to offer an opposition candidate.

But the Republicans under Jefferson were more willing to fight Adams. In March, Adams had informed the Congress that negotiations with the French were not going well and made recommendations for arming American vessels and protecting the coast. The Republicans denounced Adams as a warmonger. Half a dozen Massachusetts towns sent petitions to the president protesting the arming of merchant ships, and the Republicans in Congress demanded to see the correspondence with the French.

With great relief, Adams sent along what came to be known as the "X Y Z dispatches," since those letters were used in place of names of the French agents. The revelation that Tallyrand, the French foreign minister, had demanded a bribe to sign a treaty with America struck Republicans dumb. Fisher Ames crowed gleefully, "The Jacobins were confounded, and the trimmers dropt off from the party like windfalls from an apple tree in September." The response of Pinckney, one of the American envoys, that American wouldn't pay "sixpence" was translated into the facile slogan "Millions for defense, but not one cent for tribute."[12]

The Massachusetts towns changed their tunes and their petitions. All over the country "the most magical effects" were observed on the public feelings. Addresses poured in on Adams supporting his firm stand. The students at Harvard offered "the unwasted and unimpaired energies of our youth to the service of our country," pledging to defend with their lives "that soil which now affords a peaceful grave to the moldering bones of our forefathers."

On April 21, 1798, Perkins sent along to Harry Otis, in the House of Representatives at Philadelphia, a copy of the Boston address. They had opened it for signatures on Saturday and "received in a few hours 150 names." It was to be handed round on Monday for more signatures. "It seems to unite all parties, except such as we shou'd feel disgraced in having with us in a good cause." While Perkins felt that it was "A melancholy concession to make" that government needed support like this, he regarded it as "a duty in us to give it." Probably after the sense of the town had been taken in this fashion, a "finishing stroke" would be to get town meeting approval too. "You may recollect," he continued, "the Knot of Jacobinism, which was concentrated at Sam. Turells shop in State Street, with C. Marshall at the head—these same people have volunteered in signing and forwarding this measure."[13]

James Perkins went to Philadelphia to see how the Perkins firm could assist the war effort. He wrote brother Tom on May 23 that he had "made my bow" yesterday to Adams "at his Levee.—The old Sage seems happy and appears to be filled with that *holy enthusiasm* which pervades all classes here." Tom had written his brother of the outcome of the local elections and James applauded the removal of all the "luke-warm men from our councils." As for the business at hand, "Write me how you should like the agency for fitting the Public Ships?—I know not if 'tis disposed of, but am confident from some circumstances I have heard that we can have it." Have it they did, with all the commissions that accrued to the holders.[14]

The war spirit was whipped up on every hand. When Josiah Quincy gave the Fourth of July oration in Boston at the Old South Meeting House, his audience was greatly impressed. Eliza Quincy, his wife, noticed that Major T. H. Perkins was "affected to tears," as were many gentlemen in the audience. The *Centinel* trumpeted that Quincy's oration ranked "among the most masterly productions . . . ever originated in any nation or on any epocha."[15]

The military spirit was still strong that August 1798, when the president came up to Quincy from the capital for a rest. The Boston calvary escorted him to his farm, and the *Centinel* hailed him as the "American Herschel." That October the president's birthday was honored several weeks late with Major-General Elliot ordering out the troops for a parade. Major Perkins was there commanding a sub-legion. The ships in the harbor made a handsome appearance "displaying the Eagle and Stripes."

There were no flags flown on Thursday June 27, 1799, though perhaps Perkins wanted to. That night he was chosen captain with the rank of lieutenant-colonel in the cadets, the top rank of that unit.* At noon on the Fourth of July, the new lieutenant-colonel and his cadets escorted a procession of civil, ecclesiastical, and military gentlemen to the Old South Meeting House to hear an oration by John Lowell.

The year closed with a momentous event, marking the close of the first years of the new republic. Writing in his diary, December 23, 1799, Dr. Bentley had to use capital letters to express the immensity of it. "This evening the News reached this town of the DEATH OF GENERAL WASHINGTON." The country nearly fell apart. "Liberty's temple is rent

* Because of a now-obscure cause, Perkins resigned this position the following June.

in twain," wailed one New England divine, "Her spotless high priest hath retired to rest, through the portals of everlasting fame." Everywhere the preachers mounted their pulpits to pronounce eulogies. The military organized funeral processions. The Masons had their own services in honor of their dead brother. Ladies wore armbands with the initials G. W. on them. Towns voted to print the sermons of their ministers upon this occasion. Monuments were conceived and erected. The cadets under Perkins took part in the Boston ceremonies. On Washington's birthday in February 1800, the whole performance was repeated. Americans began the new century feeling somewhat fatherless.[16]

# Colonel T. H. Perkins III 1799–1820

So your little John . . . grunts like a little pig, . . . pray frequently remind him that he is no pig but a little Boston boy.

Letter of the Byles sisters
May 1795

# 12

# See How We Grovel Here Below

In early September 1800, Perkins and his friends Captain and Mrs. Magee set out across Massachusetts. Showers late in August had brought the fields to peak, and the abundant harvest was being gathered in. On either side of the turnpike road, the three travelers could watch the busy panoramas of farm households attending to their fall engagements with the earth, and could almost taste the apple sweetness on the air.

They did not linger, covering about forty miles each day. Mornings, the colonel rode horseback until they stopped for dinner. "My object," he explained in his journal of the trip, "was exercise." In the afternoons, he joined Captain and Mrs. Magee in the carriage. They were heading for the springs at Ballston, just over the Massachusetts border in New York State, hoping the waters there would "prove efficatious" to the captain, who was suffering from a "stroke of Parylitics."[1]

One of the colonel's delights as he traveled was to quiz everyone he met about the people and places he was passing through. As befitted a business gentleman, he was particularly interested in the small mills and incipient factories along the way. What did they make, how did they make it, was it any good?

They had left Boston on Wednesday, September 3, and by Sunday they had reached the baths at Lebanon, New York. The water did not taste much different from rain water to the colonel, but it was invariably supposed to cure cases of scrofula. Four kinds of persons frequented these baths, and Perkins put them down as "the Halt, the Blind, the Lame, and the Lasy." Few persons, either sick or well, came to the baths without also going into the pool. This was leased to Andrew Craigie of Cambridge, Perkins learned, and he tried to discover from the operators how much Craigie was paying for it, but "I could not learn." What he did know was that the waters were "of a temperature to be very agreeable and are very soft to the touch."

One of the sights of Lebanon was the Shaker community of Mount Lebanon, two miles away, a pleasant village clustered in the hills. Founded not much more than a dozen years before Perkins's visit, by 1800 it was the principal community of the sect.* Perkins attended the worship service there in the large gambrel-roofed, white meeting house. Sixty feet long and forty feet deep, the building stood upon a green and was enclosed in neat Shaker fashion by a picket fence. This obsession of the Shakers with neatness and order was noted by all visitors. No weeds, no filth, no nuisances were allowed on or about their property. It was contrary to good order for Shakers to spit on the floor, to speak loudly, to shut doors with a bang, even to knock at a door for admittance. When entering a room, they scratched on the door first.

Perkins went into the meeting house by the men's door on the left side; women used the right-hand door. He found himself inside a large room without any divisions, a chimney at either end which, he uncharitably remarked, was "necessary to their comfort *the influence of the spirit notwithstanding*." Perkins was not too sympathetic to this new sect with its strange doctrines that Christ had returned to earth in the person of the founder of the Shaker sect, Mother Ann Lee, and that the Saints even now were judging the world.

The room he was in was about twelve feet high with planked whitewashed walls, the whole uncluttered and neat. Between the two doors

* It survived until 1947. In its 160 years, it had a maximum membership of 600, and a total membership of 3,202. The surviving members moved to the community at Hancock, Massachusetts.

T. H. Perkins, by Gilbert Stuart, 1805

were benches for the "strangers," again segregated by sex. As he sat on the long side of the room, Perkins could see the male Shakers, about fifty of them, at the left end of the room, while about seventy female Shakers sat on the benches at the right end of the room. For about ten minutes after he entered "all was perfect stillness." Then an Elder got up and came to the center of the room, "keeping near to the Wall." A woman Elder did the same thing. When the two Elders got to within six or seven feet of each other, all the men and women participants rose and "place themselves in what was not altogether a Hollow Square, but it was upon the same principle."

The group at first stood perfectly quiet, "with the eyes cast down and the deepest cast of distress and anguish painted on their faces." After a time, the Elder spoke to the spectators, asking them to make no noise and remember that "the house of God ought to be a house of Order." Then he spoke softly. "Now and then I caught a sentence which recommended perseverance in the good works they had begun and others which chided for their want of zeal in the works of Christ."

The short talk ended with "a song of Zion." The principal singer set a melancholy strain and the group joined in, but no words were uttered, only meaningless syllables and sounds. "The eyes are principally closed, and they all seem to be wrapt up in this sad melody. The sounds are distressing, and the countenances of the singers still more so."

After a second song, the Shakers went back to their seats. After a bit, the men got up, took off their coats and began one "of their modern exercises"—a dance. The chorister struck up a new tune more melodious than the ones first sung, and they began to dance. The dancing was patterned and regulated, and Perkins found it "not unpleasing in its effect, did you not necessarily connect other ideas with it" than the worship of God. Shortly afterwards, the service ended. The Shakers marched out two by two, climbed into their wagons and rode off to the various houses where they lived as "family" groups, even though absolute chastity was believed in and practiced by the sect.

Intrigued by what he had seen on his Sunday visit to the Shaker meeting, the colonel went out the next day with the Magees to find out more about the Saints and their settlement. "It consists," he wrote, "of but four Houses which are occupied as dwelling houses, and the number of persons who reside in them is about 200, the greatest half of which is female. The Houses are perfectly neat; well built and commodious." They took a walk in a six-acre garden that was highly cultivated with onions, beets, potatoes, and other vegetables.

Some of the women members were working in the garden and "Mrs. Magee endeavoured to make some conversation with them, but all she could get from them was yea or Nay." When Perkins walked towards them "they moved off in a body and left us to ourselves." Perkins found the men as laconic as the women. Finding one who seemed to be an Elder, he cornered him and found himself talking to David Meachem, one of the leaders of the settlement. Perkins fired questions at him, and Meachem answered "but avoided entering into any more conversation than was necessary." However, when he found that Perkins did not come to deride them, he opened up. But Perkins "was cautious however of asking any which I thought could possibly give offense."

And Perkins was far too practical. He was more interested in their "curious inventions for cutting and heading nails" and their "other improvements in mechanics which are worth notice," than in theology. Having learned all they "were able to get out of them in so short a time" they reluctantly left the village, "much inclined to know more of these people." His mood was reflective. "They stile us—the *World's people* and affect to pitty our wretched and forlorn situation as much as we do in fact pity them."

The next day, following partly on the new turnpike road being built from Lebanon to Albany, they left the springs for the New York capital. Albany was building and expanding, although "Dutch prejudice does much to impede it." The old Dutch were still in the majority, so the improvers "must wait with patience their removal to another and a better world before the present plan of improvement can be effected." Still their hotel and coffee house "made me blush for my native town," wrote Perkins.

Wednesday they rode a few miles out of Albany to visit the estate of Stephen Van Rensselaer, an amazing place with 4,000 tenants who paid a yearly rent of 20,000 bushels of wheat. "His lands," Perkins recorded, "are leased for *999 Years* or *Forever*—for my part I should like as well one as the other—" The estate was the largest in America and brought Rensselaer, who was lieutenant-governor of New York, at least $50,000 a year.

By noon of the next day they had reached famous Ballston Spring, passing many more log homes than they had previously seen, each swarming with children. They made a brief excursion to nearby Saratoga Springs, but Saratoga was several decades from coming into its own and replacing Ballston as *the* place to go. They also drove to the head of Lake George and viewed Glen Falls on the way.

By mid-October Perkins and the Magees were back in Boston. Perkins found himself being nominated for the House of Representatives from the first district of Massachusetts. The *Centinel* of October 18, 1800 reported receiving "several communications" all nominating the colonel "who as a Merchant, a Man of Information, and an active and unwavering Federalist, will unite the Federal vote of the District."

Perkins dashed off a letter to the editor the same day, flatly refusing the nomination. "To prevent the Federalists unnecessary trouble, I take this early occasion to say to the public what I have always declared to such of my friends as have conversed with me on the subject, that were I certain of combining the suffrages of the whole district (however my vanity might be flattered by the circumstance) my private concerns would lay me under the absolute necessity of declining the honor intended me."[2]

It was a wise move on the colonel's part. The election of 1800 was a nationwide sweep for the Republicans. While it was temporarily undecided whether Jefferson or Burr would become president, it was certain Adams was out. Even the first district, which included Boston, had elected a Republican.

The trip in pursuit of health did not prove "efficatious" for James Magee. Back at the elegant old Shirley mansion in Roxbury which he had recently bought, at the early age of fifty-one Magee succumbed to his "stroke of Parylitics." James Scott, the master of the Boston Marine Society, notified its members to attend Magee's funeral on Thursday, February 5, 1801. Magee's widow was appointed executor of the estate, with "T. Handasyd Perkins, her Attorney."

It was the end of an epoch in Perkins's life. For more than a dozen years he had been actively associated in business and pleasure with his wife's uncle. With him he had made one of the early Boston trips to China and gone through a moment of mutiny. As partners they had pondered the intricacies of making a profit in the first independent store Perkins had down on Merchant's Row. How many forgotten afternoons they had dawdled at dinner swapping stories over Madeira as the cigar smoke staled on the air. Now, like the cigar smoke, Magee was gone and some of Perkins's past vanished with him.

The period of the close friendship with Magee had coincided with the first years of Perkins's life as a married man. Those years had seen him setting up a home and fathering a family. Tom and Sally's married life had begun in a rented house on Summer Street, on the southerly corner of Chauncey Place. It was a good neighborhood, with Barrells, Russells, and Geyers nearby who extended a hospitable welcome to the newlyweds without expecting to put them to the expense of reciprocating. As a young man just starting to make his way in the world, Perkins appreciated this and remembered it warmly nearly sixty years later.

In 1791, Perkins felt financially secure enough to buy a home of his own. From two ladies, "Ruth Hulme, widow, and Peggy Hunt, spinster," he purchased a double lot on Purchase Street near the South Battery. The larger of the two lots, containing the house and outbuildings, was on the west side of the street. The house stood in a large garden running up the slope of Fort Hill. The lot on the other side of the street, facing seaward, was vacant land, grassed over. Eight hundred pounds "lawful money" was the price he paid, half in cash and the women took a mortgage for the balance. By the end of 1793 he had paid that off.

By that time his mother had bought a two-story house just down the street from him at the head of Sears Wharf. Surrounded by a brick wall, it had a stable, outbuildings, and was handy to the pump in Purchase Street. Many years later, Eliza Perkins Cabot remembered it as a West Indian style house with piazzas all around it. "You could look right out to sea and in a storm you could hear the roar of Nantasket Beach."[3]

Eliza thought her grandmother Perkins a "silent, reserved woman," adding, "they called her 'Madame Perkins' and she seemed rather awful to us. Mother spoke of her, even to the servants, as 'the old lady.' I used to like to go there for the gardens but I was not so fond of her as I was of Grandmother Elliot. But she was a remarkable woman, very dignified, and of great strength of character. Her children had unbounded respect for her."

It was in the Purchase Street home that the first child, Sarah, died of smallpox in September 1792. Another daughter born two months later was given the dead girl's name, and this second Sally lived till

1856. To the Purchase Street home, too, Perkins brought the Cushing children. His sister Nancy who had married Captain Robert Cushing before 1782 against her mother's wishes, had taken her two children to North Carolina in 1791 to be with the captain.

"He was a fascinating sort of man," wrote Eliza, "but dissipated." News reached Boston early in March 1793 that Nancy had died suddenly of smallpox at the age of thirty-three. Someone from Carolina wrote Perkins that her husband had abandoned her and the children were left without means of support. Perkins immediately wrote to have them sent on to Boston, and they arrived shortly after a rough trip in a coaster. When they landed, young John Cushing and his sister Nancy "looked like wild Indians. Father brought them up from the wharf in a carriage and he pulled the blinds down to Nancy's great disappointment, for she wanted to see the town."

John was about five years old and Nancy nearly eleven. At first they lived with their Uncle Tom and Aunt Sally, although later, sometime after Sam Perkins and Barbara Higginson married in 1795, Nancy went to live with them. "In those days," remembered Eliza, "there were great fights on the Common between the 'Fort-Hillers' and the 'Round Pointers.' When I asked Nancy Cushing how she and John came to be so strong, she said it was fighting the 'Round Pointers.' "

Before the ropewalk fire of 1794, Perkins had moved to a large three-story house on Federal Street, which he rented for $400 a year from the heirs of Joseph Russell. This brought Sally Perkins nearer to her mother, Sarah Elliot, who also lived on Federal Street. Mrs. Elliot's husband died on January 25, 1793, not long after the death of Sally's child.

Little Eliza loved to go over to her Grandmother Elliot's house. She was entranced with the kitchen, "a nice old place with brass and pewter kitchen things about and very neat and shining." The old-fashioned air of the house, "parlours with arches at the sides of the fireplace," the hangings about grandmother's bed, what was called "copper-plate"—cotton with outline figures in red picturing the story of Robinson Crusoe—all this was part of the attraction. Then there was Grandmother Elliot herself, "indulgent and generous, always bent upon making you happy." Factotum of the establishment was "Old Jenny, who came with her from Scotland . . . I thought nothing could taste so good as what Jenny cooked."

It had taken nearly two years to settle the estate of the elder Simon Elliot. He had stores on State Street, a snuff mill in Newton, and other interests. When it was finally divided in December 1794, son Simon, widow Sarah, and son-in-law Tom on behalf of his wife, split nearly $50,000 between them. For that time $16,000 plus was a very comfortable fortune. Perkins had been singularly fortunate in legacies twice in his lifetime, first with the "stake" that came to him from Grandfather Peck's estate when he reached twenty-one, and now nine years later, in his wife's share of his father-in-law's estate. With normal prudence and care, he need have no more financial worries the rest of his life.

He could well afford to provide his family with such luxuries as the new indoor water, which he did. As the population of Boston grew towards the 25,000 of the 1800 census, the wells and springs of the peninsula were proving most inadequate. Nor did all the houses have their own wells; many depended on the pump in the street. In 1796 an aqueduct was built to bring water into Boston from Jamaica Pond in neighboring Roxbury. It would save soap, cut washing time, give added fire protection, and, best of all said the promoters, be *pure*. Forty miles of log pipe were laid and Boston became the first large city in the country with an aqueduct. A "tube" was fixed into the subscriber's house, and a "drawing or perpendicular stand" provided to "draw" the water from. Houses not connected with the aqueduct (only the wealthy center district was at first served) could send someone down to the fish market, where aqueduct water was sold for thirty cents a hogshead, eight cents a barrel, and one cent a pailful.

By the end of the decade, Perkins had a good-sized family to feed and water. Sally was pregnant almost every other year: the first Sarah, 1788; Eliza, 1791; the second Sarah, 1792; Ann, 1794; Thomas Jr., 1796; Mary Ann, 1798, and Caroline, 1800. These first twelve years of marriage produced seven children, two of whom died. Other children, like John Cushing, lived with the Perkins, as well as connections, like Walter Burling's nephew, Sam Curson. Then there were the servants and the governess, Mrs. Sarah Tucker, to be provided for. Eliza's comment was to the point: "My mother was an excellent nurse. Having so many children she understood it thoroughly."[4]

The children lived in the nursery and were not permitted to eat with the grownups until they were ten. Instead, "Nanny" Tucker served them their meals. "There was a large fireplace with a crane and a kettle always hanging," Eliza recalled, "and she cooked a beefsteak or mutton chops in the frying pan. Mother thought that butter was not good for children. We had biscuits and milk. We had *clams* given us in the Spring 'to purify the blood.' "

The house bubbled with children coming and going. Uncle James had only two, but Eliza remembered having a "museum" with James, Jr., who was her age. Uncle Sam had started on his family. There were Sturgis cousins by the barrelful and assorted Magees, Elliots, and neighborhood friends. Like children everywhere they passed through what Lucius Manlius Sargent termed "all the epocha—rattles—drums—go-carts—kites—tops—bats—skates."[5]

The "epocha" of parenthood can be followed in the business ledgers, for family expenses of both brothers and of Madame Perkins were paid through the daily account books. Give us this day our daily bread? Principally, THP bought it from William Breed, ten dollars' worth a month, and Sam Thwing, five dollars a month. Thwing's crackers were famous, and a son with the odd name of Supply Clap Thwing worked for the brothers later. Special family treats stand out in the items: a barrel of apples, melons from Charleston, a jar of soy, sweet potatoes, and gallons and gallons of "cyder." What Madeira was to the adults, "cyder" was to the children and servants, although milk consumption was not small. Perkins's milk bill for March 1797 came to $5.75 for 103 quarts, or more than 5½ cents a quart. Other items also seem cheap by today's prices, such as coffee at 25 cents a pound. Actually, in terms of purchasing power they were quite a bit more expensive. In the ledger books are other family items: a hat "for John Cushing, $3"; "three children's chairs"; a stair carpet and a straw carpet; painting a chamber; shoes for the servant girl; a muff and a tippet ($27); a clothesline. "Fresh beef" was bought from several dealers, a bill for a year's groceries paid to another. "Sundries" came from Eben Eaton. A barrel of soap, or candles, was frequently noted. Twelve cords of wood were bought and Hermann Pierce hired to saw them. Chimneys had to be swept at 50 cents each.[6]

Schooling for the children had to be arranged. Payments were made for this purpose to a Mr. Chapman, and later for Mr. William Payne's "Federal Street Academy." Perkins explained this in a letter of September 14, 1797: "Mr. Payne, who kept school in N.Y. is now here and we have erected a little Academy for him in this Town.—he is certainly the first Preceptor for Children in N. Engl. The expense of schooling will be but trifling, $6 pr. quarter." The "Academy" was formally organized and Russell Sturgis served as president of the trustees and "T. Handasyd Perkins" as secretary. Printed shares were sold.[7]

Eliza vividly remembered Payne's wife, who was her teacher. "She was a jewess, a handsome woman and a good teacher; a woman of taste. She read English poetry well and encouraged us to read it. She allowed us to pick out pieces to learn. Cowper was a favorite and we used to read Goldsmith and Burns."

Expenses for horse and chaise run through these household expenses; bills for hay and oats, for trimming and "shewing" the horse, repairing harnesses, varnishing the chaise, paying taxes on it, and buying whips. Town taxes and pew taxes recur yearly. After Belknap's death in 1798, Perkins shifted allegiance to the New South Meeting House where the eloquent John Thornton Kirkland, later president of Harvard, was preaching.

Personal expenses show something of the man. He buys a walking stick, has his angling rod repaired, pays his hairdressing bill at Keith's (hair was powdered and still worn in a small pigtail at this period), and buys hats including "one military hat, $7." As he travels about town, he often hires a hack. Tickets are bought for theater performances, for Washington's Ball, or dancing at the Assembly. Servants' wages are paid, and they often stop by the counting room on Foster's Wharf to pick up pocket money for Mrs. Perkins, or to get money for shopping. Perkins himself frequently takes five or ten dollars, which is faithfully recorded and eventually charged up to his share of the profits of the business. During September 1797, for instance, he picked up on various occasions a total of $56.38.

Among the trials of childhood that nobody liked to think about were the everyday perils of life. There was the "feaver" that carried off Ann, four and a half years old, on February 12, 1799. Perhaps it was a lingering touch of the yellow fever that had infected the town the previous autumn. That had been the most severe epidemic since smallpox had taken the first Sarah. On August 29, 1798, the *Centinel* reported that "a great number of stores and shops are closed; and business is at a stand . . . the neighborhood of our office has the appearance of a deserted city." The Perkins brothers had moved their operations out to Roxbury where James had a summer place on Jamaica Pond. Tom rented a house on Canterbury Lane near Forest Hills.

For the children it was a great change from routine. Eliza remembered the clerks of the countinghouse making a puppet show for the children under the tall desks. She and young Jim Perkins, both lively seven year olds by then, also used to coast down a steep hill of sand as if it were snow.

A drenching rain ended the long summer drought, and the coolness of fall abated the fever. The Perkins family stayed out in Roxbury until they were sure it was over. By the middle of October they were back in Boston and busy at their regular activities. Perhaps this brief experience of the benefits of country living, persuaded the colonel of the value of a summer retreat.

James had been enjoying a farm in Roxbury, later to be called "Pine Bank." Both Sam Perkins and his Higginson partners had bought land in Brookline, a small village on the outskirts of Boston next to Roxbury that was becoming popular as a summer place for some of Boston's more affluent families. Then, in 1799, Perkins purchased sixty-one acres of land and began to build a country house, which was called "THP's Brookline Farm" in the account book and subsequently styled the "Mansion House," ultimately becoming one of the show places around Boston.

About the same time he changed his town residence from elegant Federal Street to the even more elegant Pearl Street, just two streets away. Russell Sturgis had not the highest opinion of some of the people who lived on Pearl Street and when the name was changed from Hutchinson Street to Pearl Street he commented that it was casting pearls before swine. The ropewalk fire of 1794 had destroyed the whole west side of the street and the subsequent banishment of the ropewalks to the lower end of the Common had opened up the Pearl Street area for development. Sometime near the end of the century Perkins moved there, first to a rented house, which he eventually bought.

This house on the east side of Pearl Street was actually a double house. The colonel and his family had the southerly half and James Lovell and his family lived in the north half. It was a large three-story brick mansion, standing about fifty feet back from the street with beautiful horse-chestnut trees growing in the front yard. Behind the house a large garden area rose in a gentle slope towards Oliver Street, with a summer house on the topmost terrace. The interior of the house was as sumptuous as the outside was pleasant. Elaborate oak paneling (which had been painted white on the Perkins's side) graced the parlors, and Eliza particularly remembered a rich mantlepiece of white marble with purple streaks running through it. Panneled shutters were at each window, with green stuff curtains that were caught up in sweeping festoons.

A month before he bought his house on Pearl Street from George Erving, the colonel had purchased for $3,000 a piece of land almost directly opposite on the west side of the street. He would later build on this lot, selling his former house to Russell Sturgis.* As was characteristic of many Bostonians of this period, families tended to cluster. The Elliots, the Magees, and the Perkins were always just within a few streets of each other, throughout most of their married lives. They were to repeat this pattern in the next generation with their children's families grouping around the parental home.

It was in the sumptuous setting of Pearl Street that Sally Perkins had the great scare that became a family joke for years. Her nephew Jim Elliot, on a trip to Baltimore in 1803 or 1804, carried some letters Perkins gave him to deliver to a certain Mr. Grundy. When located, Grundy behaved peculiarly and swore he had never heard of Colonel Perkins. It turned out that the letters were from a third party and Perkins was simply doing a courtesy in having them delivered. Young Elliot on his return related the story to the colonel. Grundy and his odd behavior became a standing joke between them.

One day, the colonel sent Jim a clipping from a Baltimore paper about the death of Grundy's grandmother. Along with the clipping, he sent a note of consolation on the death of a venerable relation of Jim's *dear friend* Mr. Grundy. Jim dashed off a reply in the same strain, including some rigmarole verses beginning, "And is my Grundy's granny dead?" He sent the note over to Pearl Street embossed with a black mourning seal as was then customary.

The colonel was at the store and Sally Perkins was dining with the children. Handed the note by a servant, and recognizing her nephew's handwriting, she concluded before opening it that something dreadful had happened. Hastily scanning it, her eye caught the words "granny

* Sturgis bought the property in 1811 for $15,700. Sixteen years later his widow sold it to John Odin for $23,900.

dead" and she promptly fainted. The children screamed and the flustered servant summoned Mrs. Lovell from next door, who rushed over but could not read the note for in her excitement she had left her spectacles at home. Thinking it must be something very bad, she sent the note down to the colonel at the store. When the servant burst in upon him, all excited by the tragedy, the colonel demanded to know what had happened. The fellow replied that old Mrs. Elliot was dead, Mrs. Perkins had fainted, and they wanted him home at once. Without bothering to read the note, the colonel rushed home, put his wife into the chaise, and hurried over to Federal Street, only to find the old lady alive and well. Oddly enough, however, when she did die, on January 17, 1805, it was "suddenly." Perhaps reality copied some of this comedy of errors.

To the Merchants of the United States—
Long credits—short voyages—good stocks—
great profits, and an hearty perseverance in
federalism.

Toast at banquet to Alexander Hamilton,
*Centinel*, June 21, 1800

# 13

# A Solemn Protest Against the Ice, Winds, Tides, and Rocks

Early in his partnership with his brother, T. H. Perkins set out a credo for their careers. "Now is the heyday of life," he wrote, "let us improve it, and when the inclination and ability for exertion is over, let us have it in our power to retire from the bustle of the world and enjoy the fruits of our labour."[1]

The inclination to retire was furthest from their thoughts in the busy decades on either side of the new century. Now they were scrambling for some of the "ready": now they were part of the bustle. With true Boston zeal they pursued the dollar. A contemporary, Nathaniel Goddard, said that his mother would often chide him for his impatience at getting rich. "Something will turn up by and by." "Perhaps so, ma'am," he would reply, "but not until I turn it up."[2]

The Perkins fortune was to be made by taking risks. The brothers began their commercial life as commission merchants, doing business for others and charging for their services. "You speak of the commission of 2½% as too low. It is, but it is what everybody charges. They are a set of poor pitiful devils who first introduced it. Though I have no doubt there were advantages to them *sub rosa* which ammounted to more than an *honest* 5%." So Perkins commented to his brother just before their association started. It was the standard charge, so they charged it. They were happier when they could write, "For this business we are to receive 5% on outfit and 5 on sales."[3]

That particular business was outfitting the brig *Katy* for a slaving voyage to the coast of Africa for Daniel McNeil. An Act of the General Court clearly outlawed such practices. "Whereas," the law proclaimed, "by the African Trade for Slaves, the lives and liberties of many innocent persons have been . . . sacrificed to the lust for gain . . . Be it therefore enacted" that no person in the Commonwealth, "either as master, factor, supercargo, owner, or hirer . . . cause to be imported or transported any of the inhabitants of any state or kingdom in that part of the world called Africa as slaves or servants." The fine was fifty pounds for each person so enslaved and two hundred pounds for the vessel.[4]

McNeil and the Perkins brothers were in no danger. The brig *Katy* sank, carrying her cargo—at fifty pounds fine a head—many fathoms beyond the reach of the law. But the law itself provided a loophole for those wishing to use it. How far did Massachusetts law stretch? To the Middle Passage? It could not, clearly, control the actions of Massachusetts citizens on the island of Santo Domingo.

But their staple business was not slaves but the handling of lumber, fish, flour, horses, and such for their clients. And as quickly as possible they began speculations on their own. "Adventures" they were called in the terminology of the period. With the advantage of an office in the islands as well as Boston, they were in a good position to conduct trade to the best advantage. They knew the markets and the people they were dealing with. Both brothers, having had experience in the West Indies and speaking French, and perhaps a smattering of Spanish, were in an ideal situation. The collapse of the Cape in 1793 temporarily upset this advantage, but the brothers rapidly rallied and sent their ventures to other ports untroubled by revolt.

As early as December 1792, they had investments in seven vessels; this in addition to sustaining the *Hope* and the *Margaret* in the China trade. They were now beginning to develop a pattern of three types of ventures. Short-term speculations in the West Indian markets; medium-term investments in the European market; and long-term adventures in the China trade, which involved an extended journey and a stay on the Northwest Coast to secure skins to trade with in Canton.

Their ventures in 1793, for instance, combined the first two types of speculations. Ships went first to the West Indies and secured sugar, coffee, indigo, or cotton to take to Europe. The outbreak of the European war made these trips profitable. But ships went wherever they might buy or sell a cargo. The brig *Bee* was in St. Petersburg in 1794 looking for iron.

The brothers put their profits back into ships, sometimes in partnership with other merchants like Stephen Higginson (brother Sam Perkins had married Higginson's daughter and was in partnership with him), sometimes with the captain of the ship, sometimes on their own. One of the first of their regular vessels was the brigantine *Dolphin,* built in Gloucester in 1782 and just over one hundred tons, thirty tons heavier than the *Hope,* and nearly half the weight of the *Mayflower*. A double-decked, two-masted brig, it made at least nine or ten voyages for the firm before it was sold in the West Indies. It soon fell into a pattern of making a spring voyage and a fall voyage to the Indies, which was repeated with other ships.

The *Delight* was another of these workhorses of the firm. Slightly larger than the *Dolphin,* it was much like it with the addition that it was reported to have a serpent figurehead. Starting life as a schooner in Amesbury, it was only four years old when the brothers acquired it. In the next six years it made approximately a dozen voyages for the firm, was captured once by the British, and, suspected of being British property, was carried into Jamaica. Ultimately it was released, and several years later the firm received $2,000 compensation for a cargo worth about $10,000 that had been confiscated.

The brothers had already gone far beyond the kind of business that their grandfather Peck had engaged in. He had merely put freight on vessels somebody else owned. The brothers not only took adventures on ships other merchants were sending out, they owned ships and had what they might have called a "fleet." It increased the risks, but it increased the profits too. It also increased the complexities of doing business. Owning ships meant finding captains to sail them, outfiting them, and recruiting sailors.

This "outside" part of the business was handled by Perkins. In 1813, to a committee of the General Court investigating the subject of impressed seamen, he deposed that he had "always had the particular care of that part of our business which relates to the shipping of our seamen." He concluded his statement with the observation that the firm had employed "in vessels fitted for sea by them from this place upwards of 2,500 persons from the year 1793." The twenty year average of this would figure 125 men per year, though it certainly was not that large early on. That is a great many men to hire. It also indicates the unsettled nature of the market in sailors. Few of the men stayed with a ship or with a merchant. They kept trying their luck with another captain, another vessel. The transient nature of their employment kept their wages low and their conditions of life and labor hard and rough.[5]

The hiring of seamen involved much more work than appears on the face of it. The account books show varying sums paid men on each ship. The second voyage of the *Thomas Russell,* for example, had John Purdy, listed as an ordinary seaman, being paid $15 a month, while Asa Morse, also listed as an ordinary seaman was hired at $10 a month. Regular seamen on that trip were being paid $18 a month, as was William Thomas, the cook. Ordinarily, cooks were paid less than regular seamen. Each of these agreements had to be negotiated.[6]

The outside man handled all the direction of outfitting the vessel for the voyage. Provisions—cabbage, beef, vegetables—had to be bought and put aboard. Was the vessel going to the Northwest Coast? The sailors would need warm jackets. Wood was ordered, sawed, and stacked aboard. Cargo was trucked to the wharf, unloaded by muscle power, and perhaps hoisted on board ship by horse-powered winches. Water had to be put on board, and remembering his trip to China, Perkins made sure the casks were tight and clean. If the cargo was "merchantable boards," Edmund Ranger might be called upon to come in and survey it. They would have to be taken down from the loft. Temporary labor would be employed for this job and then discharged. On the second voyage of the *Dove* this particular item of labor cost the firm fifty-five cents.

Was the ship itself fit for the voyage? Properly ballasted? Painted? What about cordage, spare spars, extra sails? Had the apothecary Ephraim Elliot stocked the medicine chest? The cable anchor must be put on board. And all the time, sugar was being wheeled down the gangplank, or barrels of dried fish were being rolled aboard. The men might be treated to grog if the day were cold or rainy. Those peppers must be weighed before being stored. Was the fish being properly packed?

The inside man was James Perkins. Of a quiet and unambitious disposition, with a strong taste for reading, his temper was "retired and domestic," and he left the active pursuits to his brother. "His virtues were those of the fireside" and the counting room. His job it was to account for the pounds and the shillings and pence until 1795 when Massachusetts switched to dollars and cents accounting. His careful watch over the money of the firm was no small part of its success. As early as his tenure with the Shattucks he had been drawn to the bookkeeping side of business life. While there, he had "engaged of his own motion in the study of the method of double entry (then but little known in this country) which had accidentally attracted his notice." Though just an apprentice, he introduced the method into the Shattuck financial books. The many-volumed, carefully, and beautifully written account books of the Perkins firm were a tribute to his care and zeal for this aspect of the business.

Of course there were apprentices to help with the copying and leg work, to run errands and sweep and clean. Many of the younger family members or connections began their business career in the counting rooms. Sam Burling, Walter's nephew, made himself useful around the shop. Young John P. Cushing was helping out by the time he turned eleven. Sometimes older men, such as John Palfrey, were hired too. Young Tom Doubleday came in, after two years at Exeter Academy, to complete his practical education.

All this work had to be done a dozen times a year as each ship left port, and in reverse order when the ships returned again. Captains and officers had to be carefully selected and instructed, for the risk rode on their abilities. An error here could doom the whole enterprise. Finally the day came when each ship was piloted down the harbor. Occasionally Perkins went along until they reached the lighthouse. Then over the side, the climb down the ladder to the rocking boat, the row back to town, and perhaps a cheering glass of Madeira.

The ship went its lonely way on the empty sea. Back in Boston men kept busy. James Perkins paid the firm's postage bill to Postmaster Hastings and bought a map of the United States to study. The partners read the *Centinel,* the *Gazette,* the *Mercury,* and even the *Chronicle.* The colonel went to Providence or Portsmouth searching for specie for their next venture. They bought sand to spread on the floor at the store, in 1807 changing to straw carpets. They paid their subscriptions to the Humane Society, the Chamber of Commerce, the Marine Society, the Boston Dispensary. They strolled down to 'Change in State Street each day at one o'clock and shared the business gossip with the merchants gathered there. And as the earth spun, the "great miracle" was performed.

What was this great miracle? For the Perkins brothers sitting in their counting room on Foster's Wharf, it was that what was sent out as "dumb fish" came back as sugar and indigo; what was sent out as thimbles, brass buttons, "chizzells," looking glasses, blankets, blue cloth, wampum, or tobacco came back as rich nankeens, fragrant teas, handsome china plate—came back as a profusion of money.

Sometimes the outcome of a voyage was an exciting cliffhanger. The *Grand Turk,* a new ship in 1795 and a large ship for the Perkins firm, being nearly 371 tons burthen, was sent to China in March 1796 shortly after Perkins returned from his first European trip. It was a long ship, just over a hundred feet in length, thirty feet wide and drawing almost fifteen feet. Ownership of this proud vessel was spread among eight investors, but it was largely a Perkins-and-family project. They took 20 percent, James Magee had another 20 percent, and Russell Sturgis had 10 percent. Magee's younger brother, Bernard, captained the ship. A Providence, Rhode Island, merchant, a good friend of Tom Perkins, William F. Megee—no relation to the Magees—went as supercargo.

On its way to Canton, the *Grand Turk* touched briefly at Sydney, Australia, the second known American vessel to visit that continent. It sailed on up to Manila, and by December 10 was at Whampoa anchorage. Wintering in Canton, they left for Boston on March 26, 1797. Stopping off at Manila again, they made a slow sail to Java Head, beating against monsoons all the way, arriving there by the end of June. A short side trip to India further delayed them. Coming back around the Cape of Good Hope, they began the long sail up the Atlantic. Troubles still dogged them. Five members of the crew died on the way.

On the fifth of November, they met another vessel in latitude 28°, longitude 60°, some distance off Bermuda. Here William Megee had a chance to write a friend in Providence some of the news of the trip so far. For sixty days, he reported, they had been on short allowances. The brig which was taking this letter to Providence was "laying to for us to get some provisions out of her." The wind was "blowing very fresh" and he expected to be in soon.[7]

A fisherman spoke to them on the sixteenth and found them in a bad state with the crews sickly, and their provisions down to an eighteen day supply that perhaps could be stretched to last forty days. He gave them what few provisions he could spare, some wine and raisins, and put a pilot on board to help. When this news reached Boston a week later, it gave rise to "much anxiety." James was out of town, probably in Charleston, South Carolina, and Tom had the worry and decisions to make alone. The firm had just moved from Long Wharf to the "White Stores" on Foster's Wharf. All was confusion and a sense of helplessness.[8]

Day after day went by in Boston and no word of the *Grand Turk*. Not only were family members and friends on board, and the vessel itself an expensive investment, but it carried a cargo estimated to be "greater in respect to value" than any previously brought back from China. After suffering "a long State of Suspense" greater than almost any he had ever experienced, Perkins could sit still no longer. He went up to Marblehead and sent a fishing schooner out in search of the missing vessel. He loaded it with provisions. Four days later, on December 10, he wrote his brother the unhappy news. "I fear she has been obliged to leave the coast from her want of provisions. If so she is dished."[9]

The easterly storm blowing lifted nobody's spirits. It might push the ship towards shore; it might equally drive it off into the Atlantic. Then they were "dished" for sure. When Captain Atkins returned the next day in the *Jay* from Havana, Perkins hired the schooner *MicMac* and sent him out on search too. The anxious days went by with no word from the three ships. The two search vessels returned with no good news. But then "authentic information" was received that the *Grand Turk* was "in at Townshend, a harbor in the district of Maine—having nine fathoms of water and sheltered from all winds." Captain Bernard Magee wrote that their situation was not as desperate as had been reported. They had caught 420 gallons of water from the storm and they had twenty pounds of beef and some biscuits. But the passage had been a long nine month's ordeal and the long beating on the coast had wearied all.[10]

Perkins hired the schooner *Rover*, loaded it with brandy, wine, and liquor, and sent it off under Captain Prebble. It seems he was determined to float it home to Boston on alcohol alone. On Tuesday afternoon, December 26, the *Turk* sailed into Portland harbor, and just in time too. The ship was entirely out of water and provisions on the day it arrived.

Suddenly an express arrived from Portland with bad news. On January 4, ice had cut the *Turk's* cables, she went on to some rocks, and was run ashore to keep her from breaking up on the rocks. When the men left Portland she had seven feet of water in her hold. Perkins and James Magee hired a sleigh and immediately set out for Portland. When they arrived they found the situation both worse and better than described.

A fair wind had come up on January 3, and it had been decided to sail the vessel on to Boston. A pilot, Captain John Thorlo, went on board and just as the anchor was "short a peak," the wind changed to the southward, compelling them to delay their departure. The next day, the weather was still unfavorable and about 2 P.M. Thorlo "hove up & cleared her anchors & properly moored her—the people being employed in taking care of the Ship, Rigging, & Sails until 8 oclock—at which time he ordered a watch" posted, starboard and larboard. To all appearances the ship was lying in safety. Then at 9:30 P.M. "the watch called & informed that a Body of Ice appeared to be approaching the Ship."

Thorlo quickly turned out all hands. He "let go the Sheet Anchor, & payed out the whole Scope of Cable—by which means the Ship was brot up & rode at her anchors near one hour." Then she drifted again "& was forced by the Wind, Tide, & Ice" on to Stanford's ledge on Cape Elizabeth, where she struck about half an hour after midnight. Thorlo sent one boat ashore for help and fired three guns as a distress signal. Then he ordered out the long boat and cleared the deck, cutting away the top masts, and everything necessary for saving "Ship & Cargo." The pumps were constantly kept working. As the tide rose, the ship which was lying on her beam ends, righted. They hove her off the ledge, hoping to get her safely up to town. But it was in vain. Too much of the hull had been damaged and the water was pouring in faster than they could pump it out. Thorlo judged it best to cut the *Turk's* cable, hoist sail, and run it on shore.[11]

In spite of the wind, the snow, and the darkness, nearly a hundred people turned out to help the ship. Although the storm increased, the small vessels in the harbor came over to help by taking off as much of the cargo as could be saved. "So indefatigable have this community been in their exertions," reported a letter to the *Centinel* of the seventeenth, "that on this day every perishable article is nearly discharged. Her lower hold is full of water at the height of each tide which must prove a great injury to the Teas." Perkins was in his element, directing these operations. This was far better than waiting on shore.

There was much to be arranged. The men had to be boarded, warm winter clothing provided, wages paid, the doctor to be consulted (his bill was $2). The men moving the damaged teas from the *Turk* and two other vessels which would bring them on to Boston were given eight-nine cents worth of grog one day and fifty cents worth on another day. Some of the sailors had come back to Boston, and one of them, Charley Groves, was hired to clean out the store and get it in order to receive the *Turk*'s teas. He thus earned himself an extra thirty-seven cents. The fellow who shoveled off the snow before the door at the wharf got thirty-eight cents. But this was not at all a small operation. The cost of the sleigh that took Magee and Perkins to Portland, and which they used there, came to nearly $173. The expense of the vessel from Marblehead on its fruitless mission alone came to almost $640. And Perkins's bills in Portland for various items came to about $4,900.[12]

After the crisis had passed, Captain Bernard Magee, Captain Thorlo, the second mate, and one of the *Turk*'s sailors went before a notary public to solemnly protest the "Ice, Winds, Tides, & Rocks" and "all other causes & things" which had occasioned the damages to the *Grand Turk*. Peter Peron, a passenger on the ship, also signed the protest, and attested to the truth of their statements. This "solemn protest" might not carry any weight with the Lord, but perhaps it would persuade the insurance companies that men were not to blame for the disaster.

Even with the losses sustained, the *Grand Turk* was a rich prize; at today's valuation it carried a million dollar cargo. The teas and other merchandise were brought down from Portland in several coasting sloops, and handbills and advertisements soon circulated announcing auction sales. When James came to total up the amount taken in on sales from February 1 to April 7 alone he could put down over $82,000. Assuredly, in spite of the unusual expense, a nice profit was made by the "meritorious adventurers" in the *Turk*.

After his ordeal in the *Grand Turk,* Bernard Magee took a six month rest at home. Then he went back to China for the firm in the *Thomas Russell.* The brothers advised him to bring home fresh teas as they sold better. "Foreigners in Canton will try to put off old teas on you." So that he could the better tell, they wrote, "new teas are heavy in the hand, greenish, with no red leaves."[13]

Magee's next trip began when he left Boston on July 21, 1800 in the new ship *Globe* for the Perkins firm. Now he was an experienced captain, having acquitted himself ably in trying circumstances in the *Grand Turk,* and having had a successful voyage in the *Thomas Russell.* His nephew, James Magee, Jr., sailed with him and the voyage began uneventfully. They had a successful season the summer of 1801 on the Northwest Coast, collecting 1,400 skins. Probably the melancholy news of the death of James Magee, Sr., would have reached his brother and his son by August or early September. But the year 1801 was not yet finished with the Magee family.

On Sunday, September 13, Bernard Magee sailed the *Globe* into Shaker Harbor on the Northwest Coast. In a short time he was "snug moored." Three natives in a canoe had welcomed them to this new harbor and showed them where to anchor. Monday, they hoisted out their long boat, hauled it on shore, and began to repair it. The three natives—"young lads appeared to be friendly"—were with them off and on. They told Magee that there were many skins at their village and went off to tell the inhabitants about the ship and urge them to come and trade because the men of the ship could be trusted.

On Wednesday four other Indians showed up. "They came on board and appeared to be quite familiar." William Cunningham, the first mate, was busy working in the hold, but thought all was going well. "At dinner time one of them came down into the cabin and took some with us and was very particular in inquiring the names of the officers, which we told them." After dinner, Cunningham went back into the hold to direct the work and only saw Captain Magee briefly when he came to the hatchway and gave some orders about stowing the hold. Cunningham thought he went aft, "but it proved to be the contrary, as he got in the boat and went on shore by himself. Soon after, the natives went from alongside, and when passing the cove where Magee had landed, he hailed them and asked them to come on shore, which they did.

"While they were talking to Capt. Magee, the carpenter was at work on the long boat on shore and Cunningham's boy was attending the pitch pot." One of the Indians whipped out a pistol from under a skin he was carrying and fired at the carpenter, hitting him in the thigh. A second Indian stabbed young Cunningham several times. The carpenter and boy ran for the water and swam the few yards across the cove to the other side, shouting to Magee to make for the woods. When they got to the safety of the other shore, they turned and saw that three of the Indians had grabbed Magee, while the fourth picked up an ax and swung it directly across Magee's face, cutting him from "the left eye all through the nose to the socket of the right jaw, cut his right eye out entirely and let his right jaw drop."

One of the men of the *Globe* going on shore at that moment in the whaleboat gave the alarm as soon as he came in sight of the long boat with Magee leaning against it and bleeding. The men of the ship had no boat now, and had to wait until the whaleboat got back before they could give chase to the Indians or help Magee. When they brought Magee on board, they knew at a glance it was a mortal wound. "A shocking sight it was I assure you," wrote Cunningham. They dressed the wounds as well as they knew how, but it was no use. "We could not stop the blood." He died in three hours. Cunningham's own boy had died before Magee did.

The Indians were firing some scattered shot at the ship from the point. Cunningham fired three guns directly at the point "and we heard no more from them." After great difficulty he managed to get the ship's anchor up and sail out of the narrow cove. He took the ship to Kaganny and found several vessels there which offered him officers and men to finish the voyage.[14]

For Bernard and James Magee the bustle of the world was over. And the time of retiring was not of their inclination, but one of the hazards of life that could be met either in the quiet of a Roxbury mansion or on the wilderness shores of the Pacific. Money is not made out of paper; it is made out of the blood of living men.

If in Lo-yang, my friends and home folk ask about me, Tell them my far-away heart is a splinter of ice in a jade jug!

Wang Wei

# 14

# The Principal Agent of An Important Establishment

After some dozen years in the Northwest Coast and China trade, the Perkins brothers decided in 1803 that it would be advantageous to establish a branch office in Canton with trusted associates permanently stationed there. The benefits would be many: the opportunity to buy teas and nankeens and china when prices were low and competition was absent, storing them until the ships arrived; the chance to establish better credit and business relations with the Hong merchants than the itinerant ships' captains could; and, as a by-product, to service these captains and thus earn a commission on the business of their competitors. It was the logical next move in the China trade, and the Perkinses, along with some other Americans, took it.

The leading commodities in the trade in 1803 were specie and sea otter skins. The fur trade on the Northwest Coast had been British at the start; by 1798 it became principally American. Two years later it was almost a Boston monopoly. The Perkins firm was already thinking about making that a personal monopoly if possible. Specie, however, was the more important item by far in trade with China. From half to three quarters of the exports to China were in that form. Spanish-milled dollars were used, there being then no source of gold or silver in the States, nor a mint to coin it. American merchants had to procure specie wherever they could find it.

Since the China trade required large resources in ships, capital, and credit, it gradually settled into the hands of a few merchants who could afford to take the great risks involved in long hazardous voyages and expensive cargoes, largely of gold and silver coins. An office in Canton would reduce those risks that could be reduced. It all depended on getting the right man.

In Ephraim Bumstead, the Perkins thought they had the right man. He had been apprenticed to the firm, knew their methods and ways, and they had had several years to judge his character and ability. In 1798 Bumstead had gone to China for them as supercargo of the *Thomas Russell* and they had been pleased with the way he handled their affairs. Since then he had been in business for himself and had acquired a small stake.

They proposed a partnership to Bumstead, to be called E. Bumstead & Co., he to manage it and reside in Canton; they to furnish roughly three quarters of the capital stock ($20,000) and he the balance ($6,500), their money to bear interest at 6 percent from July 15, 1803. In today's terms it was like being capitalized at a quarter of a million dollars. In addition, Bumstead took with him another $47,500 in specie to spend on behalf of a dozen other individuals and firms. Russell Sturgis alone put in $10,000 of this. So Bumstead was to be established in Canton with the *equivalent* today of perhaps $750,000. The Perkinses meant this to be a major operation and made sure it was financed as such, although actually only furnishing about one third of the cash. "Share the risk" was an old Boston motto.[1]

The team they assembled for this venture was basically family. Bumstead, then about twenty-six years old, while not related to them, was a product of their counting house. His assistant was John P. Cushing, Nancy's child, who had been raised by Perkins and had been working in the counting house too. In addition, James Magee, Jr., then twenty, went as mate on the vessel taking them to Canton, and his brother, eighteen-year-old Charles Elliot Magee, shipped along.

The ship that took the lads and the money to Canton was a fairly new Providence vessel—the *Patterson*—quite large, being 447 tons, three-masted, with two decks and a male figurehead. It was owned jointly by four men in Providence and James and T. H. Perkins. One of the owners, Samuel Snow, went as supercargo, returning to his post as the American consul in Canton. Through June and July preparations went forward to prepare the vessel for its long trip. On the twentieth of July 1803 the ship sailed out of Providence harbor, carrying young Cushing on the most exciting adventure of his short life.

The colonel settled back into his regular pursuits, putting the *Patterson* and its passengers at the back of his mind, though they were ever forward in his heart and care. The death of Samuel Adams in October came like an echo of times gone by; the thought that these United States had ever been mere colonies of Great Britain seemed almost like something out of a dream. That world was gone forever, and the men who were of it, were fast going too. The Perkins family continued to change too. His third boy, George Cabot Perkins, named after one of the Massachusetts senators, was born September 25. But two months later, the two-year-old second son, Charles Elliot Perkins, died of "the Quincy"—as it was spelled in the family Bible. This left Tom and Sally with six children.

Eighteen hundred and four. On the first day of the new year the *Patterson* arrived in Canton. The world that opened on John Cushing's startled eyes was even stranger than any dreamt of in Boston. There was Canton itself, which no matter how much his uncle might have described it to him, could not compare with the living reality that passed before his eyes. The pagodas on the far horizons, the distant bluish hills becoming green as one came near the city, the balconied villas of the rich with their gay adornments, the white-walled city itself with its indescribable noise and hum, like some giant hive of yellow bees. The crowds of people, a staggering sight to a Boston eye, more than one might have thought there were in the entire world. Crowds that spread right out onto the river itself, making houses on little boats, junks, sampans, anything that would float, spending almost their whole lives on the water.

The people of the city: men carrying live fish in buckets through the streets; beggars who would cut themselves until they were covered with blood, hoping to draw a coin from the foreigner's purse; naked men who would swallow all of a sword, then pull it out again before your eyes; paupers who would smear themselves with excrement and be paid to go away where they could not be smelt; a man who clinched an adder to his tongue, was seized with convulsions, his tongue swelling so that it couldn't be drawn back into the mouth, frothing and bleeding in a most distressing manner, but given alms, he applied an ointment to his tongue and the swelling went down in a few minutes. Decidedly, this was not Boston![2]

Should a New England boy look at such things? At first there was hardly time to look, there was so much to do getting themselves established. Bumstead hired House No. 3 for five months at one hundred dollars per month. A house compradore, Aryune, was employed to manage their living needs, hire coolies, cooks, and arrange the mundane necessities. Furnishings had to be bought for the new establishment, among them two card tables. The "necessary House" had to be cleaned out, which cost two dollars. And the *Patterson* had to be made ready for its voyage home.[3]

Back in Boston, the brothers were busy writing letters to the new firm, keeping a steady stream of advice and information going by the various vessels leaving for the East. In November they wrote that dollars were "very scarce, 2 or 3 percent advance" wanted. In December, "we send a box of Scotch snuff as a sample." The fine hand of Simon Elliot there! "Shipments from India to Canton now possible. Check the price of cotton." In January 1804, "The scarcity of Dollars will make it very difficult to make any remittances in Specie." "War very possible in Europe. That reduces competition, so extend credit as much as possible. What price lead? Can teas be bought at Amoy?"[4]

Always a word was added for the benefit of nephew Cushing. "Encourage John with a small adventure in such vessels as you ship in. We hope he conducts to y'r satisfaction." "Enjoin on J. C. to write to us all and more particularly his Grandmother, who will be very anxious to hear from him." "Make our regards to Jno. Cushing, we enjoin on him close application and attention."[5]

Finally, word reached Boston that Bumstead had arrived and set up his establishment. On May 25, 1804 the Perkinses wrote a notice for the papers that "they have formed a Commercial Establishment at Canton, in China, with Mr. Ephraim Bumstead, under the firm of Ephraim Bumstead & Company whose services in the purchase of China Goods, Sales of Merchandize, or the transaction of other business, they now tender to their Friends and the Public. The terms may be known by applying at No. 11 Foster's-Wharf."

At this important juncture, James Perkins and his wife left for a European trip, sailing from Boston in June. Jim, always frail, had been poorly of late and was hoping a prolonged tour of the continent and visits with some of his friends from Santo Domingo, now residing in France, might improve his health. He would not have been a Perkins however, if he did not intend to do a little business on the side! This left the entire management of the firm in Boston on the colonel's shoulders, including all the increased work attendant on making a success of the new establishment. It was not many months before the statement appeared in a letter that "Such are the many avocations of our T. H. P. that he has more to think of than accords with his wishes."[6]

The things he had to think of ran quite a gamut. With Josiah Quincy he was on a committee to have a sewer put in Pearl Street and all the business of that went through the office. He was continually improving the house and stable and grounds of his Pearl Street mansion. He wanted a couple of marble figures to be put on a pedestal in his garden and was hoping they could be purchased in Italy. "Modest figures such as will not violate the feelings of those to whose eyes they may be exposed."[7]

A new counting room was being built at Foster's Wharf. Walter Burling wanted his farm in Cambridge sold. Keeping an eye on the stock market, Perkins sold seventy shares of Boston bank stock for almost $8,000, clearing more than $1,000. He had a new coach coming in from Philadelphia which cost him $680. He was overseeing the education of B. F. Gomez's son at Hingham. One daughter told him the piano forte needed to be tuned. Two daughters were sick. His mother was seeking legal advice about some property she owned on School Street. A carpenter who had sailed on the *Thomas Russell* was bothering him about the loss of an elephant's tooth, the loss of which the carpenter felt should be made good by the firm. They settled for $6.75. And there was all the regular work besides. No wonder he paid for five operations on the new Galvanic machine, which gave a mild electrical charge said to be good for the nerves.[8]

Perkins was having a new ship constructed at Edmund Hartt's shipyard in Charlestown. "As good a ship," in Perkins's opinion, "as can be built in this country. We have furnished her in a masterly style, and she will cost a masterly price—say not less than $30,000." The 358-ton ship was launched on June 4 and christened the *Mandarin,* quite likely in honor of the new Chinese establishment.

The *Mandarin* nearly did not make it to sea at all. A late September hurricane, after doing extensive damage in the Carribean and the southern states moved up the coast and late Tuesday, October 9, lashed into Boston. The steeple of Christ Church was blown down and the roof of King's Chapel was lifted off, carried two hundred feet, then dumped on a shed, smashing two chaises to smithereens.

All day long Wednesday the storm raged. Much damage was done on the windward side of the wharves. "A small sloop foundered at her anchors opposite our wharf," Perkins wrote a correspondent, "and it was impossible to give relief to a couple of poor fellows who were on board." The *Mandarin* was in great danger, but Perkins sent three men who made it fast to the wharf. For the job they were given eighty cents to split between them.[9]

The same issue of the *Centinel* that gave notice of the launching of the *Mandarin* also announced the sale of the teas that had been shipped home in the *Patterson,* the first effort of the new establishment. After listing them, came this cautious boast: "The above Teas were purchased by a gentleman who has resided some years in China and who is considered an excellent judge of Chinese goods. They are presumed to be as good in quality as any imported from China."[10]

Now that Bumstead seemed to be well established in Canton, the brothers decided that the China trade should be pursued with all their resources. Snow had returned from Canton and the position of consul was vacant. What a plum if Bumstead could get that appointment! The colonel was not so staunch a Federalist that he was above asking a Republican president, even the impossible Thomas Jefferson, for something that would advance his own interests. He also wrote to Bumstead telling him of the financial support they were going to give him. "We shall send $60–80,000 in the *Montezuma* and as soon as we can command funds, we shall throw 50 or 60,000 more into the Concern, confident that with your management that is the best business that can be followed."[11]

There were increasing problems with the Northwest trade, and the West Indies trade was proving a vexatious one too. It involved strategems to get a ship into port, or else one had to get them in by taking a few Negro slaves on board. But the fines for this were very stiff. "We prefer," wrote Perkins on July 16, 1804 to his Havana correspondent, "losing a little upon a few horses than gaining upon human flesh." But by January of 1805 he was enough disgusted with the West Indies trade to write James Gorham "we shall probably conclude to take a few Negroes off the port and depend on getting in with them." His intentions were to keep in the trade long enough "to get away our property and then relinquish the West Indies business altogether, as it perplexes and does not pay in proportion to the vexation."

Under the combined effect of these two forces the China trade looked more rewarding every day, and they relied heavily on Bumstead: "We hope to send not less than $80,000 for the owners of the ship, $150,000 on freight." This was all specie, the idea being that Bumstead would obtain "a great advantage by having so much money pass thro' your hands and being able in consequence to take up a valuable credit in fine goods." The brothers were anxious to take advantage of all openings while the hostilities were going on in Europe. When the peace finally came, the colonel felt it would be more durable than the last one. "We have determined to concentrate our property in the Canton trade, and shall make our arrangements accordingly."

Perkins busily went on his way dispatching ships to China. The *Mandarin* sailed on December 10 with $300,000 in specie on board and the *Montezuma* was due to leave Lisbon, where she was to pick up $80,000 more in specie, touch at the Isle de France for Black Wood and then head for Canton. The ships *Hazard* and *Caroline* were trading on the Northwest Coast for furs. The *Globe* was on the Malay coast, the *General Washington* was already at the Isle de France, bound for China. Here were six large ships with enormous cargoes of goods and money, all due to arrive in Canton in a few months. Bumstead was to organize the sale of their contents and select quality cargoes to load on them and send to Boston. All very fine and just as planned—except that Bumstead was desperately ill.

It took four months for that news to travel from Canton to Boston. About mid-March letters were received that had been written in Canton the previous November. Bumstead was so ill he planned to return to Boston "this spring." Here was a crisis calling for quick action. On March 18, 1805, the colonel wrote to England, where another of their former apprentices, Sam Burling, nephew to Walter, was completing a mercantile adventure that had first taken him to South America. Perkins wrote with even more of his usual directness: "We request you to return to the U.S. with all dispatch." Briefly he explained the situation to Burling. "Even if he should so far recover as to be able to go back, we think it unsafe that he should be there alone, and wish to associate you with him. This is an opportunity which seldom occurs, to make your fortune." The colonel then sounded the trumpet call: "You will lose no time therefore in embarking at some Northern port." But Perkins still didn't know the worst.

On March 20 he wrote to Canton, "Pained to learn of the indisposition of Mr. B. We are in hopes Mr. William Paine, supercargo of the *Gen. Washington,* will remain during Mr. B.'s absence." He too had been trained in the Perkinses' office and the colonel felt he could be relied on. He added a word of encouragement for his nephew: "We have great confidence in the correctness and activity of Jno. P. Cushing, but he will require the counsels of Experience."

At the same time, he wrote directly to Cushing, we "shall rely upon your utmost exertions to make good his place. You will have a great charge on you, and such as few young men ever met with." He could not resist a few words of fatherly advice: "Your future well-being depends upon y'r conduct in this crisis. We shall calculate upon your throwing off all juvenile pursuits and acting up to the situation in wh. circumstances have placed you." Then if the fatherly advice of an uncle was not sufficient, he added, "Let the sage counsels of y'r good grandmother still vibrate on your ear, and let them sink deep into your heart."

By the twenty-second of March he knew that Bumstead planned to sail with his brother, Captain Samuel Bumstead, to the Isle de France. The colonel thought that perhaps the sea voyage might allow him to recover sufficiently so that he could return to Canton in the *Montezuma.* Since there was nothing to do but write, the colonel advised Bumstead. "If you can buffet the Climate for a few years we must make as much of the Lucre as we shall have occasion for in our journey thro' life."

All the time he knew very well how drastically changed the situation might be not only by the time his letters were received in Canton, but even as he was writing them. It was with a preoccupied mind that he went through the excitements of voting on April 1, when he won his first election to the General Court as senator from Suffolk County. The pleasure that he might otherwise have enjoyed in this honor was overridden by his concern for what might be happening in Canton.

As each day went by with no further news from Canton, he brooded more and more on young Cushing and the "heavy charge" that lay upon him. He sat down and wrote him again on April 2, "not to be dazzled with direction of business on so large a scale." He congratulated himself on giving Cushing a good foundation, but he worried about "the excitements of youthful minds to dissipation." He then expressed some mild criticism of John, "we have been a little surprised that you have not written us since your arrival in Canton; should you be so silent on the subject of business . . . We shall have much reason for pain and mortification." He reminded his nephew that the firm's reputation was "deeply involved in your good conduct," and reminisced how happy he would have been if such a "conspicuous situation" had been thrust on him in his youth where "I could serve my employers most importantly, and thus distinguish myself in the Mercantile World."

On April 5 he finally received some news from China, but not from John. The situation was worse than he thought. Bumstead had left Canton at the end of November in the *Guatamozin,* captained by his brother Samuel, and bound for Boston. But going through the Straits of Sunda, between Java and Sumatra, Captain Samuel Bumstead had been washed overboard and drowned. The colonel immediately wrote to a correspondent at Nantucket urgently requesting him to pass along any news that Captain Thorndike of the *Lady Adams* might have concerning Ephraim Bumstead's state of health. Still, all the colonel could do was wait. If only John would write!

The final blow came on April 27 when the *Guatamozin* arrived in Boston and the colonel learned "to our grief and distress" that Bumstead had "survived the dreadful stroke occasioned by the death of his brother but a few days." All the expectations that had been posited on this able young man's talents were blasted. The equivalent of millions of dollars worth of business were now in the untried hands of the seventeen-year-old boy eight thousand miles from home and five months away from advice by letters.

All the colonel could do was hope. How would young Cushing meet this situation? It did not look good. Since Cushing had sailed for China in July of 1803 there had not been a single letter from him. Nor had any of the ships that had reached Boston before the *Guatamozin* brought letters. The silence was ominous. In a stern mood the colonel sat down to write his nephew the next day. "We have the extreme mortification of not having received a single line from you after the sailing of Mr. B. . . . no not a single line from you to say that Mr. B. had sailed; to give your opinion as to his sickness, to remark on the situation of the *Hazard,* or even notice the arrival of the *Washington;*—had we not had a letter from Mr. Paine, saying you was at Canton, we should not have known you had been left behind." He informed Cushing that he hoped to send Burling to Canton, and would bring Cushing home when he was twenty "for a season"; then he would get a share of the business "provided your good conduct should warrant it." At the moment, the colonel was not too highly impressed with the good conduct of John Perkins Cushing. Still, he consoled himself with the thought that "we must encourage a hope that you did write and that your letters miscarried." It was a slim hope however. Vessels that sailed in January had arrived with no word from the errant nephew.

By early May the teas from the *Guatamozin* were all landed and the colonel wrote again to tell Cushing that the teas were "we are sorry to say rather in bad order, the chests are much broken." Lean upon the advice of Captain Magee, he urged. Take the advice of Mr. Thompson, whom Bumstead had asked to oversee Cushing. "Avoid dissipation in every form." But even more urgent: "write fully."

An answer was not long in coming. By May 6, the colonel had his first letter from his nephew. It had been written in December so that the scolding he had been given was not deserved. The colonel read it with "great delight" for he saw that his nephew was taking a firm hold of affairs in spite of his youth, and had been busy shipping teas home. Just how competent young John was, was soon made evident. The ship *Hazard* arrived in Boston on May 7 carrying teas from Canton that had been loaded under John's supervision, and with more letters. The colonel was delighted with the letters—"they are a proof of attention and activity," he wrote John. To Grant Forbes and Co. he commented on these "very satisfactory" letters, by giving John his highest accolade: "He writes like a man of business."

He not only wrote well, he purchased well. Part of the colonel's delight may have been a deep feeling of relief that his expectations of commercial disaster were not only groundless, but that Cushing was proving to be an excellent man. Part of it too may have been to give encouragement to young John. Mostly, however, his comments must have been a fair statement of the situation: "We have never been more pleased with a cargo than with that shipp'd by the *Hazard*." Had John then sent the best teas in twelve years in the China trade? Apparently. "We have good reason to expect that the teas will bring much more than those lately sold, in proportion to their cost."

Having gone through one scare with Bumstead's ill-health, he stressed that John "be particularly careful of your health, and if possible pass the summer months at Macao, where you will have some little variety of scene, and will get yourself prepared to encounter a busy winter." Gone from the letters too was any mention of avoiding dissipation. A man who sent teas like those in the *Hazard* had apparently earned his right to dissipate as he chose!

Perkins informed the Grant Forbes firm that Cushing would be handling the business of three or four ships the present season with the disposal of $300,000 to $400,000. This should certainly show the confidence they had in him. "He has loaded two of our vessels much to our satisfaction." Nor did he feel that the business "of our friends will suffer" in consequence of the change in Canton. He asked Forbes as a favor, to write Cushing and say "some handsome thing of the manner in which he is conducting."

By the middle of May, the *Washington* had reached Boston with William Paine aboard. The letters asking Paine to stay at Canton and help Cushing had all been written when Paine had already left Canton, as Perkins had feared. Never mind. A few weeks before and he would have been greatly upset. Now he could relax. Indeed, with typical Boston understatement, he could inform Samuel Williams, the firm's London contact, "We have a nephew, Jno. P. Cushing, now in China, who is very competent."

Soon Perkins was addressing his nephew as a principal of the new Canton firm, which he proposed to call Perkins & Co. As a gift, he sent along some books. "Shakespeare is a library in itself, the Spectator, Rambler, etc. contain much information, and may be read once a year to advantage." Again he urged upon John the value of spending the summer at Macao. But most important, "You will consider yourself as the principal agent of an important Establishment. Your mode of living and dressing you will conform to your wishes," but they were allowing him $500 for his private expenses and the right to ship home any adventures on his own account which he thought proper.

When the teas from the *Hazard,* John's first cargo, were sold at auction by Samuel Bradford for the Perkins firm, they brought over $93,000, which the colonel reckoned gave them a clear profit of more than $23,000. Not a bad day's business for a youth of seventeen. Greatly moved, the colonel closed his August letter to John with a heartfelt, "God bless you my dear John and make you happy."

In this letter, the colonel set the standard John was to follow, which was quite simply that of quality. "It is expected we shall supply this market with the best of teas, and it is my firm belief we shall." To do this and to stay competitive, it was essential to have a competent man year round in China. The colonel had found his man. Now he set out to consolidate the venture.

In October he had John purchase an interest in three "factories," as the stores in China were called.* This decision gave his firm the cachet of being permanently established. When Burling finally returned to Boston, Perkins offered him the partnership in Canton he had promised in his letters. While he was delighted with John's efficiency, still he had learned from Bumstead's sudden death what could happen. A competent partner was needed at John's side.

Much to Perkins's surprise, Burling turned the lucrative offer down. Burling's first Latin American venture had been a disappointment, but he thought another would work out much better. Then the colonel offered the job Burling had turned down to William Paine, who jumped at the chance and agreed to sail out on the *Mandarin.* Articles of co-partnership were drawn up making both Paine and young Cushing full partners in the enterprise. "We do it as a tribute to your manly, unremitted attention to your duty," he wrote John. In fact, so proud was Perkins of his nephew, that at the end of 1806 he enclosed a testimonial he had received from one of the Dutch firms for whom Cushing had organized a shipment. Hope and Company in Amsterdam had been very pleased and well rewarded. They were "laboring," remarked the Colonel, "under the idea that the cargoes were selected by Dutch factors." "We," he added proudly, "have taken care to let them know that no Dutchman had anything to do with the business." To out-Dutch the Dutch! Even a yankee couldn't do better than that!

* Because it was where the Dutch factors had lived and worked.

Is this a pistol which I see before me
The muzzle t'wards my breast! —Nay, do not
  shoot me—
I squat and dodge and yet I see it still,
Art thou not, fatal vision, capable
Of "noon-day execution?"

The *Repertory,*
March 17, 1807

---

# 15

# Party Provoked To All Its Rage

One of the least political men in Boston at the turn of the century must have been Ebenezer Eager, proprietor of a tavern in Back Street. Seeking an inexpensive tavern sign, he picked up a second-hand one at an auction in Cambridge. A few days later he was out superintending its erection when a violently partisan Republican militia captain, who lived next door to the tavern, came by. Recognizing the face on the sign, the captain's blood pressure shot sky-high. "What have you got there—a head of old John Adams? You are not going to stick that up there! We won't have it here! Do you think that we are going to have that old face stuck up so that we can't look out of our windows without seeing it?"

"But it is a handsome picture," said the neutral Mr. Eager. "I have bought it and paid for it." Nothing for it but it was to go up, it had been *paid* for. The captain, after more Adamic cursing, finally realized the operative nature of this remark. "If you'll go to some good painter and have the face brushed out, and have a good likeness of Tom Jefferson put in its place, the neighbors here will make up a purse and pay for it."

Now the captain was talking. He invoked that sensible word—money. Eager thought it over. After all, Jefferson was now president. There were many Republicans in his neighborhood. It would be good for business, and he would have a freshly painted sign free. So what might have become the Adams Tavern became the Jefferson Tavern, and soon the local meeting place for Republicans. Over all their sessions there, bibulous and nonbibulous, swung the two-faced sign. The genial countenance of the Sage of Monticello smiled down on all their doings. But underneath the layers of paint lurked the grim visage of the Sage of Quincy, keeping watch above his own.[1]

"His own" had things pretty much their way in Boston at the beginning of the new century. When it came time in May for electing representatives to the General Court, the Republicans rarely bothered to offer candidates. The Federalists had a steady margin of some 1,000 votes over them. About 900 Federalists would stroll down to Faneuil Hall, take a slip from one of the vote distributors (perhaps Colonel Perkins), march into the hall and vote in what the *Chronicle* derisively called "The Boston Host."

Throughout the Commonwealth, however, it was becoming increasingly apparent that at least the appearance that the candidates had been officially chosen by the party was needed if the Federalists were not to be ultimately overwhelmed. It required, said many businessmen, the application to politics of the same techniques that had brought them business success. It meant the development of political machines. It meant the organization in every town of a committee of leading Federalists to "get out the vote." The Republicans had shown the way, but the Federalists had been loath to follow. The older leaders, labeled the "Essex Junto" by their opponents, felt that gentlemen did not solicit votes. Not so the younger Federalist leaders like Perkins. The election of Jefferson had been a lesson to them.

Eliza Cabot never forgot that defeat. She and her father were on the stagecoach for Philadelphia. The election results were still uncertain when they left home, the tie vote between Jefferson and Burr having thrown the election into the House of Representatives. Thirty-five ballots had been taken without a winner. At one stage stop, "Father got out to get a paper. I was frightened at his look when he came back; he was so white. He thought the Devil's reign had begun. We all did."[2]

It was a time when that partisan parson of Salem, Dr. Bentley, in a nonpartisan moment admitted that "Party is provoked to all its rage and Truth is not much known." What was certainly "not much known" was the history of the formation of the central committees of the two parties in Massachusetts. These were conceived in darkness and born in secrecy, only becoming visible in 1804. Otis wrote a Portland man on August 29 of that year that if they intended to save the Commonwealth and New England, "our organization must be more complete and systematic; it must extend through every county and town, and an ample fund must be provided for the distribution of political truth." He expected "wonders" from such an effort.[3]

The *Chronicle* noted on October 24 that the Federalists were sending out "circular letters calling upon every county and town to associate for the purpose of consolidating the federal vote on the ensuing election. They even propose committees of correspondence and communication from one extreme of the Commonwealth to the other." Yet the Federalists were only copying what the Republicans had already done. "The whole of this plan," said the Federalist circular of April 1805, "it is perhaps unworthy the Federalists to copy but a part of it is certainly their duty not to neglect."[4]

Once established, the organization was carried over from the presidential election of 1804 to the state election of 1805. A Central Committee was organized to direct the election. It appointed the county and town committees, and through these appointments was able to control who was sent to the General Court. There were towns then that did not bother to send their full slate of representatives to Boston because they were required to pay their travel expenses. Since every Federalist was needed at "his post," it was vital that not one Federalist town be unrepresented.

Prominent on the Central Committee, which in effect controlled the Federalist party in Massachusetts, was Colonel Perkins. He took an active part in the planning and work of the organization. In the spring of 1805, he was one of their five candidates for state senator from Suffolk County. The announcement was made on March 20 and ten days later somebody signing himself "A Northend Mechanic" wrote to the *Centinel* praising the slate offered. Of the colonel he said: "I like too Col. Thomas H. Perkins—I have known him, boy and man, above thirty years.—I have always found him true, generous, and up to his word. I have been an Engineman; and I have witnessed his activity, and courage as a Fireward; and the attention he always paid to us Enginemen, during and after the fire."

In Suffolk County (essentially Boston) the entire Federalist slate was elected. The colonel ran third with 2,563 votes, out of a total of 3,844, more than 600 votes over what was needed, and some 127 votes ahead of his friend Otis, who was much better known to Boston voters. Russell Sturgis was a candidate on the Republican ticket, and though he lost, he polled the highest Republican vote.

The twenty-six Federalist representatives from Boston were safely elected that May without opposition. At the end of that month, the members of the General Court assembled at the Bulfinch State House atop Beacon Hill to organize themselves. Of the thirty-nine senators present, twenty-one were Federalists, and when the Senate elected its president they chose Harry Otis. At noon they marched down to the Old South Meeting House for the election sermon, escorted by the Independent Corps of Cadets so recently commanded by Colonel Perkins. More than once he had escorted the General Court on such an occasion, now he was among those being honored.

Perkins continued his involvement in the work of the Central Committee. On February 8, 1806, he wrote William S. Shaw, a former secretary of John Adams, "I send you also one of the circular letters of last spring. We must have another underway immediately. Will you take this, examine its drift and sketch something which you can show to Otis and on Tues. eve submit it to the Gentlemen of the Central Committee." Perkins himself had decided not to run for another one-year legislative term.[5]

As the legislature neared the end of its session there came a colorful diversion. Ten Indian warriors, belonging to the "Osage, Sacks, Missouri, Pawnee, Reynard & Powtooatomee tribes" arrived in town and were feted by the state government. Simon Elliott was on the committee to arrange the reception of the chiefs. On Saturday, March 1, they called with due protocol first on the governor and council, then the Senate, and finally on the representatives. They were dressed "in a very fantastical style," reported one of the legislators. "Their hair is all shaved close to the head except one small lock which hangs down the back and is painted in various colours. The skull ears and cheeks are dyed in various hues and the brow crowned with a wreath of feathers and ribbons. The ear is slit into strings and adorned with rings. There are scarcely few stouter men to be found in Boston, any one of them would eat you for dinner and me for the desert." President Otis of the Senate gave an impromptu speech which was then translated by one interpreter, who knew no Indian, into French. A second interpreter, who knew no English, translated it from French into the Osage tongue.[6]

The chiefs expressed a wish to see the troops parade, and on Monday morning they were escorted to the colonnade in front of the State House and watched the Winslow Blues, Independent Fusiliers, the Washington and Boston Light Infantries, and other troops deploy through a variety of exercises, firings, evolutions, and charges. The Washington Light Infantry should have been led by Captain Joseph Loring. It was not. If he was one of the many spectators that fine day, he was there in mufti. The reason he was not there in uniform was a good example of "party provoked to all its rage."[7]

On the surface it looked like a mere matter of military prestige. But the trouble had been triggered by the violent politics of the times. In 1796, the colonel's brother-in-law, Simon Elliot, a staunch Federalist, had been appointed major general of the state militia by a Federalist governor. Among General Elliot's new troops in the militia was a Captain Davis, a Federalist, who had enlisted two months earlier than Captain Loring, a Republican. Since the position of a regiment in parades was determined by the date of a captain's commission, this meant that Davis's regiment preceded Loring's. But then Davis transferred to a new regiment, was given a new commission, and had to march behind Loring. In the spring of 1805, Federalist Davis arranged with Federalist Elliot to have Federalist Governor Strong predate his original enlistment. This put him and his regiment ahead of Loring again. Loring protested and ended up being court-martialed in the fall of 1805.

The court-martial found Loring not guilty, but Elliot set the verdict aside and ordered the court to reconsider the case. Loring petitioned the legislature in which Perkins was sitting, for redress. The Federalist legislature gave him "leave to withdraw" his petition. Loring responded to this rebuff by publishing, early in March 1806, a pamphlet on his case. He had no intention that Elliot and the Federalists should eat *him* for dinner and desert.[8]

This brought public attention to the matter and the *Chronicle* embraced their partisan's cause. A young Charlestown lawyer, William Austin (later to be famous for writing the popular short story "Peter

Rugg"), attacked Elliot in the *Chronicle* in the most scathing terms. Elliot was compared with Caligula and Marat, and they came off his superior.

Now Elliot's son, the colonel's nephew James Henderson Elliot, got into the act. On his father's behalf, he challenged Austin to a duel, which had to take place in Rhode Island as dueling was outlawed in the Commonwealth. On March 31 the duelists met, shot off their guns, satisfied their "honor," and fortunately kept their lives. Loring's second trial was about as conclusive. The judges still found him not guilty, Elliot still disagreed, but did discharge him from arrest. The whole ludicrous episode was typical of the fierce passions aroused by politics, which were building towards a dramatic encounter.[9]

This was the situation:

Item: *An unpaid bill.* Landlord Eager, of the Jefferson Tavern, was hired to cater the Republican Fourth of July banquet atop Copps' Hill. The Republican committee planned one menu, decided to expand it when they heard the Tunisian ambassador and retinue would walk in their procession and attend the feast. These colorful Easterners would be sure to attract a crowd. But when Eager rendered his bill the committee called it too high and flatly refused to pay. Eager took it to his lawyer, Thomas O. Selfridge, and insisted, in spite of the lawyer's efforts at conciliation, on suing the committee. Selfridge got a writ and the committee quickly paid up.

Item: *Some letters.* Ben Austin, of the *Chronicle* and cousin to dueling William, was the principal committee member involved. In an insurance office on State Street, twitted by some Federalists about the matter, he accused the "damn Federal lawyer" (unnamed) of instituting the suit against the wishes of Landlord Eager. This was quickly reported to Selfridge, and he demanded a retraction from Austin. Austin found out the truth, and told the emissary from Selfridge that he had gone round to the people concerned and corrected it. Selfridge, however, had an affidavit from one of those men stating that Austin had not seen him to retract a word. Selfridge felt his whole reputation was at stake in this matter. He wrote another letter. Getting no reply from Austin by Sunday night, August 3, he took a further step towards jail.

Item: *Two newspapers.* Selfridge put a notice in the *Boston Gazette* for Monday, August 4, labeling Austin "a coward, a liar, and a scoundrel." Austin replied in the same day's *Chronicle,* calling it "insolent and false" but refusing "to enter into a newspaper controversy with one T. O. Selfridge."

Item: *A black hickory cane weighing nearly nine ounces.* Austin told a friend of Selfridge's the morning of the publication that he should not meddle with Selfridge himself (he was fifty-four years old and Selfridge only thirty-one) but someone his own age "should take him in hand." This was relayed to Selfridge as a definite threat, which it was not, for Austin had no idea his son was in the shop of William Schaeffer selecting a cane. "Do you think," young Charles Austin said to the proprietor, "that this is a strong stick and will take a good lick?" Schaffer allowed it would. Austin bought it and then waited until it was one o'clock and 'Change opened. Then he headed for State Street.[10]

Item: *A brace of pistols.* His office boy testified that Selfridge kept a brace of pistols in a desk drawer in the office for protection. Saturday, the boy had been sent out to buy four and a half pence worth of shot.

That Monday at one, just before Selfridge left the office to meet a client on 'Change, the lawyer loaded the pistols and put them in the pockets of his long coat just in case the threat was true. Since a lawyer must dress properly, even in August, he put on his stiff black fur hat and likely saved his life. He went out the door of the old State House where he shared offices with Lemeul Shaw, chatted with some men outside for a moment, then started slowly to walk down State Street. Selfridge's path brought him near Mr. Townsend's shop where young Charles Austin was waiting, hickory cane in hand, chatting with two people. When he saw Selfridge, he pushed between the men and out into the street. What happened next was a matter of dispute that was to be resolved in court.

Meeting a few days after the events of that Monday afternoon, the coroner's jury called it "willful murder." The fact that Selfridge was a prominent Federalist lawyer and Austin a leader of the Republicans meant that the whole business was being judged by its political overtones and not necessarily on the facts of the case.

Under Massachusetts law the state was obliged to present its case against Thomas Selfridge to a grand jury. This jury would decide whether the state had sufficient evidence to bring the accused to trial. If they did, they would bring in a "True Bill of Indictment." If they brought in a "No Bill," the accused would go free. A grand jury proceeding is not a trial since only the state's evidence is heard. The result of a "True Bill" would be a regular trial before a petit jury in open court. Grand jury proceedings were held behind closed doors.

When the grand jury was organized on November 21, 1806, was it just a happy coincidence that appointed as the foreman of that jury was a former Federalist senator to the General Court from Boston, a prominent member of the Federalist Central Committee, and a present Federalist representative to the General Court—Colonel T. H. Perkins? Was it not fortunate for the accused Federalist lawyer that the chief justice giving the charge to that grand jury should be the founder of the Federalist party—Theophilus Parsons? Was it not lucky that "the clerks who issued venires for grand and petty jurors were all on one side . . . and knew to what towns to send" for "safe" jurors, as the *Chronicle* was to complain?

The grand jury of twenty-one was impaneled and sworn and "T. Handyside Perkins, Esquire" was named foreman. Among the other twenty names were many with a solid Federalist sound to them. The jury considered the evidence presented to them and on Tuesday, December 2, they returned into court and Colonel Perkins stood and declared, "That he the said Thomas Oliver Selfridge, the said Charles Austin then and there, in manner and form aforesaid, feloniously, wilfully, and of the fury of his mind, did kill and slay against the peace of the Commonwealth aforesaid, and the law in such case made and provided." It was a true bill and so signed by the foreman, "T. Handyside Perkins," and attested by James Sullivan, attorney general. But there was a "but."[11]

Their true bill was not for murder, as the Republican press was demanding, but for the lesser charge of manslaughter. This verdict was furiously attacked by the Republican papers. In particular the charge of Judge Parsons was criticized. The irate Republicans claimed he had failed to give the grand jury all the distinctions between the crimes of murder and manslaughter. Had he rigorously applied the law, said the Republicans, the jury would have had no alternative but to bring in an indictment for murder.

Had the grand jury under Perkins been fair? Selfridge came to trial two days before Christmas in a crowded courtroom. Prosecuting Selfridge for manslaughter on behalf of the Commonwealth was Attorney General Sullivan. Selfridge was represented by the "big brass" of the Boston Federalist bar, Samuel Dexter and Christopher Gore, with

Fisher Ames, and Harry Otis, assisting in the preparation of the case. The most important question was: when had Selfridge fired the fatal shot?

Republican Sullivan put three witnesses on the stand who saw the whole thing. Their evidence made it look like murder. Mr. Howe, who had been on his way to lunch and a Mr. Frost both said that Selfridge had fired at Austin before Austin stepped off the sidewalk. Barber Lane said he had seen the whole shooting match from the door of his shop and he agreed that Selfridge fired first.

But the Federalist battery moved in with twice as many witnesses who testified they also had seen the whole affray and saw it entirely differently. A Mr. Bailey claimed that the first blow of Austin's cane was descending when Selfridge fired. Three other witness agreed that blow and shot were simultaneous. But the most telling witness for the defense was Lewis Glover, who expected to see a quarrel because of the publication and went on 'Change expressly to watch it. He never took his eyes off Austin and stated most positively that Austin struck the first blow and only after that did Selfridge fire.

Christmas day, no holiday then in Boston, the lawyers began their final arguments to the jury. The judge instructed the jury regarding the law, this time to everyone's satisfaction. After the furor he had caused at the grand jury hearing, Judge Parsons pleaded illness and assigned Isaac Parker to preside in his stead. The jury retired to consider their verdict. Was it manslaughter or self-defense? Should the grand jury have called it murder? In less than fifteen minutes they were back. They had reached a decision. The jammed courtroom was tense as Foreman Paul Revere said—"Not guilty."

It was a landmark decision: a successful defense of the right of self-defense. Selfridge was free. As the Republicans saw it, a murderer had been freed to walk the streets of Boston. From Salem, Parson Bentley saw it as a "wanton act of political prejudice." What was worse was "his release without censure." The Republican press frothed at the mouth in every issue. Selfridge and Parsons were hung in effigy in Boston. The fury spread—to Charlestown, to Marblehead, to Salem. It was thought the mobs might stop hanging effigies and hang Selfridge instead. Taking the advice of his friends, Selfridge left town soon after until things could calm down a bit.[12]

Some years later, in 1815, Selfridge died, considering himself "a sort of victim" Dr. John Warren remarked, "to the cause he had undertaken to defend."[13] Long before he died, however, that cause was to suffer severe tests and be led to the brink of secession. The troubles arose, not from the domestic disagreements which agitated the Austins, the Elliots, and Selfridge, but from the foreign policy of Mr. Jefferson.

No words were too strong for Federalists like Perkins in denouncing this "Madness" of "our present Dictator." For Jefferson's policy was putting the merchants in what the colonel styled "Commercial purgatory." Since "God" was the last name any self-respecting Federalist would confer on Mr. Jefferson, they could not grant him the right to send them to such a place. But for fifteen months that was exactly where the "Embargo" of Mr. Jefferson placed them. A Federalist walking up Back Street in those days might have been forgiven if he detected a faint smell of sulfur exuding from the sign swinging before Mr. Eager's tavern.

So we go up, up, up,
And so we go down, down, downy,
Now we go this way and that way,
And now we go round, round, roundy.

*Columbian Centinel,*
December 22, 1804

# 16

# Strong Nerves and Long Purses

"It is our wish," wrote Colonel Perkins regally in May of 1806 to his nephew in Canton, "that you sh'd return home the next spring." So, late that fall, young John Cushing sailed home to Boston. Home to the town he had left four years before for a minor position in an uncertain enterprise as a youth not quite sixteen. Now he was returning a full-fledged partner in a successful firm, whose success rested in good measure on his capable shoulders. A man who was still four months short of being twenty.[1]

William Paine had gone out in the *Mandarin* with the co-partnership and the temporary reprieve for Cushing. Paine was then twenty-three, and a nephew of James Perkins. Because of his work in the counting house and his experience at sea, the Perkins brothers felt he would make a good partner for Cushing in Canton. Insurance, too, in case of a repetition of what happened to Bumstead.

The colonel thought it would be "pleasant" if Cushing could return in the *Mandarin,* but was afraid that would not give John enough time "to initiate Mr. P. fully into the business." It was a sign of Cushing's eagerness to come home and the good order in which he had affairs, that he did embark for America on the return voyage of the *Mandarin.*

One hundred and thirty days later, the *Mandarin* arrived at Martha's Vineyard. It was Thursday, April 19, 1807. Being so near Boston made Cushing doubly eager to get home. He left the *Mandarin* and came up to Boston on another ship, arriving in town a day early. It was difficult to believe that he had done so much and was still only in his teens. He was in good health and full of news. During the homeward journey, the *Mandarin* had been stopped twice by British vessels. On April 3 the warship *Leopard* had sent a party aboard and taken a Scotsman, James Johnson, from the crew. Otherwise they behaved politely. Two days later, in sight of Bermuda, the *Halifax* had examined the *Mandarin*'s papers, and finding nothing amiss, permitted her to proceed.

The stopping of American merchant vessels by British warships, and taking off seamen claimed to be British deserters was becoming a great nuisance. Working conditions for sailors, bad everywhere, were at least better on American ships than British ships, and far superior to conditions in His Majesty's Navy. With American vessels carrying more and more of the world's trade while Europe wallowed in the Napoleonic wars, deserters had no trouble finding berths on American ships. This sorely limited the supply of seamen for the eight hundred ships that were Britain's greatest weapon against Napoleon. Rather than improve conditions on their ships, it was easier for the British simply to stop American vessels found in international waters and remove any of its crew suspected of being deserters. If a British captain was in desperate need of seamen, his standards of determining British citizenship were apt to be correspondingly accommodating. It made for a situation that any moment could prove explosive.

Cushing's homecoming was happy and sad. "The Dowager Mrs. P." had been fluctuating between sickness and health for several years. Now she went into a decline that led to her death on May 24. "She left us with the utmost tranquility and resignation," the brothers wrote to sister Esther Sturgis in Charleston, South Carolina. Reporting the event to Paine in Canton, they remarked that "she had the gratification to see JPC before she took her leave; which was a great source of comfort to her in her dying moment." She too, "returned home in the spring."[2]

After a short six weeks home, John Cushing returned to duty in Canton, leaving early in June in the *Levant*. His real vacation was the five-month sea voyage each way, for the weeks at home were crowded not only with the death of his grandmother, but with intensive talks about the business in China. Letters written to Paine in Canton at the time reflect these extensive speculations.

The tea market was oversaturated and prices were dropping. Teas that cost an importer sixty-three cents by the time he had brought them to Boston were selling for fifty-five cents. "Such business would sap the mines of India!" Seeing no relief in less than eighteen months or two years, the brothers decided "it will not answer to meddle with Teas." The question then arose, "how shall we apply our Ships and our Capital?"[3]

One way that seemed profitable to them was to ship sandalwood and tin between Canton and Hawaii, "as long as Vessels and Crews will hold together." The other way was to place money at interest, the rate of which in Canton, Cushing told them, was now 18 percent. Perkins calculated that $50,000 lent at that rate in China "with the Accumulation of the Compound Interest" would double itself in four and a half years. This was about four times better than they could do on trading voyages without the risks of depressed markets, bad debts, wars, and such. The brothers decided to use their "private funds" in China for such speculations and suggested that the firm there do likewise.

It was always difficult to find an article that would do well in the China market. "For once," they observed in another letter at this time, "we have fallen on an article for your market which has done well. The Lead has exceeded our expectations." They were sending fifty or sixty tons of it on the *Levant* with Cushing. But as for "Brimstone and opium"—"we shall meddle with neither of those Articles." Nor were they to be tempted by the example of another trader "and pickle our finger with the Salt speculation." They explained this to a correspondent: "Even salt has been carried to Canton, but the adventurers in this wild essay have experienc'd great trouble as well as Loss. The Chinese w'd neither permit it to be landed or thrown overboard, and they have been obliged to smuggle it into the sea by night."[4]

On the surface, the glut of tea in the home market was easily explained. Too many merchants were shipping too much home; more than seven million American mouths could swallow no matter how diligently they gulped. Since all the Chinese teas for America were funneled through Canton, the brothers felt that in planning tea shipments home it would be well for the Canton establishment to consider the total amount being shipped out by all ships to all ports in the United States. "It is very possible to ascertain and to govern your Shipments, by the annual supply, and the wants of the Market." It didn't matter which port in America they were shipped to. Teas would always find "their level, and be shipped from one port to another until the prices in each are nearly brought to the same point."[5]

Of course there were "accidents" that could not be foreseen and therefore could not be avoided. Such was the capture by French privateers of a British tea ship whose cargo was then sold at very reduced prices at the Isle de France, bought up by an American, and sent to Boston—temporarily undercutting the local market. The best planning, the brothers admitted, "may be contravened by unexpected events—but there are hazards in all business; contingencies to which every operation is liable." So on the whole it were best to stick to the "general rule of calculation": shipments must equal consumption.

But other factors also complicated the Canton operations of the brothers. One was the delivery of the factories, arranged for by their Providence friend and fellow merchant, William F. Megee, several years before. Now it turned out in May 1807 that another Providence businessman held a lien on the property and would not release it until sums owed to him by Megee were paid.

Megee was just then returning from a long trip to South America and the colonel presumed he would come back empty-handed. After a most cordial friendship stretching back a dozen years, he had discovered that "this man has a wonderful facility in blasting everything he touches." They wrote him at Charleston about his debts to them, only to learn as they had foreseen that he had made "a most wretched voyage to La Plata and nearly sunk all his Property." It was doubtful if they would recover anything on what he owed them.[6]

It took more than talent, hard work and a knack for business to bring a man success. Luck played a part too, and Megee had had no luck. Of the dozen years they had known him, he had spent at least five of them on voyages to the East. He had done much business with the brothers, of mutual benefit. Relations between the families were very close. Mrs. Perkins, who was not overly social, became quite fond of Megee's wife, Susan Nightingale, and visits back and forth between family members are frequently referred to in their letters. The Colonel was urging Megee to stay at least a week with them in June 1804. "There is a great deal of business to be done here—Nahant is to be seen, Salem Turnpike & the Canal to be visited, and half a thousand other things to be done which require time."[7]

Perkins made frequent business trips to Providence and seems to have stayed there with the Megees. A number of ships were sent out in combination with Rhode Island merchants, and sometimes it was better to hire crews there, than to have to send sailors down from Boston. Perkins looked into every detail of the business too. "It appeared to our THP that the bread shewn to him was not dry enough—it must be as dry as tinder."[8]

But business can break up good friendships. Embarrassed by his failures, Megee fled the country, abandoning wife and family. He ended up in the East, running a boarding house in Macao for some years, where Cushing must have seen him on occasion. The firm eventually secured the factories in Canton, but there were other complications affecting their China business. One of them they had inadvertently caused themselves, with their efforts to secure a monopoly of the declining Northwest Coast fur trade.[9]

By the middle of the first decade of the nineteenth century, the fur trade on the Northwest Coast was gradually coming into the hands of three Boston firms: the Perkinses, the Lambs, and the Lymans. There were a few Russian ships probing the area, but the British were, for all practical purposes, out of it. The increased use of firearms was slaughtering off more and more of the sea otters. With scarcity came higher prices. The old days of baubles, buttons, and beads were fast disappearing. Now it was axes and helves, gunpowder and shot, kettles and pots, molasses and tobacco that the Indians demanded in trade for skins. Fewer skins, higher prices, narrowed the profit margin for the merchants.

As competition sharpened, so did the selfishness, greed, and jealousy of the captains. Ships had to stay longer to make a profitable voyage. Many remained on the coast for three years, which meant five years away from home port, and a longer period before the merchant made any money on his venture. Only firms with several ships, large assets, and adaptability could survive the changing conditions of the trade.[10]

While the British had given up sending ships to the coast, they were still the most important factor affecting the fur trade. Montreal was the headquarters for the two companies that dominated British efforts—the Michilimackinac Company and the Northwest Company. Enjoying government-granted monopolies, between them they gathered furs from all the area east of the Rocky Mountains, and were particularly active in the northern section around the Great Lakes and the Mississippi River. These companies supplied not only all the furs the British shipped to Europe and the East, but three quarters of the furs bought in the States.

The Northwest Company coveted the rich fur country west of the Rockies, the region where the Boston merchants traded. Perkins was aware of this interest, which threatened to diminish even more the dwindling supply of skins. During a trip to Canada in 1806 he had talked with the men of the Northwest Company, including McGillvray, one of the leaders. From him he learned that the Northwest Company had sent agents over the Rockies to organize the trade there. It would take some time to do this, and Perkins reasoned that if they could get the trade into their own hands there might be a few good years left before the British efforts began to hurt them.

The principal Boston competitor of the Perkins firm was Theodore Lyman. A York, Maine, man who had moved to Boston in 1788 just as the China trade opened, he had been in that trade and made enough money to build a comfortable country estate in Waltham. By 1807, Lyman was fifty-four years old and there was some talk of his retiring from the China trade, even though his two sons, Theodore, Jr., and George, were also merchants. Perkins followed up the rumors to see if he could put his plan of a coastal monopoly into effect. By June 8, 1807, negotiations with Lyman had reached a satisfactory stage. On that day J. & T. H. Perkins gave him their note for $8,000 payable in six months without interest. In return they got full rights to the ship *Vancouver,* and a free hand on the Northwest Coast. Lyman agreed not to send any vessels to the coast for seven years. Working in close partnership with the Lambs, the only other important coastal traders, the brothers effectively had the field to themselves. June and July of 1807 found them readying two vessels, the *Pearl* and the *Vancouver,* for the coast. But they did it under great uncertainties.

By now the struggle between France and Britain had been going on almost continuously for fourteen years. Who could have forseen it would drag out another eight? The present commercial prosperity of

Boston and the States rested on this extremely artificial base. As the only sizable neutral, America received, by default, the carrying trade of the world. Naturally, American merchants were sensitive to every change of relationships in the conflict. By the summer and fall of 1806 England and France had fought each other to a standstill. Rumors of possible peace between the two spread consternation among the merchants. In September the *Centinel* published King George's July statement to Parliament that he was "engaged in discussions with a view to the accomplishment of peace." Within a week Perkins had written to a European firm that this news had "paralyzed the markets of New England."[11]

As international traders the Perkinses had to keep in constant touch with the changing situation. The news did not take them so much by surprise as it did some of their fellow merchants. They were able to tell their contacts in Amsterdam that "we have withdrawn ourselves from every active business for the last six months, which may prove beneficial." They intended to act with great caution. "Such times require strong nerves and long purses." Fortunately the Perkins brothers possessed both.[12]

Early in February 1807 the *Centinel* informed its readers of Napoleon's decree given in Berlin the previous November. "England," read the *Centinel* heading, "Declared in a State of Blockade by France." By this decree Napoleon prohibited the importation of British goods into Europe and forbade any ships that had gone into English ports to enter ports under his control. The effect of this, as James Perkins wrote Williams, was that "everything here is perfectly stagnant." The brothers were not caught unprepared. "Thank God, the State of our particular concerns is such as to involve no Hazards."[13]

The uncertainty extended into the spring. In April the Perkinses wrote their Amsterdam contacts that they had thought proper "to remain quiet and have preferred to remain Spectators, than to become actors in the mercantile transactions of the moment." They were waiting until the time "when the Prospect brightens." But hearing that Napoleon's decree would not go into operation in Holland for the time being, and tea prices being so low in the States, they decided not to unload the *Mandarin* in Boston, but to see if they could chance getting it landed in Holland. Arriving in Boston on April 24, the *Mandarin* was quickly overhauled and by May 3 had cleared for Amsterdam. They admitted it was a "choice of evils," but hoped to pull it off. Strong nerves indeed![14]

Their nerves were stronger than the copper on the bottom of the *Mandarin*. Captain Cunningham wrote them a sea letter informing them of the ship's poor condition. They replied in July telling him to wait in Amsterdam until he should hear from Williams in London. "From some recent occurrences," they wrote cryptically, "we are led to Suspend the Voyage of the Ship." Williams, being on the spot where actions that could affect the *Mandarin's* voyage would be taken, was in a better position than they to determine whether the ship should go on to China or not. Writing Williams at the same time they asked him to be guided by "the temper of the British government and the possibility of getting Insurance."[15]

But the matter was academic, though they didn't learn this until August. In early June the *Mandarin,* that elegant ship, was wrecked on the coast of Holland "in fine weather and under circumstances of great aggravation." Now was a time for "long purses." They had no insurance on the ship, though the cargo was partly covered and most of it saved.[16]

And what were the "recent occurrences" that would have led the firm to suspend the voyage? On June 22, 1807, with the *Mandarin* lost, and John Cushing and the *Levant* three weeks out of Boston bound for China, an American warship, the *Chesapeake,* sailed out of Hampton for the Mediterranean to protect American shipping from the Barbary pirates. Aboard the *Chesapeake* were four men who had deserted from one of the British vessels anchored off Hampton Roads. Because of the European war, British warships frequently patroled in American waters for French vessels and put into American ports for provisions and refitting. No one was disturbed when the British frigate *Leopard* left Hampton shortly after the *Chesapeake*. Once in international waters, the *Leopard* pulled close to the *Chesapeake* and sent a demand aboard for the four claimed deserters.* When this was refused by the American commander, the *Leopard* immediately opened fire on the unprepared and unsuspecting *Chesapeake*.

In fifteen minutes the *Chesapeake,* with three killed, eighteen wounded, and no hope but for more punishment, "struck her colours and declared herself a prize." So Perkins described it to Cushing when

* Three of the men were actually native Americans who had only recently escaped from long impressment in the British navy.

he got around to detail the affair in a letter of August 2. The *Leopard* contented itself with taking the four men and the *Chesapeake* was left "in a crippled and disgraceful state to find her way back to Hampton."

News of the event took eight days to reach Boston. The *Centinel* reported it on Wednesday morning, the first of July. On Friday the *Palladium* headlined it an "outrage." The Saturday edition of the *Centinel* screamed "WAR! WAR! WAR!" "Never, since the battle of Lexington," commented President Jefferson, "have I seen this country in such a state of exasperation." That was a mild word. Norfolk and nearby towns had passed what Perkins called "the most inflammatory resolution" immediately on hearing the news. All provisions were refused British ships and mobs roamed the streets looking for British sailors to beat up. Protest meetings were held in all coastal cities. Even the West joined in the outcry. "The genuine fervor of Mobacy," as Perkins termed it, was "displayed in every direction."[17]

Boston Federalists, accustomed to taking the British side of every argument about the European war, were stunned. Republicans, however, knew how to react. Mechanics, laborers, people in the street all demanded action. The leading Federalists met to discuss their dilemma, and decided the best policy was to do nothing. Their celebration of the Fourth of July was held as usual.

Five hundred Federalists gathered at Fanueil Hall at three o'clock for their banquet. Christopher Gore presided, assisted by Otis, Paul Revere, and Colonel Perkins. Former President Adams and Revolutionary War hero Robert Treat Paine were the guests of honor. Federalist toasts were drunk to Federalist heroes—only the newspapers shouted about the *Chesapeake* affair. "If we have a War," mourned the Perkinses two days later to a Philadelphia correspondent, "it will be owing to the Madness of our Rulers, or their Masters, the Sovereign people."[18]

John Quincy Adams, though a Federalist senator from Massachusetts, felt in this crisis that his state should support the government, even though it was not one of their liking. A violent argument on 'Change on July 9 between Adams and Judge John Lowell, a diehard Federalist, led to Adams's ostracism by the Federalists for his apostacy. On the tenth, when the Republicans of Boston held an informal meeting at the State House (since the Federalists would not allow the Republicans to have a town meeting) Adams showed up. Adams accepted appointment to their resolutions committee. The resolutions strongly backed the Jefferson government and passed by acclamation. Yet Perkins was able to say of them that "under the circumstances" they were "extremely moderate."[19]

The Federalists now felt pressured to take action and called a town meeting for July 16. Federalists packed the meeting, although many Republicans attended. Federalist merchant John Coffin Jones was chosen moderator. On their resolutions committee there was a safe margin of Federalists including Otis, Perkins, and the doubtful Senator J. Q. Adams. They brought in as weak an approval of the government's position as could be drawn up. This too was carried by "acclamation" and the Federalists considered they had satisfactorily disposed of the affair.

Time laid its soothing hands on the affair too. The slowness of communications had its advantage as well as disadvantages. Jefferson, not disposed to war despite what the Federalists thought, sent a dispatch boat to Britain with a protest and a demand for reparations. The Perkinses felt that most people "seem inclined to await the return of the Governmental Dispatches." Fortunately "three months will probably elapse before" that would happen. By then "the first moment of effervescence" would have passed. In spite of "the folly and prejudices of our rulers," the Perkinses hoped that "a rupture between the two nations" could be avoided.[20]

No matter which way the decision for war went, the Perkins house had to make the best decisions it could to protect its interests. The brothers had told Cushing to keep all their China ships "out of danger till the storm blows over." If they were unable to communicate with him, he should weigh well the advice of Williams, "and all your measures must be taken with due deliberation."[21]

At first the attitude of the brothers to the *Chesapeake* affair was judicially impartial: "There have been faults on both Sides. The protection of Deserters, contrary to the usage of Nations was no doubt an act of the most flagrant Injustice and impolicy. The mode of redress was equally unwarrantable and more flagrant in its nature." But soon their thinking hardened into the official Federalist view of the matter: "We believe that the orders given by Berkeley [to seize the four sailors] may be considered as a justifiable reprisal for a deliberate wrong, and that our Gov. revolts at the protection of British Fugitives at the moment G. B. is struggling for her existence, and fighting the Battles of the Civilized World."[22]

The Perkinses hoped that the British reply to Jefferson's protest would be conciliatory. If the British government chose to disavow the attack, "the door of conciliation" might "be yet open." It was "our nasty Government" that they and the other Federalists did not trust. But as time passed they grew more uneasy and uncertain. In September it was "we hope from appearance G. B. will act with temperance." By late October their state of uncertainy was "extremely distressing." By mid-November "we must remain in suspence until the arrival of the Express Boat *Revenge,* when we hope in God, our fears may be dissipated." They continued to fret that Jefferson might plunge the country "into a Contest which would be ruinous and to defend a Principle not worth a Cent to us."[23]

When the British reply came, it was stiff. No negotiations until British vessels were permitted to re-enter American harbors. Accompanying this was the text of a Royal Proclamation strengthening the navy's policy of impressment, and word of a forthcoming Order in Council which would prohibit trade from ports where British ships were not permitted. Napoleon quickly hit back with a decree ordering every ship confiscated that complied with the British order.

This put American ships in the middle. If they traded with the British, the French confiscated them; if they traded with the French, the British seized them. Jefferson's answer was bewilderingly simple. American ships would stay at home and thus stay out of trouble. The howls from the merchants were immediate and loud. Gone in a flash were their worries about a war. This stoppage of commerce meant one thing, as Perkins glumly pointed out to a British contact: "It leaves you the whole field of Commerce without a rival."

No overseas trade meant no profits. What were traders to do? Disaster stared the merchants in the face.

One unemployed seaman met another on the streets of Hartford: "Holla! messmate, where are you bound!" "Bound to Halifax by the pipers, which way are you steering?" "By the powers of Moll Kelly, I am steering the same course, for there's no standing this *dambargo* any longer."

*Connecticut Courant,*
January 13, 1808

# 17

# No Boat, Raft, or Float Can Pass Our Castle

A good merchant is nothing if not adaptable. The embargo required the maximum of adaptability for a merchant to survive unscathed. It changed all the rules of the game with great suddenness. No vessels could sail from an American port to any foreign port, except an occasional public dispatch boat on official business, which might be allowed to take business letters. Only coastal traffic was permitted, and this under increasingly stringent regulations. Merchants who customarily imported merchandise for re-export, which was unsaleable on the local market, found tremendous inventories piling up in their warehouses.

The Federalists at first saw the embargo, as Perkins phrased it in a letter to London, as "a mere 'raw head and bloody bones' " to use in negotiations with the British over the *Chesapeake* affair. Nevertheless, Perkins wanted his London contact, Samuel Williams, to "be prepared for the worst" and to "secure *your Friends* from the Hazard of losing Property in England."[1]

Since nobody could predict whether or not war might come with either France or Britain, Perkins asked Williams to write to their Amsterdam connection and request them to put "whatever Property they may have belonging to us" safely "out of the reach of accident, in case of a rupture between this Country & France." He presumed there were still "some Catwick communications" between England and Holland even if not more "open Intercourse." This, then, was a time to take stock of one's position. The first rule of warfare, as any colonel worth his braid should know, was to secure flanks.

When the embargo began that December 1807, the Perkins firm had five vessels at sea in which they were the chief owners. Three others had only recently been wrecked, though they then knew of only two, the *Mandarin* in Holland and the *Cordelia* off Boston. They had not yet heard of the wreck of the *Eclipse* off Alaska. Of the five still afloat, three, the *Derby,* the *Pearl,* and the *Vancouver,* were sailing between Canton and the Northwest Coast. The *Hazard* was about to leave Canton for Boston, and the *Levant* had just taken Cushing back to China.

Since ships were allowed to come home, but not go to sea again, it was common sense for a merchant to keep his vessels away from America and actively trading. The brothers had already advised Cushing to do this. The previous November, they had instructed him that "should this letter find any vessel in which we are concerned in China, we wish to have our Property retained there until you hear further from us." There is a time to adventure boldly, and a time to be cautiously prudent. The Perkins brothers had the happy faculty of knowing what time it was. But the letter reached Cushing too late for him to follow their counsel about the *Hazard.* It was more than halfway home to Boston by the time Cushing got that letter.[2]

Since Boston could not write directly to Canton, the brothers had to use roundabout channels. A public dispatch boat going to England gave them a chance at the end of March 1808 to write to Williams and enclose a long letter for him to forward to Cushing. In miniature, this letter embodies their "theology" for coping with the effects of the Embargo.[3]

Their general creed they stated thus: "Our Govt. seems determined to destroy our Commerce and we shall be unpardonable not to profit of the Situation of things, as far as in our Power, by Continuing to keep our Ships abroad as long as we can." Clearly, this was one of their main strengths in this commercial crisis: a base of operations outside of the country in charge of a competent man authorized to act independently.

They recited their rosary of troubles: teas would be a drug on the market for two years so they thought; coffee which had been selling for thirty-one cents had fallen to nineteen; sugar had sunk too; cotton in the South had dropped ruinously; rice couldn't find buyers; over one hundred establishments in New York had failed; "in short, every joint and articulation of our Commercial System, has felt a Shock."

In giving Cushing the history of these things they adhered strictly to the Federalist Gospel. Great Britain had been reasonable in the negotiations, "disavowing" the admiral whose order had prompted the *Chesapeake* affair and bringing him home in "disgrace." The British envoy had been unable "to appease Mr. J and his adherents." France, of course, was "wicked"; American vessels had been taken by the French on any pretext; "burned at sea without form or Process"; or condemned out of hand on arriving at French ports. "God only knows what will be the measures of him, who seems to direct the destinies of Europe." However, the true devil of the piece was not Napoleon but "the Executive of the U.S." who had recommended to Congress the "annihilation" of our commerce. "The little Federal Phalanx" had gone down in defeat heroically fighting this "disastrous measure." A measure they saw no prospect of having "taken off" for many months.

What road should be taken to Salvation? They were full of passages and texts. Perhaps Cushing, with no other American competition, could corner the fur market in China and "get the Price of Sea Otter Skins up again." It might be possible to do business with the Russians. One advantage not to be overlooked was that the interruption of the usual business should "renovate" the market and "give us an opportunity to run off the old and present stock of Teas at saving Prices." Commercial Hell might be heavenly after all!

Their benediction to Cushing was couched thus: "You must in the mean time remain firm at your Post and be consoled by the reflection, that your disappointments cannot equal or exceed those of your Friends in America." There was no telling what the full effects of the Embargo would be or how long it would last. A merchant had to play his cards close to his weskit.

One of the cards was political. In the election of 1807, the Republican candidate for governor, James Sullivan, had defeated Federalist Caleb Strong. Colonel Perkins had been re-elected to the Senate by a two-to-one majority in the same election, but he ran from a safe, overwhelmingly Federalist Boston district. In the election of 1808 Christopher Gore, a fifty-year-old lawyer with a distinguished career in public service, ran against Sullivan. The election was warmly contested. The embargo, as Dr. Bentley put it, "touches the bone and the flesh and few reason about it." The candidates ran neck and neck and it was not until all votes were in that Sullivan could claim victory. Though the Republicans held the governorship, Perkins was able to tell his brother-in-law Forbes that there was a "Federal majority of 32 members in the House and a sufficient number in the Senate." He felt that Massachusetts had "in a great degree" been "revolutionized," and that they had come from a condition he termed "the vilest democracy."[4]

Perkins had not run for re-election, but had been very active on the Central Committee. The Federalists particularly wanted to control the new session of the legislature because it was to elect one of the Commonwealth's senators to the United States Congress. The six-year term of John Quincy Adams was not due to expire until March 1809, but the Federalists were unhappy with Adams. None more so than Adams's colleague in the Senate, Timothy Pickering, the "Old Sachem" himself.

Pickering was an able, clever, and ultra-conservative politician, a leader of the so-called Essex Junto. Ornery and stubborn, he more than met his equal in Adams. Popular fable has long been able to categorize to whom the Lowells speak and to whom (or what) the Cabots speak; nobody would try to predict to whom any Adams might choose to speak or even if he would speak at all or what he might say if he did choose to speak. In the matter of the embargo, Senator Adams had spoken in favor of Mr. Jefferson's scheme and to Senator Pickering this was the last straw.

The legislature was organized on May 25, 1808. Pickering successfully pressured them into choosing a senator now, though Adams had nine months left to serve. The candidate the Federalists decided to propose was James Lloyd, almost a political unknown. After he had been chosen, a leading Republican asked a friend if he was known by anybody out of Boston? He could find no one who had ever heard of him.

Colonel Perkins had heard of him. He had been a partner in many of the firm's commercial adventures. Five years younger than the colonel, he graduated from Harvard with John Quincy Adams. While a good student, his arrogant manners and violent temper had made him unpopular in college. As far as the Perkins brothers were concerned, it would be very useful to have such a good friend in the halls of Congress.

When the Massachusetts legislature came to consider the selection of a senator, the vote was 219 for Adams and 248 for Lloyd. Adams immediately resigned his seat, and for the moment, his public career came to an end. But the Federalists were not content to break Adams politically; they ostracized him socially too. Christopher Gore described for a friend what happened. "He walks into State Street at the usual hour of Exchange, but seems totally unknown."[5]

But the selection of a friendly senator did not solve the problems of the Perkins brothers. In June a Perkins ship joined the scores of vessels hauled up in the harbors. The *Hazard* arrived loaded to the gunwales with tea, nankeens, and china. The ship had lost five sailors overboard in a heavy sea on the outward passage, and homeward bound it had been stopped off the Cape of Good Hope by a British frigate and three seamen who were unable to prove their American origin were "pressed" into the British navy. In August the *Levant* arrived home and added to the stock the firm was storing in its warehouses. The brothers had decided to sit on their merchandise as long as the market was glutted. They were in a fortunate enough financial condition to be able to do this. Many a small merchant, and some of the larger ones, were not in such a liquid situation.

Many were seeking to "secure advantages" to themselves from the embargo. It had now been in force some eight months, and merchants saw little prospect of its being lifted. But perhaps ways around it could be found. Perkins reported to his brother-in-law Ralph Forbes that it was daily becoming "more rigorous. No boat raft or float of any description Can pass our Castle," (referring thus to Fort Independence in the harbor) "without Permit, even our Coasting trade shackled and embarrassed to annihilation."[6]

But a loophole did exist. President Jefferson had authority to grant permission to American merchants to send their vessels out in ballast to bring back property owned by them prior to the embargo. John Jacob Astor of New York applied in June to be allowed to send a ship to Canton to bring home some property he alleged was there prior to the embargo. In mid-July the Perkinses filed a similar petition asking to send a ship to Europe to bring back cargo that had been on the shipwrecked *Mandarin*. They also wanted to be allowed to send a ship to the Northwest Coast in order to reprovision ships trading there. All three petitions were denied on general principles.

But one defeat does not mean that the war is lost. The frustrated

Astor prepared an ingenious plan. The Perkins brothers were essential to its implementation because of their branch office in Canton, although it cannot be stated positively how much they knew of Astor's intrigues. Astor knew a Chinese man by the name of Punqua Wingchong. Astor said this Chinese "mandarin" had come to New York nine months before on business and wanted a letter of introduction to the president. Astor got a letter from New York's senator Samuel Mitchell on July 12, 1808.

With an interpreter, the mandarin went to Washington to see Jefferson, but Jefferson had left for Monticello the same day. Deprived of a personal interview, the mandarin wrote to Jefferson asking for a passport. Secretary of State Madison was induced to support the petition with a letter. Jefferson quickly granted permission, sending a blank passport to Gallatin, the secretary of the Treasury, along with a note indicating that Jefferson thought this goodwill gesture "might be the means of making our nation known advantageously at the source of power in China."[7]

On the third of August Gallatin officially informed the collector of the Port of New York, David Gelston, that the Chinese mandarin and his suite had permission to leave, taking with him all his personal baggage and $45,000 in specie or goods. However, the return cargo of the ship he charted for his trip could only consist of goods belonging to American citizens that had been owned by them prior to December 22, 1807. Gelston reported to Gallatin within the day that the mandarin had hired Mr. Astor's ship, the *Beaver*. Gallatin, being more suspicious than Jefferson, wrote to Jefferson, hinting that had the affair been left to him he would have "hesitated."

In New York, Astor was busy preparing the *Beaver* for sea. It made a great stir in the quiet harbor. Merchants from Philadelphia even came over to see what was going on and to get a look at this mandarin. On August 10, some Philadelphia merchants wrote an official protest to Gallatin stating that some of them had lived in China for years and knew the mandarin to be a fake.

The New York newspapers joined in and charged that the mandarin was nothing more than "a Chinaman picked up in the Park" or a "Common Chinese dock loafer." But there being no immediate reply from Gallatin, the *Beaver*, its preparations completed, was free to sail. On August 17, it weighed anchor and headed for China, carrying a letter from Colonel Perkins to Cushing, dated August 11 from Boston.

"We have just heard," he wrote Cushing, "that the *Beaver,* by which this goes, is permitted to sail for Canton, for the Purpose of Carrying out a *Chinese Mandarin & his Suite.*" They were not allowed to remit funds, however, and could only hope that their Chinese creditors would wait patiently until they were permitted by the government to do so.

Jefferson had brushed Gallatin's suspicions aside, saying the gesture was "likely to bring lasting advantage to our merchants." Gallatin delayed his answer to the angry merchants until August 17. Diplomatically, he replied that not much could be done since the *Beaver* was scheduled to depart as he wrote, but for whatever solace it might be to them he said he understood the property to be brought home was that which Mr. Astor and Mr. Perkins had previously petitioned for and been refused. Why that made it all right now he did not bother to explain.[8]

In his next letter to Canton, Perkins was much more explicit to Cushing. "We hope you have done all you can with the *Beaver;* the result of that will be great, if you succeed." The letter was a short one, sent through Williams in England, but their anticipation of a coup, made him add once again before he closed "If you Ship largely in the *Beaver,* it will be a great thing."

As the embargo continued, the hopes of the Federalists rose. Fall elections were nearing. The economic situation had steadily deteriorated. Ports that had been filled with shipping, whose wharves had been crowded with bales, barrels, hogsheads, boxes, crates, parcels, and packages; whose streets had been filled with noise and bustle, with carters driving in every direction, sailors and laborers pushing through the throngs, merchants and clerks busy in their counting rooms or on the piers, auctioneers chanting wares; carts, drays, wheelbarrows, horses, and men making a terrific din, the coffee houses or the 'Change packed with underwriters, merchants, traders, politicians, all busy selling, buying, insuring, gossiping, plotting, planning, scheming—all this was a thing of the past.

Now the ships were dismantled, laid up. There was no bustle and stir. All was as quiet as a New England Sabbath. The decks of ships were cleared, hatches fastened down, spars housed on deck, lower mastheads covered with boxes against the weather, and decks matted or roofed over. Many shop windows had "for sale" signs in them. Grass had actually begun to grow in the streets. There was so little business in town that Perkins was able to spend nearly all of September in Vermont on a new project. But in Boston the politicking was intense.

In Washington, Jefferson had decided that his successor should be his present secretary of state, James Madison. The Federalists nominated Charles Pinckney, but when the electoral votes were counted, Madison was the victor. Still, the Federalists had more than tripled their electoral vote of four years before. All of New England had returned to the Federalist fold. The Perkins brothers could happily report their satisfaction in electing their friend, neighbor, and staunch Federalist, Josiah Quincy, to Congress.

Perkins reported to Canton his belief that if the embargo was not taken off in this present session of Congress, it would stay on all through 1809. The president, supported by one third of Congress, could keep it on indefinitely. "The writer of this," Perkins continued, "is however of the opinion that it cannot be left on so long, that if relief is not given thro' the legal channel, the Northern States will be so impatient as that the President will be under the necessity of using the Power vested in him and take off the Embarrassment, or See a general Insurrection against the general Government and its arbitrary measures."[9]

Insurrection? This was not the first time—nor would it be the last—that secession had been spoken of in New England. In 1804, when Jefferson had annexed Louisiana and the Federalists feared that this new territory would in gratitude vote Republican and forever foreclose their party from power, the flame of rebellion had been fanned by dissident politicians with a long list of other grievances. The death of Hamilton had eliminated their potential leader and the plans came to nothing. But the sentiment lingered, and as the embargo screws tightened on the Northerners, the 1804 idea seemed more and more attractive.

The winter was cold and snowy. In Salem the rich Republican merchant William Gray had been supplying flour to the poor since the start of the new year. Almost alone among the merchants he had supported the embargo. Charity concerts were held and a soup house was opened. A thousand applied in Boston. The Byle sisters reported that "The present unhappy time is felt by all classes of people." "We are full of alarms," noted Dr. Bentley, "Boston has been violent, Newburyport outrageous, Gloucester ridiculous."[10]

Eliza Quincy, writing to her husband Josiah, the new representative, on January 15, 1809 described how some Bostonians intended to submit to the new enforcement of the embargo. "Mr. James Perkins said this evening, that a letter he had received from you today had been taken by his brother, T. H. P. to Judge Parsons; and they had agreed with other gentlemen to meet this evening to concert measures. They only fear they shall not be able to prevent all premature violence. Mr. Perkins desired me to relate this to you on his authority."[11]

The measures included an agreement among the merchants that they would not give bond that their vessels might be carrying embargoed goods, nor would they permit the government to examine their vessels or shops. If the government broke open the ships, they agreed to institute suit. And they called for a town meeting. It was scheduled for the afternoon of January 23.

Rumors of secession were current in town. The *Chronicle* printed a call to action in its paper of that day: "The Republicans of the town of Boston who are adverse to a Separation of the States and to a connection with Great Britain or any other Foreign power and who are willing to rally around the standard of their country in defense of its laws are earnestly requested to attend the meeting at Faneuil Hall this day."

The *Centinel,* on the contrary, called the meeting the "Second Rocking of the Cradle of American Independence." Colonel Perkins, by a show of hands, was elected moderator of the meeting. He graciously declined the honor for reasons that soon became evident and Stephen Codman was elected in his place. Codman immediately recognized Perkins, who rose and said a few words explaining the purpose of the meeting. Then he pulled from his pocket a piece of paper and started to read it. The paper contained a petition prepared for the occasion calling upon the General Court to study "means of relief against the unconstitutional measures of the general government." A heated debate followed, but the Federalists were firmly in control. The motion to appoint a study committee carried overwhelmingly. Perkins and six other staunch, reliable Federalists were appointed to the committee.[12]

At 10 A.M. the next morning the meeting reconvened. A very strong resolution was presented by the study committee which emphatically stated that they were "not voluntarily to assist in carrying the Embargo Act into execution and all who should do so ought to be considered as enemies of the Constitution of the U.S., enemies of the State of Massachusetts and hostile to the liberties of the people." Four hours of emotional debate followed, but the Federalists had packed the hall and, when the vote was called for, carried the resolution by better than 85 percent.

New England was now in a "feverish state." Theodore Sedgwick, writing to his son early in February, stated that the men leading this resistance to the federal government "are not only the most sensible, but also the most temperate among us." It was precisely this group who had lost faith in the government. They wanted to preserve the union "if it can be done withont ruin," but were becoming convinced that this was probably impossible without a change in the government's policy. Sedgwick expected only "the most dreadful consequences."[13]

A fever is worst just before it breaks. So it was with the embargo. The good news came on March 4 that a bill to raise the embargo had passed Congress and was on the president's desk for signature. On March 5, in a letter to William Paine's father in Worcester, Perkins said he planned to have a ship ready to go to China by the first of April. The March 8 letter of the Central Committee signed by Perkins and others jubilated that "the mists of error are dissipated." They claimed that "the exertions of Massachusetts, and a few of her sister states," had saved the country from "an unjust and ruinous war." But Jefferson could not bring himself to sign this bill. He had invested too much emotion in the embargo to do that. He did permit it to become law, however, without his signature on the expiration of his administration.[14]

By March 15, plans to send the *Levant* to China were well underway. Captain Proctor was given his official instructions. On his arrival off the China coast he was to offer incentives to the boat captain to get a messenger to Canton quickly. Nobody must know the embargo had been lifted. "Report your ship as being from the North West Coast." None of the officers or men on the ship were to communicate with the mainland. The happy news from America would cause prices to rise precipitously.[15]

The demise of the embargo was celebrated in Boston by a subscription dinner in honor of the "Federal Phalanx" that had fought so valiantly in the Congress for its repeal. The dinner was held on March 27, three days after the *Levant* sailed.

Otis was toastmaster and the brothers Perkins had prominent places at the head table. Seventeen formal toasts were tossed off, then came the volunteer toasts from the banqueters. As the members of the head table left the room, their departure was heralded by extravagant remarks. When the colonel left he heard, no doubt to his deep satisfaction, a toast proposed to "Thomas H. Perkins whose public enterprise has given sinews to our government—whose private conduct an illustrious example of virtue."[16]

What actually had been the effect of the embargo on the Perkins firm? Nothing equal to their complaints. They had found the fifteen months hiatus a good time to pay off debts. Prices of goods, which they could afford to sit on, had risen to great heights and they were able to skim off an extra profit. The market had been "renovated," and old stocks of teas and other goods "run off." Having an overseas base with a man as competent as themselves in charge of it, enabled them to a large degree to keep part of their commerce alive. Cushing was able to buy teas, nankeens, and other China goods at low prices and hold them until the embargo was lifted. He was able to push the price of furs up to extremely profitable levels. And they had high hopes for the *Beaver*.

While all other merchants had to start even when the embargo went off in March, the Perkins were already there, thanks to Astor and the *Beaver*. As Perkins wrote Cushing in the fall of 1808, "If you have loaded the *Beaver,* we shall have no occasion to regret the embargo as she will have several months the start of others."[17]

Perkins was right. During the last week in May 1809, the long-awaited ship from China, the *Beaver,* sailed into New York harbor. It was the first ship to arrive from Canton since the lifting of the embargo. Her holds were crammed with teas, nankeens, silk, and china. Cushing had purchased $64,000 worth of teas alone, charging his 5 percent commission. Astor had fat cargoes, but so did J. & T. H. Perkins. On July 24, 1809, their share of the cargo was sold for more than $113,000. Once again the golden links of commerce had been rejoined. "Business as usual" was the order of the day.

There is something consummately sullen in a rainy day in the city . . . How different is a shower in the country! How pleasant is it, then, to sit at the window of my country house, and listen to the gentle hisses of rain-drops and leaves; to hear the drooping bird chirp faintly from the orchard, and the dripping cattle, gathering close, low at the gate.

Col. Benjamin Welles,
*Monthly Anthology,* 1807

---

# 18

# Short Blast on the Otter

Great Otter Creek begins high in the Green Mountains of southwestern Vermont, on the edge of Long Trail, and about six miles from Stratton Mountain. It is the longest flow of water wholly running within the state. For perhaps a third of its length it ripples along the border of the present Green Mountain National Forest, through towns with such rough hewn country names as Barnumville, East and North Dorset, Mount Tabor, Wallingford, then down to plain old Rutland.

The creek babbles by the marble mountains of Proctor, glides under covered bridges in Pittsford and Florence, and rushes down to Leicester Junction, where it picks up water from the three lakes of Fern, Silver, and Dunmore. Then it meanders through Salisbury and on into Middlebury. On speed the waters, by the Morgan Horse farm, by way of Weybridge, by Waltham, until they come to Vergennes.

Here at Vergennes, with all that distance behind it, the stream plunges thirty-three feet over and down a gauntlet of rock, then runs smoothly seven miles to its end in Lake Champlain.

For an engineer the most important part of Otter Creek is that fall of water at Vergennes. In an age of manpower, windpower, and horsepower one of the most wanted, most exploitable sources of power was water. Perkins Nichols, sometime Boston merchant and lawyer, was listed as an engineer on the occasion of his visit in the spring of 1807 to Vergennes. As such he was interested in the power represented by the Vergennes Falls and the fact that in the nearby village of Monkton there was a large bed of iron ore lying close to the surface of the ground. Iron ore and water power; put together the two spelled money.

Through that spring, summer, and into the fall, Nichols quietly bought up ore land in Monkton and neighboring Ferrisburg. He was apparently acting for a group of Boston merchants. The idea appears to have been Frank Bradbury's. Bradbury was forty-two years old and with his younger brother Charles had been operating a store on India Wharf for five years. The Perkins, having moved from Foster's Wharf to Stores 30 and 31 on India Wharf that spring, were now neighbors of Bradbury. Like many men with ideas Bradbury had to turn to others for the elusive "wherewithal." The Perkins brothers, the Higginsons, William Parsons, who had often joined in ventures with them, Bradbury, and a rising young lawyer, Col. Benjamin Welles, made up the group that in the fall of 1807 organized the Monkton Iron Company.

Eighteen hundred and seven seemed a good time to get into the iron-making business. The uncertain foreign situation, the large amount of idle capital, the desire of the country to attain self-sufficiency in the iron industry all combined to attract these astute businessmen. Iron manufacturing was then largely concentrated in Pennsylvania and New Jersey, where the best ore deposits were found. Because of transportation difficulties, most ironworks were located near ore beds. This added heavily to the costs of getting the finished product to the market.

Right from the start, four of "the concerned" took the lead in the project of making a success of the Monkton Iron Company. Two of them were younger men, Welles, twenty-six, and George Higginson, twenty-seven. Welles brought his legal skill to bear on the company's problems. Young Higginson was proposed by his father Stephen as secretary and treasurer of the company. Although he had not made much of a name for himself in commercial circles except as his father's son, he was accepted for the dual job, which meant, in effect, he became the chief operating officer for the firm, working mostly in Boston.

Two of the others were in their forties: Frank Bradbury and Colonel Perkins. Bradbury agreed to move to Vermont and become the resident manager of the company for a yearly salary of $1,200. The colonel had a care for every detail of the company's business, but especially seemed to make it his concern to get and give technical advice. This was fine, but neither he nor any of the others connected with the company had any experience in this field. It was a case of the blind leading the blind. They had to feel their way at each stage of the project.

Very quickly the dominating personality in the company became the colonel's. Young Higginson had been a private under Perkins in the cadets and so would have been accustomed to taking orders from him. Welles and Perkins seem to have been of a mind in most matters. And Bradbury was in Vergennes.

Aside from its excellent waterpower, Vergennes had several advantages for being headquarters of the operation. A small village of some five hundred people built on the ridge above its falls, it was surrounded by miles of virgin forest. Abundant timber was essential, at that stage in iron technology, for smelting iron. It was turned into charcoal and blast furnaces consumed charcoal in tremendous quantities. A "blast" in such a furnace would ordinarily last nine or ten months, each "blast" consuming more than two hundred acres of timber.

From Vergennes to Lake Champlain Otter Creek is a narrow, winding stream, but deep enough to float a sloop and provide easy access to and from the lake for the transport of charcoal and ore. And trained people, of a sort, were available in Vergennes. When the Boston entrepreneurs came on the scene, there was already a grist mill, two saw mills, a carding mill, a rolling and slitting mill, and a bloomery forge all operating at the falls. These provided a pool of men with some experience in small-scale iron manufacturing.

One of Bradbury's first moves when he arrived in Vergennes that winter of 1807–08 was to arrange for a long-term lease of the water rights of the falls, along with buildings already on the land, plus six acres on the west side of the stream. He got all this for $3,000 and an annual rental of $300. Now the money started to flow out. In Boston James Perkins entered in the firm's large account book, "Blotter N," the first of many such items, "Paid to Benj. Welles $2,500 as first assessment of the Monkton Iron Co."[1]

The colonel was busy the last month of 1807 writing to find out how they should go about the new business of being iron men. To Dr. Nathan Hayward of Plymouth, Massachusetts, who had some experience in the subject, he honestly admitted "we are novices in this Business."

Dr. Hayward had already supplied him with the name of Daniel Johnson, one of the men who built the water wheel for his furnace. Perkins wrote Johnson the same day to arrange a trip to Vermont for the end of the month. "It is our intention to erect several forges and at least one furnace, and we shall probably put in rolling, slitting, and nail machines." The ambitions of the company were not small. If Johnson could come to Boston a few days before the trip, "we could have a consultation with the whole of the Gentlemen engaged in the Business."[2]

By the time Perkins, Welles, and Johnson were on their way north, the Embargo Act had gone into effect. But in Vergennes, the seaboard and its troubles were far away. Bradbury had plunged into this work, tackling two of his big problems almost immediately: "Coal"—as charcoal was called—and money. A dozen miles away was the largest town in his immediate area, Middlebury. He traveled there to place a notice in the paper for coal and to talk with the bank directors to see if they would advance him Vermont money against drafts on Boston. A couple of days later he wrote Higginson to send up "ten good Irishmen" so he could get started clearing the earth off the ore beds.[3]

The plans for the company were on an extensive scale, almost unprecedented. They proposed a completely unified operation: a single company that mined the ore, smelted it, provided the coal from their own lands for the smelting, had the sloops to transport the ore and coal, refined the pig iron, wrought it into nails, pots, kettles, sheets, bars, provided boarding accommodations for the many laborers involved, and even contemplated furnishing library books to them! It was unique for its time, and incorporated elements that a dozen years later would be hailed as pioneering efforts when introduced at the textile mills in Lowell.

There would even be a company store! Since a sizable work force was planned, these would require supplies. Why not open a store for their convenience, where the company could make a tidy little profit as well? To a company made up of so many erstwhile storekeepers, such a thought would have been most natural. It became one of Bradbury's first tasks.

Bradbury was operating on four fronts at one and the same time. His first job was building the iron works itself. This required engineering knowledge which neither he nor the directors possessed. They made do with what they could pick up from books, what they learned from talking with people who were operating furnaces, and the skill of the few "experts" they were able to hire. Perkins had heard of an improved form of air blast that was used in some furnaces, employing two wooden cylinders instead of the leather-type bellows. He strongly advocated using this, but Bradbury complained justifiably that he had no one available who had any knowledge of how to make the new cylinder bellows. So he proposed continuing with the ordinary bellows. Besides he had already purchased the leather for it.

Bradbury's second task was getting the ore beds into a workable condition. Through that first spring he had a gang of Irishmen, under the direction of his brother Theophilus, removing the banks over the ore. The ore itself was found in rock ledges very near the surface of the ground, and it was relatively easy to obtain. Lacking power tools the entire work was pick and shovel, with some blasting to break up the rock and ore ledges.

His third job was to obtain a dependable source of charcoal for the furnace. Not only did a great quantity have to be prepared beforehand and coal houses built in which to protect it from the weather, but a continuous supply line had to be arranged to insure a regular flow of the coal. This was done in two ways: contracts were let with local farmers and others for specified amounts of charcoal at an agreed upon price; and the company itself also had a crew of men making coal on lands the company owned.

His fourth job involved the organizing and supervising of all this work. He did an amazing amount of this entirely by himself. Running the store, writing and copying the letters, keeping the financial accounts, arranging the boarding accommodations, inspecting timber land to be purchased, getting a sloop built, and buying all the tools, horses, carts, needed for the multitudinous jobs.

That is, he did it himself, with the constant "advise and consent" of the directors in Boston every step of the way. The Boston group kept Bradbury on a strict rein. Even minor decisions had to be cleared with them. Perkins had the major voice in the Boston decisions, but all took part. And Boston was constantly admonishing Bradbury to practice rigid economy and to avoid "designing" men.

By the first of March 1808, the slitting mill, which had been shut down by the cold weather, was back in operation. A gang of men were at work digging ore, and Bradbury advised the directors that twelve men were required for every thirty to fifty tons dug per week. In the woods he had a large gang cutting timber for the charcoal making.

While Bradbury was getting underway in Vermont, the Boston gentlemen were busy trying to find men with experience who could supervise the technical aspects of the project and manage it when put in operation. Daniel Johnson, the wheelwright from Plymouth, was hired to construct the mechanical works. He was supposed to arrive at Vergennes in March or April, but by May he had not yet come. A foundryman by the name of Bates did arrive, however, and with an excellent reputation. He was to construct the furnace and run the foundry. Bates arrived with two stone masons, to be used first to build the furnace foundation. Bradbury, who was eager to speed up the construction, asked Boston to send up more. He was dissatisfied with the local "mechanicks" and complained that they expected high wages. The embargo might have caused wide unemployment in the coastal towns and driven down wages, but as far as Bradbury could see, it had not had that effect in Vergennes.

Perkins and Higginson decided to go to Vergennes themselves to see how Bradbury was progressing. Leaving Boston about May 15, they had reached Walpole, New Hampshire, by the morning of May 17. The stage was delayed for awhile, and they decided to walk along the road until it caught up with them. It was only four miles to the Connecticut River and the town of Bellows Falls. Higginson wrote his wife the next night that "I never enjoyed a walk more in my life." Both the road and the countryside were "most beautiful." Learning that their next stage would not leave Rutland until Thursday the nineteenth, they spent most of Wednesday leisurely fishing near Rutland. On horseback they rode to a pond on the top of one of the mountains where famous trout were said to have been caught. After fishing for a while with no luck, they decided to follow up a little brook into the lake. "I became tired & gave up the chace. THP—who caught a few small ones was delighted with the fatigue as the thing he most wanted."

That night they slept in Rutland, taking an early stage the next morning. By the afternoon they had arrived in Vergennes, after traveling over very rough roads from Rutland, "hardly fit for our ladies to travel on," wrote Higginson. Greeted by the Bradburys, he found Mrs. Bradbury "a sweet little woman—she is at last likely to have a child, as she appears quite near being confined." They rode over to inspect the ore beds in Monkton and "a furnace in the neighborhood." Higginson, in spite of his poor health, rode part way and found himself stiff, but "I shall persevere." He was glad, he told his wife, that he had not taken his "thin clothes." It had been very cold and the beginning of the week, the frost "hereabouts was severe for several nights."

During the next two days, the men traveled across Lake Champlain to see the ore beds in New York. Higginson still felt well "notwithstanding that I have rode 16 miles on horseback—walked 5—& rowed myself about 8 miles." The excursion left Perkins "unwell with a violent sick headache." In a few days they planned to travel on to Burlington and then return to Boston, hoping to arrive early in June. After their inspection they concluded: "There is a great deal to be done here, to get well under way—when we are so—it will be a good affair."[4]

Work continued into June. Bradbury had increased the number of men at the ore bed and experimented with sinking a shaft to try out deep mining. It quickly filled up with water. This was just another in the series of frustrations the whole project was to experience. The houses for the laborers were nearly finished. Earlier Bradbury had suggested to Perkins that perhaps he could find in Boston "two good ship Cooks to come up" and "Cook the provisions" as he had been unable to find any suitable person in the area. With the embargo on, there should be plenty of such available and willing to work at a low wage. The blacksmith shop was busy, the coal houses completed, and men were chopping wood and making charcoal. Three teams carted ore from Monkton to Vergennes. Three more brought in the charcoal, but even these, thought Bradbury, were not enough.[5]

July came and went, and still Johnson did not arrive. Bradbury had been expecting him since March and was increasingly annoyed. Construction had reached the point where they were beginning on the waterworks that would power the machinery and Johnson's experience was badly needed. With the season so far advanced, Bradbury did not dare wait any longer, and decided to go ahead with the work himself, depending on as much local advice as he could get.

During Perkins's visit in May, the men decided that it would be cheaper to move the vast quantities of charcoal by water rather than by the primitive roads. The colliers need only bring the coal to the banks of Otter Creek and boats would take over. Bradbury sent one of his chief carpenters into the woods in July to cut the necessary timber for a sloop. The boat's hardware was ordered from Boston, but to carry the heavy ironwork overland was a problem. The solution was to send it by boat from Boston to New York, up the Hudson River to Troy and then cart it overland the one hundred odd miles to Vergennes.

Now that summer was upon them, their location in a farming community began to cause problems. The local workers started to drift away. It was time to hay. With labor short, the work slowed down, just in the best season of the year to complete the project. On top of this, in the middle of July, Bradbury came down with the "billious fever."

He was ill for ten days, although some work continued in his absence. The flumes that were to carry the water from the millpond to the waterwheels were raised. With the outside of the furnace completed, the masons were at work on the walls of the casting house that surrounded it. The end of that month Bradbury sat down to report to the directors his efforts to date. He began with an apology: "I am sorry our works have progressed so slowly, in the beginning of the season I did not drive business in expectation of Mr. Johnson & Col. Perkins being on the spot to give directions to their mind." As for the ore, "Mr. Smith thinks in one month we shall have at least 2000 tons out." As to when the furnace would actually be started, he hedged a bit: "shall endeavor to get ready if possible for a Blast this fall but there is much to do." In spite of everything his hopes of realizing a rich profit for himself and the other directors was not dimmed. "I am more than ever persuaded it may become more than ever I calculated."[6]

The long-awaited Johnson finally arrived in September and set to work. It was well into October, however, before Bates had the furnace finished. Johnson had not yet completed the waterwheel. At the end of October, Bates went to Boston to confer with the directors about starting the blast. It was felt that everything could be ready by December. But perhaps it might be better to wait until the spring? They had to remember, however, that they were not the only ones in the business. Nearby in New Haven was another furnace already in blast, and Bradbury reported it as "doing very well." Bradbury had recommended purchasing that furnace in the spring to stop "the spirit of others interfering with us." His advice had not been followed. Now the effects of that neglect were being seen. "They take much coal that might come to us and continually [are] seeking out ore that may eventually diminish our establishment."

Bradbury was doing some seeking himself. He had been offered five hundred acres across the lake in New York state with a fine stand of hardwood from which the best charcoal was made. The owner wanted $3.50 an acre, and although Perkins had favored the purchase all the directors had to vote. Bradbury wanted a quick decision as the owner's "situation for money is such that I think a better bargain may now be made." All through October he tried to get a decision out of the directors. Finally in November they agreed to the purchase.

Also in November came the fifth assessment. This represented $150,000 paid in by the shareholders. Bradbury observed "your alarm as to the expenses" and acknowledged that the works far exceeded his calculations "but they are executed so differently from my calculations." Enough ore was now on hand for a nine to twelve months blast, the establishment was "on a good footing," and he could see nothing to prevent "a permanent good profit arising from the business." But the only immediate source of profit from the business was the store. "We sell much Rum, besides all our supplies, & at a good profit, every 10 Days takes a Hogshead, & our other goods turn into all our Coaling payments, & in a variety of other channels, & it is an object to be well supplied with every article for our workmen, with our Colliers, miners, & Carpenters etc. we have as many as an Hundred men at work & all draw their supplies from us." Money made the work go, and rum made the men go.

The proposed date for starting the blast came and went. They were still not ready. An unusually cold winter had set in. Thick ice sealed up Otter Creek and heavy snow covered everything. They had to shut down until spring. Bradbury sent encouraging predictions to Boston as to what they might anticipate. "The furnace will turn out 4½ tons of common castings a day, if she goes well, the lowest wholesale price will be $50 per ton and in heavy ware much higher, it may be stated $112 per day clear money, if she continues 12 months it will give . . . $40,000. This sum is more than 20% on the amount expended." The figures were comforting, but the "ifs" were many.

With the works soon to be started, it was necessary to locate iron workers. This was not easy. Men with the needed skills were not readily found behind the stone walls and in the cow barns of Vermont. By January 1809, Otis Pettee, a refiner by trade, had been hired. He was the only experienced ironman on the place besides Bates. Slowly through the winter help drifted in as word spread. In February a stove moulder who had worked with Bates in Canada made himself available. Another Canadian refiner was engaged in March. Bates also hired two firemen "and a sufficient number of moulders to begin" work with, "and as we are daily applied to we think we shall do better than to send out for workmen."

When the ice melted the waterwheel could begin to turn. The end of March came and still no end to the cold weather. Bradbury tried cutting the ice to release the wheel but it only froze again so quickly that he soon gave it up as wasted effort. In the woods the snow was two feet deep. By mid-April the snow had gone and coaling operations could begin again. The wheel was now free of ice, but the conduit that led water to it was still frozen solid. When it finally thawed they discovered it had been damaged by the ice and had to be rebuilt before they could start the blast. One problem followed another.

Johnson regulated the bellows so that on the first trial they exceeded their expectations. Now the end of the beginning was in sight. On Friday, May 11, "Mr. Bates put fire into the furnace." When it was sufficiently hot—in ten or twelve days—they would charge it with ore. The machine to wash the ore was finished and in operation.

On Sunday morning, May 20, 1809, water was let into the conduit and the great wheel slowly began to turn. The bellows engaged, the charge put into the stack, and at long last the blast began. "Mr. Bates," Bradbury reported to Perkins with understandable pride, "as well as all the workmen are much pleased with the work of the furnace, that they make iron fast and the prospect is good for a successful blast." Bates was gradually increasing the charge, and in the last twenty-four hours they had drawn off the furnace three times. Bradbury was impressed with the caution and prudence of Bates and predicted that "he will make more Iron per Week than he ever made in any Furnace."

The satisfaction in Vergennes was as nothing compared to the joy of the directors in Boston; after eighteen months of patiently doling out money, they had reached the eighth assessment and had $200,000 tied up.

Had they rejoiced too early? Soon there were disquieting signs. "The

Blast," Bradbury reported, "is much more powerful" than any Bates had known. "This will wear out the Hearth I fear sooner than we expected." When they put in the new hearth it would have to be thicker and longer. By Thursday of the first week of blast, the furnace was turning out more iron than Bates expected "or desired." "He took of[f] three Tons in the 24 hours." They had been using Swanton ore, and Bates now changed to Monkton ore to see if he could lighten the burden, and keep the furnace in a good state. "The stack Stands very well, the intense Heat makes the stones sweat and some small cracks but not as much as is common." But still "she exceeds expectations, and I know of nothing to prevent a successful Blast."

Through June, Bradbury reported good progress. They were putting in eight boxes of ore at each charge, and were charging it fifteen times a day. It was now producing about a ton and a half a day, and as the furnace worked well at this pace, "they conclude not to augment it untill the Cam Rigs are on." Perkins had gone to New York and at the end of the month Bradbury wrote him there to tell him the furnace was "gaining" and "the Blast is as good as Need be, and everything looks well." It seemed as if they could relax their anxiety and turn to other matters.

By early July they were slowly increasing the number of charges to eighteen a day. Bradbury was rebuilding the dam and dickering to replace the small saw mill of the firm with a larger one. He was worried about the flume, which he considered the weakest part of the works. Perkins had been to Vergennes and seen how well the blast was going. Bates thought the iron was good "and works kindly." The wooden cams, put in during Perkins's visit, seemed to be making the blast go more steadily. They were still increasing the charge cautiously. When they had been in blast for two months, Bradbury felt relaxed enough about conditions to advise a gentleman in Hartford, Connecticut, that "our establishment will become not only a valuable one for the Country, but a profitable one for the proprietors."

Then at the end of July Bates came down with summer fever and the blast started to go poorly. "Mr. Bates says he has blast enough but still we do not make iron as we ought. He now says the hearth was not laid as it ought to be." Bradbury was mortified to have to report this to Boston. Nor did he quite know what to do about it. He was too preoccupied with the over-all concerns and lacked the skill to take a greater charge of the furnace operations. He now began to have some doubts about Bates's ability. "I do think there has been a want of energy." On top of this, Johnson fell ill, and the weather turned so rainy that all outside work came to a halt. The furnace soon was running so poorly that Bradbury had no alternative but to suspend operations. On August 6, after only seventy-nine days in blast, the furnace was shut down. The trouble appeared to be in the hearth, as Bates had said. With Bates still sick, Bradbury supervised the rebuilding of the hearth himself, for his confidence in Bates had vanished.

"He has blundered from the foundation." As Bradbury examined Bates's work more closely he saw that "the stack ought to have been a larger square, the arches to have been higher, and as for the interior, it was all wrong." With Johnson's help, he was repairing the damages. As for Bates, "he has conducted so much like an old cat that I do not want him around me." George Higginson had arrived in England and Colonel Perkins wrote the sad news to him. "We have taken out the old hearth, altered the lining, added to the highth of the stack, and discharged Bates, so that an entire revolution was worked." The one consolation he could report was that the "ore was all we could wish it."[7]

Unfortunately, all the troubles were not in the production. The prospects of a killing in the iron market had vanished too. Any hopes of taking advantage of the embargo or a possible war had been frustrated by the long delays in getting started. With the end of the embargo in March 1809, cheap foreign iron once more began to be imported. Monkton iron could not compete. But this was somewhat academic to Bradbury and the directors, for at the moment Vergennes had little to sell and its future was problematical.

O, how sweet did it seem
What a feast, what a dream
What a pleasure to smoke the segar!

Philip Freneau

# 19

# Far Different from Our Calculations

The end of the embargo not only sent many ships scrambling overseas in pursuit of a quick profit, it released a fresh spirit of enterprise at home in the men of business and trade. New projects were proposed on every hand. Perkins was discovering, for example, that money could be made out of land and bridges.

Cambridge adjoined Boston, but the Charles River and a state of mind completely separated them. In 1809 the town of Cambridge was essentially Harvard College and the houses around it. The original way to Boston had been a long seven and a half miles through Roxbury and over Boston Neck. In 1786 the Charlestown Bridge shortened the trip to four miles, and a second bridge in 1793 from West Boston to a point on the Cambridge shore cut another mile off the traveling.* Both were private toll bridges.

Watching this activity was a promoter par excellence, Andrew Craigie. Craigie's schemes usually benefited only Craigie, such as his nefarious Scioto project which sold unowned Ohio land to French refugees.

* Now called Longfellow Bridge.

Craigie had a bridge of his own in mind. Further down the Charles, where it is joined by Miller's River, and the two empty into the harbor, was Lechmere's Point—then a barren upland surrounded on the west and south by swamps. At high tide it was sometimes an island. There were about three hundred acres of land here going to waste, at least as promoters view land. Opposite Lechmere's Point on the Boston side was Barton's Point. If a bridge connected these two, Craigie saw the possibility of making some money out of this "worthless" land.

As early as 1795 Craigie started to buy land in the area. By 1803 he had most of the tract in his possession. Early in 1805 he petitioned the legislature for the right to erect a toll bridge. Opposition immediately arose. The West Boston Bridge people naturally argued against it, foreseeing a loss of revenue to their bridge.

After much political maneuvering, Craigie got his bridge in February 1807. Then a title dispute delayed actual construction until the summer of 1808. A bridge which goes nowhere is of little value, and so Craigie planned a road from his bridge to the Cambridge Common, where the main roads from the west converged. He began construction, but a crucial strip of land, which the owners would not sell, blocked its completion.

In the middle of 1808, Craigie received a letter from Harry Otis, president of the State Senate. Otis bluntly offered a deal. If he was let into the land speculation "upon such terms as would make it an object," then he would use his influence in the legislature to help Craigie get the needed piece of land by eminent domain. He not only wanted a large slice of the pie "as to justify exertions on my part," but he wanted to let in "a cooperation of friends as will tend to promote the new settlement."[1]

Otis's "friends" turned out to be five Federalists in the legislature, including Colonel Perkins. On November 30, 1808, Craigie sold ten of sixty shares in the Lechmere Point Corporation to this group. Perkins paid $1,000 for his share. Otis took three shares. At this price, Craigie had already tripled his profits on his original investment.

The group, in Perkins's name, petitioned the legislature in June 1809 for a committee to mark out a highway from the new bridge to the Common, and the right to use the state's power of eminent domain. Republicans rose in righteous indignation at this Federalist trick. They bewailed the "incessant machinations and intrigues of Mr. Andrew Craigie." It was pointed out that he had tried twice before to get the state's help in securing his road, "and the same game he is evidently now playing, by the petition signed by T. H. Perkins and others."[2]

Despite the political prestige of the Otis group the petition failed. Back to the Cambridge town authorities went the tireless Mr. Craigie. This time his persistance paid off. In July his road was approved, but so that his victory would not be complete, they laid the road out over a different route than that which he had used for the part of the road already under construction. Craigie's Bridge was completed that summer and its opening timed for the commencement exercises at Harvard, August 30, 1809.

The event was doubly important for the Perkins family. Their first member graduated from Harvard that day, James's son, James, Jr. Since he played no part in the graduating exercises, he apparently had not distinguished himself, but at least he had graduated. His cousin Eliza remembered him as "a nice boy, not handsome; short and thick-set, with blue eyes and sandy hair; very fond of athletics, the best fencer and dancer about." When he went to college, she said, "he got into a gay set, Kirk Boott and others, and I remember wondering as a girl to see Aunt James putting up bottles of wine to send over to Cambridge to Him."[3]

Early that September, the colonel's oldest boy, Thomas, Jr., went back to Exeter Academy in Exeter, New Hampshire, where his uncle, Dr. Benjamin Abbott, was the strict and successful headmaster. Young Gorham Palfrey, whose father once worked in the Perkins countinghouse, went over and spent the night with young Tom, as he was going to the academy too. With several other returning Exeter students they crowded into the coach early the next morning. Tom Jr. was almost thirteen. That he may that early have been following in his cousin Jim's grapestained footsteps is suggested by the report that Palfrey "was constantly jostled by his rowdy and drunken companions."[4]

Colonel Welles was also traveling that month of September 1809. He had gone north to Vergennes, where the furnace was being rebuilt. Heavy rains and cold weather slowed the work down, and it was not until the twenty-eighth of the month that Bradbury reported the furnace in blast for the third time. To replace Bates, he had hired a man who had been working for the Salisbury Furnace in Connecticut, Joseph Brinton, to "blow my furnace." By October, he was able to write Perkins that "Mr. Brinton behaves as well as he was recommended to."

Brinton was satisfied with the working of the furnace, and predicted he would soon have it producing twenty-five tons a week. By the end of October they had only been able to get twenty-one tons, far lower than the thirty-one tons Bradbury had first estimated. His crying need now was for molders. The men he had were making stoves from patterns Bradbury had at the works. They were using many of these themselves at the establishment, and a sale was beginning to develop. Customers were "constantly calling." This was cheerful news to Boston ears, but Bradbury still hoped that Perkins would "be able to make us a visit as you proposed."[5]

Perkins was unable to visit Vergennes at that moment. Instead, he was out on another prospecting trip with Perkins Nichols. Nichols had located an abandoned lead mine in Northampton, Massachusetts, and invited the colonel along to look at it. It had been first discovered in 1679, mined a few years, abandoned for a century, and then, shortly before the Revolution, worked rather assiduously. But the Revolution had, strangely enough, put it out of business and it lay idle until Nichols came along. What the two men saw looked good to them and Nichols bought the property, Perkins agreeing to take a third interest for $2,666.66.

While his brother was inspecting the lead mine, James attended the next stage in the development of Mr. Craigie's land speculation. The owners of the land now included Christopher Gore who had acquired ten of Craigie's fifty shares, still leaving Craigie with a controlling two-thirds interest. On Saturday, November 4, 1809, the group met at the Exchange Coffee House and organized the Lechmere Point Corporation.

Otis, Ebenezer Francis, and Colonel Perkins formed a committee to study the building of a dam across the mouth of the Charles River. Three weeks later another meeting was held, at which Craigie proposed that his partners in the land company might also like to buy into the bridge company. Perkins and Francis were to study this proposal.

The next meeting was held at the palatial Otis residence on Beacon Street, but Perkins had finally responded to Bradbury's urgings and gone to Vergennes. His fellow proprietors, however, voted to accept Craigie's proposition and buy into the bridge company. They decided to build a blacksmith shop, put up hay scales and a wharf, and heard a progress report on the construction of a brew house. Every incentive was to be offered the wagon men to use their bridge and road.

Perhaps the colonel's trip to Vergennes was the one his eldest daughter remembered later. "We passed through Chelmsford," she wrote, "which was a clearing in the forest, with burnt stumps, fire-weed, and raspberry bushes about. We stopped there and some of the party went up to see where a bear had been trapped the night before. On that journey we met Beza Tucker, who thought he could live only on human milk. Father said he supposed he was looking for a *wet-nurse*."[6]

They needed more than a wet-nurse to help them with their iron works. Higginson, who was still in England, had been implored to send "any new works which are practicable on the subject of Iron making." The unsubstantial nature of their enterprise is revealed in the remark the colonel made to Higginson about the construction of the hearth and lining of their furnace: "we were governed by a plate . . . in the Philosophical Magazine of Tillock."[7]

That fall the temp stone on the furnace gave way, and the blast was again suspended. When the furnace cooled down it was evident that the hearth needed to be replaced as well. The discharged Bates was again cursed. Such had been his "miserable calculation" that "a large substantial hearth cannot be put in." The furnace repairs were completed by January 13, 1810, but now Brinton had left the job. Bradbury felt by this time that he had learned enough to give it a try himself. He had hired two "careful sober" firemen and with their "united" knowledge put the furnace into blast. For the moment it seemed to run smoothly.[8]

Good molders were now his problem. The ones he had been able to get were "lazy intemperate and drunken dogs." Nor were his refiners doing as well as he expected. Bradbury was just too deficient in technical knowledge to know what was wrong. "I have no books that treat on this subject and nobody of any information here on the business. If you find any treatise on the refining of iron and can send it me, it may assist me." Nor had the refiners time to show whether they were good or bad before the cold weather arrived and froze the water wheels. Once again the iron making ceased.[9]

When the hearth was examined it was found to have worn badly in the few short months the furnace had been operating. It had to be replaced, but they did not have enough stones to do the job. The stones came from Troy and the bad weather made transport impossible. They would have to wait until the weather changed.

By contrast the lead mine in Northampton seemed to be proceeding with encouraging rapidity. Twelve men were employed and the shaft had been sunk fifty feet through sheer granite. The deeper they went the richer the vein appeared. The ore was embedded in a vein of white spar, which "is said to produce 60% of lead." Each ton of ore also yielded between fifty and seventy ounces of silver. They had found some specimens of zinc, but not in any great quantity. Traces of barite and copper showed up and "the workmen say this is a favorable indication, we should rather have this confirmed from higher authority." So the colonel asked Benjamin Silliman, professor of chemistry at Yale, to visit the mine with him. It was Silliman's report that encouraged them.[10]

Confidence was strong enough for Samuel G. Perkins and Isaac Davis to buy a sixth interest. The Perkins brothers sold half of their third to David Hinkley, who seems to have paid $8,750 for his sixth, a rather neat profit in a few short months for the brothers; and they still owned a sixth!

As if running an ironworks, a lead mine, the Massachusetts branch of the Federalist party, a worldwide trade, and a land and bridge speculation in Cambridge were not enough to fill his working hours, the colonel decided this was a good time to build a house! He had ten years earlier bought land across the street from his house on Pearl Street, and on it started the construction of a home of his own where he would spend the next two decades of his life.

In Vermont, Bradbury was continuing to have problems with his help. The work of the refiners turned out to be "far different from our calculations at first," a text that could apply to their whole venture in the iron business at that point. It took most of the winter to get a new crew of four. A new blastman had been hired from Canada, a Mr. Salmon Washburn, to fill the job Bates and Brinton had vacated. Johnson had returned to Boston for the winter, and now the work of coaxing him back to Vergennes had to be begun again. Bradbury was beginning to become disenchanted with Mr. Johnson as well: "a very expensive fellow. Our works have cost an immense sum yet the forge bellows works bad and the hammer gates I have altered." Two weeks later, Bradbury was warning Boston, "I am quite displeased with Johnson. He has cost us double the expense of his wages by his delays. You must not consider him so highly. I do not expect him here until June or July."[11]

Most of the potash kettles Bradbury had cast the fall before were still at the works, unsold. When questioned about this by Boston, Bradbury blamed the bad traveling throughout the winter and the difficulty of carting the huge kettles to possible customers. They were scarcely the kind of item a Yankee peddler could put in his pack. Another reason, he had to confess, was that "every Furnace has been making them." Too many kettles, too few buyers. So the colonel had been right after all. He might not know much about the technical matters of running an ironworks, but he knew the "market." Still a few dollars were flowing in.

Perkins had one diversion that summer from the dispiriting news from Vergennes. The minister who had been sent from Great Britain to settle the Chesapeake affair, Francis James Jackson, had behaved so undiplomatically that Madison declared him persona non grata. Sensing a chance to embarrass the administration, the Boston Federalists invited Jackson to visit there on his way home. Tactlessly, he agreed to come.

Perkins was prominent in Jackson's escort when he arrived on Friday, June 1, 1810. The Federalists had invited Jackson to be present at the annual dinner of the Ancient and Honorable Artillery Company on the following Monday. He was to march with them in the parade to Faneuil Hall, but he failed to appear. After stalling the parade as long as possible, it finally took off without him. Perkins was sent to locate Jackson, whom he found waiting at his boarding house. Together, the envoy of King George the Third and one of Boston's leading merchant princes had to scurry through lanes and alleys and cut across vacant lots to catch up with the marchers.

Perkins headed for a spot on State Street near the Old State House where he thought the procession might be. He miscalculated and they arrived too early. It would not do to be found lurking on the sidewalk, so he took Jackson into a nearby jewelry store to wait. At the proper time as the procession swung down the street, he hustled Jackson out of the shop and smuggled him into the line of march.[12]

Vergennes had no such diversions. They were busy repairing the furnace. By the end of June, the work was done, and the night sky was lit by a dull red. They were in blast for the fourth time. The new foundryman, Mr. Washburn, like those before him, was predicting a long and successful blast. The iron was flowing, and Bradbury had ten molders to shape it. Johnson had finally arrived and was hard at work. But it was the usual story. Two hours after the blast began, the flume carrying water to the waterwheel sprang a leak. This was quickly repaired and for twenty-four days everything seemed to be all right. Then Washburn came down with the "fever and ague." Four days later, Bradbury gave up hope for him. Next, the water supply to the wheel dwindled and the bellows came to a stop. Since all the workmen were busy building the flume for the new grist mill and saw mill, the furnace repairs had to wait.

By July the fever had spread among many of the crew. Washburn died, Johnson came down with rheumatism, and to cap it all Bradbury wrote to Boston that he found himself "so unwell that I must take a journey to see if it will reinstate me." His wife too had had a fever. He decided to visit "the Springs" and then go on to Troy and Albany. He left for two weeks and all activities of the Monkton Iron Company ground to a halt.[13]

With fall, prospects at Vergennes again showed their seasonal upswing. Bradbury had returned from his vacation full of energy; Johnson had the forges nearly done; and Brinton had offered to come back. Boston sent Welles down to New Jersey to see if he could find some good men to take charge of the refining. A clever mechanic and inventor, Jacob Perkins, no relation to the colonel, had been sent up from Boston to improve the mechanical operations. The bellows did not give a steady enough air blast, and the hammers in the forge were so erratic that half the time was spent just keeping them in running order.

The sickness of the men, however, continued into the fall. When Perkins arrived, he was most reluctant to stay and risk his health. Bradbury persuaded him to stay long enough to correct the main deficiencies of the bellows, hammers, and one of the forge bellows. Welles had had good luck in New Jersey. The men running the Union Forge were most obliging and sent five refiners who arrived near the end of October. Bradbury was quite pleased with them; they seemed to know their business and were willing to work at it. They repaired the forges to their satisfaction and began work. Then, "before they finished one Soupe they said it was impossible to work with the blast they had." The air could not be regulated—it had only one speed. It had to go faster or slower, as needed. "It is very strange," wrote poor Bradbury, "that Johnson, Kinsley, & Perkins did not discover this defect." But the men told him how to correct it, and Bradbury set to work to do it.

Brinton was ill when he arrived to take charge of the furnace. The fifth blast began on October 22, yet Bradbury was troubled. It had become second nature for something to go wrong. On November 23 it was stopped once again, and it looked like repairs on it would have to wait until spring. The refineries were the one bright spot. They were averaging five soupes a day (six soupes weighed five hundred pounds), and claimed they would soon be making six or seven a day. Even this was not to last. "The severe weather froze up the wheels" and that was that. Bradbury's health was such that he was not giving much time to the work and he ended this report to Boston on the lowest tone ever. By New Year's Day, 1811, the last piece of equipment still functioning, the slitting mill, gave way and silence fell over the Monkton Iron Company once more.

These times touch monied Worldlings with dismay:
Even rich men, brave by nature, taint the air
With words of apprehension and despair.

William Wordsworth, Sonnet XII

# 20

# With No One To Tell My Cares To

Amid general commercial gloom, war suddenly provided a market. Wellington's armies on the Spanish peninsula had to eat. Europe was too busy fighting to till its fields and grow its own wheat; and the grain it grew was often destroyed by the combatants. Outside trade had to supply flour and breadstuffs. The Perkinses joined with the Higginsons and "entered pretty largely into the flour business."[1]

They told Henry Higginson that spring of 1811 that "the shipments to Spain and Portugal are the only speculations we have engaged in this Year." This was not quite true. The war in Europe had encouraged the colonies of Spain and Portugal in South America to revolt. "Will not all Spanish America be bitten by the Tarantula of Liberty, and set to dancing? It appears to us that there will be a general attempt to throw off the subjection under which they have been held to the Mother Country, and that a new speculation will be opened to us, provided our wise rulers keep out of a war with Great Britain, which by the bye, we have some fear will not be the case." They tested some ventures on the Latin American market but for the moment nothing much came of it.[2]

What was to be done? Perkins Nichols had an answer. It was the usual one: sink some more money in the ground. With an iron works that was in trouble, with a lead mine that was not yet in full operation, the Perkins brothers went out and bought a third interest in a marble quarry. Too much money was a problem—there was no profit in keeping money idle. They had been more than successful in times that had bankrupt other entrepreneurs. Excess capital brought in no return unless it was invested. Nor were there that many opportunities to invest in at that stage of American business life. The result was this rather desperate leap into enterprises over which they had a chance of exerting some direct control and which, if they could be successfully developed, would be additions to the country's welfare as well as their own.

Too much money was the direct cause of the other venture of the colonel's that year. This money was in England. The firm now had 80,000 pounds sterling there, which they were unable to "realize." The brothers felt that the money was now an urgent matter, since they deemed a war with England to be imminent. August 22, 1811, the colonel sailed for England on the brig *Reaper*. His wife did not want him to go, and she cried when he left. He was not too happy himself, but it had to be done. More than he could know at the time, it had to be done. An unpleasant surprise was waiting for him on the other side of the Atlantic.

Eating, much sleep, a little reading, and a great deal "of listlessness" were the routine of a voyage when there were only one or two passengers on board a vessel. The colonel's sole fellow traveler was twenty-eight-year-old Henry Lee, who was also serving as supercargo. Lee was a kin of the Cabots and Higginsons. Hoping to recoup losses in the East Indian trade, he was on his way back to Calcutta carrying letters of credit from a dozen Boston merchants amounting to some £40,000, with which he intended to buy English cargoes for speculation in India.[3]

Good winds sped them rapidly across the Atlantic the first two weeks. They were averaging, the colonel figured, 155 miles a day. This was pleasing, but he worried about the danger of hitting the huge "ice islands" floating down upon them from the pole. The disasters or near-disasters of friends, and the remembrance of a drawing he had at home of the loss of the packet *Lady Hobart* to an iceberg, kept him uneasy. He fretted too that perhaps a whale might run into the ship some dark night and with a "stroke" of its tail wreck them. It was all very well, he thought, for the officers to tell the seamen to "Keep a sharp look out ahead." Jack sings out "Aye aye sirs" and thinks no more of his charge.

Then the winds failed, and they made little progress east, though the weather was pleasant enough for them to sit on deck. Lee tried to interest Perkins in venturing money on his Calcutta trip. While tempted, Perkins wanted first to discuss it with Stephen Higginson, Sr., who was then in England.

By September 20, they were sailing up Bristol Channel, admiring the abundant harvests and the green landscape that contrasted so strikingly with their colorful New England autumn. They disembarked three days later, and left for London via Bath.

Perkins took rooms at the Globe Coffee House, "one of the most classical spots in all England," another Bostonian called it. One of the oldest coffee houses, "it was here that learned Jonson, rare Ben Jonson," wrote Alexander Everett, "put his sock on. He and old Will Shakespear have drank many a potation together within these very walls and chanted many a woodnote wild." Rather purple that, but then Everett was Harvard-educated. Perkins was undoubtedly aware of the literary hangover, but he was equally impressed with the fact that the Coffee House was cheap, and being on Fleet Street was handy to the mercantile district.[4]

Perkins had his own bedroom and shared a sitting room with Joseph Dorr and William Tudor, Jr. Young Tudor had literary pretensions and had been active in the Anthology Society with Colonel Welles, and in the Boston Athenaeum, a library that the society had spawned. Tudor, "destined to wander over the world, like Ulysses" said his cousin, was as much of a financial "success" as his father, which was none at all. Young Stephen Higginson had offered him a job helping to smuggle British goods through Napoleon's blockade onto the continent and this not too time-consuming project left him plenty of hours to accompany Perkins around London. "I think I shall be a great walker before I leave this country," Perkins wrote to his wife from London. He had hardly engaged rooms before he was out exploring the city and visiting Henry Higginson's house for letters and on business. When Higginson had opened his agency in London, the Perkins firm, out of family loyalty, had henceforth split their English business between Higginson and Williams.[5]

Mrs. T. H. Perkins, by Gilbert Stuart, 1822

T. H. Perkins, by Gilbert Stuart, 1822

James Perkins, by Gilbert Stuart, 1822

Monday, September 30, with Lee and Tudor, Perkins took a "skul" up the Thames, after having stood on the bridge and marveled in silent astonishment at the busy life on the river. Being in the neighborhood, they visited the Abbey, Westminster Hall, and other sights. Perkins went off with Nancy Higginson to a play starring Mrs. Siddons. "She is still Mrs. Siddons and astonished me with her powers." He closed his first letter to his wife with the admonition to "kiss those who are not out of kissing years—would to God I was near enough to you to do it myself."

The "bevy of Bostonians" at the Globe was augmented that week by the arrival of young Alexander Everett. Son of a well-known Boston clergyman, Everett had studied law in the law office of John Quincy Adams and, mostly for a lark since he paid his own expenses, had gone to Russia as one of Adams's secretaries. Having his fill of Russia in a short while, Everett was on his way home to Boston via Scandinavia and England. Perkins, who knew him as a friend of Eliza's, thought him a "very pleasant fellow." He joined the others in providing a walking companion for the colonel, though what was needed was someone to run interference. London, Perkins wrote his wife, contained more inhabitants than Massachusetts and Maine put together, by two or three hundred thousand. The daily crowds on the streets looked like Boston "when our churches are coming out." "It is enough to addle the brain of people" accustomed to live in such a backwater as Boston. He fussed at the haste and speed of the people, all of whom seemed to be rushing somewhere.[6]

That same week Higginson returned to London and there was a grand reunion. Perkins had spent Saturday, October 5, inspecting a beer house that brewed eight and a half million gallons per year, and by way of penance he squired the Higginson ladies to Westminster Abbey on Sunday to hear the celebrated boys choir. The age of the Abbey, the relics of the great men, of the kings of England—"the tombs and ashes of the mighty dead"—induced somber reflections. The day, however, was damp and cold and so was the Abbey. After a bit, the solemnity wore off, the charms of the music diminished, and the delights of a glowing fireside rose proportionately. They rose to leave only to find the verger had, as was the custom, locked the door when the service began and vanished. There was no escape. Motet followed motet, canon succeeded canon. At length God was satisfied, the verger materialized, undoubtedly after toasting himself at some comforting grate, and they fled. The colonel began the next letter to his wife by remarking that he had a cold.

That England was waging a war was brought home graphically when Perkins toured Woolwich Arsenal. Here, hundreds of boys were preparing cartridges to tear French flesh. It was mass production: in one room the boys formed the cartridges and tied the ball in. In a second room more boys filled the tube with powder. From here the bullets went to a third set of boys who tied the cartridges at their tops to prevent powder leakage. A fourth set bunched them in twenties and packed them into kegs, which were carried to the magazine. The speed of the operation astounded Perkins.

Other sights of London included people as well as places. One day Perkins dined with sharp-eyed, sharp-nosed Sir Alexander MacKenzie, who had traveled from Montreal to the Pacific Ocean, and whose account of his travels "speaks him a man of no ordinary character." Another day Perkins dined at Henry Higginson's with a large party of twenty, of whom eighteen were Americans and thirteen of those Bostonians. William Gray, uncle of Harrison Gray Otis was present, and a few days later wrote his nephew to tell him that he had met a "staunch and sincere friend of yours," namely "a very sensible pleasant man Thomas H. Perkins." Perkins was equally impressed and wrote his wife that Gray was "seventy years old, with the appearance of fifty, and the vivacity of twenty-four." Gray lived about three and a half miles from Higginson and walked down to dine and at half-past ten set off "to foot it back."[7]

At 4 A.M. on Monday, October 21, Perkins set off by public coach for a week's trip to the Isle of Wight. His traveling companion was a Mr. Thompson, an uprooted Bostonian, working for Samuel Williams. The island was a convenient communication point for Boston merchants, with ships from Boston or the East stopping there for instructions from their owners about future ports or late news. The two men explored the island, using a book written several years earlier by that lead mine expert, Prof. Benjamin Silliman. Hearing that a gentleman he had met and entertained in Boston in 1809 was lying ill at the town of Ryde, Perkins paid him a courtesy call. By so doing he would find himself part of a congressional investigation in a very few months.

The man he called on was John Henry, a tallish, thirtyish, Irishman with skimpy brown hair and hazel eyes. Henry had first shown up in America in the late 1790's. His Irish good looks won him a rich wife, good connections, and then a military commission. A widower when Perkins met him in Boston in 1809, Henry was invited around to all the Federalist houses and heard much talk of the cursed embargo. He kept his ears open and particularly cultivated the friendship of Harry Otis. So frequently did he visit the Otis household that Otis's spinster sister jotted romantically in her diary about the eligible widower, this "rolling stone who fluttered about without any apparent aim than his own amusement, a romantic, generous spirit that seemed too sublime to grub this earthly hole in low pursuits."[8]

But even "romantic, generous spirits" sometimes descend from their sublimity and "grub this earthly hole" with the rest of us. Henry's particular hole was not yet exposed to the light of day, but he was digging. He was staying at Ryde in a house rented by a flute-playing Frenchman, a Comte Edward de Crillon. The two men had booked passage for Boston on the *New Galen,* which was presently detained in London. It would be another month before the *New Galen* arrived at the Isle of Wight to carry Henry and Crillon to America and their niche in history.

Perkins and Thompson, after leaving Wight, landed in Portsmouth and explored that town's naval base. Learning of letters waiting for them in London, they took a stage and rode back through a night of pouring rain. Three drunken sailors from the base rode outside the coach on top. Apparently they were so little bothered by the rain that they slept and snored through it. Perkins, warm and dry inside, could get no sleep because they were "blowing their bellows." Three women rode up on top too. "Of that class who are as much exposed to weather as a Jack Tarr, and whose home is as much on the top of a Coach as *any where else.*" A warm bath and a good night's rest restored Perkins, but even without that, the letter from his wife that was waiting for him would have sufficed to restore his spirits.

The next Sunday, November 3, Henry Higginson came to Perkins with shattering news. Funds he had advanced to some of his correspondents had not been paid back. While actually solvent himself, this deficiency of others—of half a million pounds—did not permit him to meet his obligations. The Perkins share of his disaster came to about thirty-one thousand pounds, around a million dollars today. The colonel took the news with as much good grace as possible.*

That Sunday evening it was a dejected gentleman who sat down in his bedroom at the Globe to write to his wife. The house was quiet, a single candle burned in the stand, his mind and heart were three thousand miles away. "You will very readily conceive how unpleasantly situated I am, knowing as you do the interest I feel in supporting you and your family in the way they have a right to suppose they should continue. No less a sum than £30,000 sterling locked up, if not lost, in a foreign country and with no one to tell my cares to—this is bad indeed and the only consolation I have is that it would have been worse if I had not been here."[9]

The next morning, after a sleepless night, Perkins reread his letter. The gloomy reflections of the night did not look quite so bad by the light of morning. He cautioned his wife that he was showing the worst side of the picture, but immediately qualified his qualification by adding that "even the best is bad enough." He had so little expected this blow "that I am led to fear every thing." He regretted building his new house and was afraid they might lose it. He knew how quickly she would be able to give up their luxuries but feared that he would be "the most restive." He hoped there would be no need for such sacrifices, but "the present state of the walet is awful."

As the days passed the extent of Higginson's failure became clearer. The news spread rapidly in London and of course reached Boston as soon as ships and letters could get there. Lee urged a relative to transfer his business to Samuel Williams's office. "He is good against all events, his credit is better than almost any man's who goes into the London Exchange." If Williams's credit was so good then Perkins's must have rated equally high, for he and Williams were appointed assignees of the estate and effects of Higginson. In due time they began the work of bringing order out of the situation and sending out the forms to creditors and debtors that had to be completed so that an early dividend could be paid.[10]

* Later, Boston mercantile circles whispered that the Higginsons had told their Perkins kin of the impending failure and that was why the colonel had so precipitantly left for England, to salvage what could be salvaged before the other creditors learned of the failure. Henry Lee maintained, however, that Perkins was as surprised and shocked as everyone else, and greatly admired Perkins's sense of honor that he did not press Higginson to give him any preference in payment.

The Higginson disaster stimulated Perkins's acquisitive nerve. The British navy had brought in a number of prizes, vessels bound from Bourdeaux to America, and the ships and cargoes were up for sale. The silk cargoes particularly interested American merchants, for silk could not be imported into England and so was useless to the prize agents. But an American could buy the cargo and have it transshipped to Lisbon. This was too good an opportunity to miss. Perkins bid on the ship and cargo of the *Catherine Augusta* for a fraction of its value, and early in December left for Plymouth, England, to complete the purchase and see that the merchandise was well on its way. Here was a chance to recoup part of what might be lost through Higginson's failure.

It was a good thing, Perkins wrote Sarah, that her tears had not kept him home or she would have shed more if Perkins had not been in London when Higginson failed. "There is very little doubt that all the property we have in Europe would have been swallowed up in the same vortex." Bit by bit as he and Williams worked their way through the accounts, the Higginson situation improved. But though he had had his eye on a horse for young Master George and a carriage for Miss Nancy, those were out of the question now. Worse, the failure meant he must stay in England as long as his presence was necessary to save more property from the wreck.[11]

On Christmas Eve he was back in London after an excursion to Plymouth. The Bow bells were chiming in his ears; he had just returned from a fine walk with Samuel Williams on as fair a day as in New England in September; and he wished his far-away wife "a Merry Christmas." Christmas day he dined at Samuel Williams's with a party of friends. The Higginsons were there, young Tudor and his sister Delia to whom bachelor Sam Williams had proposed only to be turned down, Boston painter Washington Allston and his wife, and others Perkins did not know. The exiled Americans forgot their cares and woes in the cheerful company and the cheering glass. Perhaps even their host so far forgot himself as to say a few words. Allston, who did a portrait of Williams sometime before 1818, shows him grave and reflective with dark brown hair, firm face, large jaw and forehead. This was entirely in character. Everett, like nearly everybody else, found Williams taciturn. "He makes it an invariable rule never to say anything. If he is asked a question he replies in one syllable or the briefest explanation that the nature of the subject will admit." It was a wonder he ever mustered up enough words to ask for Delia Tudor's hand. Wordless or voluble, it is certain that more than one toast was drunk to family and friends in Boston, who, after a warm December, had been buried under a blizzard on Christmas Eve.[12]

Arriving in Boston just before the blizzard struck was the *New Galen* with a packet of letters from Perkins to his family and friends. A most welcome Christmas present. Less of a Christmas present and more of a surprise package were two passengers who took lodgings at the Exchange Coffee House, John Henry and the Comte de Crillon.

On the long voyage, Henry and Crillon exchanged confidences. Henry revealed that in 1809 he had been a secret agent for the governor of Canada, to see if contacts could be made with Federalist leaders in Boston dissatisfied with Jefferson and the embargo. Together, he and Crillon concocted a scheme whereby Henry could get his revenge against the British who had never paid him, and be handsomely paid for it.

Shortly after their arrival they saw the governor of Massachusetts, Republican Eldridge Gerry, and told him they had evidence of a Federalist plot to dismember the Union. This was good news to Gerry who faced a stiff re-election contest against the Federalist Gen. Caleb Strong, who was a Revolutionary War hero like himself, and much more popular than Gore. Gerry sent the two to Washington with a special introduction to President Madison.

In Washington, Henry contacted James Monroe, then secretary of state, and repeated his tale of Federalist treason. Monroe was extremely anxious to get his hands on the documents Henry claimed to possess. Complicated negotiations on the price developed, with Crillon acting as an intermediary. Finally, Henry accepted $50,000 plus the deed to Crillon's valuable estate in France. The government also promised not to release the papers until Henry could sail for Europe, which he did on March 7 aboard an American naval vessel.

Two days later President Madison sent a message to Congress stating that a British secret agent had been active "in certain states, more especially at the seat of government in Massachusetts," and that his aim was "destroying the Union" and secession. The effect on Congress was electric.[13]

When the documents were read aloud in the Senate there were shouts of indignation from every quarter. However, Senator James Lloyd of Massachusetts put his finger on the vital spot. He moved that Monroe be directed to reveal the names of those alleged to have been involved in the plot. For while the documents were full of insinuations, they named no names. The papers were turned over to the Committee on Foreign Relations for investigation.

On Friday, March 13, they called Comte de Crillon as a witness. He gave a long rambling story of his association with Henry but through some oversight neglected to reveal his part in the negotiations. Henry had also not mentioned the names of those with whom he had conferred in Boston in 1809. But then, gratuitously, Crillon volunteered the information that Henry had been visited on the Isle of Wight in October 1811 by several persons including a Mr. Perkins of Boston. When asked if he had heard his Christian name, as there were several Mr. Perkins in Boston, Crillon said no. Then he was asked whether he had observed anything unusual in Perkins face. Crillon replied that he had a strong natural "wine mark" on the outside of his face. The only Mr. Perkins who was at the Isle of Wight in October 1811 and had a prominent birthmark on his face was Thomas Handasyd. But what did that amount to? Crillon's testimony did not link the Boston people Henry talked with in 1809 and the Boston gentleman who visited him in 1811. At best it was inuendo.[14]

Now the Federalists got in their licks. It became known that Monroe had used $50,000 of public funds to buy the papers, and the public did not like that. Those innocent carefree days! The letters named no names. The government named no names. No one was prosecuted. No proof of anything was brought forward. The government's disclosures amounted only to insinuations, which had cost the taxpayers a goodly sum.

By April the political atmosphere was so hot that Crillon decided to decamp. He was paid $5,000 by the government for giving his estate to Henry. Then he disappeared. And Henry? Arriving in Paris, he called on the son of the Comte de Crillon to claim the estate deeded to him. The son of the *late* Comte de Crillon declared that the person who assumed his name was an imposter. The Comte turned out to be a well-known swindler named Soubian.

Perkins missed all this excitement, which had tangentially touched his good name. His pleasant circle of friends in London began to break up after Christmas. Working on the Higginson business and his own, he watched Twelfth Night come and go. His chief thought was of an early return home. Letter after letter, the very abundance of the letters themselves, bespoke his homesickness. "I pant for the delights of domestic life." Always he kept in mind the time difference between London and home, about four hours and forty minutes. He pictures himself sitting down to supper as his wife was sitting down to dinner, so that they were eating together although they were 3,000 miles apart. "I shall most gladly take my leave of England," he burst out in one letter, "where there is more wealth and poverty, luxury and wretchedness than in most countries." If he had to choose between living in London on $10,000 a year or in Boston on $2,000, it would be "Dear Boston for me, with all its cold winds and democracy."[15]

London winds were hardly kinder. Perkins was having a great deal of trouble with the chimney in his new chambers. It smoked up the room and he ordered it swept. Early one morning while he was still in bed, a man and boy arrived. Since the chimneys had to be narrow to give a good draft to the dense smoke, only small boys could climb up them and clean them out. With some difficulty the boy worked his way up the chimney, the man staying in the room and directing him. Suddenly, Perkins heard the boy cry. "The Master asked him what was the matter, he feebly announced in a most distressed tone that the bricks had given way at the side of the chimney and that he could not 'get out'—his Master spoke to him several times, but got no answer.—I sprang out of bed in great distress, and proposed going on the top of the house; when at the moment down came several bricks, and the boy again spoke and said he had got clear—When he came down the skin was stripped from his arm several inches in extricating himself." Perkins could not help but notice that the child was no older than his own eight-year-old George, and nowhere near as large.

By February he was down in "the dumps." He had not heard from his wife for almost three months. "I make no comments," but then the hurt burst out and he did. He had letters from his brother as late as January, but none from Sarah or Eliza. He explained it to himself as the delay occasioned by sending letters through New York, but this did not satisfy him and he felt she could have done better. He hoped the next ship would have a letter from her, if it did not "I shall have at least one regret the less, as I shall presume my absence is not very severely felt by *you,* and therefore be the more reconciled to it *myself*—however, I will believe that I shall not be forgotten by you." Soon, the long-awaited letters from his Sarah arrived.

By the end of March Perkins planned to go to the continent on business. When he arrived in Paris, Napoleon was preparing for the break in relations with Russia. A mob was about to attack the Russian consulate in one of those "spontaneous public demonstrations" so familiar to the twentieth century. On leaving London, Perkins had been entrusted by the American chargé d'affaires in London with some despatches for the Russian minister at Paris. This was then a common practice. Seeing the mob, Perkins decided to rid himself of the Russian messages immediately, and he promptly delivered them to the minister. That night, Perkins was roused from his bed by the French police who insisted on searching his rooms. Finding nothing, they apologized and left. Except for that mob, they might have found the embassy despatches.

While in France, Perkins visited Lafayette for a few days, inspected the paintings of Jacques Louis David, and viewed an exhibition of 250 trained birds. There was a memorable visit to the Paris catacombs: "A large company each with a candle looked like a procession such as I have seen painted (Hollens, Bridge, & Everett with me)." He gawked at the royal robes and regalia on display at Notre Dame, and was shown in that cathedral a globe containing "the *Crown of Thorns* which was placed on the head of our Saviour!" The large pearls in the crown of the Empress impressed him more; they were the largest he had ever seen.[16]

A few days later, Perkins attended the theater on an evening when the emperor was present. He saw Napoleon publicly cast angry glances at the Russian minister, who wisely left the city the next day. Napoleon was not the only celebrated or notorious person to be seen in Paris. John Henry was there, and all the Americans made a great point of having nothing to do with him. After all, to what government might he not sell their conversations? And with the irony that life so seldom exhibits, Mr. Henry received partial retribution for his swindle. It seemed he had lent the false Comte de Crillon $6,000, accepting a check on the Banque de France which turned out to be bogus. Swindled while swindling. Henry complained bitterly.

The first of June Perkins was back in Cherbourg waiting to go to England. A batch of letters from home was there for him. Given them at 11 o'clock at night, he read them straight through "till day light." Then he began writing his answers. It was hours later before he was content to go to sleep, happy in home thoughts.

Back in London he was in time to join the celebrations when Parliament, in response to repeated American requests, repealed the hated Orders in Council. With these dead, relations between America and Great Britain were bound to improve. The joy lasted one week. Then came news that President Madison had requested the Congress to debate a declaration of war. Seventeen days later the news came that he had signed the declaration. It was to be war and not peace. A general exodus of Americans took place, none of them, especially Perkins, wanting to be interned "for the duration."

The next day he was on the road to Liverpool to arrange passage home. Depressed with thoughts of the coming conflict, he was yet exhilirated to be finally homeward bound. On the morning of Independence Day they arrived in Liverpool and found the *New Galen* in the harbor loading for Boston. The Higginsons, the Amorys, Delia Tudor, and others were sailing on the *Galen*. Perkins was tempted, but found he was able to get better accommodations on the *Liverpool Packet*. The vessel was not ready to sail, so with two others he took a trip through Wales. They visited a lead mine at Hollywell, with a conductor leading the way. They were dressed in miner's clothing "and put an handkerchief on our heads in place of our hats." Each man took a candle between his fingers and went down the ladders. At 120 feet they watched the miners blast out some ore. Coming back out they went down to the foot of the mountain where a tunnel had been driven in horizontally to provide a drain for the water in the mine. They took a boat and were rowed into the heart of the mountain about a mile. Coming to a level where some workmen were, Perkins stepped out, took a pickaxe from one of the miners and dug some pieces of stone loose as a memento of the occasion.[17]

Finally, on July 25, the *Packet* cast off the ropes binding it to England and trusted its wooden bulk to the wind and waves blowing toward Boston and Sarah. The Perkins luck held true. The *Packet* arrived in Boston on September 2. The *New Galen,* though it had left before Perkins, limped into port a full week afterwards. Storms at sea had battered the ship and the captain had had to rig jury masts to bring her in. The town was joyfully celebrating the first triumph in the new war, the victory of the *Constitution* commanded by Captain Hull in capturing the *Guerriere*. The colonel and his lady had a more private celebration of their own.

Ye, whom Washington has led,
Ye, who in his footsteps tread,
Ye, who death nor danger dread,
  Haste to glorious victory.

Philip Freneau
"The Volunteer's March"
July 1814

---

# 21
# Sticking by the Stall

A twenty-five-year-old Boston spinster scratched into her diary for Wednesday, June 24, 1812, the overwhelming calamity that had "befallen our Country." Underlining it for proper emphasis, she wrote *"War Unqualified War."* As a properly reared Federalist she knew that it had been "accelerated by our Rulers," and with a proper flourish of the exclamation point, noted that "the people of America are to consider France as a friendly Nation, and in peace with them!" The Bible being a good New Englander's first line of defense, she concluded, "Tell it not in Gath, publish it not in the streets of"—and here emotion got the best of her spelling—"Ascalon" (II Samuel 1:20).[1]

"Madmen may, to be sure, be expected to do mad things," James Perkins wrote. It was madness, Federalists thought, to go to war because of impressment—Madison's foremost reason for asking Congress to declare war. His other official reason for the war had been removed by the British repeal of the Orders in Council. But other factors were involved. Those included the resistance of the Indians to American expansion westward, the temptation of conquering Canada, Texas, and Florida, the frontier prejudice against Britain and in favor of French trade, the personal ambitions of men like Henry Clay and John Calhoun, the blunders and naïveté of Madison in his dealings with the British, and his complete misreading of Napoleon's mind.[2]

The Northeast decided to have as little to do with the war as possible. Federalist Caleb Strong, chosen governor in the 1812 spring election, at first ignored the demand of the federal government to turn over to them forty-one companies of the Massachusetts militia for service in Canada. When he got good and ready he flatly refused to send them, citing an opinion of the Massachusetts Supreme Court, dominated by Federalists, that the militia could only be commanded by its officers and the governor of the Commonwealth was the only person who could decide its employment. He was not about to send them to invade Canada on behalf of Mr. Madison.

The Perkins brothers had nothing good to say of the war. Invariably in their letters it appeared as "this most distressing state of things," "this most ill-judged conquest," "this most unnatural war." The epithets that flowed most readily from their pen in describing it were "unprofitable," "ruinous," "unhappy," and "most vile." From the counting room on India Wharf, it seemed that "all the men of reflection and Character" wanted a speedy end to the conflict. "Let a union of honest men on your side meet our exertions to produce this most desirable result."[3]

The business of New England was business, and merchants did not want to stop to play war with Mr. Madison. Once again the rules of the game of trade were changed, and the Perkins firm had to adapt themselves to the new conditions. American privateers had flocked to sea, and were busy seizing everything they could subdue, including some ships in which the Perkins had ventures. Communication with Canton was cut off and Williams was asked to write Cushing "the state of things" and advise Canton "they must keep snug" until things got better. "Tell them to hold fast what they have got, to ship nothing until they hear that war has been put an end to." They charged Williams to keep an eye on their concerns in Europe, and particularly to send them British licenses permitting them to trade with Spain and Portugal.

On that war-ravaged peninsula Wellington was laying the foundation for Napoleon's defeat. As the armies swept back and forth across the countryside, near famine continued. The Perkins firm had been sending cargoes there, and, Perkins told Williams, it was "a great object to continue." "The miserable population," he reasoned, would be even more miserable "if deprived of our supplies." He hoped something could be worked out to permit more shipments and prevent vessels being captured. Returns were so high that a merchant could lose two out of three ships in the trade and still make a handsome profit.

Equipped with proper licenses, they had seven ships that fall bound for Cadiz or Lisbon. Amory and the Higginsons were sharing these voyages with them, but disaster dogged the little fleet. One was wrecked in the Chesapeake. Two were captured by American privateers, and one by the British, and only released with much difficulty. A fifth, the *Miser,* was intercepted and, lacking proper papers, was taken by British cruisers as a prize into Gibraltar. Samuel Storrow, the supercargo, had put the papers where he thought they would be safe, but they "were destroyed by vermin." Duplicate papers were sent across the Atlantic by the roundabout Halifax route, with hopes that Williams could straighten things out.

Another prize closer to home was being captured. Near to the Perkins family, on Fort-Hill, lived the Cabots, descendants of the distinguished Cabots of Salem and related to Senator George Cabot whom Perkins so much admired. These Cabots had an unmarried son, Samuel, whose mother was a shrewd matchmaker. As early as 1808 she had written to him in Philadelphia, where he was on business, that she had "discovered a prize," and that if his heart was free "to keep it so until you come to Boston and then do your best to obtain it."[4]

The prize was the Colonel's eldest daughter, Eliza. On a spring visit that year, twenty-four-year-old Sam fell promptly in love with his mother's choice, an emotion apparently reciprocated by Eliza, then seventeen. The colonel was the only roadblock. Twenty-one was early enough for Eliza to get married, he said. The years passed, with Samuel returning to Boston to work where he became an expert in silks, even handling some silk imports for the Perkins firm. Finally Eliza reached her majority and on November 2, 1812, the colonel squired his daughter down the aisle of the Federal Street Church and joined her hand in marriage to Samuel Cabot Junior.

After the ceremony, the couple moved in with the colonel on Pearl Street. This was a mistake. "It is not a good thing," Eliza commented years later, "for a man to live with his wife's family." The reason was the old one of mother-in-law trouble. Sally Perkins was a strange woman in many ways. "My mother thought," said Eliza, "that any of her daughters were fools to marry *anybody*. They had all they wanted at home. My husband felt that he was treated with a want of consideration and I felt it for him and it made me cross and jealous." As soon as possible, the young couple rented a home in the Bulfinch-designed Colonnade Row on Common (now Tremont) Street, and Samuel got out from under his mother-in-law's tongue.[5]

Sixteen-year-old Thomas, Jr., who had been studying at Phillips Exeter in New Hampshire, was entered that fall at St. Mary's College in Baltimore, Maryland. He was no scholar and the colonel did not try to enter him into Harvard. But with a married daughter and a son in college, the colonel must have been vividly reminded that he was very close to being a half century old.

Hopes that fall of 1812 were high that the presidential election might end the war. Federalists backed Governor De Witt Clinton of New York, a dissident Republican who favored peace, as their candidate. "All our hopes," the Perkinses wrote Williams, November 24, "hang upon the change of President." Federalist Rufus King, a power in New York, had not gone along with the idea of running a sometime Republican as their candidate against Madison, and likely his opposition had proved strong enough to let Madison squeak in. New England, except for Vermont, gave solid electoral support to Clinton, but the South and West went completely for Madison. Hopes for peace were dashed, the war was to drag on. It was a close thing, however.

By the end of November 1812, the brothers were convinced that Madison had won, and they were already predicting to correspondents that the war would continue for two years at least, probably until December 1814. So they battened down for the long pull. "Under such circumstances," they wrote Williams, "we are disposed to lay by and keep out of harm's way if possible."[6]

"Laying by" did not mean doing nothing. They decided it would be useful to send a special messenger to Cushing in Canton and selected a nephew of James, Frederick W. Paine—a younger brother to William Fitz Paine, to give him his newly adopted middle name. Having a large property on the Northwest Coast which probably would be in China by the fall of 1814, they wanted to be sure it would not be shipped and seized by the British. Also they intended him to carry some very large sums with him—up to $200,000 if they could scrape it together—to be invested in Calcutta goods on his way to Canton.

"Laying by" really meant doing everything possible. Early in January 1813 they wrote Williams wondering why he had not sent them more licenses for shipments to the Spanish Peninsula. If England still permitted such voyages, the Perkinses wanted to avail themselves of its chances. What about salted provisions, they inquired? "Beef, Pork, Butter & Lard are the articles we could furnish, with Codfish." Licenses they told him a few weeks later were selling for as much as $1,500 in Boston, which in London cost only ten or twelve guineas ($44). "We are quite disposed to scold you for not having sent us some, when they were to be had, as you knew we were much in the flour trade."[7]

"Laying by" only meant that one worked much harder, even if the returns might not be as good as in former years. For the Perkins brothers were managing an intricately interwoven operation. The Spanish business, profitable in and of itself, even humanitarian in many ways, also provided them with money or negotiable credit *in* Europe that could be easily and quickly transferred to Williams in London and used to fund investments in their China business. No part of their concerns stood alone and remote from their other involvements. All were made to fit into their total operation. In a time of unusual strain, one cleared the decks for action. So brother James tracked down outstanding bills owed to them and scratched up cash from every available source. As the war lengthened, they re-emphasized the commission business. And brother Thomas saw in the war renewed possibilities for the iron works in Vergennes.

While the colonel had been abroad, the Monkton Iron Company stumbled on its unprofitable way. James had gone to Vermont once to look in on things, but seems not to have felt competent to give it direction. George Higginson had died. Bradbury, in Vergennes, continued on his vague but busy course, having an aqueduct built to supply water to one of the boarding houses, making benches for the school house, ordering some Cape Madeira wine for himself and gin to sell in the store for the workers, subscribing to the village minister's salary, making fire-brick, doing everything but make the company a success.

Shortly after Perkins returned from Europe, busy as he was with a year's accumulation of tasks, he turned his thoughts to Vergennes. The basic decision was made: Bradbury had to go. Sometime in October 1812, he either quit or was asked to leave. He stayed on in Vergennes and worked as a miller. Benjamin Welles was selected as the new manager of the works. The owners of the company were now reduced to the Higginsons, the Perkinses, William Parsons, and Welles, and its active direction was in the hands of T. H. Perkins and Welles. However much, as good Federalists, they might deplore "this most unnatural war," that same war was to prove a great stimulant to their sagging iron works.

On Lake Champlain the Americans were face to face with their foes in Canada. Both Britain and America had small fleets of gunboats cruising the lake and small military garrisons in the vicinity. Some military action was inevitable. That meant cannon balls for the artillery—a difficult supply problem when the nearest American arsenal was 260 miles away across a wilderness broken by a few roads and those bad, plus the high price of slow transport by oxen. Aware of these bargaining points, Perkins offered the services of Monkton to the government—for a stiff price.

His price was $120 per ton. He figured it cost him no more than $25 per ton to cast pig iron and only a little more to cast cannon balls. Mr. Madison could have his war if he wanted it, but it was going to cost him. The commandant of the Boston Navy Yard thought the price exhorbitant, but considering the cost of transport, the government was not in a position to do better and the colonel knew it. They gave him an order for three hundred tons of shot and Perkins went up to Vergennes at the end of January to see how Welles was progressing. "We have got our sheet iron on a very good footing," he reported to a friend in Philadelphia, "and are rolling it as thin as tin plates, and 8 ft. long." Maybe thanks to Madison, the long losing venture at Vergennes might finally show a profit.[8]

But while the left hand made shot for the war, the strong right hand worked to stop it. No sooner had he returned from Vergennes than he appeared before a committee of the Massachusetts House of Representatives that was looking into the subject of "Impressed Seamen." This committee, controlled by the Federalists, questioned the principal merchants from Boston, Salem, Marblehead, Portland, and other seaports, plus men from the Custom House and the Navy. In all it heard fifty-one witnesses.

Each merchant interviewed told how long he had been in business and how many seamen he employed in an average year. The Perkins brothers testified they had been in trade for twenty years and employed an average of 100 to 150 seamen a year. The hiring end of the business, said the colonel in his deposition, was done by him. "In our vessels we have usually had a fifth part and I think a fourth part of the crew foreigners, chiefly English and Irishmen." In some cases he said, foreigners applied to him without having the "protection" which prevented them—so it was hoped—from being impressed. They could always get some from the owners of the boarding house they told him. "In several instances they have brought me protections that did not agree with their persons, and told me they gave two dollars a piece for them." They often secured extra "protections" by going down to the Custom House and swearing they had lost their originals.[9]

The committee concluded that out of an average of some 21,000 seamen sailing on Massachusetts ships in the previous fifteen years, exactly thirty-five sailors had been "pressed" and of these only twelve were Americans. Of the twelve, they claimed nine had been discharged, one escaped, and one held. This left one unaccounted for. Was this worth fighting a war for? Gratuitously they added that the cases they had heard of throughout the country totaled only 147 or 157. Even adding in all the cases they could find, they still got only 175. Far from the 6,000 Madison claimed in his war message.*

A more important fact was that the government was finding itself hard-pressed to pay its bills. Expenses, drastically inflated by the war, were soaring to the fifty million mark. The firm wrote to William F. Paine that the government would have to borrow this sum, "as they dare not lay direct taxes for fear of losing the support of the people." A war loan was opened in March 1813 in Boston "and not a cent subscribed except in the Democratic State Bank, where the pitiful sum of $62,000 was subscribed, principally by persons living out of town." Samuel Williams was told why: "None of the monied men will lend them money, and without it they must abandon the prosecution of the war." If Madison wanted his war—let him pay for it himself.[10]

The spring election in 1813 gave cause for satisfaction to the dissenters from the war. Strong was re-elected governor and his margin of victory increased from 5,000 to 14,000. The colonel was nominated one of the senators from Suffolk County, and was elected by a plurality of 2,100. His career in elective office had been one year in the state senate in 1805 and two in the state house in 1806 and 1807. He was now to serve regularly in the state senate from 1813 through 1817.

* A figure historians agree was grossly exaggerated.

Still the war crept nearer to sheltered New England. The British navy had begun a blockade of American ports soon after the war started, beginning in the Chesapeake Bay area. Gradually it spread up and down the coast. Cannily they had allowed the port of Boston to remain open, hoping that the forces that had been working for separation in 1804 and 1809 might come to the fore and remove New England from the conflict. British warships had cruised along the coast intercepting shipping, but it had not been difficult to avoid them. By the middle of April, however, Bostonians were "tortured with the view of two frigates for the last two days" in their harbor area.[11]

A Canton ship, the *Sally,* in which J. & T. H. Perkins had a venture, had only just escaped the British by running into Plymouth harbor. With British cruisers outside the harbor, there was no chance to bring the *Sally*'s cargo to Boston by sea. The colonel went down to Plymouth and found that the teamsters knew a good thing when they saw it. They now wanted $1.50 per hundredweight, "which is double the price formerly paid on the Providence road."[12]

Boston realized its exemption from combat was ending when, on the first of June, the British frigate *Shannon* was chased out of Boston bay by the American frigate *Chesapeake.* Crowds took to the hills and rooftops to watch the fight. There was soon little to see as the ships fought their way beyond Salem. Dr. Bentley went out with the crowd to follow with "eyes and hearts" the chase. "The American Frigate hove too and fired a gun, but the English Frigate suffered herself to be chased till she was out of sight." Ultimate victory, however, went to the Englishmen; the young Captain of the *Chesapeake* being killed in the battle.[13]

Republicans tried to make propaganda out of the death of the *Chesapeake*'s captain. They sent to Halifax for his body and arranged multiple funeral pageants for the dead hero. The Federalists refused to go along, and the General Court would not pass a memorial vote, so deep were political passions and feelings. They even had appointed a committee to end the war, on which the colonel was serving.

Federalist hopes were pinned on the attempt at mediation being made by Russia. Madison, in a corner, sent three of his best men to St. Petersburg to see what could be worked out. Writing to Liverpool in late June, the Perkins firm spoke of their "most ardent wish that the Mission of our Ambassadors may end in peace." But by then England, invigorated by Napoleon's defeat in Russia, was filled with renewed fighting zeal for pushing the American war to a successful conclusion, and nothing came immediately from the Russian proposal.[14]

By the middle of June, the colonel had gone to Vermont to check the progress Welles was making at the iron works. It was most satisfactory. "We make 7 tons of iron, 3 tons of sheet-iron, and 12 tons of shot, per week. In a few weeks our blast furnace will also be at work, and our establishment have the appearance of another Etna." The twenty-two ton weekly production was about what Bradbury had been able to coax out of the works, but the chief difference was that Welles had, in the federal government, a good customer paying top dollar.[15]

While things were booming at Vergennes, they were dull elsewhere. The financial disaster that hit Henry Higginson in 1811 was not yet settled in 1813 when his father's firm went bankrupt. Perkins reported to Williams on July 10 that "There have been a set of Vultures preying upon Sm. H. and they have succeeded in destroying him." Out of the wreck of S. Higginson & Company came a new firm, S. G. Perkins & Company, which essentially continued the Higginson interests and concerns.

The Perkinses themselves were involved in a court case with Theodore Lyman, and might have been forgiven if they thought him a "vulture" too. When they had purchased the ship *Vancouver* from him in 1807, Lyman had promised not to engage in the Northwest Coast trade for seven years. They sued him in March 1813 because they claimed he had broken that agreement.

On March 16, 1809, they asserted, Lyman had fitted out the ship *Hamilton* for the coast. Lyman argued it was done not by him but by his son George and others and that the Perkinses knew this. He had had a conversation with them about it and advised them to take a part of the voyage, which they did. They replied that was not the way of it at all. There was no conversation, the ships were not up for sale, and they did not buy in. They did agree they bought in on October 25, 1809, only after the ship had sailed, and then only to protect themselves, and at a great advance and profit to the defendant. Similar pleadings were entered for the brig *Lydia*. The defendant argued that a clause in the contract exempted from its provisions, vessels which were then on the coast or on the way to it. He contended that these vessels came under the clause.

The court ruled that restraint of trade did not apply to this case; that Lyman had made an agreement not to trade for seven years, and had done so in spite of his agreement. The jury could only consider the Perkinses buying into the two vessels in question in relation to setting the damages. They had won, but Lyman immediately appealed the decision to the next term of court, and the case ultimately ended up in chancery, with an inconclusive result unsatisfactory to either party.[16]

While hoping that the Russian mediation would eventually terminate in peace, the brothers made plans in case it failed. If the war was to continue, they decided to send a vessel to Canton that winter and "let her run the gauntlet," of blockading ships. If they sent it out without funds, they would "hazard nothing further." The ship they planned to send was a new one—the *Jacob Jones*. "She is 500 tons, and promises to be as fine a sailing vessel as can be built here." It was also the largest ship the Perkins had owned up to that time. "We think she will sail in December." They planned to send T. H. Perkins, Jr., out in the vessel, so something was being "hazarded." But if the war was coming to an end, it would mean that the *Jacob Jones* might be one of the first ships to return to America with a cargo from Canton. It turned out that their planning was almost on the button. Their incredible luck for shrewd guesses and taking their risks at the right moment was an indefinable but definite factor in the success of J. & T. H. Perkins.[17]

New England ports continued fairly open, though the rest of the country was closed. This meant that the Northeast, and particularly Boston, was being enriched at the expense of the remainder of the country. Specie flowed into New England, and their nonsubscription to war loans kept funds from going back to Washington for the war they did not believe in. The privateers sailing from Massachusetts ports proved lucrative. Beside the legal piracy of privateering, New England was perfectly located to engage in smuggling and trading with the enemy. A busy traffic developed with Canada and the West Indies under various guises.

Even the Monkton Iron Company was tainted with what was treasonable activity if viewed with strict legality. The company owned three sloops, the *Francis,* the *Dash,* and the *Maria*. These were used for different purposes, but were frequently employed carrying ore from the New York mines up the creek to Vergennes. On Saturday, October 9, the

*Maria* sailed from Vergennes and on the following Tuesday was stopped off Hog Island by Major Roberts of the U.S. Army on patrol of the lake. Roberts claimed the *Maria* was smuggling and seized it in the name of the government. When Welles heard about it, he immediately protested to Commodore MacDonough, commanding the American fleet in Lake Champlain. Along with the protest went the suggestion that if the *Maria* was not returned to Vergennes forthwith, they would not be able to keep their commitment to produce cannon balls for him. The *Maria* was promptly released.

There was little activity in Boston. Wellington's victories on the peninsula ended the need for flour shipments there. The Perkins kept their counting room open more from habit than need, and they scratched around for business. Much of September was spent fussing with some shipments from Havana they were handling in their old role as commission agents. It did not bring much profit but it gave them something to do. And five per cent was five per cent.

Still the war went on. No one could tell, they complained to Williams at the end of October, when this "wickedness and folly" would end. "Many think it will continue as long as the present rulers are in their places." Then, significantly, they commented, "They are execrated every where and yet we cannot help ourselves, except constitutionally." In light of later charges made against the Federalists' loyalty, this qualification seems important to note.[18]

In Vergennes, Commodore Thomas MacDonough went into winter quarters with his little fleet up Otter Creek. Here was a place secure from attack by the British, where there was plenty of timber and iron. He knew if he were to have half a chance against the British the following spring he would need more ships. Vergennes offered what he needed. Safely away from the lake, he need fear no surprise assault by the enemy. Great stands of virgin timber were all about, and at Vergennes was one of the largest and most complete iron works in the country.

In January of 1814 MacDonough got his authorization to build a ship and three or four gunboats. Thirty shipwrights were brought up from New York City and more than a hundred lumberjacks swarmed into the woods to provide the timber needed. The flat ground just downstream from the iron works became the shipyard. Sawpits and steambox were set up, ways constructed and a keel soon laid. While the valley rang with the sound of saws, axes, adzes, and sledge hammers, a bit further up the creek the iron works roared away casting the cannon balls and the ironwork the new ships would need.

Another new ship, the *Jacob Jones,* slipped out of Boston harbor on January 14 with Tom Perkins, Jr., aboard. Companion with him was seventeen-year-old Horace Bucklin Sawyer of Burlington, Vermont. The colonel had privately enjoined Captain Roberts to give the young men neither favor nor indulgence, but to require them to bear their part. This was probably more than young Tom bargained for. The crew felt the two youths were interlopers, but they soon showed they could manage the ropes and sails handily, and were not adverse to swabbing the decks. "Jack," said Sawyer later, "agreed they were no shirks" and soon took them into favor.[19]

The new year brought an extraordinary feeling that things were about to change. Bonaparte's power had been broken. "Peace will be the consequence in Europe and this country," the brothers predicted. Prices which had been rising rapidly, quickly plunged. Brother James found himself writing letters everywhere and with each letter his spirits grew higher and more excited about the possibility "we shall be at liberty to pursue our own affairs in our own way." To agents in India he advised investing funds of the firm in indigo, for prices were very high, likely to remain so, and "the day of delivery is near at hand." By March 1814 when Madison had sent new commissioners to Gothenburg to seek peace, "we are so confident of this result that we have written our China friends to purchase two Cargoes of tea suited to the North."[20]

For all their surge of hopes, there was a note of caution. Writing on March 21 to Welles at Vergennes, the colonel observed, "the sooner we touch the cash for all our debts to the Government, the better." Earlier that month he had written Bradbury, who was looking for somebody to buy his interest in the Monkton Iron Works, that no purchaser could be found. He advised Welles to get all his dealings with the government on paper. The iron must be good too. "The iron in the bottom of the vessels will last as long as the timber and the quality as respects both them and us, is not of importance; but for the Gun Carriages, rigging, and other work upon deck with the mast work they ought to have the best we can make."

By the end of March, however, peace prospects were fading and it looked like the British were preparing to make "red hot war" the ensuing summer. Perkins grew fearful that all the activity at Vergennes would bring the enemy down upon his iron works. Skirmishes were constantly reported on the Canadian border, and the ice was starting to go out of the lake. If MacDonough's new boats were not ready by then, the British could bottle him up in Otter Creek. Welles was treated to some advice by Perkins: "a few pieces of heavy artillery below the ferry would be well placed to prevent an attack by boats which I should think the only mode in which one would be made."[21]

The government's big problem that spring was not protecting the Monkton Iron Company but paying for the war. The national treasury was nearly empty. The first war loan, boycotted by the Federalists, had largely failed. In March 1814 a second loan was authorized to raise $25 million. Early in April a private meeting was held in Boston of the principal Federalists of that town and Philadelphia, the chief money markets. The hardliners were for boycotting the loan again, reasoning that the government then would be forced to sue for peace. Let the loan, advised the *Centinel,* "be filled by those who urged the Government to declare an unjust and ruinous war."[22]

Otis and Perkins were among those who disagreed. Money was plentiful and difficult to place at interest. Massachusetts banks found their hard money holdings had quadrupled in the three-year period ending in June 1814. Otis pointed out that the government could get the money in Europe if it failed at home, and the high premium the government offered was most tempting. Still, the firm reported in a letter of April 14 to a Philadelphia correspondent, "the loan will not go here. Our monied men have resolved to give no aid to the dominant party in any shape whatever."[23]

Knowing of the split in Federalist thinking, however, the brokers handling the loan advertised that mail applications for loans would be accepted and "the names of all subscribers" would be kept secret. The Federalist press raged at this trick. "How degraded must our government be," the *Gazette* screamed. "They know right well that the cause is so sneaking and vile that nobody would be seen in broad daylight to lend them money."[24]

But the government loan was just too good to miss. Eighty-eight dollars bought a hundred dollar bond and paid 6 percent interest. This was a good return even from Republicans. Perkins subscribed quietly. After all, somebody had to pay for his shot. Not enough Federalists thought as the Perkinses did however, and the government only raised ten million from the new loan.

As summer approached the British began striking nearer to the "Home of Correct Principles." Few of the New England coastal towns had made much preparation for a war most of them did not want. Fortifications had fallen into decay. Powder was short. Men were less trained than formerly. After two years of war, the British had given up hope that New England might be split from the rest of the country. The blockade was extended to cover the entire East Coast. On May 6, 1814 the British frigate *Nymph* arrived in Boston bay for blockade duty, cruising up and down the bay, harassing the shipping. All boats except fishing boats were stopped. Some were burned, others ransomed.

At Vergennes, it had been touch and go, but the ship builders had worked miracles and MacDonough's flagship, the *Saratoga,* had been finished twenty days ahead of schedule. The *Centinel* reported that as of May 11, his flotilla in Otter Creek was getting ready to move into the lake. Just in time, too, as a British squadron of twelve ships was laying offshore nearby Burlington. Panic spread through that town and many lake dwellers moved inland. Ten days later the air furnace of the Monkton Iron Company burned flat. Whether it took fire by accident or design was not known, but sabotage was suspected. Indeed, the war was "hotting up."

But Federalists took a moment off from their troubles to celebrate what for them was "Glorious News From Europe!" The *Centinel* of June 4 announced to Boston, "Bonapart Banished to Elba—the Ancient Family and Ancient Boundaries of France Restored—A General Peace in Europe Made." Column after column of detail followed. Federalists met and decided that a Grand Religious Celebration would be the only fitting way to celebrate this news of the century.

Two thousand people, Federalists claimed, crowded into King's Chapel to hear former Governor Christopher Gore orate. That evening, fireworks on the Common gathered ten thousand spectators. Carbonic comets were shot off on Boston neck along with glowing, heated cannon balls. Five hundred rockets soared aloft from a scaffold on a remote corner of the Common. The State House shone with the light of 2,600 blue lamps. An illuminated *fleur de lys* shimmered from the attic window of the Hancock house beside the State House.

British sailors on the blockading ships must have wondered at the racket and rockets. Had the American's won the war or some great victory? How amazed they must have been to discover they were celebrating England's victory! An insult to "fallen greatness" fumed Parson Bentley. The *Chronicle* too, joined in to attack this "solemn mockery." Particularly inappropriate, they said, while the enemy "were illuminating our coast with bonfires of our vessels and our adjacent villages." For the dangers that threatened at Vergennes and at Boston were "clear and present," and the war was far from over on this side of the Atlantic.[25]

This is the most joyous day that I ever remember for the news of Peace arrived this morning, that sweet guest so long banished from our land.

Eunice Callendar's diary,
Monday, February 13, 1815

# 22

## A Great Shaking

The gentleman's nose was large and red. His face was marked by the smallpox and some thought him ill-looking. He was about forty years old, nearly six feet tall, and when he spoke it was "very full and quick, with a Dutch or German accent," although he said he was French.[1]

The gentleman's name was Charles Sandos. With his wife, he had fled France and its Revolution. After a period in England, they had come to America and had been living quietly for two years past in Worcester. Known and liked by friends and relatives of James Perkins, he and his pretty wife made an amiable addition to the society of that interior town. His credit was good too. A Worcester merchant handled his financial drafts on a London agent, and the money had always been promptly paid.

When the news of Napoleon's defeat and exile to Elba reached Mr. and Mrs. Sandos they made plans to return to France via England. They booked passage on a Spanish ship, the *Naderhda,* sailing from Boston at the end of June 1814. With a letter of introduction from Dr. Paine, James Perkins's father-in-law, Mr. and Mrs. Sandos arrived in Boston and were immediately invited to stay with James at Pearl Street until their ship was ready to sail.

There was more than mere hospitality behind the invitation. The firm was looking for a responsible neutral—"a confidential person"—to deliver some "few thousand dollars in gold" for them to Samuel Williams in England. Perhaps Sandos was the man. He was not in the house twenty-four hours before James took him aside and broached his plan. Sandos replied he knew nothing of commercial affairs, but would do anything to oblige Perkins, if in doing so there was no risk or danger, and nothing contrary to the honor of a gentleman. Such a reply struck exactly the right tone with Perkins.[2]

Accordingly, a few days before the *Naderhda* was ready to depart, James, Jr., and some clerks from the counting house came to Pearl Street with forty thousand dollars worth of gold coins, rolled in paper, to be packed in the trunks of Mr. and Mrs. Sandos. Perkins instructed Sandos to say the money was his private property if the ship was boarded by the British, otherwise it would be confiscated. As soon as they landed in England, he was either to deposit it at a bank or deliver it to Mr. Williams in London.

Sandos was given a letter for Williams explaining that since gold was at a premium on the London market, they thought this was the best way to remit "the amount belonging to you in our hands" rather than by bills of exchange. If bills were to drop however, they would send "the balance belonging to you in that way," unless Williams preferred specie.[3]

On June 20, the *Naderhda* sailed for England with Sandos and the Perkins gold. Even without a war, it would be at least two or three months before the brothers could expect to hear of the safe arrival of their gold in England. In the meantime, rapid changes in the fortunes of war gave them something far more urgent to think about. The defeat of Napoleon, celebrated so joyously by some Bostonians, freed the British to take care of the long-neglected American skirmish. It released thousands of battle-hardened veterans for duty in the former colonies.

The *Naderhda* was just two days out of the harbor when a Republican paper published a note that had been sent ashore by the commander of a British warship blockading Boston harbor, telling how he had sailed around the harbor, inspected its defenses, and burnt a sloop. He "strongly" recommended Commodore Bainbridge to put the *Constitution* "in the best possible state of defence." This impudent note aroused a flurry of alarm over the state of harbor defenses.[4]

By mid-July Charles Sandos, safely across the Atlantic with his precious cargo of gold, was writing a disturbing letter to James Perkins from London. Five days after their ship left Boston, it had been stopped and searched by a British cruiser. Sandos had been so sick during the search, he said, that he could scarcely stand.. The British sailors doing the searching had rifled his trunks and his writing desk, "pilfering whatever they could lay hands on." Part of the gold had been stolen, and he blamed it on the searchers and not the crew of the *Naderhda*. Fortunately, he reported, the "English visitors" missed the trunk containing most of the doubloons, which was under his wife's bed.[5]

Their troubles had not ended there, Sandos continued. At the customs house in Portsmouth, he had been asked to declare "upon my honour" that the gold was not American property. Only by a bribe to the customs officer (of some of the gold) and a declaration that he would not put the gold into the hands of any American citizen until peace had been declared between England and America, was he allowed to bring the gold into the country.

Arriving in London, he found gold dropping daily in value, but it was said to be higher in Paris. Therefore, he intended to dispose of it there, but he wanted to assure the brothers that no loss would fall on them, and he annexed an I.O.U. for the forty thousand dollars at the bottom of his letter. He had not called on Williams, he wrote, since the man was a "total stranger" to him. Nor did he mail the letter then, but took it to Paris with him.

On August 9, Sandos, now in Paris, wrote another letter to James Perkins, telling him that he had disposed of the gold, after having it smelted into ingots, and while he didn't get as much as he hoped, he did better than he would have in England. The receipts would be "punctually paid" when peace was concluded. His own reception in Paris had been all he could have hoped for, and his wife was writing to "all her female American friends" the particulars of the voyage. In a "P.S." he added that several of the doubloons were "clipt" and some of base metal and of no value. He would deduct those from the accounting in the spring. In the meantime, they could reach him by writing to an address in Rome, which he gave them. Sandos mailed this letter and the London letter of July 19 to Perkins in care of Williams in London, asking him to forward them to Boston.[6]

For Perkins, the war was coming closer. When British troops landed at Eastport on the Passamaquoddy and occupied it, Boston had cause for concern. After all, Eastport, in the district of Maine, was then still part of the Commonwealth of Massachusetts. When the news reached Boston the end of August that the British had captured Washington, burned the public buildings before withdrawing, and were threatening Baltimore, the nature of this war came home to them. Washington in flames was one thing, but Boston in flames was a matter of their houses and their goods and their families.

Late in August a group of gentlemen, including Colonel Perkins, met with the selectmen to ask for a town meeting to discuss measures for defending the town. The selectmen complacently replied that the governor had taken all necessary steps. The gentlemen did not agree and applied to a justice of the peace to call a meeting over the heads of the selectmen. They got their warrant for a meeting and on Thursday evening, August 30, met together in the Exchange Coffee House to plan their strategy. Perkins, with six other Federalists and three Republicans, was appointed to a committee to draft resolutions to be discussed.

By the time of the town meeting on Saturday, September 3, it was reported that the president had returned to a smoking, ruined Washington. The *Chronicle* cried that Boston was next. People were more concerned than at any time previously and began gathering early at Faneuil Hall. After a moderator had been elected, the colonel rose to present his committee's resolutions. These stated that the main threat of the British was against the public ships and naval arsenals of the federal government; that even though Boston uniformly despised the present "calamity," it now felt itself exposed to danger because of the warships in the town; that the federal government was providing no protection for the town; and that having every confidence in Governor Strong, it was proposed that the town cooperate with him by building fortifications and making loans and contributions for this purpose. After bitter debate the resolution that the colonel and his group wanted, was overwhelmingly approved.

Strong, who had been dragging his feet, now swung into action. The previous June, when Commodore Bainbridge of the Navy Yard had tried to get him moving, Strong had appointed a committee of three (Gen. David Cobb, John Brooks, and Timothy Pickering) as a Board of Commissioners of Sea Coast Defense. Their principal suggestion was that Bainbridge move his war ships into the outer harbor so that if the British came, it would not be necessary for them to bombard the town to destroy the warships. Bainbridge turned a deaf ear to this extraordinary suggestion and the committee reciprocated by ignoring all his advice.

Strong now ordered militia companies to Boston to aid in defense of the capital, and summoned the General Court to meet on October 5. The selectmen rushed plans to sink hulks in the harbor to prevent British ships from entering, and arranged for gangs of axemen to destroy bridges if the British landed. They also had men at Faneuil Hall from twelve to one o'clock each day to collect donations to pay for these measures.

The excited town heard that the British, moving down from Eastport, had captured Castine and Belfast. Portland was seized by "moving fever," families taking their valuables and themselves into the countryside. The frenzy hit Salem, and made, said Dr. Bentley, a "great shaking." Federalist Nathaniel Bowditch noted that "almost all the influential democrats" had scampered, while the Federalists generally were sticking "by the Stall." But just to be on the safe side, he sent off most of his library and astronomical instruments.[7]

In Boston, plans were made to build a new fort on Noddles Island (now East Boston), two on Dorchester Heights, and a battery at Dorchester Point. Others were to be built later. A suburbanite coming into town on September 8, found it "in considerable alarm for its safety." But alarm was only one side of the picture. There was a resolute firmness to stand and protect families and homes. Volunteers clamored eagerly to work on the new fortifications.[8]

A regiment of "Sea Fencibles" in smart blue uniforms marched through town on Friday, September 9, with four pieces of artillery they were taking to Dorchester Heights. They were armed with cutlasses and pikes, not much use against British canons. The merchants on State Street greeted them with three cheers as they filed past. At Dorchester Point, they fired thirty-two rounds at targets stationed a mile off shore and even hit them a few times.

Through the weekend, militia companies began arriving in Boston from the hinterland. Passengers reaching town on stages from the north and west reported troops on the march for Boston. On Saturday morning at 6 A.M., 150 mechanics assembled at the ferry way opposite Noddle's Island to begin work on the new fort, which was to be named Fort Strong.

Each day new recruits took their place. So seriously did Boston view the danger that it even permitted work on Sundays. Six hundred crowded down to the ferry ways, but only four hundred could be used. Members of the Suffolk Bar volunteered, as did the dry goods dealers, Long Wharf merchants, India Street Wharf merchants, printers, housewrights, "200 of the jolly tars of the Navy Yard," and students from Harvard. Unused to such hard labor, many of the respectable men got "completely fag'd" as one of them wrote. Even boys from the public schools turned out, marching down State Street in military order, flags flying, drums beating, to spend a few days carrying sod and pickaxes.[9] *

The Perkins family was actively involved in the defense effort. Samuel G. Perkins had organized the "exempts," men of fifty or under who were legally exempt from military service but who still wanted to help. They formed a cavalry, an artillery, and an infantry, which was captained by Sam Perkins. The colonel was notified by Governor Strong that he and Israel Thorndike were being added to the Board of Commissioners of Sea Coast Defence which had been set up in June.

There was much to be done and the commissioners plunged into furious activity. Boston Neck had to be fortified, so did Charlestown Neck. A fort ought to be erected on Bunker's Hill. Who could tell what Bainbridge and his public ships would do? Or how much help they would be to the defense of the town? Pickering's advice was to leave them "to their fate." Both the forts on Governor's and Castle Island were in bad shape. Field officers were not yet acquainted with the terrain around Boston. Signals of alarm were not yet fixed. Weapons were in

* At an anniversary of the Latin School, Ralph Waldo Emerson remembered that as a boy of eleven he had gone with his whole school to do his share. He confessed he couldn't recall a stroke of work that he did. Mostly he remembered the thirst brought on by the dry and dusty work, and how they spent much time filling their tin pails with water. "Whether the news of this action on the part of the Latin School reached England and decided that government to sue for peace I have never heard. (laughter and applause)" (*Proceedings of the MHS*, vol. 34, p. 149).

short supply, and the selectmen needed warehouses and buildings to house the troops daily pouring into Boston.[10]

There was one piece of good news on September 15, and salutes fired from vessels at the Navy Yard and harbor forts celebrated it. The militia on the Common aimed their muskets at the lowery sky and shot holes in the clouds to announce the great naval victory on Lake Champlain. Colonel Perkins received the news with private gratitude as well as public pleasure. The British warships that were threatening Vergennes and the Monkton Iron Works, among other more important objectives, had been decisively defeated at Plattsburg by the fleet of Captain MacDonough on Sunday morning the eleventh in a battle lasting two hours and twenty minutes. The army of invasion accompanying them had retreated to Canada. Writing to Welles at Vergennes, the colonel acknowledged the debt: "I believe in my heart that MacDonough saved our works, but I believe too that our works saved his ships by furnishing a large supply of shot. So that I think it is an even bargain."[11]

It was even a better bargain than the colonel could know. For news of the crushing defeat of the British at Plattsburg and the subsequent retreat of the British army without risking battle, was carried across the Atlantic to the peace commissioners at Ghent. It played a distinct role in softening the position of the British negotiators, so that an end to the conflict came sooner. Thus Monkton showed a profit that would never be recorded in any account book.

Back in Washington, Pickering was still fretting about the defense of Boston. The plans for fortifying Boston Neck bothered him. The plan had been given to Perkins to expedite, though who drew it up is not known. When still in Boston, Pickering, sitting at Colonel Thorndike's table, had suggested to Perkins some of the deficiencies of the proposal, marking them out on the map, "loosely, with a pencil." Thorndike, replying to Pickering on the eighth of October assured him the steps he was concerned about had been taken. The works on Noddles Island and Dorchester Heights were nearly finished too, he reported, but those on Dorchester Point and Neck were barely begun. With General Brooks and Colonel Perkins he had been on the "clift grounds proposed to be fortified several times." Bainbridge, wrote Thorndike, was still keeping his ships in the background and letting the town protect them, and he wanted Pickering to let the navy secretary know this.[12]

Perkins was apparently responsible for the works protecting Charlestown. A star-shaped fort was planned for Bunker's Hill (not Breed's Hill this time), and a defensive line for the neck where the Medford road crossed the Middlesex Canal. This was to guard Boston from an attack from the rear.*

On Wednesday, the fifth, the General Court met at the State House in extraordinary session to consider the distressing situation that faced the Commonwealth. Governor Strong cataloged their woes: the coast blockaded, two counties in the district of Maine held by the enemy, invasion of Boston imminent. Rumors were circulating that 15,000 British troops would soon be marching on the town. The citizens were being taxed to support the national defense, being given none by Washington, and so obliged to provide and pay for their own. A joint committee of the legislature was appointed to study and report on this situation. Several resolutions resulted, supported by Colonel Perkins and all the Boston members, one in particular calling for a committee of twelve to meet and confer with delegates from the other New England states, "upon the subjects of their public grievances and concerns, and upon the best means of preserving our resources and of defence against the enemy." Suggestions of secession from the Union were openly discussed in the Federalist press.[13]

But fear of invasion diminished as the fall days passed. By the time Fort Strong was finished and dedicated at the end of October, it was no longer needed. The dignitaries, including the five Commissioners of Sea Coast Defence, embarked from Long Wharf for Noddles Island and were met at the gate of the fort by the regiment of Winslow Blues. At a marquee pitched in the center of the fort the lieutenant-governor gave a speech, flags were hoisted, cheers cheered, guns touched off, answered by salvos from the town, and then the company sat down to a huge collation. A month later, to the day, Brooks could report to Pickering that the troops "are all discharged except 1100 at Fort Independence and Warren."[14]

Everywhere in New England, the fall elections witnessed the defeat of many Republican candidates. This encouraged Federalists that a groundswell of public opinion favored the convention of New England states called to meet at Hartford. The Federalist papers outdid them-

* A note on the map found among the papers of the colonel would indicate that only part of this plan was to be constructed during the "present exigency"; the rest could be finished later if found expedient.

selves in speculation on the coming meeting; the *Centinel* talking of it as a "new Federal Edifice," John Lowell writing inflammatory letters to the papers, and a most perceptive editor in Georgetown, Maryland, a month before the convention was held, outlining almost all the amendments the convention finally adopted.[15]

Twenty-six delegates attended the Hartford meeting, all of them from New England states and all Federalists, making it purely a party meeting. The Massachusetts delegation of twelve was headed by the venerable George Cabot, seconded by Harrison Gray Otis, who became the principal man at the meeting. Like nearly all the men chosen to go, he was a moderate. John Lowell thought him even worse: "today bold, and tomorrow like a hare trembling at every breeze."[16]

Though Otis greatly distrusted his "skill and talents as a pilot in a revolutionary storm," he could feel in the air "an evident suspence in expectation of great changes and events." He put his thoughts into an aphorism: "If the clock has run down, why try to move the hand by pushing it round—Wind it up if you can, otherwise buy a new one." Would the men of Hartford be clock winders or clock buyers?[17]

The sessions concluded January 5, 1815, and it was clear that the men at Hartford had not bought a new clock. It was not even clear if they had wound the old one up. The "pilot in a revolutionary storm" had counseled against rocking the boat. Instead, the convention issued a strong protest against the abuses of "bad administrations"—which in their eyes were non-Federalist ones, and complained against violations of the Constitution, which meant almost anything the Republicans had done. They proposed all the Federalist remedies urged during the years out of power, and suggested seven amendments to the Constitution that would correct the abuses they noted.* Further action was referred back to the concerned states.

There was a great sigh of relief by the administration and by those who had believed the newspaper agitation and feared the conference might recommend secession. Radical Federalists were disappointed at the moderate tone of the report, but made the best of it. The Massachusetts and Connecticut legislatures acted promptly, appointing three commissioners each to go to Washington and discuss the two main mat-

* None of these amendments was then adopted, but two, in much modified form, are now part of the Constitution as Amendments 14 and 22.

ters that had most concerned the delegates: militia and money. Who was to control the state militia and pay it, and where was the money coming from: these were the matters in the report that required immediate attention.

The governor and Council of the Commonwealth appointed Otis, William Sullivan, and Colonel Perkins to be their three agents to Washington. Of these three, only Otis had been at Hartford. Perkins and Sullivan had both agreed with the calling of the convention and its report by their affirmative votes in the legislature. On January 31, 1815, Perkins received his official notification—the most important task he had been given or accepted in political life—and on the following Friday the three men left for Washington in a private coach supplied at the expense of the Commonwealth.

The Republican newspapers gave the three emissaries a sarcastic farewell, hailing them as the "Lords High Commissioners," and anticipating the "awe, the dread, the astonishment and dismay that our backwood men at Washington will be struck with when they first behold the three great men of Massachusetts." The editor, showing a poor ear for rhyme, then delivered himself of a jingle:

> This high and mighty trio
> Must awe the reptiles from Ohio
> And he who contradicts it—tells a lie-o![18]

Saturday night, the three reached New Haven, where they were forced to spend Sunday, since the blue laws of Connecticut forbade travel on the Sabbath. Otis fumed to his wife that such laws are "unworthy of the State of Connecticut and discreditable to the age we live in." He conveniently forgot in his indignation that the Massachusetts General Court had only the year before reaffirmed similar laws forbidding Sabbath travel, although it was not generally enforced.[19]

Four days later they reached Philadelphia, though not without incident. The coach broke down, which delayed them an hour or two, but nobody had been hurt. They lost a day at New York since the ice was running "so violently down the river as to render the passing dangerous and nearly impracticable." Watching their chances, they finally made it across the next day in a rowboat, dodging the ice cakes. The road to Philadelphia was covered with eight inches of packed snow and made a smooth surface so they reached that town without "fatigue or inconvenience." Spending the night there, Otis sketched, for his wife's benefit, a homey scene of the three of them: "My two fellow-travellers are my chums and at each elbow interrupting me every moment both expressing their love to my wife and Sullivan adding that he is in love with my daughter who he thinks is as like her mother as one pea is like another."

A flock of crows accompanied the coach on the drive from New York to Philadelphia. Every so often the flock would alight and three large black crows would separate from the rest and stalk about, "waddling and looking wise," until the clatter of the approaching coach would scare the whole flock up into the sky again. The obvious implications were not lost on the travelers: "These are ill-omened birds and in days when augury was in fashion, would have been considered as sad precursors of the three Ambassadors. What the blackbirds at Washington will say or do with us remains to be seen."

Staying but one night in Philadelphia, they arrived in Baltimore three days later. There they heard the news that Andrew Jackson had defeated the British in a decisive battle at New Orleans. This would certainly accelerate the peace negotiations at Ghent. It was now apparent to the ambassadors that the war was not going to last much longer, and the success of their mission had depended upon the continuation of hostilities.

By Tuesday, when they arrived in Washington, rumors of a peace treaty were everywhere. The three took up lodgings in the same boarding house where Senators Gore and Rufus King were staying. Wednesday, they met with members of the Massachusetts congressional delegation and it was decided, since peace seemed so imminent, to hold off any application to the government until they heard one way or the other.

They did not have long to wait. The messenger with the peace treaty shortly rode into Washington, and the Senate ratified it quickly and unanimously on Thursday, February 16. The Republican press found the sight of the "three wise men of the east" a suitable butt for satire, cartoons, squibs and verse:

> Billy, Harry, Tom
> What the Tophet ails you,
> Better now go home
> Before your courage fails you.[20]

But they could not go home; Otis had come down with the gout! They were compeled to wait out his attack in a Washington rejoicing in peace. Although it was the worst thing that could have happened to their mission, Perkins could not have been happier. "Thanks to the Giver of all good things," he wrote, "we are once more restored to peace, and I trust I shall never see another war."[21]

Boston rejoiced too when the news of a treaty reached it. Monday, February 13 was a "day of Jubilee"; Schoolhouses were opened "to let the boys run and kick up their heels." All day long, guns were fired off, military companies turned out, people roamed the streets cheerful and animated. In the evening, the Exchange Coffee House, the Province House, printing offices, shops, and dwelling houses were illuminated. Eunice Callendar went home and wrote naïvely in her diary that there could be no doubt Madison would be glad to sign the peace treaty; "after ruining our country he must begin to see he has gone too far."[22]

While the ambassadors waited for the swelling in Otis's foot to subside, they passed the time by attending a few balls. Those held by the Federalists in Georgetown were enjoyed. "The ball here on Washington's birthday night was select and genteel. The party consisted of gentlemen and ladies," Otis wrote his wife, whereas the one held by Madison at the White House was attended chiefly by the "Court Party, and strangers allured by curiosity." Two of those strangers were Perkins and Sullivan. A guest in the president's drawing room, on the twenty-second watched as Perkins and Sullivan "presented their respects to him, Madison, and talked of nothing." But when they got home they told Otis the affair was all "tinseled vulgarity." Otis was glad he had been unable to go.[23]

Then, on Sunday morning, February 26, the weather was fine, and Otis, still weak, but feeling much better than he had for days, greeted his fellow-travelers that morning with a cheerful "Suppose I should tell you that I am ready to march in one hour."

"Why" said the colonel, "you must judge of your own feelings, and ought not to expose yourself, but if you could bear it, it would certainly be a great affair to get on to Baltimore. The thaw is already rapid; the runs [fords] will be full, the roads frightful, and every hour is worth saving."

"Order the carriage, Sir," responded Otis, "I am ready in an hour."

"You are not serious," said Sullivan with a look of incredulity.

"Sir, I say I go with you in an hour."

In half an hour, the horses were hitched to the coach and the party was ready to start. All the boarders—who solemnly voted Otis mad—

assembled to see them off. Otis made them line up on either side of the entrance and exited brandishing his crutch, just as if the commissioners had triumphed on their mission.[24]

The Republican papers let no chance escape to mock "the three wise men." The *Boston Yankee* on March 3 published an imaginary letter purportedly written by "Tin Ware" living in "Indigo-and-Feather-Town" Connecticut. Hearing that people wanted information on these three men who seemed mysteriously to have disappeared in Baltimore, he sends the editor information of them as they passed through his town. On the Sabbath, just as people were gathering for worship, "three men on horseback came in from the South full drive." Two deacons, grabbing the horses by the bridles, stopped them for Sabbath traveling. "The rider whom they called Oat-es, the prettiest man of the three, flew into a most violent passion and threatened them with instant death and made use of the most profane language."

The second rider, whom "Tin Ware" called "Sully-vung," appeared troubled in mind and looked like he needed sleep. He said they had traveled a great distance, mostly by night so as to avoid being seen. The tears ran down his cheek profusely as "he begged and pleaded most piteously to pass."

The third ride was "the stoutest man of the three" and "had a conspicuous mark on his face." He was called "some such name as Purkkens." "He kept himself quite still and seemed willing that Oat-es should take the lead, He however tried to pacify Oat-es and told him that it would not do to break the Laws of Connecticut. D-m the Laws of Connecticut says Oat-es. If we can break the Constitution and separate the Union, cannot we break the laws of this little paltry state?"

Late in the evening of March 14 the ambassadors finally entered Boston. No illuminations, no cannon, no bells greeted their return. Instead, a month later, the *Yankee* was attacking them again. The legislature had voted an expense allowance for the three, and the *Yankee* computed the Federalist folly had cost the Commonwealth at least $996.

The Commonwealth was not alone in paying for wasted missions; Perkins himself had some stiff bills to pay. Back in October, when fear of invasion was strongest, Perkins received news from London that must have momentarily driven away thoughts of the war. On the thirteenth of August, Williams had received some letters supposedly written in

Paris, which he was asked to forward to James Perkins in Boston. The letters to Perkins were sealed and the gentleman writing him, Mr. Charles Sandos, was unknown to him. Two days later, he received a letter from Perkins dated June 19. This letter gave him his first news of the intended gold deliveries by Mr. Sandos. On getting Perkins's letter he broke open Sandos's letters to James Perkins, and quickly saw what had happened. His indignation poured out in a letter to the brothers: "Were I to exhaust Johnson from one end to the other I should not find description of the Villany of the unworthy character in whom you reposed confidence and who has shamefully abused and betrayed that confidence." In a word, Sandos was nothing but a swindler. The gold had never been delivered by him to Williams nor did he intend to deliver it.[25]

This was more than enough evidence to cause Williams to take action. After all, the money if it could be found was his, though the loss, if it were not recovered, fell on the Perkins firm. He selected John B. Greene of his office to go to Paris and see if he could find Sandos, even though the trail was a month cold. "In a pursuit of this kind, though apparently desperate, no Expence ought to be spared." None was. Greene set off that night for Paris.

The same mail contained the first report from Greene. Greene said he had employed an assistant and contacted the bankers the Perkinses used in Paris to aid in the search. All thought Sandos was in Paris and "if the man is here he can hardly escape."[26]

Whichever brother first read these letters, the other must have quickly been called in to share his distress. The colonel, however, was the one who replied to Williams. Their knowledge of Sandos's background while in America was sketched in for Williams's benefit. Calling it "this apparent atrocity," they remained puzzled over why Sandos would have written the letters he did if the case was as hopeless as Williams thought. This was grasping at straws, but the letters were strange, unless they were to delay pursuit or at least lead the pursuers off on wild goose chases. The brothers approved the measures Williams had taken, but in any case wanted no publicity either in Europe, where it might hurt Williams's claim on the money, or in America where it might embarrass them.[27]

The pursuit of Sandos continued. Williams reported that Sandos's trunk had been found. Breaking it open, they found "books, newspapers, a few old letters—some of yours to him while at Worcester." The name of Sandos's wife was Ann Ford. It appeared that she was a poor illiterate girl whom Sandos had got with child. Williams did not believe they were married even though they called each other husband and wife. "Such fellows never marry." Also in the trunk was a small diary Sandos had kept for two or three years, "by which I should suppose that the man was then deranged for it is a record only of his dreams."[28]

The wild goose chase went on. Now Aix La Chapelle. Now a town nearer Paris. By January 9, 1815, Greene, who had been 147 days on the chase, was forced to turn his attention to other matters. He submitted a bill of nearly 7,500 francs for his expenses. But pursuit was not abandoned. Brother-in-law Ralph Forbes, then in London, was asked by Williams to check a report that Sandos had been seen in Coblentz, Germany. But the week after Forbes had left for Germany, Williams received word that Sandos had been seen in London with his wife at Covent Garden Theater. A Major James who several years before had been victimized by Sandos and had him arrested only to see him escape, was the informant this time. When Sandos had seen James looking at him, he and his wife had left hurriedly and disappeared in the crowded London streets. The major told Williams that Sandos was "one of the most infamous men" who ever lived. While Greene was chasing will-of-the-wisps around Europe, Sandos had been quietly living in Saint-Omer, a short distance from Calais. Forbes, of course, found nothing at Coblentz, but billed the Perkinses about $500 for that nothing. In all it had cost the Perkinses more than $2,100 *not* to recover their $40,000.[29]

Sandos himself had the last word. Purportedly in Leghorn, Sandos picked up his quill and wrote a letter to James Perkins. A chevalier, no less, would shortly visit Boston and "settle with you for that unfortunate gold." As for himself, why "a nervous fever confines me yet to my bed," and he expected to leave it only in a coffin. Failing that heavenly dispensation, he and his wife (for they *had* been legally married) intended to pass their remaining days "in a religious retirement, disgusted with a world that for the most part we cannot but despise." Undoubtedly, the $40,000 in stolen gold went far to sweeten the poverty of their religious retirement.[30]

The birthday of American Independence announced as usual. May generations yet unborn hail with Joy, this auspicious day. But if vice should pave the way for civil discord and Faction rend the bonds of Union, may Liberty with her attendants still smile on the cold mountains of New England.

Aaron White's diary,
July 4, 1817

# 23

# A Cavalcade of Boston Gentlemen

When the second war with England ended, Colonel Perkins was fifty years old and his brother fifty-four. For more than twenty-two years they had been associated in business; a partnership that had made both of them wealthy, and enabled them to afford elegant townhouses as well as extensive country estates—James at "Pine Bank" in Jamaica Plain, the colonel in neighboring Brookline. They had pursued the activities that interested them: James the more sedentary pursuits of real estate and reading, the colonel the far-flung concerns of the partnership, of sports, politics, and civic service. Both now had sons near the age they were when that first war ended.

The comparison might have occured to the colonel on Monday, May 8, 1815, when the ship *Jacob Jones,* together with the brig *Rambler,* arrived in Boston harbor and fired salutes to the town. The ships were 108 days out of Canton, loaded with rich cargoes of silk, tea, and other valuables, and were two of the first ships from China since the war had ended. The fresh goods they bore were welcome to merchants, and one young man on the *Jacob Jones,* completing his first turn before the mast, was joyfully welcomed back by his parents on Pearl Street.

The colonel's son had had an exciting voyage. On its outward trip, the fast-sailing *Jacob Jones* met one British warship and engaged in a long cannon duel, until the Britisher ran out of shot. Subsequently, the *Jones* captured two British ships, one loaded with opium, the other with opium and gold dust. The colonel's comment on hearing this was eminently practical: "The crew will all have a handsome interest in defending the ship."[1]

On June 7, the *Jacob Jones* had arrived off the Pearl River. The port of Canton was blockaded by British warships, and several American vessels were sitting out the war in Whampoa. The *Jones* was spotted by one of the blockading British vessels, which gave immediate chase, but being a faster ship, the *Jones* reached the safety of the port. Cushing was happy to welcome his young cousin and hear the news from home. Early in September, the *Rambler* slipped through the British net, to join the American ships at Whampoa. Acting on the theory that there might be escape in numbers, five American ships—including the two Perkins vessels—made a break for it on January 18, 1815.

The joke of it was that a paper already signed in Ghent had put them all at peace. Since it would be summer before the news could reach Canton, they went through the motions of escape and pursuit in deadly seriousness. The dash was successful, and three days later the two Perkins ships parted company and sailed separately for Boston. It was not until the *Rambler* was almost into Boston that it spoke to another ship and heard the news of peace. The *Jacob Jones* learned it only two weeks before arriving.

The end of the war with England left the dispute between the two countries nominally unchanged. None of the "principles" Madison claimed the war was fought over were conceded by the British. Federalists were relieved that the country had gotten out of the war without having to yield any territory. The crisis of the war having passed, people turned to making a living in the new world created by the defeat of Napoleon and the social ideals of the French Revolution. Merchants found new trading conditions and opportunities calling for men with venturesome spirit. Though now middle-aged, venturesomeness was still a hallmark of the brothers. The firm explored new areas of profit and one of these was the cargo captured by the *Jacob Jones*—opium.

The British East India Company, the major factor in trade with China, had discovered the advantages of opium as early as 1773. Since

Western demand for Chinese products far exceeded Chinese demand for Western goods, the adverse balance of payments had to be met with specie. There was no chance for a double profit in specie, however, such as the Perkins and others obtained with the furs of the Northwest Coast. Opium gave such a double profit to the British East India Company who had a monopoly on the drug. Introduced first for its medical values, the pleasant physical sensations quickly became the main reason it was wanted, giving the peasants and coolies a quick release from the misery of their daily life.

By 1800, alarmed both by the pernicious effects of the drug and by the fact that its use had grown so that the balance of trade was now draining specie *out* of China, the emperor forbad its importation. Because of its paramount position in the China trade, the East India Company had to follow the law to the letter. However, the sale of opium in India, had become a large factor in the economy of that country and in British interests there. The company was not about to see this disturbed. Fortunately, there was a way out. The company's monopoly covered trade only between China and England. Independent British merchants, trading between India and China, were not under the company's jurisdiction. It was these ships—called "country ships"—that carried the opium to China, buying it at the great opium auctions in Calcutta, keeping the revenue of the East India Company intact, and allowing the company piously to assure the Chinese that they had no control over what other merchants did. This, and the unbelievable corruption that existed among the Chinese themselves, permitted the trade to flourish.

Turkey also produced opium, most of which went to the European market, to be prescribed as pain-dulling laudanum for almost any ailment. Shortly after they opened their Canton office, the firm wrote Cushing for "information respecting the article of Turkey Opium; its value in China, etc." Nothing further was done, although other American merchants began to export Turkish opium to China as early as the 1809–10 season.[2]

Turkish opium was considered inferior to the Indian and had to be sold at a discount. However, the Perkins were not ones to ignore this profitable commodity for long. As time went on, the Chinese in the northern provinces developed a taste for the harsher Turkish opium, and the trade increased. In August 1815, Perkins sent the brig *Monkey* to Havana for a cargo of coffee and sugar for the Mediterranean. The supercargo had instructions to invest the proceeds in quicksilver and opium, the latter known to be in short supply in Canton. The fact that they were entering a trade forbidden by China was known to all the merchants involved. Nor was the fact that many considered it immoral to use opium any deterrent to the traders. They cheerfully rationalized that the opium habit was not nearly so debilitating as the habit of drink.

The reports that came back from Cushing indicated that the first ventures with opium would produce good profits. Having tested the market, the Perkins firm decided to go into it heavily. If they were to make the most advantageous purchases of opium and realize the biggest profit possible, they needed an agent on the spot. As was customary, they looked within the family group first. Their choice again fell on the Paine family. William F. Paine himself was not available since he was running a kind of branch office of Perkins & Co. in the Isle de France, but his younger brother was.

Fred W. Paine was then twenty-eight years old, unmarried, of medium height, both hair and complexion dark. Of a rather melancholy disposition, aggravated by indigestion, he left Harvard after one term. Having decided his future lay in the mercantile field he had gone as supercargo for the Perkins when only eighteen to the Northwest Coast on a trip lasting three years. Satisfied with his work, the brothers had sent him to Canton in 1812 to warn Cushing of the war. He had spent the war years in Canton, was fully acquainted with the demands of that market, and presumably well-trained by Cushing. After the war, he had captained the *Levant* to Rotterdam for the firm with a cargo of tea. In point of experience and trust, he was ideal for the job of Mediterranean agent of the firm.

In the spring of 1817, supplied with power of attorney from the firm, he left for Leghorn. His pay was to be $2,000 plus expenses. His principal job was to buy opium for transshipment to Canton, to see that the various cargoes sent to his area were profitably sold, and generally look after the interests of the firm in the region. It was not long before he was sending back to Boston, page after page of detailed commercial memoranda written in his neat, precise script. Apparently without any sort of masterplan behind it, the firm was moving towards a pattern of local offices in various areas of the world, run by competent semi-independent agents, under the general direction of the brothers in Boston. What prevented this from maturing was time: the time needed in those days to communicate back and forth around the world, and the fact that time was running out for the brothers. They were just too old now to carry out such an operation on a large scale.

Changes had taken place, too, in the situation on the Northwest Coast. The Russians had extended their settlements down along the coast of Alaska where formerly some of the greatest collections of furs had been made. The sea otter had drastically decreased in number, for the reason Perkins noted in a letter of November 14, 1815: "the indiscriminate destruction of old and young." John Jacob Astor had hoped to move in and take over this trade by establishing an outpost, Astoria, on the coast. But the London-based Northwest Company, pursuing their plans to move westward, planted a post nearby and Astoria became one of the early casualties of the war when the Northwest Company took it over for a small indemnity.[3]

Now that the Northwest Company had cornered all the fur trade in the Northwest Territory, they had to decide how best to exploit their position. It was too expensive to transport the furs over the mountains to the East Coast. The obvious solution, to send their furs by ship across the Pacific to Canton, as the Americans had been doing, was balked by the monopoly of the East India Company. In this impasse, William McGillvray of the Northwest Company turned to J. and T. H. Perkins, who, because they were Americans, could trade with Canton without permission from the East India Company, and who had, in Perkins & Co., the most practical outlet to market the furs.

The colonel had suggested an arrangement of this sort some six years before. Now it was in the interest of the Northwest Company to explore it further. It looked profitable for both parties. Perkins, talking with the ship captains who had gone to the coast, had always been persuaded that there must be "immense quantities of land furs" in that quarter. "We presume," he wrote McGillvray, "that you would direct a considerably quantity of peltry, that is, beaver, otter and fox, which are collected on this side of the Rocky Ridge, to the establishment at Columbia."[4]

Perkins's proposal was to supply the Northwest Company outpost, have his ship do some trading along the coast for sea otter skins, then return and load the Northwest Company skins, take them to China, sell them and invest the proceeds in China goods. The gross profit of the sales of the China goods would be split, by a formula, between the two groups. The crux of the plan was that the cargo of furs was to be represented at Canton as Perkins property, thus bypassing the East India Company.

It was a shrewd bargain. It took the speculation and risk out of the business for the Perkinses. It gave them a sure profit at each end of the trip, speeded up the frequency of the voyages and thus the returns, and put the trips on a regular basis. How it would work out for the Northwest Company remained to be seen.

Yet to be seen too was the future of the elder sons of the two brothers. Both were juniors by name but neither seemed to be cut from the same cloth as their fathers. They were the sons of rich men, they were young, and their own pleasures seemed to be the most pressing concern to them at the moment. T. H. P., Jr., as he is styled in the letters of the firm, had been born with an infirmity like his father, though not the same one. He was nicknamed "Short-arm Tom," because his left arm was about three inches shorter than the right one. In his boyhood fights this sometimes gave him an advantage. He would lead with this left, and his opponent would think that was the extent of his "reach," then suddenly he would swing around the much longer right, catching his adversary off balance.

He had apparently been a problem to his parents. References in the colonel's letters hint at extravagence with money and general intractability. He had been put under the care of his uncle-in-law, Benjamin Abbott, at Phillips Exeter. From there he had gone, not to Harvard, but to St. Mary's Academy, in Maryland, a Roman Catholic institution. There an escapade caused his expulsion. When morning Mass was celebrated, the Protestant students were obliged to remain outside the chapel in a sort of porch area. Winter mornings it was very cold, and the young Protestants protested vigorously but to no avail. One morning, the Catholic students comfortably inside with their God and the Protestants out in the cold with theirs, someone suggested making a fire. Young Perkins looked at the wooden steps leading up to the chapel, then started "pulling off the treads and risers, split them into small pieces" and soon had a fine fire blazing. The Catholics emerged from chapel into smoke and flames—a reverse inquisition! But Perkins was suspended for six months and sent back to Boston in disgrace. It was then that his father found it prudent to send him off in the *Jacob Jones*.[5]

The colonel was not taking any chances. Six weeks after his son returned to Boston in the *Jones,* he was headed back for China again in the *Ophelia,* captained by Samuel Hill, a thirty-eight year old mariner, who had been at sea since he was seventeen. Hill had risen in the ranks, at the same time acquiring "a superior and practical knowledge of all the modes of vice and profaneness known among seamen." The Perkinses knew him well, rated his nautical ability highly, and made him a good offer in order to secure him as captain of the voyage.[6]

The *Ophelia* was carrying a cargo of seventy thousand dollars, and by June 17 this was safely stowed on board along with its complement of twenty-two officers and men. J. and T. H. Perkins had a five eighths interest in the voyage, S. G. Perkins & Company held two eighths, and Bryant & Sturgis took the remaining eighth. On Sunday morning, June 20, the ship was ready for sea. As usual, several of the owners came aboard to ride down the harbor with the ship. The colonel was there to see his nearly nineteen-year-old son off.

While the ship was making its way out, the colonel and his friends were below having dinner with the departing officers and T. H. P., Jr., who was acting as supercargo under Captain Hill. After tacking and hauling and anchoring five miles below the lighthouse, the colonel and his companions went down the ropeladder and returned to town, while the ship waited for another boat to bring back some light sails they had inadvertently left ashore. About sunset, the ship got under way again with a pleasant gentle evening breeze, and by morning they watched Cape Cod disappear behind them.

During July their weather was mostly pleasant as they sailed down the Atlantic. By the middle of October they were rounding Cape Horn, and early in November they had landed in Valparaiso, Chile. Here the colonel's son showed his temper. Captain Hill tells the story:

> On the 13th November, some gentlemen of Valparaiso dined on board the *Ophelia* by invitation with Captain Edes and Mr. Brown of the *Beverly.* We sat late after dinner and perfect harmony prevailed. Towards evening I went on deck and was conversing with Mr. King when I heard some noise and disputing in the cabin. I immediately went below and found Mr. Perkins and Captain Edes warmly engaged in a dispute. I sat some time and after hearing Mr. Perkins make use of very indecent and abusive language to Captain Edes, such as calling him a liar and telling him he would deprive him of a living by his father's influence, *etc.* I begged Mr. Perkins to desist and not make my company unhappy.

He then diverted the same kind of language to me and after repeated attempts to pacify him I urged him to go to his room.[7]

The upshot of the affair was that Perkins left the ship and returned to Boston via London.*

James Perkins Jr. was equally lively, and already too fond of the cheering bottle. What were their parents to do with two such spirited lads? Put them to work was their answer, but it seemed best not to take them into the senior firm. A new firm would be formed for them. To their two sons, the Perkinses added son-in-law Samuel Cabot, who brought several years active experience as the Boston agent of the Philadelphia firm of Perit & Cabot, into the new combine. It was upon his knowledge, stability, and skill that they were principally relying to keep the new firm from any major disasters until the juniors could acquire "seasoning." The fathers intended gradually to switch much of their minor commission business to the new firm in order to get them going. On New Year's Day, 1817, the new partners met in the colonel's house on Pearl Street to sign their articles of co-partnership.

One of the witnesses to the signing was the new firm's first apprentice, twelve-year-old Robert Bennet Forbes. Young Forbes was the son of the colonel's sister, Margaret, and Ralph Bennet Forbes. Forbes the father had spent the last quarter of a century in a vain pursuit of the fortune that showered on his Perkins brothers-in-law. Whatever he touched, he seemed to jinx. After the war, he had returned ill and penniless, a forty-year-old failure. A second Captain Cutting, his finger was always in his mouth.

His wife and six children were living in a farmhouse on top of Milton Hill with the Blue Hills behind them and Boston harbor and its islands in front of them. The brothers had supported their sister and her family, and continued to do so, for Forbes was no sooner home that he was seized with what was called "gout of the Head" brought about by overindulgence in what Forbes euphemistically termed "eau medicinale."

Since a college education seemed out of the question for the boys, the obvious profession was that of merchant, particularly since they had such well-placed uncles. The oldest, Thomas Tunno Forbes, was thirteen years old in 1815, a good age to begin his apprenticeship in the counting

* Presumably he was back in Boston by the spring of 1816, and there is a hint in the letterbooks that he was in Canada in the fall of 1816. At any rate, the colonel's problem was back on his doorstep.

house of his uncles. The job was not demanding. There were fires to be made, the store opened in the morning and swept out, and closed again at night. The account books had to be delivered to James's house the last thing every evening for safe keeping and picked up again the first thing each morning. There were innumerable errands to run, notes to fetch and deliver around town, the copying of invoices, letters, and such. All these tasks were well within the capacity of a thirteen year old. Two years later, his younger brother, familiarly called Bennet, had begun the same work for the firm of the junior Perkinses.

After the signing of the co-partnership papers, Tom, Jr., disappeared into the wine cellar and came back with a bottle of his father's best and oldest wine. The health and prosperity of the new firm was toasted by all, including the new apprentice. Thus festively was the firm of S. Cabot and J. and T. H. Perkins, Jr., launched.

Young Bennet moved into town and lived with the colonel on Pearl Street. Uncle James had even proposed that young Bennet might sail to China in one of the spring ships, although this was not too agreeable to his mother and father in Milton. Yet, as Forbes wrote the colonel, "I most cheerfully resign him to your joint management." A retired ship captain tutored Bennet in the elements of navigation and, though nothing was said of the future, the colonel dropped broad hints now and then. Casually during dinner, while they were eating a good pudding, he would comment: "You won't get any so good off the Cape of Good Hope." But an odd accident delayed Bennet's chance to eat poor pudding off the Cape.[8]

The colonel was planning to send Bennet to China on the *Canton Packet,* one of the finest vessels owned by the brothers. On Monday morning, June 2, 1817, it was preparing for sea just a short distance from the end of Long Wharf. A cargo of lumber had already been loaded, but the chief freight was to be specie. Thirty thousand dollars worth of bullion had already been stored in the hold, and the crew was organizing sixty thousand dollars more on the wharf to be loaded in half an hour. Such a vast sum of money required great precautions against theft and robbery.

Mr. Stickney, the chief mate, was superintending the job. He had much on his mind. During the hurry and confusion of the morning, the steward of the vessel had been acting most strangely. Just before noon, he came up to Mr. Stickney with a request to go ashore. This was out of the question, and Stickney refused. Angered, irrational, the man went off, took a loaded pistol, and went to the stern where the gunpowder was stored. He fired point blank into the powder kegs.

The steward and the stern of the vessel went sky high in a tremendous explosion. Those of the crew who were on board were either blown into the water or jumped, for the whole rear of the ship was on fire. The men on the dock, after the first surprised moment, immediately made for the ship to put out the fire, heedless of the danger of more explosions. A nearby government vessel sent men to help; a burning ship in a busy harbor threatened them all. They cut the mooring cables and began to tow the heavy ship out toward the mud flats north of the wharf. The men from the dock had boarded the vessel meanwhile, and were busy putting out the fire.

The noise of the explosion had startled the whole town. Bells quickly spread the alarm. Smoke towering into the sky from the harbor area sent hundreds running to see what had happened. They watched excitedly while the crippled ship was grounded on the flats and the fires sloshed and beaten out.

No sooner had the fire been put out, than the colonel, who had rushed to the disaster area, hired a sloop to unload the precious cargo of coins and bring them to the wharf. He arranged to use a room on India Wharf and here the specie was carted. While the coins were not damaged by the fire, they were soiled and had to be cleaned and repacked. They also had to be counted to make sure none of it had disappeared into the pocket of some "firefighter." The clerks from the counting house of both the senior and junior firm (including young Bennet), as well as the clerks from Sam Perkin's office were employed in the task.

Because of the valuable nature of the cargo, the clerks were locked into the room where they were working. They were required to stay there until the job was finished. In his usual magnanimous fashion, Tom, Jr., saw that they were repaid for their inconvenience. When the job was finished, he arranged for Boston's best restaurant, Julien's, to feast all hands on lobster and cherry bounce. The pen of James Perkins had the last careful word on the matter, neatly putting down the cost of the whole process, from the first boom to the last watchmen, into the account books at $296.45. All the specie was recovered except $154. So quickly had the work been done, that in a week another ship, the *Ophelia,* put to sea with the specie aboard, though not young Bennet.

The ship Canton Packet, which was blown up in Boston harbor, 1817. The Perkins house-flag is on the mast.

The Colonel decided to send him on a later ship. The delay gave him a chance to witness President Monroe's good-will tour of the northern states.

The visit planned by President Monroe to view military establishments in the eastern states was most timely. Colonel Perkins had a pressing matter to discuss with the president.

When the second war with England ended, British merchants glutted the reopened American market with surplus goods that the impoverished European continent could not afford. For the British there was a happy calculation in the event. Perhaps they could "stifle in the cradle those rising manufacturers in the United States which the war has forced into existence." One of the infants thus stifled in the cradle was the Monkton Iron Company. Perkins had recognized the debt owed by Monkton to the war. In March 1814 he predicted that if the war "was to continue half a dozen years, we should be able to do something. But should it terminate soon our fair prospects would be blasted." The good management of Colonel Welles plus the excellent prices of iron during the war finally made the venture profitable. But, as the colonel foresaw, this was only temporary.[9]

Peace came and gave the *coup de grâce* to Monkton. The costs of transportation made Monkton iron too expensive to ship elsewhere. When customers in Boston could import bar iron from Sweden and Russia at $75 a ton, they were not interested in buying Monkton iron at $85 a ton.

The experiment that began so hopefully in 1808, that had been continued so bravely so long at such a cost to the investors, was at last terminated. "Satisfied that we could not stand in competition with the ironmakers of Europe, we sometime since stopped the Vergennes works." The October 2, 1816 issue of the *Centinel* carried a long advertisement that gave the last chapter of the venture. "The original proprietors of the extensive Iron Works, water rights, mills, and estates belonging thereto, situated in the town of Vergennes, state of Vermont, offer the whole establishment for sale to any body of individuals who may be disposed to form a company to carry on the same."[10]

For whatever slight consolation it might have given them, the Monkton ironmakers were not the only failures. Production of pig iron in the United States, under the influx of cheap European iron, dropped from a high of 54,000 tons to 20,000 tons. In such conditions, where were the Monkton proprietors to find "any body of individuals" who would be "disposed" to take Monkton off their hands? The colonel had a candidate in mind: the new Republican president!

Perkins had been acquainted with Monroe since his visit of 1795 to Paris. He had liked him then, and in spite of Monroe's association with the Jeffersonians, found him the most acceptable of the lot. Even though Monroe had been Madison's secretary of state, he was known to have more moderate leanings than any other Republican. His private views were thought to be not so far removed from those of the Federalists. Should they support him, perhaps the bitterness of the past sixteen years might be lessened, and Federalists once again find a place in the government. Monroe, it seemed, was a man they could do business with.

Conservative Federalists were not convinced, and a split developed at the election. Although a considerable number of Boston Federalists supported Monroe, the conservatives were still able to control the Massachusetts electors, who voted officially for Rufus King. Only Connecticut and Delaware electors joined them, and Monroe was elected. Shortly afterwards, Otis and Perkins left for Washington, on what they termed a "pleasure" trip. Christopher Gore wrote Rufus King on Christmas Day 1816 what local "gossip" said was the real reason for their trip: they were looking for federal appointments. "The want of their services," wrote Gore drily, "is not felt now."[11]

Even though Monroe was not about to distribute federal jobs lavishly to Federalists, they looked forward to his coming visit to New England with great anticipation. More than one hoped for a bit of personal gain out of the political thaw. The colonel, whether or not he had been interested in a federal job—there is no evidence other than Gore's remarks that he was—had something else he was pushing. He had a turkey to unload and it just might be, he thought, that the government was in the poultry market.

A federal arsenal was going to be built somewhere near the Canadian border. What better spot could the government choose than Vergennes? In June 1817, Colonel Welles had written to Major General Macomb in Detroit and to Commodore MacDonough requesting their assistance in recommending Vergennes. Both had replied favorably. However, the final decision was not theirs but the president's. The colonel hoped to promote his scheme directly with the man who had to decide.

Monroe was to be in Boston for the first seven days of July. The Federalists now prepared a royal welcome for him; Republicans were largely ignored in the plans for greeting the Republican president. Of the thirteen men selected to be on the welcoming committee from Boston, only three were Republicans. Two of the other ten were those redoubtable "Wise Men of the East," Otis and Perkins.

Wednesday, July 2, was the day of his entry into Boston and one of great public prominence for the colonel, for he was to be the chief marshal. The day was cool and clear. The colonel mounted and rode to the Common where the welcoming procession was forming. He had two aides and forty-two assistant marshals to help him in organizing the five hundred riders taking part in the grand procession. The marshals were the sons of Boston gentry, and both THP Jr., and James Jr., along with Harrison Gray Otis, Jr., were among those riding out to the town line. James Perkins, Sr. was absent on a trip to the West Indies.

It was one o'clock when Monroe crossed into Boston. One eyewitness thought Monroe looked "as became the head of a great Nation, plain and dignified." He was wearing a simple old-fashioned New England suit and riding on an elegant horse with "superbly caparisoned stirrups and other trappings of solid gold." A committee of the selectmen greeted Monroe and a short address was made, "by Mr. Perkins."[12]

The officials now entered town, with Colonel Perkins and his cavalcade following. All along the route ladies saluted the president by waving handkerchiefs and tossing garlands of flowers in his direction. Miss Eunice Callendar had been invited with her mother into one of the houses to watch. She thought the grey charger which Monroe was riding was beautiful, and of the president: "He is in his sixty-fourth year and never was in town before." Imagine waiting that long to visit Boston![13]

At five o'clock, an official state dinner was held in the main hall of the Coffee House. All the local dignitaries, including former President Adams were at the head table, as was the colonel. Indeed, during the whole visit, the colonel never let Monroe out of his sight for long.

Thursday, the third, after a breakfast in his honor, Monroe, with the colonel and others in tow went on a tour of the defense of the harbor, the ostensible reason for his visit. The next day was the colonel's turn to be privately honored. It was Independence Day and the president of the United States was in Boston. Bostonians felt duly honored. Orations were given in the churches, collations were provided for distinguished guests, and Monroe—making a side trip to Waltham to see the new cotton factory of Lowell and Jackson and the arsenal at Watertown—stopped off at the colonel's mansion and gardens in Brookline.

Over the years since 1800, the colonel had turned this into the very model of a gentleman's country estate, and he took great delight in escorting the president round his extensive gardens with their elaborate greenhouses and exotic plants. It may have been here too that he had a chance to suggest that the president visit the iron works at Vergennes when he was in those parts.

The social peak of the visit was Saturday night, the fifth of July, a cloudy day, but it was brilliant inside the Bulfinch mansion of Senator Harrison Gray Otis on Beacon Street. The president's entertainment in Boston on Sunday was, as might be expected, a chance to go to church. In the morning he went to the North Church, while Susan Quincy went to Federal Street Church to hear Dr. Channing: "When we entered the congregation were standing singing a hymn. Colonel Perkins, whose pew was the second before ours, on seeing us, started out of the pew and opened the door of ours for Mrs. Quincy and stood until we had entered. The people all looked round thinking, I believe, the President was coming." In the afternoon he did come and heard Channing deliver a sermon on patriotism and general benevolence. *And* he sat with Colonel Perkins in his pew.[14]

On Monday the president had a whirlwind tour of Harvard in the morning. In the afternoon, he reviewed troops on Boston Common and then was rushed out to Quincy to dine with former President Adams, the troop of gentlemen attenders right at his heels. On his way back, he stopped off at Senator Quincy's country place, visited the great barn, was introduced to "the Oakes cow and her calf," climbed a fence and stared at the men raking hay.

No one told him that Senator Quincy, like some New England Potemkin, had ordered a few loads of hay to be carted from the barn and spread on the fields, to give a properly pastoral look to the place. There seemed to be no limit to the hospitality of the Federalists. That evening when Monroe spent an hour at George Blake's house, the Republicans got *their* chance to entertain him. But his visit had been mainly a Federalist monopoly.

Tuesday morning, the colonel and his committee were at the Coffee

House to speed the guest upon his way north. For the president, in spite of all the ceremonial folderol, had not forgotten the business he came upon, which was the inspection of military posts. This included that potential arsenal near Canada. On July 24, when he was leaving Burlington, Vermont, to sail across Lake Champlain for Plattsburg, New York, he traveled out of his way in order to go up Otter Creek. Not only did he view the place where MacDonough's fleet had been built, he also "examined the extensive iron works."[15]

Somewhere in the marathon week in Boston, the colonel had been sufficiently persuasive to accomplish that much of his objective. But not persuasive enough. Perhaps he should have gone to Vergennes and welcomed the president to the iron works. Perhaps, like Quincy, he should have "spread hay"—that is, fired the works up and had them operating. For the president was not sold by what he saw, the arsenal was not built at Vergennes, and the Federalist investors in Monkton were not bailed out of their adventure by the Republican president. The "era of good feelings" did not go quite that far.

The Serpent's tail is caught, pray what's all this?
Where's gone his head?—this is some hoax, I wis:
Bring me his head, or dead or 'live, and then—
I will believe that sin has fled from men.

*Centinel,*
May 23, 1818.

# 24

# A Plain Unvarnished Tale

President Monroe was not the only distinguished visitor to Boston in the summer of 1817. A creature given the Latin name of *Scoliophis Atlanticus* followed in his wake. The president had long since left Vergennes and New England when the skipper of a coasting vessel reported in early August that he had seen a sixty-foot-long creature at the entrance to Gloucester harbor. Quite soberly he described it as a sea serpent. At first his tale was ridiculed, but then everybody, including some most respectable people, began seeing what Parson Bentley carefully defined as the "something."[1]

Having satisfied himself by talking with people who claimed to have seen the "something," Colonel Perkins decided to go and have a look. With one of the Lees, he drove down to Gloucester. On the way, they met several people returning from that town who said that the serpent had not been seen for several days. Still it was a fine day for an excursion, and they rode on.

When they arrived at Gloucester, they found everybody on the alert. Many said they had seen "him"—though nobody claimed they had actually gotten close enough to verify the gender. The sea was perfectly smooth. Lee and Perkins picked out an advantageous spot on a point of land projecting into the harbor. Perkins had brought a powerful spyglass with him just in case.

Scanning the water, he suddenly noticed an "agitation" at the harbor entrance, "like that which follows a small vessel going five or six miles an hour through the water." Knowing of no shoal where the "agitation" was, he exclaimed to Lee that he had no doubt but that he had seen the sea serpent in pursuit of fish. Lee had not been looking in that direction, and by the time he did, the "agitation" had ceased.

In a few minutes, however, the colonel saw on the opposite side of the harbor, "at about two miles distance from where I had first seen, or thought I saw, the snake" the same object moving rapidly up the harbor on the western shore. Now Lee saw it too. As the object approached them, they observed that its motion was not like that of a common snake, either on land or in the water, "but evidently the verticle movement of the caterpillar." As nearly as the colonel could judge, about forty feet of the creature's body was visible at any one time.

As a veteran of numerous sea voyages, long and short, and armed with a good glass, the colonel's report could be considered that of a trained observer: "It was not, to be sure, a continuity of body; as the form from head to tail (except as the apparent bunches appeared as he moved through the water) was seen only at 3 or 4 feet asunder. It was very evident, however, that his length must be much greater than what appeared, as, in his movement, he left a considerable wake in his rear." The colonel was within half to a third of a mile of the creature. He could now plainly see in his glass the flat head of the animal, two or three feet above the water, and its chocolate color. "I was struck with an appearance in the front part of the head like a single horn, about nine inches to a foot in length, and of the form of a marlin spike."

A great many people had now collected along the shore, watching the sight. Some of them had seen it before and said it agreed with their previous observations. The creature did not wait around to be stared at. From the time the colonel had first seen him, until he passed by the point of land where they were standing and disappeared, only about fifteen or twenty minutes had elapsed. Yet they were highly gratified with their chance encounter.[2]

When Perkins returned to Boston he wrote down exactly what he had seen. Years later when the noted geologist Sir Charles Lyell was visiting in Boston, Perkins showed him the memorandum. Lyell copied it and included it in his travel book, published in 1849: "He counted 14 projections, six feet apart, on the back, which he imagined to be verticle flexures of the body when in motion; but he also saw the body bent horizontally into the figure of the letter S." From the colonel's descriptions, a friend made a sketch of it, which Lyell thought resembled a "Pontappedan figure."[3]

So excited was his family by the colonel's report that they wanted to see the serpent for themselves. So a few days later, Perkins "went again to Cape Ann with the ladies." All they got out of it was a pleasant ride, for this time the serpent was not so cooperative and they did not see a single chocolate scale of him. Perkins did get to talk with a skeptic from Marblehead, who had become a believer when he had finally seen the animal stretched out half on the beach and half in the water. He asserted the snake was at least a hundred feet long. Another viewer of the serpent, Captain Tappan, told Perkins that the "horn" he had seen was actually the serpent's tongue.[4]

The fancy for seeing the "something" gripped the whole North Shore. It was even more exciting than the newly introduced steamboats. The Gloucestermen took out their boats to bring the "newcomer" in. One fellow fired at it, thought he had hit it when it sank like a rock, only to see it reappear some distance away, healthy but wary. Others started to weave nets that would be strong enough to bring in their catch, for a prize of $5,000 had been offered for the serpent. Vessels were fitted out by men from several ports, but all returned with "their fingers in their mouths."

"The ladies" other than his wife, who had gone to see the great sea serpent were four: Sarah, now twenty-five, Mary Ann, nineteen, Caroline, seventeen, and Nancy, the youngest at eleven. With Eliza married, it should have been fat and jolly Sarah's turn next, but she had not attracted any suitors. Mary Ann, however, had caught the eye of a younger brother of the captain of the *Levant*.

Thomas G. Cary was the sixth son of a retired West Indian planter living on an elegant ancestral farm which comprised an extensive part of present-day Chelsea. After graduating from Harvard, he studied for the law and opened an office on State Street, though he spent much time on legal business in Brattleboro, Vermont. The Perkinses had employed him to collect bad debts and other such legal "errands," with the unforeseen result that by 1818 he had become engaged to the colonel's daughter, Mary Ann.

William, another of the Cary brothers, was in Boston at the end of January 1818. Like a good brother, he visited Mary Ann and sent long reports to his brother Tom in Brattleboro. On the next visit William took a third brother, George, when he called at the Pearl Street mansion. He found Miss Sarah there alone. "After being seated a few moments upon the sofa, which you know is concealed from the door by a screen, Miss C[aroline] P[erkins] came in, in great spirits." Presently, Tom's intended arrived, wearing a red Canton crepe without any ornament. "We sat there an hour during which there was no cessation of conversation, Miss Caroline keeping us all merry with a little deluge of words."[5]

Two days later, he went to a tea party at Samuel Cabot's and again met Mary. She sang several songs, including *Blue-eyed Mary*. "Her little laugh," he wrote his brother, "is killing, absolutely." Thursday evening, attending a ball at the Exchange Coffee House, he again saw her, this time with her father. Introduced, the colonel "gave me his hand in a handsome and easy manner and at several times during the evening made occasional observations to me which entirely eradicated from my mind the idea which I had always entertained of his extreme coldness and reserve." It was fortunate that William got along so well with the Colonel, for in ten years he would marry the colonel's youngest daughter, Nancy.

Tuesday of the next week, February 3, William Cary again called in Pearl Street and for the first time met Mrs. Perkins, finding her "an amiable and agreeable matron." Later, walking up Beacon Street, he passed the colonel "who turned around after I passed him and called to me and very cordially invited me to dine with him." A man with four unmarried daughters finds it well worth his while to cultivate the company of eligible young men. The dinner was a little formal, but the colonel appeared in good spirits. After the ladies retired, the men talked "upon mercantile subjects" over their wine and cigars. Since the colonel had to attend a session of the legislature, he asked William if he would join the ladies, which he did gladly. "Mary was animated in conversation, sat opposite me and did everything with a great deal of loveliness."

Thursday night "a famous ball" was given by the colonel, and this eligible young man was invited. He was received in the drawing room "most cordially" by Mary, the colonel, and all the family. "We found the whole party tripping it in very fine style—heart, soul, and foot." He danced with "many pleasing young ladies."

The next day William was taking the mail coach to New York, where he and his brother Henry had a commission business. They were often used as the New York agents of J. and T. H. Perkins. The colonel was traveling with them in the coach, but when it called in Pearl Street to pick him up, they found he had been detained in the Senate by some important business.* Off they went without him, but he overtook the stage in Brookline. "He was in very pleasant humour and good spirits and spoke to me in an easy and familiar manner. He paid my stage fare at one tavern and I his at another." What had put the Colonel in the pleasant mood that William mentioned? Perhaps it was the progress of one item of "his" public projects that the Senate had acted upon favorably that day: the proposed new hospital for Boston.

Efforts to provide a general hospital for Boston went back eight years. At that time only Philadelphia and New York had general hospitals for their citizens. Boston had its almshouse for the indigent, a filthy, wretched place; a dispensary for ambulatory poor; and the Marine Hospital in Chelsea for sailors. The need for a general hospital furnishing care for both the physically and mentally ill was obvious, and the time was ripe for building one. A strong committee of incorporators, including Perkins, had been granted a charter early in 1811. Former President John Adams moderated the first meeting of the corporation that year, but all that came of it was a set of bylaws.

Two doctors, however, kept prodding—Dr. James Jackson and Dr. John C. Warren. Finally, on February 2, 1813, a board of trustees comprising twelve prominent Bostonians was selected. The colonel was one of them. He invited the group to gather at his new house on Pearl Street for their organizational meeting. A draft of an appeal to the public to raise the sum of $100,000, large for the period, was discussed, and a committee appointed to have it printed and distributed. This was the first large public subscription undertaken in Boston.

* The usual practice then was to reserve a seat on the coach a day before. On the day of the journey, the coach came round and picked up all the passengers at their lodgings.

A legacy of $5,000 had been left to the town by William Phillips early in the century for a hospital, and his son Deacon Phillips added $15,000 to it. It looked like the project was well underway, but, as Perkins wrote Samuel Williams on March 7, 1814, the decline in the value of real estate and the effect of the war militated against the success of the drive. Perkins had agreed to write "to such of our friends as were abroad on this most interesting subject," and the question he put to Williams was: how much would he give? "I think a few thousands placed in this fund will give you more satisfaction than an interest in all the funds in 'Change Alley." He sent Williams "documents" to distribute as well as a subscription book to circulate. "Please to get as much subscribed as you can and return it to me." Then he closed with a joke, obscured by the slang of the day. "We do not expect above a plumb." The word was slang for £100,000 sterling, or half a million dollars—five times the sum to be raised![6]

Solemn Samuel Williams did not respond to the humor: he only gave $100. The colonel and his brother James each gave $5,000, after Phillips the largest contributions, and only equaled by two others. Brother Samuel gave $100, which was as much as Paul Revere and the Reverend William Ellery Channing contributed. Two of the wealthiest men in the Commonwealth, Israel Thorndike and Peter C. Brooks, contributed $2,000 a piece. Somewhat later, John Perkins Cushing matched his uncles' donations. By early 1817, they had nearly raised the $100,000.

Since the trustees felt that the needs of the "insane" were more pressing, their first efforts had been in that direction. They purchased the fine Bulfinch-designed mansion of the late Joseph Barrell on Cobbled Hill in Charlestown.* The house had been repaired and two extensive wings added, in order to ensure the separation of the sexes, "a circumstance in modern institutions of this sort deemed absolutely indispensible." Boston, after all, was promoting faith, hope, and charity—not love.[7]

The asylum (now McLean Hospital) had cost them $60,000 and much effort, but they had not neglected the General Hospital. Four acres of land had been bought in the West End, on the windswept banks of the Charles River, and the trustees were examining eight or

* Now part of Somerville, the hill removed, and become part of the marshalling yards of the Boston & Maine Railroad.

nine designs for a building. They would, they warned the public, need more money. On January 25, 1818, the colonel was chosen chairman of the trustees. Brother James was elected vice-president of the institution. The colonel had every reason to feel pleased with the progress of the hospital.

At this same period, Perkins was involved in the Boston and Roxbury Mill Corporation that Uriah Cotting had conceived. This group planned to build a dam enclosing the Back Bay which would connect the end of Beacon Street to Sewall's Point in Brookline. The idea was to utilize the flow of tidal water to and from the dammed Back Bay to power a series of water wheels that would, the promoters hoped, provide energy for several manufacturies located along the dam. The top of the dam would be a toll road, providing convenient access to the country estates in Brookline.

Another interest of the colonel's that had been forwarded during the first month of the year was what the *Centinel* styled the "Massachusetts Grand Canal" in imitation of the New York Grand Canal (the Erie), then being constructed. Among the eight proprietors of the Massachusetts Bay Canal Corporation, as it was legally called, in addition to Perkins, were his old friends, Israel Thorndike, William Tudor, Jr., and Uriah Cotting. This group was given six years to build a canal across the isthmus of Cape Cod from Buzzard's Bay to Cape Cod Bay. Ten thousand shares at $50 per share were to be issued, and they were given the power to take lands through the courts and to set tolls.

They started right by hiring the leading civil engineer of the day, Loammi Baldwin, the engineer of Fort Strong and son of the builder of the Middlesex Canal, to survey possible routes. His suggested plan called for a canal nearly eight miles long, sixteen feet deep, fifty feet wide at the bottom, and requiring just two locks. The cost was estimated at about $750,000, half again as much capital as the group was authorized to raise. It may be that this unexpectedly high cost killed the project. In any event, no further work was done, though interest simmered under the surface to erupt a few years later with other promoters.[8]

Such public projects were not allowed to absorb all of Perkins's attention. Business matters kept intruding. While the colonel was in New York that February of 1818, a letter arrived from the U.S. consul at Canton enclosing an address from the eleven members of the Co-Hong there, about the importation of "that foreign Opium, the dirt used in smoking." An incident the previous spring involving an American ship had caused the members of the Co-Hong to be severely fined by their government for their complicity in the forbidden trade. Not eager for a repetition of this, the Hong engaged in much debate with the foreign traders that eventually resulted in a ban against importing opium at Whampoa.[9]

Far from upsetting Perkins, this news struck him as most favorable. He foresaw less competition for the "smoking dirt" and a consequent drop in its cost. The only competitor he feared was John Jacob Astor. "It is our intention," he wrote Fred Paine in March, "to push it as far as we can." Once again, the advantages of having a base in Canton were shown. The Perkinses' ships could keep the opium on board, while Cushing could make the arrangements for purchasers to pick it up "alongside." Perkins saw a possible market for 100,000 pounds of opium, small potatoes beside the British importation, but quite profitable nevertheless. "We think by keeping a vessel on the spot, even this large quantity might be disposed of to advantage."[10]

Quicksilver was another commodity that might prove profitable for the firm in China. In the summer of 1817 James Perkins had purchased a quantity in Jamaica where he had gone for his health. The quicksilver was shipped that October to China in the *Canton Packet*. Young Ben Forbes, togged out in a new checkered shirt, roomy duck trousers, and a pea jacket, went along too. Even with the addition of opium and quicksilver to fur as trading items to Canton, the Perkinses' principal means of remittance was still specie. By the spring of 1818 the available supply of specie in the United States was drying up. Silver dollars were at a premium of five percent. The revolutions in South America had disrupted mining activities there and reduced the supply of precious metals. Most of the world was caught up in a commercial depression brought on by the end of the Napoleonic wars. America, experiencing expansion and twin booms in land and cotton, was largely insulated for the moment from this depression, but there were danger signs in the economy.

With no national currency, paper notes of 246 state banks circulated as the medium of exchange, supposedly backed by a reserve of specie in each bank. This was not true in too many cases. Worse, the national bank established by Congress in 1816 had followed the dangerous practice of many state banks, over-issuing banknotes. The normal flow of specie in the country, from the South and West, which bought goods, to the eastern merchants, was reversed, since only eastern banks were redeeming their notes. This squeezed Eastern merchants who needed specie to finance their foreign ventures.

By May 1818 specie was so scarce that Perkins determined to see what supplies he could find in Europe. On the second of June he sailed from Boston on the *Galen* with Captain Tracy, for London. His object, "to put remittances in train." He took with him a deep sea fishing line, intending to get some time in at his favorite sport during the crossing.[11]

While he was gone, the cornerstone of the new General Hospital was laid in a ceremony held early in the morning to avoid conflict with the usual celebration of July the Fourth. Marshall Prince, treasurer of the hospital, held an early "dejeune" at his house with tables spread under awnings in the garden. Then the dignitaries paraded to the meeting house in West Boston, afterwards marched down to Hospital Square where James Perkins introduced the Most Worshipful Grand Master of Masons to lay the cornerstone in proper fashion.

In England, awaiting his father with outstretched hand, was Perkins's eldest son. He had gone to Europe the previous fall as supercargo of the ship *Independence*. Writing to Fred Paine about his prospective visitor, the colonel asked him to "advise THP Jr. what he has to do and see at Leghorn." Then he suggested "perhaps you may as well take your jaunt to Rome and Naples with him." Sober, staid Fred Paine was hardly the chap Tom, Jr., wanted to do any jaunting with, but exactly the kind of guide his father thought best for him.[12]

Hardly had the colonel arrived when he handed over £150 to Tom, Jr. These contributions continued on a regular basis until the colonel sailed for home in September. In all, he gave his son (it was carefully recorded in the account books) almost $5,000. Perhaps the reports current in the family later that young Tom gambled in England explain this princely sum. The colonel, who could be so stern and economizing with others, seemed to have been, like many a father, a soft touch when it came to his eldest son.

The colonel spent less than three months abroad, and booked passage home on the *Galen*. One of the passengers sailing with him was the celebrated painter, Washington Allston. Perkins had known Allston when the latter was last in Boston from 1808 to 1811. He had purchased several of his pictures including an amusing genre scene called "The Poor Author and the Rich Bookseller." Now the painter was returning home, bringing with him one finished painting and several others that were, as he put it, "on the stocks." One of these was the famous "Belshazzar's Feast," which he had begun in the spring of 1817 and on which he would still be working when he died in 1843. During the forty-one day trip from the Isle of Wight, a storm caught the *Old Galen* in its throes, and the artist did a watercolor of one particular vivid moment, which the colonel promptly bought for his collection.

Perkins returned home to find that the financial situation had not improved. The price of silver dollars continued to rise and specie grew ever scarcer. For America, the future seemed to hold grim disaster. The directors of the Bank of the United States decided to remedy the situation by ordering their branches only to redeem their own bank notes. Next they were forbidden to make new loans. Eastern branches went along with the order, but the southern and western branches had to ignore it. To do otherwise would have resulted in economic chaos, for the pioneers to whom they had made loans had no specie. The result was that by the fall of 1818, the Bank had immediate liabilities of over thirteen million dollars, and reserves of only two and a half million in specie.

The federal government unwittingly brought the shaky house of finance tumbling down. Since an installment was due on the Louisiana territory debt and had to be paid in specie, it called upon the Bank for two million dollars. The bank staved off the crisis by arranging credit for the government in London, but the close call precipitated a panic. Once started, it kept spreading. Hard money became scarce in important financial centers. Stock prices began to fall. Some midwestern banks had to suspend specie payments altogether. The *Centinel* saw this as the "kindling of a flame which will extend its ravages far and wide."[13]

In spite of the worsening financial climate, the Perkinses were pushing ahead vigorously to take advantage of the opportunities they foresaw for that year in China, where they would be comparatively alone. Over a year before they had capsuled their philosophy thus: "The speculator does not wait for the event which would frustrate his views; he anticipates it, and if his anticipations are warranted he makes a profitable speculation."[14]

In January 1819, they backed their anticipations with solid specie. The cost of the *Canton Packet*'s cargo came to $315,000; the ships they were sending to the Mediterranean added another $200,000; and the *Bocca Tigris* would take at least $250,000. This came to $765,000. To restore the equilibrium, they wrote to Paine, they would need twice that. "We must have large remittances made," they warned him.

At home, financial panic was spreading and affecting more basic industries. The cotton-based economy of the South had been prosperous for many years. But British manufacturers started importing cheaper Indian cotton and fear gripped the South. Within days cotton, which had been thirty-two cents, was selling in New Orleans at just over fourteen cents a pound. When the bottom fell out of cotton, it also fell out of the lands on which cotton was grown. The great bubble burst.

The president of the Bank of the United States resigned. Southern and western branches were ordered to issue no more notes. A chain of foreclosures started. Other branch banks called in the notes of state banks, and a wave of bankruptcies began. What economic historians termed the first modern depression was closing in on the House of Perkins. The brothers plunged ahead. By late March they estimated they would be sending out nearly $1,300,000 in "Gold, Quicksilver, and Coral." A truly enormous speculation. Paine was told in April, "we must go straight forward in our operations, *coûte que coûte,* and let the hardest fend off."

By May, the "commercial embarrassment," as the brothers called it, was affecting the seaboard towns as well as the interior. They listed for Paine some of the important firms that had failed. "In this town we meet less difficulty; payments are made punctually though the pressure for money is great." Paine had written them that he feared they were overextending the China investment, but they assured him once again that with their advantages of almost an American monopoly, it could not be overdone.

They even made several adjustments in their trade. Cushing had decided to take the China establishment out of the commission business and recommended turning it over to the company started by Samuel Russell. The colonel wrote urgently to England to his prodigal son that "it is the particular wish of his father that he returns forthwith, as his duty to his partners makes it absolutely necessary to him to do [so]." Rather than having him spend a lot of money in Europe, he had better be in America earning a little.

Business continued dull through the summer and was "expected to be more so." In the West, the Bank became the principal landowner through its foreclosures. Senator T. H. Benton declaimed with typical senatorial hyperbole that "all the flourishing cities of the West are mortgaged to this money power." One gulp, one swallow, and they would be gone. "They are in the jaws of a monster."

While the Honorable Senator Benton was seeing monsters in the West, some Boston gentlemen, summering on the Nahant peninsula off Lynn, were seeing monsters in the sea. The weather in Boston being unusually hot that summer, Samuel Cabot stayed at cool Nahant with his family for a few weeks, going back and forth to Boston daily in his chaise. On Saturday, August 14, 1819, he rose early as usual, and by 7 A.M. was in his chaise on the way to India Wharf.

As Cabot drove along the beach connecting Nahant with Lynn, he noticed a group on the dunes and several boats pushing off from shore. At first he thought it was a party of pleasure seekers from Lynn headed for a picnic on Egg Rock, a tiny island a mile off shore. Then he saw what occupied their attention. The sea serpent!

He had often heard the colonel describe it, and recognized in what was visible just beyond the breakers and within a quarter of a mile of him, the "something." For a full five minutes, the snake stayed in view, moving slowly in the water with its head elevated fully two feet from the surface. Then it disappeared.

Hundreds of persons had now gathered on the beach. Cabot decided to go back and get his wife, but when they got back to the beach there was no sight of the serpent. Disappointed, they were returning to leave Eliza off at her lodgings, when, as they were crossing Little Beach, to their mutual delight, the serpent reappeared just beyond the surf, and within a quarter of a mile of where they were.

When news of the sighting reached Boston, the sea serpent mania again seized the town. Expeditions were launched to try and capture him. A shed was built near Faneuil Hall to exhibit him when caught. The newspapers played it up with long testimonials by those who had seen him. One of these was from Samuel Cabot in the form of a letter to Colonel Perkins. With the word of a Cabot backing up the word of a Perkins, who could doubt that the creature was not real? One Boston newspaper announced, "The existence of this fabulous creature is now proven beyond all chance of doubt."[15]

Increase of wealth is not increase of happiness.

Joshua Bates,
February 22, 1822

# 25

# The Late Event in My Family

Long before the sea serpent began making his visits to Nahant, the Perkins family had been visiting there. The colonel was an avid outdoor man, fond of hunting and fishing. It was a pleasant hour's drive to the treeless Nahant peninsula, where he could enjoy both, topped off with a fine fish chowder served by the hospitable Quakers living there. The house of Abner Hood was a favorite rendezvous of the Colonel's, and sometimes he stayed on for a few days.

It was his daughter Eliza who showed the colonel the health-giving qualities of Nahant. By the summer of 1819, she was twenty-eight years old and the mother of three boys, the youngest about fifteen months old and teething. She had lost her milk and consequently the baby became very ill. "Nobody but me expected he would live." She made up her mind she would take him down to Nahant, at the colonel's suggestion, and see what the sea air would do. One of the local lads took the baby to the beach for her each day, since he was too heavy for her to carry. By the end of the week he looked like a different child. The babysitter claimed that the baby got well "from sucking pebbles wet with salt water." When the colonel came down on a visit and saw the remarkable recovery, he vowed he would not let another summer pass without having a house there.[1]

Perkins suggested that if Samuel Cabot would undertake to build a summer cottage, he would pay for it, provided he could have the use of it when he wanted. As early as September 9, 1819, the account books show a check for $530 to Cabot "to pay for land at Nahant." This was bought from Abner Hood and was on the north shore of the peninsula. A smaller piece of land was purchased from Mr. Breed.

A modest stone cottage of two stories was planned, surrounded by a deep porch. That fall Cabot advertised for bids on the cottage and finally struck a bargain with a contractor from Weymouth, who came up by vessel and is said to have lived aboard it while working on the building. Through the fall, winter, and spring, occasional bills were entered into the account book indicating work on the cottage. An ice cellar was built. Breed was paid for carting stone. Extra work was done on the underpinning. Bedsteads were bought. When James Perkins came to total it all up in January of 1821, he entered it in the book at almost $4,400. Considering what a dollar bought then, the colonel did not intend to have anyone "rough it" at the seashore.

As Nahant brought change into the colonel's life, so he, with his characteristic enthusiasm, brought change to Nahant. The peninsula was becoming increasingly popular. A steamboat from Boston made it easily accessible, and the more affluent Bostonians could escape the heat of town by a delightful sea ride on the new invention and then have a pleasant scramble over the rocks and slopes of Nahant before returning. Why not, thought Perkins, turn an honest dollar on all this travel?

Why not build a resort hotel like those he had seen in Europe? The idea of a resort hotel by the seashore had not been attempted before in the states, although it was a natural enough extension of the idea of such inland resorts as the springs at Lebanon and Saratoga. By June 1821, for $1,800, Perkins and William Paine bought the entire east end of the peninsula from the Breed brothers as a site for their proposed hotel. It was to be another year, however, before he could organize enough people and funds to put his idea into effect. But the important first step had been taken, and Nahant would never be the same.

The discovery of Nahant was only one of the many changes coming into Perkins's life in these opening years of the 1820s. Children were being married, which brought new people into the colonel's orbit. The first was the young dandy, Tom, Jr., home from his prolonged trip to Europe just long enough to get himself engaged.

He had had himself a fine time in Europe. It was the day of the dandy, and the colonel's eldest son had both the money and the inclination to play the role. He had taken a semi-military appointment in a group styled the Liberal Army of Columbia, been promoted to a lieutenant-colonelcy in the Bolivar Rifles, and served on the staff of Major-General Devereaux. What advantage the groups were to Simon Bolivar and the revolutions in South America is dubious, since they did all their fighting in the bedrooms and gambling dens of London.

The young colonel was principally interested in his uniform. An observer described him looking as if he had been "run into his top boots and breeches, so perfect was the fit." Dressed in a buff waistcoat, blue coat with gilt buttons and velvet collar, sporting a white cambric cravat, white hat and gloves, with a little gold-mounted stick, he turned himself into the very model of a dandy. And the very model of a lady-killer. Family recollections still linger fondly over his success with the fair sex, particularly a certain Lady Jane Paget.[2]

But all good things must end, and finally the young colonel yielded to the entreaties of his father and returned to undandyish Boston to do his duty by his partners. When the old colonel saw him he was disgusted. Tom was wearing the latest English mode: his pantaloons *outside* his boots. "Such a dirty habit!" exclaimed the colonel.[3]

One who did not find it so, was a young girl from Maine, Jane Frances Rebecca Dumaresque.* She had come to Boston to visit her relatives, the family of the Rev. John Gardiner, rector of Trinity Church where the James Perkins family worshipped. With a delightful figure, beautiful teeth and complexion, wonderfully flowing raven hair (in the sunlight, said her son, it had the sheen of that steel-colored blue seen on a crow's wing) and eyes the color of dark sapphire, she quickly became talked of as a beauty in Boston society. She was a prize well worth the young colonel's best efforts. On Monday, May 15, at Trinity Church on Summer Street, he won his prize. It was a glittering wedding;

* The family pronounces it *Du-mer'-ick*.

so many of the men wore uniforms and swords, they almost outshone the pretty girls.

Mrs. Samuel Perkins wrote Fred Paine about it some months later.

> Tom P—the wild dog—has got a sweet little wife, a very very pretty and sweet mannered—pleasing woman—and if he does not make her a good husband—I shall hate him for it—at present there is every appearance that he will—he has conducted very well since his return.[4]

Fifteen days after "the wild dog's" wedding, the colonel gave away his second daughter, Mary Ann, to attorney Thomas Graves Cary. The wedding was at the Federal Street Church with Dr. William Ellery Channing officiating. They had been engaged for two long years and their wedding was hardly the glittering dashing affair of the bride's brother. It was not to be without interesting consequences one day, however, for exclusively male Harvard College. The couple planned to move to Brattleboro, Vermont to live, where Cary had set up his law practice.*

It was the emptying of the nest. With three children married, and thrice made grandparents, the colonel and his lady must have felt the passage of time keenly. Yet he was still only fifty-five years old, comparatively a young man. It was his brother Jim who was "indeed much changed—he has become quite a sickly old man—but his spirits are still pretty good—and he has a strong interest in life and its concerns." So Mrs. Samuel Perkins reported to Fred Paine.

Both brothers were concerned about the changes the country's depression might make in their own commercial ventures. From the fall of 1819 on, financial conditions became worse. The firm noted in a letter to Fred Paine that those "most engaged in business are those most losing money." But they added, characteristically, "we flatter ourselves there are some exceptions." What good would it do them to hold back? "Were we to intermit, others would come forward and fill our places." The brothers did not intend to be discouraged by a momentary depression "so long as we have such agents and such means as at present."[5]

The national harmony which succeeded the conflicts of Madison's administration was severely tried by the depression and started to disintegrate with a new debate over slavery. At the time Missouri was proposed for statehood, the matter came to a head. When, with the approval

* A daughter, Elizabeth Cary Agassiz, founded Radcliffe College.

of Massachusetts, its former District of Maine applied for admission as a state, the Southerners scented a chance for compromise.

The issue was vigorously debated in Congress and Senator Otis spoke eloquently against the extension of slavery into the new territories. His supporters in the Commonwealth backed him up stoutly: a meeting was held at the State House on December 3, with the colonel present, and it came out strongly for prohibiting slavery in these new states. But that the colonel's attitude was not quite so clear-cut is evidenced by a late remembrance of Eliza Cabot. Breakfasting with her father—"I think it must have been when the bill for the Missouri Compromise was before the Congress"—she said something about slave holding "that made Father very angry." Very likely she had no idea at that time of her father's early involvement in one facet of the slave business. "He spoke so to me that I got up and left the room. As I went, I put my hand on his shoulders and told him he was sinning against his own conscience." The outcome of the national debate was the compromise that admitted Missouri as a slave-holding state balanced by Maine as a free state.[6]

Otis was detained in Washington that April 1820, to his great annoyance, "by the accursed Tariff." It would give you a "fever," he wrote Perkins, to know all the tricks and duplicity that had been practiced by the manufacturing interests to get "this abomination" passed. The men who had invested capital in the new manufacturing industries, such as cotton mills, were demanding high tariffs to protect their investment from foreign goods. The merchants who had built their fortunes on foreign trade vigorously protested any increases on the low duties then in effect.[7]

Whether or not the colonel developed a "fever" about the projected tariff, his brother did. One day James Perkins sat down and wrote a long seven page memorandum "on the subject of Draw backs and the abolition of credits on Duties" in his wretched handwriting. At first he set it aside, but then on April 29 he decided to send it to Otis for whatever use he could make of it, since James saw the Senate as *"the only hope of our salvation!"* Whether Otis was able to read James' hentracks is not known. He had already, in a letter that crossed James Perkins's, assured the colonel that he had very little doubt but that the Senate would defeat the tariff increase by a small majority.[8]

They wanted to be sure, however, and in late May were proposing to an important New York firm the establishment of a committee of correspondence among the commercial towns so there would be "a united and simultaneous effort to defeat the projects of the Manufacturers." They thought preventive measures could not be taken too early. "We look to New York as the head of the Commercial cities in the United States." It was not just merchants who would be hurt by "the destruction of foreign commerce," which they foresaw as the outcome of a triumph by the manufacturers. All those connected with commerce would be hurt, "from the shipbuilder to the carman."[9]

And there was a danger even closer to home for the firm. Some of their agents were getting restless. The firm had been extremely lucky that Cushing, for example, had been satisfied to put up with the less than ideal conditions of Canton for so long. He had been there since 1804 with only one short visit home. Of course he was a partner with a larger stake in the enterprise than a mere agent. One of the Sturgis boys, working for Cushing, marked him down as "exclusively a *man of business* and in my opinion, as well calculated for one on a liberal scale as any I have ever met with; in manners the Gentleman, generous, intelligent, and independent, and deservedly esteemed and respected by all who know him."[10]

The Perkinses paid their agents well, and they had every opportunity to supplement their income by making trading ventures on their own. Still, after awhile, some of them wanted to move on. Fred Paine for instance. Paine had left Leghorn and was working in London, closely connected with Williams's office, but looking after the Perkinses' interests. He lodged at Richard's Coffee House, an old London inn near Temple Bar on Fleet Street, but he was not happy and longed to be home. Several times he tried to quit, but each time the colonel induced him to stay on.

Yet he was increasingly unhappy. Writing on October 8, 1819 to a friend, eighteen-year-old George Bancroft, then studying in Germany, he complained that he was as lonely in London "as though I were in the fabulous city of Shedad." He scarcely knew anyone, he confessed, "and many days pass without my interchanging a single word with any human being." Certainly silent Samuel Williams was hardly the man to remedy this condition. Some temporary relief, however, was on the way.[11]

Ben Forbes had just turned fifteen. When the *Canton Packet* had brought him for the second time to Canton, so pleased was Cushing with his cousin's progress—"he is now more competent to transact business than one half of the supercargoes sent out" he wrote Perkins—that he tried to persuade him to stay on with him in Canton. Ben was forced to refuse the tempting offer. He knew his brother Tom, nearly seventeen, was being groomed by his uncles to go to China and assist Cushing. It was fortunate that Ben made the sensible decision he did, for in November the *Cordelia* had sailed from Boston for Canton with $420,000 in specie and Tom Forbes in the cabin.[12]

When the *Canton Packet* reached London about March 1820, Ben wasted no time in paying his respects to Paine. The thirty-two-year-old bachelor gave him a hearty welcome, happy to find someone who could relieve his loneliness. But young Forbes had to leave in a month; his ship was returning to China with him as its third mate, and once again Paine was alone and discontented.

Three days after Mary Ann's wedding, the colonel boarded the ship *London Trader,* bound for England. The trip was dictated by the fact that Paine had again given notice that he was returning to America the middle of that July. The colonel hoped to persuade him to stay, but there was another reason for a personal visit. A letter from Cushing received just before the "wild dog's" wedding, urged a large shipment of opium. Little opium was on the Canton market and the price had nearly doubled. If they could load the *Ophelia* with a large shipment it would give a great result.[13]

Perkins knew that the *Ophelia,* unfortunately for their pocketbook, did not have opium in her cargo. If he was to take advantage of the market in Turkey and England, he would have to move fast. Since he had no way of knowing if Paine had not perhaps already left for Boston, it was necessary to go to Europe himself. The incident is a good illustration of the time lag under which they operated. Cushing's letter of January 1820 was based on information from Paine of July 1819. Perkins acted upon Cushing's letter in June 1820, but it would be January 1821 before the effect of his decisions could reach Canton.

Perkins arrived in Plymouth, England, Saturday morning, June 24, and was in London by six o'clock Sunday night. He went directly to Samuel Williams's house in Finsbury Square, where he was invited to stay. This was most convenient since mail for Americans was usually sent there, and it put him at the center of news from home. Once again he was able to persuade Paine to stay for another year. It is certain the idea did not come from Paine, as he later described his change of mind to Bancroft as due to "circumstances beyond my control."[14]

During the trip to the continent, Perkins received letters from New York and from Paine in London, though "no news from Boston" he noted regretfully in his diary. It may have been this mail which advised him of Cushing's latest letter on the plans of the East India Company to eliminate the growing competition they were getting from Malvic opium. This was an inferior grade of opium grown in the western area of India, then partly under Portugese control. The East India Company planned to double the usual production of Bengal opium during the coming growing season, Cushing wrote. This would mean that they would be dumping 8,000 chests of the drug on the Canton market in 1821.[15]

At first, the company had ignored the introduction of opium by Americans and other traders into China since they still controlled most of the market. Indeed, much of the drug was purchased from them in British India. The Perkins operation was still a tiny one from their point of view, even though the Perkins gamble of 1819 had paid off extremely well when their product was sold on the spring 1820 market when high prices prevailed. But opium from Portugese India paid them no money, and, added to that from Turkey, could eventually take a sizable part of the market. As early as 1818 Perkins had expected "the jealousy of the E. I. Co." to prompt them to "sacrifices to destroy all interference." He speculated that they "might reduce the price, under the idea of destroying private speculators." What he had long feared, now seemed to be coming true.[16]

Cushing argued that American merchants might be afraid to speculate on opium for the 1821 season, anticipating the price cutting of the East India Company. He also predicted a glut in the fall, 1820, market because the high prices of the spring would have tempted merchants to rush large quantities of opium to Canton. The poor prospects for the 1821 season plus the bad results he predicted for the fall would generally discourage Americans from purchasing opium. This would reduce the price in Smyrna. The risk for Perkins & Co. was relatively small, for they were set up at Canton to store the opium for long periods of time, feeding it slowly into the market so as to get the best price. Once again the advantage of having a base in China was paying dividends.

Nor did Cushing fear that flooding the market with Bengal opium would necessarily hurt the sale of Turkish opium. Since the Turkish product was consumed almost entirely in the northern provinces of China, where they had become addicted to its harsher taste, he reasoned they would still buy it at a higher price in spite of the availability of cheap Bengal. His advice to his uncle was that for "those who have faith enough to adventure in it" it would be a "great opportunity."*[17]

The colonel had the faith to adventure, and was willing to gamble that the market would hold. The *Canton Packet* had already gone, so it was too late to send opium by her. The next available ship they owned was the *Augusta*. She would arrive in Boston from China about the end of June. This would give time enough to organize a cargo of opium for her to pick up in Europe on her return trip to Canton. With any luck the *Augusta* ought to be in Canton in the early part of 1821, perhaps even before the East India ships arrived.

By the middle of October all the British East India ships had arrived and the market price of opium was still $1,250 a chest, or just under $10 a pound.

Perkins had returned to Boston arriving on October 23. Before he left he had made arrangements for his Smyrna agents, Woodman and Offley, to buy 300,000 pounds of opium for the cargo of the *Augusta*. He discovered when he reached Boston that that vessel had had an unusually long trip from China and instead of arriving in June as was expected, had not reached port until September. When Cushing heard of it, he worried that "other importations may reach here before ours in which case it might operate very much to our prejudice."[18]

He was increasingly disturbed when the *Canton Packet* arrived that same month and he discovered that its cargo contained no opium.

By the end of February 1821 Cushing could report much better news. The East India Company were not going to double their Bengal opium shipments to China in order to defeat the dealers of Malvic opium, because they had gained control of the Malvic opium. They were selling it publicly in Bombay in the same manner that they sold the Bengal

* Opium that Perkins & Co. could buy for about $2.50 a pound in Turkey, they could sell from $7 to $10 a pound in Canton, depending on the market.

opium in Calcutta. But now Cushing worried that the high price the Chinese had been paying for Turkish opium in the past year and a half would attract other merchants to speculate in it, and drive the price down. He was expecting the *Augusta* at Canton in March. She had been refitted when she finally showed up in Boston the previous fall, and was then sent to Turkey for opium. Unfortunately, the agents in Smyrna had only been able to purchase about 120,000 pounds of the drug instead of the 300,000 ordered.

The *Augusta* did not arrive at Canton in March. The going price then for Turkish opium had risen to $1,500. It started to drop when the East India Company ships arrived with larger than expected amounts of Bengal and Malvic opium. The Chinese opium merchants were concerned that there would be a glut of Turkish opium too. Finally, on the eighth of April the *Augusta* arrived at Macao. By now, opium was selling for $1,150. Cushing decided that it would be impractical to hurry its sale. There was so much on the market that the Chinese were only buying "for their immediate wants." He had thought it would take him only two or three months to dispose of the drug, but now he felt pressured by the large British supply and so was selling at the lower price. It was still a good profit. By April 15, he was able to advise Fred Paine that what had been sold so far would bring a "benefit" of $50,000. Not to the addicts, unfortunately.[19]

Other opium ships from American merchants arrived after the *Augusta*. To counter this increased American competition, Cushing devised a scheme whereby some of the opium would be landed at Batavia and stored there, maybe half of each cargo. He would then keep one of the firm's ships shuttling between Java and China, supplying both markets wherever the price was highest. Since opium was still contraband in China, it had to be kept on board the vessel until it was sold. This was inconvenient and expensive, particularly where vessels with large cargoes would be tied up for as long as a year as a floating warehouse. Cushing's new arrangements would avoid all this.

Other than opium, the Chinese market was feeling the same depression that was disturbing the world market. British goods and other imported merchandise would only result in "a very heavy loss." Cushing recommended a total suspension of shipments, no matter how attractive the prices were. The only thing that would sell profitably was opium. The addicts had to have it.

But Fred Paine had finally decided that he did not have to have his job in England any longer. A year later than he intended, he had finally resigned his "sceptre and authority," taken his holiday in Paris, and headed home to Worcester. The sense of change was everywhere; in the family, in the nation and world, and in the affairs of the firm.[20]

That fall, as every fall since 1816, the Perkinses sent the annual ship to the Northwest Coast with supplies for the Northwest Company's outpost. It was the last one. The Northwest Company had decided that the only company making money on these voyages was J. and T. H. Perkins. Since they received a quarter of the proceeds and since Perkins & Co. in Canton also got a regular commission, they could hardly lose. Then beaver dropped to $3.50 per skin on the Canton market, less than in London. So the company decided that in 1822 the supply of the post would be taken over by them, and the career of J. and T. H. Perkins in the Northwest trade came to an end.

After nearly three decades in business, the brothers had decided as early as January 1821 to wind up their concern slowly. In that month they advised a correspondent that "we have lately made a change in our firm by introducing our sons into our American establishment, under the signature of J. & T. H. P. & Sons." Samuel Cabot was naturally included. Again in May they advised Perit & Cabot that all future importations should be kept in their books "distinct from the old concern of J. and T. H. P."[21]

Changes came in Canton too. An unfortunate incident with an American ship, not owned by the Perkins firm, had temporarily stopped all trade. No sooner was that settled than the matter of opium smuggling came to the fore. One of the Hong merchants lost his button, his symbol of authority to trade, because it was alleged that he was involved in the smuggling. Ordinarily the viceroy would levy a large fine, and the traffic would continue as before. This time there had been so much publicity that the authorities were forced to carry out the letter of the law. The Hong merchants were very disturbed. They notified the foreign merchants that the vessels used as opium storage ships at Whampoa had to leave immediately. All future ships that arrived would have to post bond that they carried no opium. Until such assurances were given, no further trade was possible. Obediently, the opium ships moved down the river to Lintin Island, where they anchored and carried on their business as before.

Cushing advised Boston that it would not be prudent under the new conditions to "meddle with opium" unless it could be bought quite cheap. Captains arriving in Perkins's ships with opium should use the codeword "gum" in letters to Cushing and remain in Macao or the islands to the east. Cushing would let them know when it was safe to bring the cargo nearer. However, it was difficult even to find purchasers as the dealers had momentarily gone underground.[22]

As the months wore on and nothing happened, the regulations were gradually relaxed, and Cushing devised a better method of handling the ships, having them go directly to Lintin, where he had set up a system to get the opium delivered. An unforeseen effect of the new regulations was that they made the business profitable only to those firms with facilities in China. It reduced the competition Perkins & Co. faced from other Americans. Yet the colonel was not satisfied by this; he wanted complete control of the American opium trade. The only way he could do this was by a monopoly of the source of supply.

There were other problems too. A good understudy for Cushing had to be found. He would certainly be wanting to be relieved of the responsibility of his office one of these days. Perkins had had such good reports from Cushing about the work of Thomas T. Forbes that if he "can be made to be able to do your business, it will be very desirable." And there were other matters just as important to the persons involved. Chinese kites for instance! Could Cushing have Forbes "find some Chinese kites in the form of birds for Eliza's boys who are playing at my elbow and being told to refrain as I was writing—They ask to whom when upon being answered to you, they beg not to forget the kites."

The business of gradually closing out the activities of the senior firm and transferring their business concerns to the new firm of five men continued slowly. On March 14, 1822, the brothers advised Charles Vaughan that they were winding up their old concern, and they asked him to adjust one of their accounts. That the young colonel was not carrying his weight in the new concern is evident from a comment in another letter that he looked more to his pleasures than to business. This two years after his marriage!

James Perkins too, was being forced by failing health to take a less active role in the firm as well as outside activities. The most difficult outside position to leave probably was that of trustee to the Boston Athenaeum. He had been a studious, bookish man all his life. When it was suggested that a private library, the Athenaeum, be established in Boston in 1807, he was one of the initial subscribers. Even before that both brothers had been members of the Boston Library Society since the early 1790s.

The Athenaeum was an outgrowth of the Anthology Club, formed in 1805 to promote literature, produce a magazine, and to discuss books. The volumes accumulated by the club formed the nucleus of a library similar to one formed a few years earlier in Liverpool. Stock in the new private library was sold for $300 a share to 150 of the Boston elite, including all three Perkins brothers. As the library grew it moved into progressively larger quarters. The annual meeting in January 1821 found them in their building on Common Street discussing the need for more room. Their financial condition did not permit them to think of a new building, however, in spite of the crowded condition of their present one.

At that meeting, James Perkins resigned from the board. He was erecting a new house for himself and his son's family on the corner of Pearl and High Streets, and he suggested to John Lowell, a former president of the Athenaeum, that he might be inclined to donate his old house as a new headquarters for the library. Since his house was half a duplex, one of the conditions of the gift was that the trustees must raise enough money to buy the other half of the building from its owner. The trustees seized upon his offer, quickly raised the $15,300 needed, and moved in during May 1822. The *Centinel* announced on May 22 that "the arrangements of the new edifice in Pearl St. were now complete and ready to receive books, cabinets, etc." But the paint wasn't dry, and the formal opening didn't take place until the second of July.

Late in July, the account books show brother James paying Dr. Jonathan Jackson nearly $60 for his share of a "Water Party" in the sloop *Maine*. Several days later he made a generous contribution to promote theological education at Harvard. This completed the July entries in the firm's journal. An entry for August 5 comes next, nearly at the bottom of the page. Then, between a pair of double ruled lines, appears this laconic statement: "James Perkins died August 1 1822, Ae. 61." The partnership was ended; the "Prior" of the Firm was dead.

I was much amazed with seeing the magic Lanthorn. Mr. Gray constructed it, you stand in the dark and see figures which appear very small at first and gradually increase in size and appear to approach nearer to you.

Eunice Callendar,
January 14, 1824

# 26

# The Consequences of Leaving Off His Flannels

A few days before his death, James Perkins had left his brand new house on Pearl Street for his country seat at "Pine Bank" in Roxbury. He seemed to be as well as he had been these past few years, though his health always needed "unremitted care." At lovely Pine Bank, on the shores of Jamaica Pond, he caught a cold. One correspondent ascribed it to "leaving off his flannels." A few days later, on Thursday, August 1, 1822, he was dead from pneumonia.

The Friday newspapers announced the funeral for five o'clock on Saturday at his townhouse. Mayor Phillips asked the shipping in the harbor to fly their colors at half mast, and requested the aldermen and city council to attend the funeral of "their senior and highly esteemed associate." Boston had become a city by act of the legislature that February, and James Perkins, though he had always declined state offices, did accept election to the city council, "where," wrote his brother a number of years later, "I have every reason to believe he was useful."

How useful is a good question, since he was elected to the position on the first of May and died on the first of August. He had one distinction however, in that he was one of three men unanimously elected to the forty-eight-member council. The colonel had become involved in the same election less happily. When Boston became a city, the post of mayor was created. One diehard held out against the use of that word. "A mare is a horse, and he had as lief be called a horse or ass as a mare." Senator Harrison Gray Otis was not adverse to the word, and he ran for the post; but so did Josiah Quincy. This split the colonel's allegiance, as well as that of many other Federalists. His neighbor or his friend? He chose Otis, and worked hard to secure him the office.

Three days before the election Perkins wrote Otis that he had spoken "very freely on the subject" to Quincy. "We are of course at Swords points—he met me yesterday on the street and gave me a formal bow, and a stately 'good morning.' " Monday, April 8, when the votes were counted, Otis had about 350 less than Quincy but due to a scattering of votes for other candidates, neither had a plurality. Both men withdrew, Perkins acting on behalf of the absent Otis. In a second election on April 16, John Phillips became Boston's first "mare."

The successful candidate and the two losers were among the many friends and dignitaries who gathered in James Perkins's Pearl Street house for his funeral. Senator Otis served as one of his pallbearers. The directors of the Boston Athenaeum and representatives of Harvard College were prominent among the mourners. Thomas Southworth handled the funeral and charged the estate $27.55 for his services. The family sent the minister, Dr. Gardiner, $50 for his words of comfort and prayer.

Long, complimentary obituaries soon appeared in the Boston newspapers. The *Daily Advertiser* on August 6 informed their readers that "no private commercial house in the world had been more extensively engaged in the trade to Canton," than the firm of J. & T. H. Perkins. The profession of the merchant, they rhapsodized, had taken over the place once held by the hereditary aristocracy. And the deceased, said the *Advertiser,* was one of the foremost of this new nobility.

But since some of the "new nobles" were anything but noble, the writer took pains to point out that James Perkins had taken "no short roads to wealth," and that "not a shadow of suspicion of anything derogatory" could be said about him. Insisting further, the paper claimed Perkins as "one of the few who passed through life without spot or blemish." To cap all, his gifts were listed: to the General Hospital, the Theological School at Harvard, and the Athenaeum, which alone "cannot be estimated at less than $18,000."

To show their gratitude for his munificence, the trustees of the Athenaeum had asked the family if they might commission Gilbert Stuart to make a copy of the portrait he had been painting for them. When the colonel called on Stuart to make the arrangements, he expected to see the original completed. To his distress, Stuart had only half begun. Stuart blamed it on his poor health, adding that he and James Perkins had been so well acquainted that they had, unfortunately, spent most of the time of the sittings in conversation. Stuart, however, was well known for procrastinating. Perkins exploded and stormed out of the studio declaring, "Very well, Mr. Stuart. You have inflicted an irreparable loss by your dilatoriness, and I shall never enter your studio again."[1]

Accidentally meeting some weeks later on the street, Stuart begged the colonel to accompany him to his studio. Reluctantly, Perkins went with him. There on the easel stood the finished portrait of his brother. Working with a speed most uncommon to him, Stuart had finished the portrait from memory. By the end of October, the copy for the Athenaeum was completed too.*

When Josiah Quincy was preparing to write his history of the Athenaeum, he asked the colonel for "some notices" of his late brother. The colonel admitted that his brother's story was "soon told and contains nothing that is very important but to his immediate connections."[2]

Now, James's estate had to be disentangled from the firm of J. and T. H. Perkins. Since both brothers had habitually put most of their private financial transactions through the firm's books, it was more complicated than it would be today. It meant that the firm had to be liquidated to realize James's portion. Within ten days of his death, a new heading appears in the firm's accounts: "T. H. Perkins Liquidator."

A schedule of what James owned at his death also gives an idea of the worth of his brother at the moment the partnership terminated. Each owned half of the joint enterprise, a third of Perkins & Co., and a fifth interest in the new concern with their sons. The appraisers' first estimate showed J. and T. H. Perkins worth about $210,000, which

* George Bancroft later said the countenance of James Perkins was "very correctly given" by Stuart. The Athenaeum copy hangs today in its reading room, presiding as calmly over the newspapers and magazines as the original once did over his books and papers.

includes all their real estate, property, stocks, and shares in various companies. They made no real attempt to estimate the value of Perkins & Co., merely stating that the seven ships owned by that establishment were probably worth $72,000. Similarly they estimated the new concern at $20,000. Even this very rough evaluation showed that each brother's share was far in excess of $133,000.[3]

The stores on India Wharf were rented out and the business activities were consolidated at the Central Wharf store. The accountants figured the living expenses of James in 1821 as $9,200, and his brother's at more than twice that. This was living in princely state.

Colonel Perkins looked over his prospects that fall, and decided that the "late event in my family will very much curtail my mercantile enterprises, which have been confined for some time past to China—I have had no vessels in the Northwest coast trade, since the Peace of 1815, although several vessels of the late firm, have proceeded to China touching at the Columbia. At present, I have no vessel in port, nor shall I send any one to the East before the Spring or Summer."[4]

In spite of his preoccupation with the upheaval in his private affairs, Perkins found time for public service. He had been elected to the Massachusetts House of Representatives in 1821, and again to the state's Senate in 1822 and 1823. When the winter session began on January 2, 1823, he heard with melancholy pride the clerk announce to the chamber that the Athenaeum had now moved to its new quarters in his brother's old house, and would be open for the accomodation of members of the Senate during the session. The next day Governor Brooks, in his message to the legislature, deplored the riots at the State Prison and suggested that perhaps a tread or stepping mill, as used in Europe and some of the neighboring states, might be employed to discourage future riots. Perkins was appointed to look into the matter.

New York City had just installed one of the stepping mills and he wrote them for details. Their device consisted of two great wheels, each five feet ten inches in diameter, one for men and one for women. The sexes were separated by a partition. When the convicts marched into the mill room at 7 A.M., the first eighteen men and twenty women would mount the millwheel. The steps of the wheel were just large enough to stand on and they steadied themselves by holding onto a hand rail. The other convicts sat on benches behind the wheels. The people on the wheel began to "walk upstairs" and the heavy wheel slowly started to rotate. Every half minute, an overseer would strike a bell, and the rear man on the wheel would leave it for the benches and his place would be taken by one of the bench-warmers. The prisoners had the same time resting and working, about 9 or 10 minutes. The group turned the wheel at a steady three revolutions a minute, which meant there was no lagging. There was a twenty minute intermission at noon, and at 4 P.M. the convicts were fed and locked up for the night.

The New Yorkers thought the project highly beneficial, the colonel reported. "There is no trade to be learned before working at it. No materials to be spoiled in an apprenticeship to it." It could be operated year-round in any weather. "Two pair of stones are kept in operation which grind forty bushels of grain per day." This only produced a small income, about $3.20 a day, but profit was not the aim of the wheel. Completely exhausted convicts, too tired to riot, easy to manage, was the aim of the wheel. "Before, when condemned to work on roads or pick oakum, they remained awake a great part of the night" disturbing the guards. Now they all slept soundly.[5]

The air in the wheel room grew extremely offensive as the many workers perspired violently. However, the New Yorkers maintained the wheel contributed to their health. Each person only had to lift his own weight, except for those convicts compelled to wear chains. They consoled themselves with the reflection that these were "sturdy rogues to whom a weight of this sort is a very proper appendage." Another benefit from the mill was that convicts were heard to declare they would quit New York state when freed and go someplace where there was no mill.

On January 20, 1823, Perkins reported to the senate that he had now received a model of the mill, and he turned all his information over to the committee on the state prison. A glowing description and a woodcut of the mill in operation appeared in the *Centinel,* but for some reason Massachusetts decided to pass up the opportunity to improve the health of its convict population by use of the stepping mill, forsaking the additional virtues of encouraging an exodus of the criminal population elsewhere.

By February 20, the process of rearranging the Perkins business was far enough along so that the colonel could formally establish the new concerns to replace the old ones. From this date began the new concern of J. & T. H. Perkins and Sons, which now had four partners.

Increasingly, the colonel came to rely on Samuel Cabot to take over many of the functions once performed by his brother. Neither of the two juniors were much inclined to business. Cabot was of a different stripe, somber and businesslike. Thomas Cary's mother, running into Cabot shortly after the death of James Perkins, remarked that he was "dressed in a full suit of black and I should say looked very serious, but I think he never looks otherwise, although it is accompanied by a very agreeable smile." His son's memories agreed with this description, James Elliot Cabot writing that his father was "a silent man, rather a dyspeptic, always kind, but not very much occupied about us children."[6]

By the middle of March 1823, the colonel had a more urgent problem confronting him than rehabilitating Massachusetts convicts and forming new firms. Letters had reached Boston from Canton, written in November 1822, with the news from Cushing that "we were burnt out of house and home on the night of the first inst. and have just got into a place where we have room to write." Shortly afterwards, American newspapers were full of the story of the Canton fire.[7]

It began in a small dyeing ship about a mile north of the factories. The wind was from the northeast, so no one felt any real threat. Around midnight the wind shifted to the north and the factories were now directly in the fire's path of destruction. Orders were sent to Whampoa for every available man from the ships anchored there to come up and help.

The fire was raging wildly. The wind blowing it towards the factories was also blowing against the boats trying to come up from Whampoa. When it became certain the factories were doomed, the merchants and whatever household staff they had started to move the contents of the factories onto "chop boats" pulled up to the river front. The sailors who had arrived were frantically put to work rescuing as much of the merchandise as possible. As the goods and specie were taken out of the factories, they were put aboard the boats that had brought the sailors up, to prevent their being plundered by the Chinese.

All was immense confusion. The narrow streets leading from the city to the river were jammed with all manner of salvage that the desperate owners hoped to save. The result was that the streets became impassable. The snapping and crackling of the flames were punctuated by the screams of Chinese ladies, helpless with their bound feet, who had been

Burning of the "Factories" in Canton in 1822. Chinese painting, second half of the nineteenth century, unidentified artist, oil on copper.

abandoned by their terrified servants, and were unable to save themselves from a fiery death.

By noon of the next day the factories had caught on fire. The wind was now a gale and driving all before it. The salvage work had to be abandoned. The view was one of magnificent destruction, the flames extending along the shore. Next morning all was a heap of blackened ruins.

"We had the good fortune," wrote Cushing, "to save most of our books and papers." The merchandise, which had not been gotten out of the factories, was lost, though its value was "but trifling." However, as near as they could ascertain, about $20,000 of specie "was plundered" as they were removing it from the vaults to the boats. Even in the rubble of the fire Cushing could see the chance to earn a few rubles. The East India Company had lost two thirds of its woolen cloth. This meant a shortage, and consequent high prices. The Americans, with their lighter, speedier ships, could easily beat the British to market with a new supply. "It may be an object," Cushing suggested, and the colonel agreed.

Two things were required to take advantage of the opportunity: to have someone on the spot in England to organize the cargo and to maintain extreme secrecy in the entire mission. By April, Perkins had written Fred Paine in Worcester in carefully guarded terms suggesting that it was "of some importance" for them to have an agent in England for a few months, and that he must go immediately. "If you cannot go let me know it, but if practicable let no one but your wife know of the intention to send anyone. If you do not go, I shall. If I go, I do not wish it known until after I have gone—nor then till necessary—others may be led into similar speculations, from knowing that I either send or go." Paine had had enough of London and declined to go. So, on Sunday, April 13, 1823, Perkins set sail once again on the ship *Fortitude* for Liverpool and what he hoped would be a most profitable adventure. He left behind him two new ventures in varying stages of completion: a hotel and a mill complex.[8]

After Perkins and William Paine had bought the land for their hotel on Nahant, another year passed before they were able to organize a large enough group to finance the project. A subscription of $19,000 had been raised and a board of directors formed, including Perkins,

Paine, John Hubbard, William Sullivan, and Israel Thorndike. In July 1822, the colonel solicited medical testimony from Drs. James Jackson and John C. Warren as to the virtues of a residence at the seashore. They responded in glowing terms, particularly praising Nahant as superior to all other places on the coast for such benefits. In the month of his brother's death, a circular letter went out seeking additional subscriptions.

The $19,000 had been spent on the twenty acres of land, the hotel building, the road to it, and like improvements. The proprietors now required another twelve to fifteen thousand to build a wharf, buy furniture, and complete their project in the style it required. There were to be floating, hot, cold, and salt water shower baths. For the gentlemen's amusement there would be bowling alleys and billiard rooms. A beautiful marine hippodrome "which twice in 24 hours is laved and rolled smooth by the waves of the ocean" was promised. Rooms were to be elaborately furnished. Meals would be served, and residents could "furnish their own liquors or have them from the bar."[9]

"This magnificent establishment," as the promotion circular puffed it, was a smallish stone building with two main stories and two more in the large sloping roof. A wide porch circled the hotel, giving a splendid view. To the south was the bustle of Boston harbor; to the north the almost unbroken greenery of the shoreline; to the east undulated the restless billows of the Atlantic. Around them were the rocky ledges of Nahant itself, offering "numerous interesting walks for health, exercise, and amusement." A rather small and shingly beach was the floridly advertised "marine hippodrome."

Having arrived in England and taken care of the woolen shipment to Canton, the colonel was unavoidably absent from the June 4 meeting of the hotel shareholders that auctioned off twenty choice rooms and twelve apartments in the hotel to those proprietors who wished to use them that season. Capt. James Magee, son of the colonel's late associate, was to be superintendent of the hotel. "Distinguished for his gentlemanly deportment and kind disposition," Magee would be "most assiduous to make everyone happy and comfortable." Or so the management assured prospective visitors.

For the times and in America, the Nahant Hotel was a marvel. With fifty-six rooms, it was larger than the newly rebuilt Exchange Coffee House, which boasted it had fifty rooms. But the Exchange was located in the "Stir of the great Babels of commerce," or one of them. It was to Nahant, "the chosen domain of youthful Hygeia" where one would flee to escape the "Babels of commerce" and to be "at ease and keep cool."

One of those fleeing to Nahant that summer was the thirty-seven-year-old spinster Eunice Callendar with a family party. "Going over Lynn Beach is really delightful to ride almost in the water and see the waves dashing up over the wheels of the carriage every moment." They went to the colonel's new hotel, which Miss Callendar pronounced "excellent." Strolling over the rocks, they watched the steamboat discharge its passengers, and then for further excitement stayed on and watched it load passengers for the return trip to Boston. After that they played a game of nine pins, fished from the rocks, had an excellent dinner at the hotel, then walked around some more. With regret she left "this fashionable place of resort" where "there is much of the sublime and beautiful to charm the eye with," tucking into her memory and diary the "lovely excursion."[10]

The colonel, his business completed, left England in July on the *Amethyst* and by early August was back in Boston, ready himself to flee that "great Babel." With his brother dead for more than a year now, the colonel was settling into new patterns of life that revolved more and more around his juniors, the younger men who were taking the place his brother once had filled. It would always be a continuing disappointment to him that Tom, Jr., was not interested in, and that George was not capable of, mercantile endeavors.*

The commercial spirit of the times was shifting from the wharf to the waterfall. The traders' surplus capital was being invested in shore enterprises, particularly textiles, and the possibilities of this field had not escaped Perkins and his brother. The colonel's father-in-law had been a tobacconist and made snuff in three mills he owned on the banks of the Charles River in Newton Upper Falls. At his death in 1793, a half interest in this property came to Perkins, the other half going to brother-in-law Simon Elliot, Jr.

Over the next twenty years they maintained an interest in the mills. When the war of 1812 interrupted their mercantile pursuits, they looked

* A fall from a horse when he was about thirteen had fractured George's skull. He was never completely "right" afterwards.

into the possibilities of keeping their capital working by investing in textiles. Their absorbing interest had been in the works at Vergennes, but there seemed a chance for profit in cotton cloth. Imported coarse cloth from India, usually retailing at about twenty-five cents a yard, tripled in price as the war continued. This looked like too good a thing to pass up. Conveniently at this time, Simon Elliot was badly in need of ready money due to some unlucky investments. In November 1814, the brothers advanced him $20,000 and took over his interest in the property at Newton. This included fifty-seven acres of land along the river, four snuff mills, a grist mill, and an iron works that consisted of a screw factory, wire mill, blacksmith shop, and an annealing house.

Further up the river, Frank Lowell had perfected his power loom and his group were contemplating their textile mill. Perkins was aware of their progress, but he and his brother went ahead with their plans to convert the manufacturing complex at Newton into a cotton textile center. The project had not gotten very far before the war ended and the American market was flooded with cheap English cottons. The plans for a textile enterprise were shelved, and the Newton mills continued to grind corn and tobacco for the next few years.

By 1823, however, much had happened in textiles. The cloth from Waltham, protected by a generous government tariff, turned a marginal operation into one that gave a handsome profit. Waltham stockholders boasted on 'Change of the fantastic dividends they were getting. During 1822 textile activities were expanded at a new town twenty-five miles from Boston, located on the Merrimack River to exploit its abundant water power. If textiles held such promise that his prudent friends would invest hundreds of thousands of dollars in the wilderness at East Chelmsford to create the town of Lowell, Perkins decided to take a second look at his plans for Newton.

The Waltham and Lowell operations were pretty much a closed group, outsiders only being let in for a stiff price. It was not difficult for Perkins to interest his Cabot and Lee connections in joining him to do at Newton what others had been doing so successfully elsewhere. The new company was named the Elliot Manufacturing Company, a nice gesture to his wife.

Samuel Cabot had four brothers, two of them, Richard and Frederick, commission merchants in Boston, but none particularly prosperous. The fourth brother, Fred Cabot, was made treasurer of the new company.

In February 1823, Perkins transferred thirty-four of the fifty-seven acres at Newton, together with all the mills, to the new company. Perkins got $22,000 for the property, so for him the enterprise had already proven a good investment.

As no one in the Perkins group had any technical competence in the textile business, a local mechanic named Otis Pettee was hired, since he was said to have had prior experience in that field. The next problem was equipment. Perkins was back from England in time to give his advice on this problem, which was to buy it from the people who knew how to make it—the Waltham concern. Perkins signed an agreement with them to build all the new machinery the Elliot company would require.

In all these multitudinous cares and concerns, Perkins had by no means forgotten his idea of controling the Turkish opium market. His scheme was simple: to corner the trade by buying up all available supplies. For every twelve pounds of opium smuggled into China, one pound came from Turkey. The Perkins firm was buying about half of this, and because of the increasingly strict regulation of the trade at Canton, hoped to get more for it during the coming season. Much depended on the goodwill of the Turks, but the best-laid plans of international merchants frequently are upset by international politics. Such was the reef the colonel's plan ran upon.

The spirit of independence bred by the French revolution finally stirred the Greeks in March 1821 to attempt to throw off the yoke of their Turkish overlords. Greek leaders wrote an appeal to the American people to aid them in their fight for freedom. By 1823 the Greek cause had caught the popular imagination. Meetings were held in various American cities, but no champion of the cause had yet appeared in Boston. Perkins was not unhappy with the lack of one. However, the Athens of America, the Birthplace of Liberty, could not long be deaf to the cries of a nation wishing to be free. When the champions arose, one of them turned out to be an old friend of the colonel's, the professor of Greek at Harvard, Edward Everett.

Everett wrote a long article for the *North American Review,* a thinly veiled appeal for aid to the Greeks. Perkins responded with a long anonymous letter to the editor of the *Daily Advertiser,* which was printed December 19, 1823. He believed the American nation fully sympathized with the Greeks, he told the editor, but wondered if the small amount of aid that could be sent would do the Greeks any good. Might it not actually do more harm to America? Turkey might very well "let loose her corsairs upon our commerce in the Mediterranean"; in fact, she might induce all the Mohammedan powers to do the same. He signed his letter, "A Merchant."

The same edition of the newspaper also carried the notice of a meeting that evening at the Exchange Coffee House "for the assistance of the Greeks." At the meeting, resolutions were voted, and a committee of twelve named to put them into effect. Perkins was named to the committee and that night, Everett wrote to advise him of his appointment.

"A Merchant" sat down the next day and wrote another letter to the *Daily Advertiser*. This time he wondered "what portion of the gentlemen named on that committee will serve." Nobody, he continued, would be against "the Greeks working out their own salvation" but "here, sir, I would stop." Then he got down to the brass tacks of the opium trade. This had amounted to nearly a million dollars in each of the last three years, "and at least half of the last crop will have been exported from Turkey for American account." He did not mention that the principal "American account" was the house of Perkins. Turning oratorical, he queried, "Shall we then go a crusade in favor of the Greeks and hazard the liberty of our citizens and a valuable trade to show our goodwill? I hope not." The lack of enthusiasm on the part of certain Bostonians for the Greek cause was reported in the *Centinel* of January 24, 1824, when it was announced that Josiah Quincy, John Welles, Benjamin Gorham, and T. H. Perkins had declined to serve on the committee for Greek aid.[11]

Still hoping for a monopoly, Perkins pushed his opium schemes. "You may think us acting a bold game," he wrote Cushing in late April, "in sending so much of the drug this year, but if a certain quantity of that of Turkey must be had and we can keep the lead which we now have, we shall not be in much hazard of losing." His fertile mind proposed another scheme to ensure that no hazards would be encountered. Besides shuttling ships back and forth between Canton, Manila, and Batavia, Cushing should have ships run along the China coast. A chain of contacts could unload the drug at many dispersed points and escape the scrutiny of the Chinese at Canton. They could also sell other European and Indian goods to great advantage.[12]

It looked as if the colonel's venture into the hotel business was succeeding pretty well too. Six Harvard students, critical as only Harvard students can be, went down on a July Saturday in 1824 to look around. They fished in the rain, then retreated to the billiard room. Finding the tables engaged, they went to the bowling alleys and amused themselves for a couple of hours. One of the young men, Charles Francis Adams, grandson of the second president, thought the alleys remarkably fine, "made of the hardest wood and very accurately smoothed." With huge appetites, they went up to dinner and found it inferior. Perhaps Adams's disappointment came from the price charged, which he found excessive, for he found the meats "well dressed and tender," the cheese "excellent," and though the first bottle of wine was not up to their taste, yet another was "much the best." A "very fine cigar," left the president's grandson feeling mellow and content. The rainy afternoon was spent at billiards, which Adams lost by what he claimed was "a lucky scratch" on the part of his opponent.[13]

The daughters of Josiah Quincy on a visit a month later, saw the hotel through more enthusiastic eyes. Up at the "peep of early dawn" they set off from Quincy for Boston, where they were told that Boston was "absolutely emptied and that every house in Nahant was absolutely crammed." Their informant thought it perfectly absurd for them even to attempt to get lodging at the hotel. Having, as girls do, an opinion of their own, they went anyway, finding the road to Nahant jammed with carriages all wheeling merrily towards the popular peninsula.[14]

They found the hotel surrounded by "a forest of parasols, veils, shawls, hats, caps, and leghorns." Margaret Quincy was immediately dragged off to visit "spouting Horn," where she found many of her Boston friends and gossiped until dinner time. Nearly two hundred sat down for dinner at 3 P.M. It was said that five hundred had applied for seats. Six musicians played amid the clatter of knives and forks, the jingling of plates, the shouts to the waiters, and the shrieking and laughter of the diners. After a saunter around the hotel, and a rest, it was time to dress for tea. Then more dressing for the evening ball, "pinned and tied and hooked and combed and curled." Cotillions and Virginia reels succeeded one another until it was time for supper. By 12 P.M. the hotel was quiet for the night. In such manner did fashionable Bostonians consort themselves at the colonel's newest venture.

Arriving back in town that same busy summer was Bennet Forbes, who in Batavia had arranged to leave the old *Packet* and Captain King and transferred to another Perkins ship, the *Levant,* under Capt. Edward

Cabot, a brother of Samuel. Forbes quickly discovered that Captain Cabot, "although a perfect gentleman," was not, "and never could be, called a sailor." Forbes soon decided he could have sailed many years more under King and never felt competent to captain a ship, but one short voyage with Cabot and he felt "sufficiently confident" to more than fill his place.[15]

Upon his return to Boston, he found his father's health quite broken, the senior Forbes having recently fractured his arm, "and it was evident to me that he could not long survive." Eliza Cabot had seen him after his paralytic stroke, when he had lost his mind and become very difficult to manage. She said to her aunt one day, "You can't wish him to live, crippled, unhappy, and senseless?" Margaret Forbes loyally replied, "I'd have him live under *any* circumstances."[16]

The *Levant* was to return to China and Bennet expected to go out as mate, until the day the colonel came aboard the vessel, and told him it was about time for him to begin looking for a mate. Taken by surprise, Forbes, not quite twenty, wondered if he was not a little too young yet? "If you're not fit to command now," replied the colonel, "you never will be." Whereupon Captain Forbes accepted.[17]

The ship was to sail the fifth or sixth of October, but on the fifth, the young captain's father died. Late in the evening of the seventh, together with a cousin, he accompanied his father's remains by moonlight to King's Chapel for burial, returning about midnight to his mother and family as a dutiful son. On the morrow, he walked the deck of the *Levant* as master of all he surveyed.

His brother Thomas in Canton seemed to be nearing a promotion too. He wrote to the colonel that he could "perceive an inclination in Mr. Cushing to leave this country." Cushing had already written Mrs. Forbes that her son Thomas was "one of the finest young men" he had ever met with, his business capacity was "superior," and that he would have no hestitation to trust the business to him. The old order was changing, overseas as well as at home.[18]

The accountants had more news to report by November 4, 1824. Perkins & Co. had made over $90,000 profit on their business with the Northwest Company, and that figure did not include the 5 percent commissions on sales in China or America. With these added in, it would total much more. The only loser had been the Northwest Company, but not because of the Perkins firm. The Lechmere Point Corporation and Canal Bridge had also brought a tidy profit, they reported, although the ten shares the brothers held in the Newburyport Turnpike were considered of little or no value.

The most interesting item in their report was the one headed "Doubtful & Bad Debts." These had accumulated during the thirty years the brothers had been doing business and had never been written off. They totaled almost $115,000 (The equivalent today of a million or more dollars). This averaged out to a loss of about $4,000 a year for each year they were in business. A sizable sum, nor does it appear that this included the money lost to Charles Sandos.

So more than two years after his elder brother's death, the sorting out and shaking down was still going on. With his brother's passing the colonel gradually began to be less interested in the business. It was not the same thing, with all these new men; and there were other exciting and worthwhile projects to be attempted. For example, over in Charlestown there was a monument that needed building.

We bow not the neck and bend not the knee,
But our hearts, Lafayette, we surrender to thee.

Charles Sprague

# 27

# Too Much for Mortal Man To Bear

Reading his *Boston Patriot* on Wednesday morning, April 17, 1822, William Tudor saw an announcement that "a lot of ground including the monument erected to the memory of General Warren and the remains of the breast work thrown up on the eve of the battle fought" on Bunker Hill, was advertised for auction on the first of May. The paper hoped that "some patriotic gentleman of wealth will purchase and preserve it."

Tudor was no "gentleman of wealth," yet he was patriotic and could hardly sleep that night for thinking of the dangers that threatened the sacred spot. The next morning he learned that the notice had been inserted by Gen. Henry Dearborn of Roxbury. Tudor interviewed him, but found that Dearborn had no money either to buy the land. Could they find such a man? He turned, next, to Daniel Webster and again drew a blank. Webster owed, in fact, rather a sizable sum to the Perkins firm (which he eventually paid off.) But for politicians, patriotic crusades rank high, and Webster was lavish with blessings on Tudor's project.

The logical choice of a rich rescuer for the sacred spot was General

Warren's closest living relative, his nephew, Dr. John C. Warren. When the plan was presented to him, he was most sympathetic, and on May 1, attended the auction and bought the property. Now that he had it, what would he do with it? During the winter of 1823, he held several meetings at his house at No. 2 Park Street to discuss this question. It was agreed that some suitable monument should be erected there. Tudor had talked over the project with Perkins, and early in the spring of 1823 the colonel invited the concerned parties to breakfast at his house to discuss forming a society to perpetuate the memory of the great battle.

Webster, Warren, Tudor, William Sullivan, George Ticknor, and George Blake, a well-known Republican lawyer in Boston, made up the group around the colonel's dining table. After eating and discussing the possibilities, they got into their chaises and rode over to Charlestown to look over the actual site. Perkins was not able to do much more just then since he was bound for England. By the time he returned, much had been accomplished. Tudor, Webster, and Theodore Lyman had sent out personal letters in May inviting some of their friends to a meeting at the new Exchange Coffee House. Twenty-six showed up and enthusiastically endorsed the idea of a memorial to Boston's only full-scale battle of the Revolution. An association was formed with a five dollar membership fee and all present joined, Tudor signing for Perkins.

Shortly, thereafter, on June 7, 1823, the group was chartered by the Commonwealth. Within a month, circular letters went out to solicit funds. At the formal organization of the group as the Bunker Hill Monument Association, Tudor was elected secretary, and Perkins, even though he was still in Europe, was chosen one of the vice-presidents. Tudor soon accepted a political appointment as consul to Peru, and Edward Everett was elected to replace him.[1]

First, they had to buy the top fifteen acres of the hill. The complicated business of raising money to buy the land and actually persuading the owners to sell at reasonable prices began. Both were headaches. William Phillips paced the subscription drive with a $1,000 gift. However, a large number of people thought that all subscriptions should be a uniform ten dollars. One of these, as the solicitor quickly discovered, was Colonel Perkins. The issue became so heated that the pros and cons were aired in a letter to the *Centinel* on October 15, 1824, signed *Civis*.

The writer stressed the desirability of large contributions. Perhaps the colonel heeded him, for he eventually contributed $100.

The land committee had its difficulties too, some landowners holding out for high prices. Putting their pocketbooks before their patriotism, some property owners were demanding as much as $5,000 an acre for their land. The average prices paid had been between $1,000 and $2,500.

By the beginning of 1825, the group had raised $59,000. Although a large sum, it was not thought large enough. They turned to the legislature for help. At first, the legislature offered to give the association what they had plenty of, the free labor of the convicts in Charlestown Prison to dress the stone for the monument. The committee replied that prison labor would neither be fitting nor practical for their project but they would be glad to take the $10,000 in cash, which was what the legislature had estimated the convicts' labor would be worth. This was another piece of pie altogether, and it was only after a hard and close battle that the tightfisted legislators appropriated $6,000 for the monument. What was more valuable however, was that they gave the association the right to take land for their monument by eminent domain proceedings. This was important, because one of the owners of a vital lot had refused to sell at any price.

What would they erect on the land once they owned it all? Solomon Willard, a forty-one-year-old bachelor, now entered the picture. Willard was a man of many talents. Originally a plain carpenter, he made himself an extra fancy carpenter carving wooden capitals for doorways and church steeples. He went to a drawing academy and qualified himself as a draughtsman and carver in wood, sculpting the painted spread eagle that decorated the old Custom House. He studied anatomy to help his sculpturing and learned French to keep his mind busy. Turning himself into a stone mason, he graduated into an architect on his own. His most recent building project was the United States Bank on State Street, and his reputation was at its highest point. Some people thought Willard eccentric for all his abilities, but Everett said that the only thing he knew about Willard that was eccentric was his readiness to do anything for anybody for nothing.[2]

General Dearborn talked with Willard about the project and in August 1824 he presented the Association's standing committee with a design for a memorial column that Willard had drawn. A month later the committee came back to Willard asking for an estimate of the cost. To help him in figuring this, Willard enlisted the aid of his partner on the Bank building, Gridley Bryant. A self-educated master mason, Bryant had worked on the fortifications for Boston in 1814, and recently had constructed the Mill Dam across the Back Bay, considered one of the great engineering achievements of the day. Perkins was well-acquainted with both men, since he had served on committees supervising the Bank and the fortifications.

But even if Willard's plan was free and acceptable, should the standing committee foreclose looking at other ideas? They decided on a great competition, and in mid-January advertised a $100 prize for the best monument design. Fifty entries were received in the competition, and the committee found they had only multiplied their problems fiftyfold. A Board of Artists was appointed to consider them. After much discussion they finally voted not to have a column, but an obelisk, using a design submitted by a Harvard student, Horatio Greenough. Then the directors ignored the board's recommendation.

Meanwhile, the project got into an embarrassing situation in regard to its chief guest. In 1824 the Marquis de Lafayette was making a triumphant tour of America, his first visit since the Revolution. The country outdid itself to honor "The Nation's Guest," the only living Revolutionary general. On June 17, 1824, when Lafayette was in Boston and at a celebration on Bunker Hill, Dr. Warren extracted a promise from the general that he would come back the next year to help lay the cornerstone of the proposed monument. This conversation had been confidential, but word leaked out. The embarrassing thing was that the newspapers announced that Lafayette was coming before the directors had officially thought to invite him. In March, Webster wrote Warren in great concern about getting Lafayette properly invited before the grand celebration became a grand fiasco.

The committee formally invited Lafayette, and asked Webster to give the major address at the ceremony. But still they had no idea of what the monument would look like. It took two more months and two more committees before they could agree on a design. It was not until June 7, only ten days before the great event, that the directors finally accepted their committee's choice. Five directors held out for a column, but eleven carried the day voting for an obelisk. Perkins was not present when the vote was taken. Dearborn, who had started the whole thing with his newspaper article in 1822, fought vociferously against the obelisk design. He predicted in a letter to Perkins that it was so extravagant that the monument might never be completed. He was very nearly right.

The public announcement of the decision brought an unexpected response from Willard, who had bowed out of the "contest" in a huff. In May, Warren had taken it upon himself to suggest to the irascible Solomon that he reconsider and come to work on the project as chief engineer. Willard had haughtily declined. Now in June he wrote Ticknor that he had "more than a common interest in its being carried into erection in a spirited and economical manner"; he hoped to be allowed to drop a "few hints." A granite quarry had been purchased for the project and he invited Ticknor to inspect it. If the directors did not want the quarry "it will be no loss."

Other plans for the great event rolled along smoothly. All the known survivors of the battle were invited to attend as guests of the association, without distinction as to ability to buy tickets. Thursday the sixteenth of June was a cloudy day with showers, but Friday the sun rose bright in a cloudless sky as a salute of twenty-four guns from the Navy Yard greeted the eventful day. People were up and doing before the sun, and carriages were rumbling over the pavements. The Thursday showers had laid the dust of the streets and made the fields about the city sparkling and fresh.

People were everywhere. They had been pouring into the city for the past several days. All the public houses were overflowing, with people bedded down on the hard floors of corridors. The regular stage lines had proven inadequate to transport the crowds to Boston; as one coach driver put it, "everything" on wheels or legs was pressed into service. Some people were paying as much as fifteen dollars for a single seat on a stage into town. The guest of honor, General Lafayette, had arrived in the city two days earlier. Accompanying him was the son whom Perkins and Russell had spirited out of Paris so long ago. They were guests of Senator James Lloyd on Somerset Street.

One newspaper sounded a note of caution that not enough people heeded, with regard to the "grand celebration." Those attending were "advised to leave their pocket books, watches, etc. at home. A strong corps of the light-fingered gentry will doubtless be in attendance."

Survivors of the battle and the officers and directors of the association,

Perkins among them, were to gather at Subscription House by 9 A.M. Among the veterans of the fifty-year-old battle were such characters as Josiah Seward of Keene, New Hampshire, who was showing everyone his coat with nine bullet holes in it, which he maintained it had acquired in the historic battle. In all, some 190 survivors of the battle put in an appearance, some perhaps attracted by the incentive voted by the General Court of a payment of three dollars, plus one dollar for every twenty miles traveled to Boston.

A committee from the association escorted Lafayette to the Subscription House where the battle veterans were lined up to meet him. Senator Quincy's son, Josiah, Jr., did the honors. The two marched down the grizzled line, Quincy taking the names of the men and repeating them to Lafayette, who immediately pronounced the names after Quincy "in tones of the deepest interest," as if they were his dear personal friends.[3]

By this time the city was bursting with people. All carriages had been barred from the route of the procession, and the sidewalks and shops along the way were filling with spectators. Since it was not customary for ladies to stand on the public sidewalks (only a certain kind of woman dared do that), they were given preferences of the best windows and the piazzas and porches. Even churches were opened and their windows thronged with viewers. But an English visitor, signing himself "John Bull" in a newspaper letter describing the occasion, reported he saw "hundreds" of ladies, "modest, refined and well-dressed," who stood outdoors, unaware of any danger. Nor did he during the whole day hear one rude remark or insult offered them.

By half past ten, the great procession got under way, with Colonel Perkins proudly in the van. The association officers marched six abreast with their six cent badges fluttering in the breeze. They were followed by the president of the United States, John Quincy Adams, in a carriage. But even he was preliminary to the next figures, Lafayette and his son. In an open coach drawn by four white horses, like some prince in a fairy tale, came the hero of the hour, of the decade, of the century. His progress through the throng could be traced by watching the violently twirling handkerchiefs with which the ladies greeted him, and the deep male cheers by which the men acknowledged his presence. Nearly six feet tall, every inch and every pound of his fine portly figure spelled out the authentic hero to the crowd.

The hero's only infirmity, a slight lameness incurred at the Battle of Brandywine, was not apparent as he sat in the open coach. Those in the front rows who got a good look at him could see the lines of age and suffering in his face. Yet he did not seem to be sixty-eight years old, perhaps because he wore a brown wig sitting low on his forehead.

On the hill in Charlestown, an enormous crowd had gathered. With great difficulty, involving very ungenteel pushing and shoving, the marshal of the grounds and his corps of assistants could barely keep open the reserved space around the monument site for the honorables who were crooking their way through Boston streets towards their destined places.

As the procession crossed over into Charlestown, the bells of its churches began to peal joyously, joining those of Boston which had clanged the parade along its way. It was half past twelve by the time the marchers started winding up Breed's Hill. A regimental drummer from the original battle, marching once again in sere and withered age, started to beat out the rhythm of "Yankee Doodle" on his old drum, and the spectators went wild with cheering.

The chief marshal directed the dignitaries into a hollow square around the hole where the future monument would rise. The Masonic Grand Master, Lafayette, Webster, Perkins, Dr. Warren, together with the other important persons, formed the first rank. The Grand Master stepped forward, armed with his instruments and with the assistance of fellow freemasons Lafayette and Webster declared the cornerstone "true and proper." A cannon on Bunker Hill banged away announcing that the cornerstone was duly laid.

As the wind gently carried the cannon smoke across the field, the procession moved down to the amphitheater for the speaking. Awaiting them was a canvas pavilion, in the center of which was a stage decorated as a temple with evergreen and garlands intertwined with flags and flowers, the whole presided over by a gilded eagle. As the procession began to assemble for the speaking, the soldiers of the Revolution were given a reserved section opposite the battle veterans. Although a shaded seat had been provided for him on the speaker's platform, Lafayette, in a splendidly emotional French gesture, cried aloud, "No! I belong there, among the survivors of the Revolution." And dauntlessly daring the sun to do its worst, he took a seat amid the old soldiers, there to bake his bewigged head for the next few hours. The crowd roared its approval.

The same chaplain who had beseeched an apparently slightly deaf Jehovah for victory on the hill in 1775, came forward and in a voice trembling with age, offered the thanksgiving of another generation to their inscrutable divinity. The assembly responded by singing a new hymn to the tune of "Old Hundred" with a full band accompanying the thousands of voices. One old man, moved by the music and the scene before him, exclaimed as the tears streamed down his cheeks, "Good God! this is too much for mortal man to bear!"[4]

But mortal man had yet more to bear, for now Webster rose. An awning had been placed to screen him from the rays of the sun, but they were running nearly three hours late and the sun shone directly into Webster's eyes. As he came forward, Lafayette signaled him to stand back where he would be shaded. Showing that handsome gestures were no monopoly of the French, Webster gracefully declined and came as close to the audience as the stage permitted. They greeted that act with hearty applause, not knowing that Webster's real motive was fear that he could not make himself heard by all.

"This uncounted multitude . . ." he began, and the uncounted multitude, their number known but to Jehovah, burst into cheers, continuing to punctuate his speech with the same at every sentimental opportunity. In his hour and a half of banalities, Webster provided many a plateau for such punctuation.

Besides an elaborate history of the battle, Webster had set-pieces for all the heroes of the occasion. When he invoked the departed shade of General Warren, he folded his arms across his breast and turned his face toward heaven. Where else would American patriots go? Mary Peabody thought that "the fire of his lightning gaze was quenched for a moment!"

When it was Lafayette's turn to be apostrophized, that gentleman rose so that all the audience could the better see him. It was the first time many realized how tall and fat he was. Not to be outshone at this tremendous moment, Webster flung his arms over his head, his ministerial robe floating behind him on the breeze, and stood on his tiptoes. It looked to Elizabeth Peabody as if "his whole person was about to take its flight," almost as if he stood "on air."

Finally the oration came to its destined end and long loud cheering woke those for whom the combination of Webster's eloquence and the hot June sun had proven too soporific. Webster generously donated the copyright of his speech to the association. The first day's printing of 3,000 copies of the address quickly sold out, and more were called for. The colonel sent some copies down to Peru for William Tudor to peruse.

Gala receptions were held that evening. At Webster's house on Summer Street, a special door was cut through the wall into the house of Israel Thorndike next door, making one large reception hall to accomodate the crowd. All of the official receptions were visited by General Lafayette before Bostonians would permit him to climb into bed to recover from the day's triumphs.

The General was to continue on his rejoicing way into other parts of Massachusetts, then up into New Hampshire and Maine. But among the many calls he made before he left Boston was one on Colonel Perkins in Brookline. He had been invited out for Sunday dinner. All Brookline, John Pierce's daughter Mary remembered, was on the *qui vive*. "Parties of ladies and children with offerings of flowers stood in the streets to do homage to him as he passed in an open barouche."[5]

A lady told Elizabeth Peabody, on her way home from church about the expected visit, and Miss Peabody exclaimed with rapture that she would "waylay the carriage and speak to him." Having arrived at Mr. Heath's, very near the colonel's estate, she sat down under some trees on a rock determined to wait for the hero to ride by. Colonel Perkins sent a billet to Mr. Heath inviting him to call and see Lafayette, and the Heath girls and Miss Peabody almost decided to waive propriety and go with him, but finally decided against that breach of good manners. Instead, the Heath girls brought out chairs and joined Elizabeth. Soon a great many ladies in the neighborhood joined them, "all without bonnets—in their Sunday-go-to-meetings."[6]

The excited group waited for an hour. Miss Peabody knew she would be unable to speak a word to the hero, but she was determined to kiss his hand. At that moment, Mr. Heath returned and brought them word that Lafayette had gone to the colonel's by the other road, but would return by this road "and the coachman had promised to stop." Buoyed by this hope, the Heath girls carried her off to tea, and thus fortified, they went back to wait.

All this while, Perkins had been proudly showing the "Nation's Guest," now for the moment *his* guest, about his extensive estate with its well-kept gardens and the great greenhouses where he grew his fancy grapes and peaches. Dinner was probably in the great square dining room hung with a Chinese wallpaper representing gardens with peacocks on a stone balustrade. Undoubtedly the handsome monogrammed silver especially made for the colonel was in use, and perhaps the blue china from Canton with the pineapple design on it. Certainly many of the colonel's family gathered for this thrilling occasion as well as the neighbors and friends that had been invited. The colonel basked in his guest's reflected glory.

At last, Lafayette had to depart, and as promised, his coach went the other road to Boston. Miss Peabody and her friends were waiting expectantly for him. Soon they heard a shouting of "coming—coming" down the road, and within seconds the hero appeared in front of her. Wrote Miss Peabody later: "I felt precisely as if I was dipped in liquid fire when La Fayette's face, glowing with delight—flashed from the carriage." She dropped her handkerchief and her feather fan and sprang towards him, caught his outstretched hand and planted a kiss on it that "had my whole soul in it." To Susan Heath it looked as if she "almost devoured the *hand* of La Fayette with kisses."

Lafayette with great fervor kept saying "thank you—thank you." Then he raised Elizabeth's hand to his lips and kissed it. "I feel his lips quiver upon it now," she wrote one of her friends three months later. Finally, leaving a string of "Ladies you make me very happy. You have my most affectionate regard," behind him, and kissing his hand to them as long as he could see them, the hero rode his exhausted way back to Boston and more of the same. "We were all trembling and shaking," wrote Elizabeth, "like the sea after a storm." For several years after the little group celebrated the anniversary of that meeting with Lafayette.

Others had been differently affected by Lafayette's visit. Three pickpockets at the "glorious celebration" on Bunker Hill had had such a profitable day relieving the "uncounted multitudes" of their money, that they had followed Lafayette's tour through New England until the hand of the law caught up with them in Maine.

This was not the only sequel to the Bunker Hill business. Indeed, that work had just begun with the laying of the cornerstone. The officers of the association, now that the glories of the glorious day were past, had to settle down to the long pull of putting the second, the third, and yea the fourth stone upon the first. This was to be a business of a different sort.

Above all, it required stone. Solomon Willard, that lethargic man, who moved so slowly that the jokers claimed he had never been seen to run, had been making a hasty search for the necessary stone. It was a search that would lead the colonel into two new enterprises: a granite quarry, and a granite railway.

Quincy granite is a medium to coarse and even-grained rock composed essentially of dominant feldspar (av. 60.02) quartz (av. 30.60) and hornblende (av. 9.37), of the fourth, fifth, and sixth hardest of all stones.

William C. Edwards
*Historic Quincy, Mass.*

# 28

# Great Means, Ardent Public Spirit, and Pertinacious Enterprise

Perkins and Willard at first hit it off well. The colonel had been favorably impressed with Willard's work on the Branch Bank. Enough so that when the building committee was considering Willard's "hint" of being willing to help again with the monument, Perkins wrote an unsolicited letter of recommendation to General Dearborn. Perkins, as a member of the committee overseeing the Bank's construction, had found Willard "to be all they could wish." Not only did he relieve them of much personal bother, but he also "saved considerable money" for the Bank. Since the Monument Association had to economize, Perkins was confident that "you cannot do so well as to employ him." He was a "man of science" and the committee could also firmly rely on his integrity. Perkins also put in a good word for "Bryant, the Mason." He had satisfied the Bank's committee, and was "well acquainted with the best ledges and at my suggestion, during the summer, secured the right to take stone from a lot in Quincy at a comparatively small sum." Willard had advanced convincing arguments that the association could quarry its own stone for the monument much cheaper than they could buy it, perhaps twenty cents a cubic foot as against ninety cents a cubic foot retail.[1]

The lot in Quincy that Bryant bought in June 1825, at the colonel's suggestion, had been discovered near the end of May by Bryant and Willard. When they came across a ledge of seamless granite on top of a hill in Quincy, only eight miles from Boston, they knew they had just the right stone. Dr. Warren advanced the $250 to buy the lot. The price was low because the owner thought the ledge worthless since it was four miles from the nearest transportation, the Neponset River, and there were no roads from the top of the hill. Willard had anticipated this difficulty, however, and reasoned that the granite could be quarried out in the summer and fall, then when the snows came, the stones could be sledded down to the river.

But there might be even a cheaper method of transportation than waiting for the snow. The latest issue of the *Quarterly Review,* an English magazine, had arrived in Boston by April 1825, containing a long article contrasting the advantages of railroads and canals, making particular reference to the newly organized Manchester and Liverpool Railway. Bryant was interested in this new development in transportation and had closely followed its experimentation in England. Perhaps a short railway from the quarry to the river might be the best mode to deliver the immense amount of stone needed. He discussed this with Willard, who agreed that it might "save much expense in so large an undertaking."[2]

Soon after the colonel's letter to Dearborn, Willard accepted the appointment as architect and superintendent of the work on the monument. He had predicted that quarry owners would ask exhorbitant prices for their stone, and so it proved. Promising the association that he could quarry stone for a third of the quoted prices, they bought the Quincy quarrying rights from Bryant, giving him $75 more than he had paid for the land. This business delayed them until it was too late in the season to quarry stone.

Since Willard's original plan of sledding the stone out could not be realized that winter, Bryant reverted to his idea of the railroad. He proposed it to the association, but they felt the scheme was too ambitious for their limited means, and so declined it. Not accepting defeat, he next tried to interest a group of private investors: Perkins, David Moody,

Amos Lawrence, and William Sullivan. He had made plans and working drawings to show exactly what he proposed.

Much to Bryant's disappointment, the group were not enthusiastic about the idea as an investment for the association. Perkins, however, saw commercial possibilities in it, particularly since there was a captive customer, namely the Monument Association. If sufficient profit could be made on the contract with them, it would underwrite the venture. Not only would it aid the association by furnishing superior granite at a bargain price, but Perkins saw the opportunity of going into the granite business. If nearby ledges could be purchased economically, the scheme might become practical. Perhaps there was also the lure of helping to pioneer in this new field.

In a dark green memo book that Perkins carried with him, he jotted down some of his financial speculations:

| | |
|---|---|
| If the railroad cost $40,000 interest is | $2400 |
| Salary of Superintendent | 1000 |
| 7 men and 1 horse @ $30 is | 2880 |
| Total annual expense | $6280 |
| 3000 tons of stone brought to Boston | $8000 |
| less expenses of Superintendent and men | 3880 |
| Profit | $4120 |

It looked good to him and he decided to adventure.

He persuaded the others who had heard Bryant's presentation of the scheme that it was not only a patriotic but a profitable undertaking. The legislature was asked to charter the group under the name of the Granite Railway Company. The petition, entered on January 5, 1826, was destined for a rough passage. It took courage for the colonel even to enter it that January, for by then he had learned he was facing the possibility of a disastrous loss overseas that would make many a man quail from launching a new and uncertain financial enterprise.

Friday evening, the second of December, letters arrived in Boston by express from New York containing rumors of a financial disaster in London. The sheriff was busy Friday evening and Saturday morning serving attachments on those Boston merchants known to hold credits payable to Samuel Williams. Since the Perkins firm did a substantial part of their business through Williams, the colonel feared a repeat of the unpleasant circumstances when Henry Higginson failed in 1811.

With this difference—this time he was not in London to minimize the disaster.

Tuesday afternoon, the new marine telegraph established on Rainsford Island, signaled the arrival in the outer harbor of the ship *Florida,* only twenty-seven days from Liverpool. It was almost sunset when the *Florida* was sighted, and it was not likely that the ship would reach town before morning.

Doubtless many in the mercantile community spent a sleepless night, but it was as nothing compared with the panic that spread when the ship docked and its news was known. Williams's failure was confirmed and the English newspapers brought by the ship estimated that his loss was a staggering seven million pounds. One local merchant summed up what this meant. Williams, he wrote, "was the Banker of New-England and had been for a quarter of a century."[3]

By Wednesday evening, however, a more complete and accurate account was available. The best news was that his failure had involved only £815,000, not the larger sum first circulated. By a "happy circumstance," a Boston merchant, Timothy Wiggin, was in London at the time and had stepped in as a temporary trustee to look after all the American business in Williams's hands when he failed. Friday's news was that the loss to all American merchants had further declined and was said to be $600,000. How much of this belonged to the Perkins firm and what could they do about it?

As more news filtered through from England, it appeared that Williams had accepted $450,000 of drafts on behalf of J. and T. H. Perkins. At the time of the failure, most of these drafts still had to be met, and Williams had no funds. Wiggin agreed to meet half of these if some of Perkins's friends in London would take the other half. Bryant & Sturgis "freely offered" to join in the responsibility, giving in a letter a testimony to the position of the Perkins firm in the business community: "their responsibility is equal to that of any house in the U.S."[4]

In spite of the assistance of his overseas friends, Perkins wanted a man of his own on the spot to protect his interests. He needed someone familiar with the English scene. Although Perkins was planning to go to England in the spring to facilitate his opium purchases, he felt there might be problems with Williams if he went now. All signs pointed to Fred Paine. Perkins felt he knew as much "of men and matters in Europe" as he did himself. He went up to Worcester and offered Paine a most generous inducement: $4,000 and all his expenses. This was too much to refuse, and on January 24, Paine left for London "to put things strait," as the colonel wrote to Cushing a few weeks later.[5]

With Williams out of the picture, the firm needed a new banking connection. Trade was now largely carried on by bank drafts rather than by the cumbersome exchange of gold and silver coin. Although many of the Boston houses had picked Timothy Wiggin as their banker, both Perkins and Bryant & Sturgis were more impressed with the ability of an expatriated Bostonian named Joshua Bates. Bates had married into the Sturgis family, which might have been reason enough for them to pick him, but Perkins had known him for more than two decades as the mainspring in the counting room of William Gray, one of Boston's leading merchants. Gray had sent Bates to England in 1816 as his agent, and Bates's success there made him decide to go it alone in 1820 as a general agent in London specializing in American accounts.

The decision to employ Bates was made before Paine left for Europe. Perkins would not have been surprised, he wrote Cushing, if Paine formed a connection with Bates, "in which case we should give them our business." But Bates had already that January entered into partnership with John Baring, the "able but indolent" son of Sir Thomas Baring, a senior in one of the most important banking houses in the world, Baring Brothers.

Despite the financial setback, Perkins went ahead with his railway. In the legislature, however, there was considerable opposition to the plan from the country members. Setting up a railroad as a commercial operation had never been undertaken in the state, and required the solution of many new organizational and legal problems peculiar to the new enterprise. For example, a right-of-way is one of a railroad's most vital assets, but its legal effect on adjoining property was as yet unexplored.

Perkins had to engage in extensive lobbying to overcome "every delay and obstruction that could be thrown in the way." Finally, on March 4, 1826, by a bare majority, he got his charter and the Granite Railway was officially born. The charter incorporated them for a period of forty years. During this time they were empowered to take land six rods in width for their right-of-way, but with certain limitations: for ten years they could charge tolls, not more than 12 percent per year, and must carry any passengers who paid the tolls. The company was forbidden to obstruct roadways and turnpikes, but must provide "safe and convenient passage," to people using those ways. The charter was to be void if there was no railroad in operation within three years.[6]

After organizing on March 13 with Perkins as chairman, a letter was drafted to be presented by Perkins and Edward Robbins, Jr. to the Milton town selectmen asking permission "to have the Rail Way within the limits of that town." Perkins, Robbins, and Amos Lawrence were to have surveys made of all possible routes for the railway, and to obtain information about the modes of construction, materials, and expenses. Milton voters, at their town meeting the first Monday in April, gave their permission, and landtaking could begin.* On March 17 the petitioners met at Sullivan's office to split up the shares. It was decided to have fifty shares, and of these Perkins took twenty-eight. At this meeting Perkins was elected president of the company. That fall he wrote Tudor in Peru that "I think I may safely call it my road, not only because I set it agoing, but because I own 3/5ths of it."[7]

Although Milton had been told that the railroad was "designed for public benefit," which in one way it was, the principal consideration was not only to convey stone for Bunker Hill monument, but to enter into the business of quarrying and transporting granite on their own account. Perkins hoped, so he wrote Tudor, that Boston would be changed "from Brick to Stone, as it has been from Wood to Brick," by the facility of getting granite to market.

One of the first actions of the new company was to obtain its own source of stone. In the same range of hills where the Bunker Hill ledge was being opened, was another piece of property that looked promising. The company bought it for $10,000. This ledge, called "Pine Hill," was much closer to the river than the association's quarry. It would save the railroad considerable money if they only had to build to this new ledge, rather than to run track further around the hill and across a swampy area to the quarry Willard was working. Could they persuade the association to transfer their activities to the new location?

* To resolve the problems of landtaking, three prominent local citizens were selected to act as referees to establish the amounts that the railroad should pay the various landowners for the rights and damages. The referees established the amounts of compensation in advance, but agreed to review their findings after the construction of the railroad was completed, thus protecting the interests of all parties, a vital consideration if the new venture were to succeed (Quincy Historical Society documents).

Willard had already quarried a considerable amount of stone from the Bunker Hill quarry when it was proposed to him to shift his operations. He promptly advised Dr. Warren that he was against the idea unless the Railway Company agreed to reimburse the association for all the money it had spent at the Bunker Hill ledge. The railway group were not about to do this, so the association continued their work at the Bunker Hill quarry.

Willard had quickly grown disenchanted with the railway scheme, and had convinced himself that it was going to greatly delay his work on the monument itself. The whole summer of 1826 would be lost while they built the track, and none of his granite blocks would be carried to Charlestown. Yet he estimated that for only $500 a wagon road could be constructed to another existing public road that would enable them to transport at least a 1,000 tons of stone to the wharf. Using this alternate route, work could begin on the monument right away, instead of after a year's delay.

Willard's idea of a $500 wagon road never was given serious consideration. The Granite Railway had gone too far to be abandoned. Since it had been undertaken to accommodate the association as well as for personal profit the directors of the association must have felt they had no choice but to stick with the railroad. Three days after Willard suggested a wagon road, ground was broken for the new railroad on the shores of the Neponset River. It was the first of April—April Fool's Day.

With his railroad begun under the capable direction of Gridley Bryant, the colonel felt free to turn his attention to his English problems. In company with his son George, the colonel left on a Perkins ship, the *Milo*. The reports Paine had been sending back from London were a little unsettling. After a fast passage, they arrived on Saturday, May 16, in London from Falmouth and went into lodgings with Paine. The colonel was relieved to learn that his cash loss was little more than $28,000, which Bates had paid the assignees of Williams in February. This was about, he thought, what the railroad would cost him. Sunday he dined with Joshua Bates, their new agent, and visited the Bates and Baring counting room on Monday. He also went round to Finsbury Square to see Samuel Williams. In spite of the situation, they had been good friends for years. Williams was upset at Perkins's new alliance with Bates; however, the colonel explained to Cushing, "I see no reason why my personal regard for him should induce me to do that which my judgment does not bear me out in."[8]

In early June Perkins left London for Leeds, to visit Benjamin Gott, one of the foremost manufacturers of woolen blankets and ladies yard goods in England. Paine had discovered this firm in 1821, and placed a large order with them for J. and T. H. Perkins. Since then, trade had grown until Perkins was Gott's largest customer. Arriving in Leeds, Perkins was conducted through Gott's huge mill, which employed 1,200 workers. Two days later, he went to the Middleton colliery just outside Leeds, which had a railway similar to the one Bryant was constructing in Quincy. A part of the road was made of wood "as we propose to make ours. Mr. Gott thinks our plan will be perfect." What else did one tell one's biggest customer? "I conclude, however, to go to Darlington tomorrow to see what is doing there."[9]

At Darlington, ten months before, the first passenger railroad in the world had opened. It was thirty-eight miles long and ran from Darlington to Stockton. Perkins studied the construction of this marvel in great detail, carefully noting down all the particulars in his diary. His entries on the subject covered several pages and would be useful to Bryant when he returned to America.

By August 6, Perkins and his son were back in Boston, having been absent about four months. "Pretty well," he wrote Cushing, "considering I travelled 1,200 miles in Great Britain and was in 29 counties." He thanked Cushing for several different varieties of excellent teas Cushing had sent him, adding, "I am a great lover of good wine, but would sooner give up my wine than my tea."[10]

Bryant and his men had not wasted time that summer either. They, too, had covered a good deal of ground. At times, as many as 150 men were employed constructing the new railway. In addition, Willard had his crew busily engaged in getting out stone. The Bunker Hill quarry and surroundings were a beehive of activity, all spurred on by a battle that had ended half a century before.

The highly gratifying work on the railroad continued through September. As the leaves died on the trees and countryside harvests were waggoned into barns and storehouses, the colonel, sixty-two years old now, was forcibly reminded by two events of his own autumnal years. One was the death of Russell Sturgis at the age of seventy-six on September 7. "A respectable merchant," eulogized the *Gazette,* "an honest man, an ardent patriot, an affectionate friend, a man of wit and honor too."[11]

A letter from Cushing, written the previous April and just received in Boston, contained news of the other change. Cushing, whose health was not very good, proposed his "quitting this country." He was forty, unmarried, and in his twenty-odd years in China had amassed a considerable personal fortune as well as enriching the company. In those years he had had only one brief furlough home, and now, if ever, was the time for him to reap the rewards of his years of effort. He intended, he informed Perkins, to close "all our outstandings in this quarter as speedily as possible, and our efforts for the coming twelve-month will be used to accomplish this object." Thomas Forbes, who would be succeeding Cushing, was being sent home via Europe for a brief holiday, before returning to China. "We hope," replied the colonel shortly after Russell Sturgis's funeral, "that you will not have remained at your post too long, and have suffered more than you may apprehend."[12]

By early October, Bryant announced the railroad ready for a test run. On the morning of the seventh, Perkins and his fellow stockholders gathered at the Bunker Hill quarry to watch the train move the first load of stone. The tracks had all been laid, but the railway was far from completed. Not enough cars had been built to keep it in steady operation for one thing. But in six months, starting in a vacuum of knowledge about railroads, having to invent or reinvent almost everything by himself, backed only by his ideas, skill, and the colonel's faith and cash, Gridley Bryant had built a railroad.

In the test, three cars were used, each weighing better than a ton and a half. It was proposed to load sixteen tons of stone on the three cars and take them down to the river. The cars were really only a long narrow platform suspended from four large wheels, each six and a half feet in diameter. The axles on which the wheels revolved were arched in the middle so that the load could be carried close to the ground.

The stones had been moved onto flats between the tracks by grunting workmen with crowbars. Then the car chassis was rolled over the flats. Chains attached to the cars were fastened to the flats. A complicated series of gears had been built into each car to raise the load clear of the ground. Once the stone had all been loaded, twenty workmen climbed aboard the cars, and a *single* horse, at the driver's signal, began to strain at the load. Slowly the cars began to inch forward. As the momentum of the cars increased, aided by the slight decline of the track, the horse was able to increase his pace to a fast walk. So far the road appeared to be a success.

Since the horse, it was found, could travel at the rate of four and a half miles per hour, he could make a round trip on the three-mile line in well under two hours—less unloading time. With only one track, until Bryant built some turn-outs, they were not getting the full benefit of their investment. Nevertheless, the brown glass bottles which had been specially blown for the occasion, and embossed with the slogan "Success to the Railroad," had every right to be raised in toasts for the event. There is a historical dispute whether this is the first railroad in the New World. It certainly was not the first horse-drawn tramway. But both legally and technically it was a successful pioneering venture. Many of the ideas that Bryant conceived played a major part in the development and expansion of the railroad system.

Among the mechanical problems that the Granite Railway tackled were those of supporting rails with heavy loads passing over them and anchoring this support below the frost line. The English railroads did not have to make provision for deep frost. To meet this problem, Bryant had had a dry stone wall laid three feet deep. Huge granite sleepers, sometimes weighing as much as a ton or more, were spaced across this wall every eight feet. The rails were made at first of pine timber, six inches wide and a foot high. On top of these pine rails were nailed oak scantling, two inches thick and four inches wide. To this was fastened a bar of rolled iron, five sixteenths of an inch thick, and from two and a half to two and three quarter inches wide. The car wheels had flanges to keep them on these iron straps. The space between the rails had been filled with small stones and gravel, and it was here that the horse walked.

The railhead at the Bunker Hill quarry was eighty-six feet above the termination of the line at Gulliver's Creek on the Neponset River. The steepest drop was two and a half inches to the rod, equivalent to sixty-six feet in a mile. A strong brake was necessary to keep the wagons from running upon the horses. The road crossed several deep ravines on wooden trestles. It ran almost in a straight line except for two considerable bends, one at the river, and the other from the Pine Hill ledge round to the Bunker Hill quarry. This section, which included a 280-foot trestle across a swamp, was the last built, much to Willard's annoyance. He had expected them to begin here. It was an "unnecessary hindrance" he complained to one of the directors. His working area had quickly become "clogged" with huge stones, "and a short piece of their railway would be important to us to transport them to a more convenient place."[13]

Bryant had enough problems that summer in building the railway, besides trying to keep Willard happy. Indeed, keeping Willard happy did not ever seem to be one of his major concerns. Perhaps he did not even keep the colonel happy, for the cost of building the three-mile line, including all expenses except the amount paid for the land, came to $11,250 per mile, considerably more than they were paying down in Pennsylvania. Admittedly, however, Pennsylvania did not have the frost problems that Quincy had.

Since the machinery for loading the stone at the river was not yet ready, Willard wrote Warren in November that they should not try to transport stone to the hill that season as it was too late. He had already taken out about 500 tons and it was estimated that it would take about 12,000 to complete the monument. It was now nearly a year and a half since the cornerstone had been so proudly laid on Bunker Hill, and though a great deal had been accomplished in Quincy and Bunker Hill, the second stone had not been put on the first to erect the monument.

With the end of the winter snows and the mud season, the railroad at Quincy came to life again. A formal contract had been signed between the railroad and the Monument Association to carry stone from the quarry to Charlestown, even though Willard opposed it. There were almost daily visitors to watch the railroad in operation. A committee appointed by the nascent Baltimore and Ohio railroad came to examine the operations and reported that two horses could draw forty tons of stone at four and a half miles per hour. The committee could see no insuperable obstacles to their own construction of a railroad after seeing this railroad in successful operation. At that point in the development of railroads, it was debatable whether horses or steam locomotives were the best means of supplying the drawing power. Horses were safer, they were cheaper, and one horse could pull "at as rapid a speed as the passengers will desire."[14]

Massachusetts was beginning to feel the effects of New York's successful Erie Canal, which was drawing off Boston's inland trade. A new and convenient route westward was required. Spurred by a petition from Mayor Quincy signed by 2,633 citizens asking for a survey to see if a western railway might be more feasible than a canal, a large delegation of the General Court visited the Granite Railway project in June 1827. Apparently they were sufficiently impressed with all that they had seen, and in the name of "Internal Improvements" and that eternally beckoning Fata Morgana labeled "Progress," they voted without dissent to authorize the railroad survey and appropriated $10,000 to do the job properly. Thus the colonel's gamble at Quincy was bearing larger dividends than he and his associates had realized.

Colonel Perkins was now older than his brother James when he died, and was showing no signs of slowing down. But there was a difference, and Thomas Forbes, who was home on holiday that winter, had noted it and commented on it in a letter to Cushing: "Mr. T. H. P. appears to wear very well—his habits only show that he is advancing. He has lost much of his interest in Commercial enterprises and feels disposed to withdraw from an active participation in them—goes rarely to his counting house and then but for a short time. Mr. Cabot has for some time taken the active management." Forbes described quite candidly the other members of the firm. The young colonel, THP, Jr., was "very much improved" and promised to be a respectable member of society, but his business talents would never make him distinguished as a merchant. Of young James Perkins, however, he could say little good. "He is daily disgracing himself—it is a melancholy subject to all his friends." For James Perkins was an alcoholic, but since that euphemism had not been invented, his friends could only call him a drunkard.[15]

Though Perkins was no longer interested in the day-to-day running of the firm, he kept his thumb on the over-all planning. By Forbes's testimony, he was the only one, with the exception of Cabot, who could. And he told Cushing in the spring that he was hoping for good business. At the moment, "slow sales and large stocks on hand are the burden of the unwelcome song." But he thought the following year promised well for China operations to America. As for opium: "I have written

Rendering of the Bunker Hill Quarry, Quincy, Mass., showing terminus of the Granite Railroad and the granite-working shops of Solomon Willard. Drawing by Draper Hill based on the archeological work of Richard J. Muzzrole.

and thought so much of opium that it gives me an opiate to enter upon the subject."[16]

Perhaps an opiate would have been useful to quiet the worry caused by the Nahant Hotel. It had showed great promise when it opened in June 1823. The second season, even though manager James Magee had died, was again a social success. However, the summers of 1825 and 1826 were poor ones. With two poor seasons back to back, it seemed clear that there were not enough fashionable people in Boston to keep the hotel solvent. The proprietors decided to sell the place at auction on February 1, 1827. Dr. Edward H. Robbins, a nonpracticing physician, bought the property for less than $12,000. Perkins was not about to admit defeat in running hotels, however, and he eventually became a silent partner of Robbins in the purchase.

Perkins also worried about making some provision for his handicapped son George, and he set him up in the commission business in New York with John Sturgis as his partner. He was making plans for John Cushing too. "After a busy life of 20 years' uninterrupted labour, we doubt if you will be content to remain quiet." The colonel knew that he himself could not. "We offer you the *Head of our Hong,* from which the writer must soon retire *nolens volens.*"[17]

Although Perkins was much admired by those around him, Solomon Willard was not about to join in the chorus of praise. In May 1827 he had complained to Warren that "through mismanagement" the railway company would not be able to deliver the stone that was first wanted for the monument. He never had had any confidence in the railway fulfilling its contract, and the agreement, he reminded Warren, had been made against his wishes. Thus, he considered himself "free from responsibility for any hindrance or loss which may be sustained in consequence of this contract." Willard was preparing an excuse for himself if any blame was to be passed around. His attitude was not about to be improved by the next developments.[18]

At noon on Monday, June 18, 1827, the members of the Monument Association met for their annual meeting. Webster declined re-election as president of the association. Being long before the days of "conflict of interest," the meeting elected Perkins as Webster's successor. He was thus president of both the association and the railroad doing business with it. Dr. Warren did not want to continue as chairman of the building committee. He had grown rather weary of the irrascible Mr. Willard and his complaints. He suggested that someone who had more time be put at the head of the building committee, and Perkins was voted into this job too.

An interlocking directorate! As president of the railroad, he oversaw the sale of granite at a profit. As chairman of the building committee, he oversaw the railway's work. As president of the association, he oversaw the Building Committee. He embarked upon his multitudinous jobs with typical vigor. Before acting on the building committee, he advised Warren that the amount spent so far "should be adjusted." Unless that was done, he would not serve. He felt that the activities of the association were being carried on much too loosely. At the rate Willard was going, they would soon run out of money. At this point a brake was needed, and he intended to apply it.

Consequently, he also wrote Willard on June 19 asking for an estimate of what was still to be done: "Mr. Lawrence is to meet me at the Bunker Hill Quarry at 3 o'clock this afternoon," and they planned to examine his estimate. "The object of the above enquiries is to enable you to continue the work in proportion to our present means and reduce the present expenditure within the means of meeting them."

The inspection of the quarry did not go off well. Perkins could speak bluntly when he felt he had to; more than one ship's captain had been hauled over the coals by him. He and the touchy Mr. Willard had words and Willard stormed off. That night Willard brooded on the injustice of it all. He had given two years of his life to the building of the monument without compensation—so he termed it, although he had gotten "expenses." Now he was told to curtail his activities. And told by the man whom he considered as the chief agent of his frustration. His displeasure with Bryant's work was transferred to Bryant's boss.

Willard sat down the next day, the twentieth, and wrote a succinct note to Lawrence. He had but one course to pursue: "I shall remove whatever belongs to me in Quincy, this day, and shall give no father [sic] direction to the workmen. Your interests there may require attention." Thursday, June 21, Lawrence caught up with Willard and listened patiently while Willard went over all his grievances. Among them, so Lawrence wrote William Sullivan, also on the building committee, was Willard's feeling that the "Chairman of the Building Committee has never felt an interest in the success of the plan, and that he will not be likely to help it along; but on the contrary, will retard it."

Two days later, however, when he had cooled down, Willard relented and offered terms to Lawrence. "The thought of returning to take charge of the work in Quincy never occured to me until this morning and although money will not induce me to return, there are other considerations which might have some weight." But the real stumbling block was still the colonel. His prejudices against Perkins were indeed strong. "The airs assumed by the present chairman in his debut at the quarry," he wrote Lawrence, were "inadmissable." Willard thought him "the most unfit person on earth for the plan." Then he too spoke bluntly: "It appears to me more safe to judge men by their acts than by their professions. I myself have seen examples of the honesty and fairness of the man in individual concerns which render his removal from that place indispensible to my return." Harsh words indeed.

Most of Willard's demands were easily met. As for removing Perkins from the scene, this could not be done without offering him the gravest insult. No one on the committee would even consider it. For the time being, Lawrence was able to soothe Willard sufficiently to continue working until some agreement could be reached on his other demands. But eventually, Perkins had to be told. It was up to him as president of the association to work out a plan that would accommodate Willard. Perkins was astute enough to find a workable solution. He wrote to Lawrence that "As I am on the move, it will be requisite to have a person who is more stationary cloathed with power to draw on the treasurer and I propose a secretary to the Building Committee be appointed." The same day Lawrence wrote Willard "I will merely state that I was appointed today secretary of the Building Committee." Everybody was satisfied. Lawrence, with whom Willard could get along, would be his link to Perkins, "the most unfit person on earth."[19]

It was not the end of the difficulties with the temperamental Mr. Willard, but his strong prejudices against the chairman of the building committee were not shared by all. Not by the president of the United States, for example. In August, Daniel Webster called on President John Quincy Adams in Quincy only to be told that Mayor Quincy had carried him off in his carriage to inspect the new railroad. They met Colonel Perkins at the stone house the company had built at the railroad the previous autumn. Together they walked to the quarry and were caught in a thundershower. They ran for shelter to the shed where the stone cutters were working. When the rain stopped and the President could inspect the road, he was much impressed with what he saw. Already, however, he noticed some wear and tear on the iron strap on the track, and even more on the timber beneath it. Perkins was not too worried by it, but had had an experiment made over a short distance of substituting a granite rail for the wood. Adams thought this desirable, but was afraid it might cause the iron to wear out faster.

Even more than the railway, Adams was impressed by the colonel. He "has great means, ardent public spirit, and pertinacious enterprise," wrote the President in his diary. It was generally reported, he noted, that the greater part of the work was borne by Perkins, "and that he is liberal even to profusion in expense upon it." Writing to Tudor, Perkins had described it as "my Reigning Hobby." The danger that Adams saw in the enterprise was that the mounting expenses might cast such "a shade" over the project as to defeat it.[20]

Presumably, Willard would have agreed with two thirds of the president's assessment of Perkins. It was indisputable that the colonel had great means, and whether one liked it or not, an ardent public spirit. But the "pertinacious enterprise"—there Willard might have drawn the line. Willard when he had resigned that June, called it "mismanagement," and had added as well sarcastic references to the colonel's reputed "honesty and fairness." Exactly what did he mean?

Who takes another man to task, should be
From all the failings that he censures free.
Are you thus faultless: did you never scrawl
A verse you'd give a finger to recall?

William J. Snelling,
*Truth,* 1832

# 29

# In the Teeth of Mr. P.

Although Willard did not specify what example of the colonel's "honesty and fairness" he had in mind, one such, in various distorted recountings, had been the gossip of the 'Change since April. In the old days of the last century at Cape Francis, when the French had restored a temporary control over the island after the slave revolt, a young Boston sailor, Unite Dodge by name, had set himself up there as a merchant. Unite was assisted by his brother John as a clerk until 1803 when John returned to Boston. The Dodge firm had occasional business dealings with J. and T. H. Perkins in Boston.

Shortly before the French army finally abandoned the island in the spring of 1804, a "loan" was extracted from the merchants by the army command. Those who refused to contribute were sent to jail. Unite Dodge was one of these. Still getting no results, the French leader, Rochambeau, threatened to shoot any who held out against the forced loan. To stimulate the recalcitrants, he shot one of the French merchants even as his friends were counting out the unfortunate man's ransom. Dodge capitulated and paid the $2,000 demanded of him. In return,

Rochambeau graciously gave him a piece of paper as a "receipt" for the "loan."

On November 1, 1803, Dodge sent the receipt, along with three others, to his friend James Perkins in Boston and asked him to try and sell them, if possible, without serious loss. When Perkins went to France in 1804, he took Dodge's receipts with him to be negotiated. He left them with the Perkins's French bankers, Hottingeur & Co., for collection. Not until Napoleon's defeat were they able to do anything with them. On January 24, 1815, they exchanged the notes for interest-paying French government bonds. This was too late to help Unite Dodge, who had died in Bermuda in 1806.

By 1814 John Dodge had settled in Salem, and was in and out of Boston on occasion. Although not as well acquainted with the Perkinses as his brother had been, they were yet friendly enough so that a chance meeting of the colonel and Dodge at the theater resulted in an invitation to a ball at the colonel's. From time to time after that, he dropped in on the brothers at their counting rooms. Being particularly interested in the efforts of the Negro Republic of Haiti, which had succeeded the French administration of the Cape, he had a long talk one day in 1819 with the brothers, trying to get their signatures on a petition to have the United States recognize the new country. By 1822 when James died, Dodge had moved his family into Boston and taken himself to Haiti to enter into a partnership in trade.

In settling the affairs of the firm after James's death, Samuel Cabot instructed Hottingeur & Co. to sell any French government bonds they held for the firm and send the proceeds to Williams in London. When the accounting arrived in Boston, it was for considerably more than Cabot's books showed the firm had due it. He took the matter up with the colonel, who could not account for the excess either. He suggested Cabot look into the old books, but after much time spent trying to puzzle it out, Cabot drew a blank, and finally credited the bonus to profit and loss.

There the matter stood until January 26, 1827. On that day John Dodge, as executor of his brother's estate, called on the colonel. Remembering the forced loan of some twenty-three years earlier, and having heard that the French government was now paying old war claims, he had recently written to Hottingeur & Co. trying to trace his brother's claim. They referred him to Perkins, saying that they had paid over the money to that firm five years before. When the situation was explained to him, Perkins said he would look into the matter, asking Dodge to call the next day.

When Dodge came back, Perkins gave him a copy of the letter of transfer of funds in 1822 from Hottingeur, and agreed that the unexplained surplus undoubtedly belong to Unite Dodge's estate. He asked John Dodge to prepare an accounting for him. When Dodge returned with the accounting, Perkins noted a claim for interest on the money from 1822 to date. This stuck in Perkin's craw; the transaction had been attended to by James Perkins without commission for the accommodation of a friend. Why should they pay interest for doing a man a favor? Whose fault was it that the money had not been called for sooner? Certainly not theirs. Dodge had never notified them that he was qualified to receive the money, and if he had done so in 1822 they would have promptly paid him. Perkins did not feel he had borrowed this money; it only "lay" in their hands; why should he pay interest on it? Interest was not always paid on such money unless the holder of it failed to give due notice to the executors. But since Perkins neither knew the money was due Dodge, nor had been asked by Dodge to produce it, he felt justified legally in refusing to pay the interest.

Things got sticky between the two men, and Perkins asked to see his administration papers. Dodge produced them. They were issued by a court in New York. If Perkins wanted to be picayune, he could legally delay the matter until papers were taken out in Massachusetts. This is exactly what he demanded Dodge do.

On April 9, 1827, Dodge was granted administration in a Massachusetts court and promptly the next day, thinking his last obstacle had been overcome, he called at Pearl Street. His official accounting showed that the Perkins firm owed him $8,668.31, of which $1,869.63 was interest on the principal since the bonds had been cashed in 1822. To Dodge's disappointment, Perkins delayed the settlement for a couple of days. When Dodge returned to Pearl Street, two days later, he was handed a note at the door by a servant. This was an offer to pay only $6,311.25, the main sum less the disputed interest, their commission, and one other small disputed item.

Incensed by such treatment, Dodge demanded to see Perkins. Once admitted, the interview got out of hand. Dodge claimed the interest particularly, he said, because Perkins knew he had owed him the money for the last five years, and although they had met from time to time in that period, Perkins had never mentioned the debt. This struck at Perkins's pride, since he viewed the affair purely as a matter of the accommodation by his brother of an old friend. The interview ended with Perkins telling Dodge that if he did not like the settlement Perkins proposed, he could sue.

And sue he did. Knowing Leverett Saltonstall was a friend of the colonel's, Dodge engaged him. A visit and a letter from Saltonstall left the colonel unmoved. Dodge was pressed for funds, so he made one final appeal to the colonel's sense of justice, offering to arbitrate. Perkins had his heels dug in, however, and replied haughtily: "The letter you have been pleased to write me is of a very offensive character, and you will please to consider this the last communication I shall make to you. You seem to desire a recourse to the law, and you shall be gratified." But it was the colonel who was forcing the matter to "a recourse to the law."[1]

Dodge now engaged Daniel Webster to file suit against Perkins. Webster approached the Perkins's lawyers with offers to arbitrate, trying to smooth ruffled feelings by implying that Dodge was disinclined to enter into controversy with former benefactors. Perkins stubbornly replied that this was "a little at variance with calumnies which Mr. Dodge has put into circulation" on 'Change. Under other circumstances, declared the colonel, these would deserve "CHASTISEMENT." Clearly, Perkins was in a fighting mood.

But so was Dodge, and the colonel's remarks set him flaring. On June 19, he wrote Perkins threatening to publish all the papers and documents in the case so that all Boston could see exactly what kind of a person the colonel really was. This threat brought a fast response from the Perkins camp. The colonel's son, THP, Jr., wrote Dodge the next day as if he had just gotten wind of the affair: "I am informed, indirectly, that some unpleasant differences exist between Col. Perkins and yourself." He offered to listen sympathetically to Dodge's side of the case, and suggested he might "be enabled to do away with unpleasant feelings in a great measure."

When they met, young Perkins made explanations that principally removed Dodge's objections. Dodge consented to leave the question of interest to two referees and would withdraw his "pledge" to give publicity to the matter, if Perkins would pay him the principal sum immediately. He put this in a letter to Tom, Jr., and added a polite remark about "the kind and gentlemanly manner in which you have acted in this affair."

Such flattery got him nowhere because legal actions had been started by other heirs of Unite Dodge, and because the colonel did not respond to Dodge's offer. Finding no softening of the colonel's attitude, Dodge wrote him on June 25, vowing not to "retract a word." Perkins's son replied immediately to say that he was "exceedingly sorry" that Dodge should view Col. Perkins's conduct "in any light but the proper one." Since the matter was now to be left to the courts, he hoped Dodge would find "the obstructions of the law and lawyers less tedious than is usual in such cases."

Webster filed a bill in equity in the Circuit Court and Perkins's lawyers objected to the jurisdiction. Judge Story sustained the objection in the December 1827 term. Saltonstall and Samuel Hubbard now took over as lawyers for Dodge, while Lemuel Shaw and son-in-law William H. Gardiner defended Perkins. Saltonstall declared that "were he in the place of Col. Perkins he would rather have paid double the amount of Mr. Dodge's claim against him than have suffered it to come before" the courts.

When the case was remanded to the February term of the Supreme Judicial Court in 1828, the jury decided for Dodge and granted him damages of over $2,000. Perkins appealed this and a second jury in the November term agreed with the first. Perkins hung on and fought it through until the March 1830 term, when the damages were reduced by about $300.

By then, Dodge not only had the money and interest due him, but the sweetly satisfying last word. Using some of the proceeds from the law suit, he carried out his "pledge," publishing in 1830 a long tract detailing his side of the case and reprinting all of the pertinent documents. Surprisingly, the Boston Athenaeum secured *two* copies of his account, in spite of the fact that Perkins was its president at the time. Dodge's concluding words in the tract took a high tone: "The end of this affair shows that neither wealth or influence can stay the march of justice in our free land; boldly, plainly is it said in the teeth of Mr. P., who has caused misery, where there could have been none; want has come where riches might have been, and the consequences as marked in the final result, are . . . ," and here the sign of a pointing hand was inserted by the printer to stress the next few words, "that the American and European markets will correctly value his goods when marked 'Reputation,' aye, 'Mercantile Faith.' " Dodge now considered his duty discharged and "now and forever he leaves Mr. P. to his own conscience and his God." Saltonstall had been correct; it would have been better for the colonel to have paid double the claim than to have had such a pamphlet printed.

Perkins was involved in another controversy during these same years—but this time with the president of the United States.

The highpoint of the colonel's relations with John Quincy Adams came in the fall of 1827. The visit to the railway, when Adams had been so impressed by the "ardent" public spirit of Perkins, had been followed by efforts to enlist Perkins and other moneyed men into backing Adams for a second term. Even though the presidential election was a year away, the electioneering had already begun. Supporters of Andrew Jackson had raised a large campaign fund and were bombarding people with anti-Adams propaganda.

The Adams family, father and son, had never cut warm, popular figures with the voters. Many of the supporters of John Quincy Adams favored him from a cold sense of duty. An exception was a congressman and classics scholar from Massachusetts, Edward Everett. He saw the deeper qualities in the president under the frosty exterior and the two became friends. Adams often consulted the scholar from Boston, and, in turn, Everett sought aid for Adams from his Boston Federalist friends. Perkins was one of those approached.

On September 14 Everett wrote Perkins asking him to place any advertising he might do in Philadelphia in the *Democratic Press,* since this paper was leaning towards Adams and might continue to do so if Federalists patronized it. He asked Perkins to use his influence with Perit & Cabot to the same end. A week later, Everett consulted Amos Lawrence on a plan to raise a fund among the Boston merchants to counteract the Jackson propaganda against Adams. They selected eleven of the most prominent Federalists to approach, including Perkins. They were to meet at Daniel Webster's, but only seven men came. Although Perkins had not gone to Webster's, he found himself heading the committee appointed at that meeting. Everett spent several fruitless days looking for the colonel to tell him of his new chairmanship, only to learn that Perkins was laid up at Brookline with the gout.

As soon as Perkins felt better, he arranged to meet Everett in Webster's office in Boston. There, plans were made for the Federalist community to come to Adams' aid. This period was probably the peak of good feelings between the Federalists and Adams. The president even received numerous offers to invest in the new cotton textile factories, which were paying lush dividends to their fortunate and highly selected stockholders. Israel Thorndike had mentioned to Adams that ten or fifteen shares might be available, and when Adams heard that Perkins had made a "large investment" in the same stock, it was a "strong inducement" to him, he wrote Perkins, to take the plunge. He asked Perkins for more information about the proposition, and found the answers "altogether satisfactory." If he decided to invest, he wrote Perkins that October, he would send his son George round to "make all arrangements for the payment and assessment." Then with a kindly inquiry about the colonel's indisposition, he wished Perkins "all possible success in the truly patriotic undertakings to which so large a share of your time and property are devoted," signing himself "your sincere old friend." Within a year however, the "sincere old friend" was to be at sword's point with Perkins and the Boston Federalists. On October 29, the Wednesday before the presidential election, an article appeared in the *Centinel,* that took the steam out of Federalist support for Adams's campaign.[2]

Boston Federalists read in the newspaper a copy of a letter Jefferson had written shortly before his death in 1826 in which the former president stated that during the efforts to repeal the embargo, John Quincy Adams had called upon him with information that "certain citizens of the Eastern States (I think he named Mass. particularly) were in negotiation with agents of the British government" and attempting to pull out of "the war then going on."

The *Centinel,* immediately after this letter, reprinted a statement authorized by Adams, which, in typical Adams fashion, while attempting to explain away Jefferson's letter, only dug the pit deeper. Jefferson had, said Adams, confused events of three different periods into one. The interview Jefferson reported was in March 1808 not during the period "pending the Embargo," as Jefferson's letter had phrased it, since that act was passed in December 1807. What he had actually told Jefferson, said Adams, was that if the embargo continued much longer certainly the legislature and probably the judiciary of Massachusetts would support a civil war against the federal government and that "he had no doubt" the leaders of the Federalist party would ask Great Britain for help. To make matters worse, he stated that that had been their object for several years: to dissolve the Union and establish a separate confederation. This was an accusation of treason made by the highest authority in the land. And the men he was implicity calling traitors were supporting his re-election.

The thunderbolt struck all over Boston. Everett wrote his brother that "I do not recollect so great an excitement." Boston's Federalist leaders were determined that Adams's insinuation not go unchallenged. It was particularly exacerbating to anyone in any way connected with the Hartford Convention, or—like the colonel—its comical aftermath. To Otis went the job of drafting a group reply. Although Adams had named no one, thirteen Federalists stepped forward to sign the answer to him, among them Colonel Perkins. The reply demanded that Adams name "the persons designated as leaders of the party prevailing in Mass. in 1808 whose object was dissolution of the Union," and to provide "the whole evidence on which the charge is founded."[3]

Adams received the letter on Tuesday, December 2, and began to draft his reply the next day. His mood was one of deep dejection; the news had arrived just that morning that he had lost his bid for a second term. "The sun of my political life," he mourned, "sets in the deepest gloom." He spent the whole day, nevertheless, on his answer to the Boston Federalists, interrupted only by a steady stream of friends offering their condolences. On Thursday he enlisted the aid of Edward Everett. After a long conversation, Everett borrowed the original letter for further study. Friday, Adams heard second-hand that Otis had been "very abusive" about him, and from other sources he learned that "some of the principal Federalists have determined to break off all personal intercourse with me, so that I shall go into retirement with I know not how many bitter controversies upon my hands."[4]

Everett was trying, however, to extricate Adams from his mess. That same Friday, Everett began the draft of a letter to Colonel Perkins. In the evening he called on Adams and urged him to delay any answer for ten or twelve days, though giving no reason for his request.

Sunday, Everett finished his letter to Perkins which he marked "Private & Confidential." It was an attempt to persuade Perkins, and through Perkins the others, not to make a public controversy out of the issue as it "can have no other effect than to break up this Union" of political sentiment, "and plunge us again into the frightful discord from which we have just emerged." He implored Perkins to use his influence to have the Otis letter withdrawn, or to acquiesce in its not being answered, or of "taking some other course which will effectually answer your object as individuals."[5]

The colonel's reply has not survived, but the tenor of it can be judged from Everett's subsequent letter. Apparently, Perkins rejected the proffered olive branch on behalf of all the Boston group and also wondered if Everett thought that Perkins might indeed be guilty of Adams's charge of treason. Everett hastened to assure him that he had no doubts whatsoever of Perkins's loyalties, or that of any of the Boston group.

During the next ten days, Adams continued to work on his reply, consulting several friends on his draft. One advised him to tone down "the severity of certain passages," and Adams struck out part of them. More and more the reply took on gigantic importance in his eyes, the consequences of which to himself and his family he saw resting "with God." Every word had to be weighed, every point had to be right. By the end of the month he had "written very few letters, and a few messages of routine." Most of his time had been spent on his reply to the "thirteen self-assumed leaders of the federal party in Mass." The affair was one of the "severe trials" of his life, but he saw nothing he could have avoided, nor anything that he ought repent.[6]

The reply Adams prepared was long but conciliatory. He recognized, he said, among the signers of the letter to him "persons for whom a long and on my part uninterrupted friendship has survived all the bitterness of political dissension." Even such a statement, intended to soothe, had a rub in the false nobility of those words "on my part," putting the onus of any interruption of friendship onto the other parties in the controversy. He tried to qualify his first statement, claiming that he had said "certain leaders of the party," neither meaning nor intending to include all leaders of the party in his indictment. In any event, he wanted no controversy, and as for the "evidence" he possessed, "no array of numbers or of power shall draw me to a disclosure which I deem premature." Instead of making things better, this made it worse. Then he dropped a broad hint that "at some future day a sense of solemn duty to my country may require of me to disclose the evidence which I do possess." But to call an unnamed group of men traitors; then assert that he indeed had evidence and would reveal it when he felt like it, left the whole group to continue to live under the imputation of disloyalty. This was no answer at all. Naturally, the Boston group had to reply.[7]

Almost a month passed before they had framed their answer to the president. When published in the *Centinel* of February 14, 1829, it ran to seven and a half columns of fine type, but it could be summed up in one of its sentences: "We solemnly disavow all knowledge of such a project." Perkins wrote Sullivan suggesting that "each Gentleman who joined in the letter to Mr. Adams should have a copy of the Printed document, signed by the whole." To him, this was a historic quarrel.[8]

Three days later the lame-duck president began a reply to the reply to his reply. But moving out of the White House so that Andrew Jackson could move in occupied Adams for the next few days. Then he mulled at length over what he should put in and what he should leave out. Everything extra he added would be "another hornet's nest that I shall disturb, and more controversy to be foreseen." If he left it for publication after his death, his children would inherit the resentments and arguments. Selfish motives induced him to be silent, but, New Englander that he was, what of the "great moral lesson to my country?" that could be taught by exposing the errors of those Federalists "who had conspired against the integrity of the Union." His present mood was to write "with the boldness of truth. I shall prune by the counsels of prudence." That was having it both ways.[9]

Adams slogged ahead with his reply, which grew and grew until by April it was over two hundred pages. Now he began to doubt the wisdom of carrying the controversy further. By May he had told a friend that although his reply was nearly finished, he doubted if he would ever publish it, and certainly would thoroughly revise it if he did. Eventually, he abandoned the project, and it was the wisest decision he had made in the whole sorry affair.

No rousing welcome was given to the defeated president by the Boston Federalists, but his leaving the last public word to them had a healing effect. When the two hundredth anniversary of the founding of Boston was held on September 17, 1830, Adams went up from Quincy to take part in it. At 9 A.M. he went into the Senate Chamber of the State House, where the state and city government and all former members of the legislature were assembling for the procession. William Sullivan was chief marshal of the day. "He and the Mayor," Adams later recorded in his diary, "H. G. Otis, and Colonel T. H. Perkins, came and offered me their hands, and their salutation was accepted." Nor did Adams, when shaking hands with Sullivan, Otis, and Perkins, make any unfortunate reference to the "Three Wise Men of the East."[10]

# The Old Colonel IV 1828–1854

Suggestive of Mr. William Gray's grim acquisitiveness and his pride in same, he was asked by a rising man 'How much it took to satisfy a man.' He replied sagely, 'A little more!'

Hugh Crichton

# 30

# Retiring from the Bustle?

John Perkins Cushing spent the better part of the winter of 1827–28 closing out the affairs of Perkins & Co. in Canton. Thomas Forbes had returned to Canton at the end of August, and before Cushing left for Boston in the spring he prepared a long letter of instruction for his successor. "I need not again remind you," he advised Forbes, "of the advantages that are derived in business concerns by pursuing on all occasions and with all persons with whom you have transactions an upright and honorable conduct." It was the philosophy on which he had successfully conducted business for a quarter of a century, including even his opium smuggling.[1]

On September 17, 1828, the firm's ship *Milo* docked at Central Wharf with Cushing aboard. With him was his chief clerk, John Hart. Cushing was forty-one years old, unmarried, "very rich"—William Sturgis underlined the word for proper emphasis when reporting this to Joshua Bates—and a virtual stranger in his native land. His health was bad; "impaired," said Sturgis, "by too much devotion to business in a climate not favorable to 'length of days.'" Sickly as he was, he was still an impressive figure to a new young apprentice who had just entered the Perkins counting rooms. This was another Forbes, John Murray Forbes, four months short of sixteen. The lad wrote his brother Thomas in Canton that he liked Mr. Cushing "better than I expected, for you know that we have always looked upon him as many degrees higher than the pope in all his glory." John had expected to feel "a proportionate degree of awe in his presence," but found Cushing had the ability of "making one feel easy." Their mother, he wrote Thomas, "looks upon him as the only unexceptional object (except perhaps aunt Abbott) in this wide world of sin."[2]

Cushing was still a young man, and Colonel Perkins was interested in what his future plans might be. Perkins proposed a new house with a capital of a million dollars. Samuel Cabot and Tom Perkins, Jr., would each put up a third of this, with the colonel furnishing them the financial wherewithal. Cushing would supply the other third, and Forbes in Canton would be cut in for a quarter interest even though he would not be required to put up any money just then.

For a bit, Cushing was tempted. It would have to be strictly a China trade agency, otherwise he would not be interested, and Cabot and Tom, Jr., would have to confine themselves merely to putting up the cash. As he confided to Thomas Forbes, "Mr. Cabot is not a popular man & the other member you are too well acquainted with to know he will not be a desirable associate in business."[3]

By Christmas time, however, Sturgis noticed in Cushing a decided "disinclination for business in this country." Partly, he thought, Cushing had been put off by the business failures of several Boston establishments. Samuel G. Perkins & Co. was one of these. Sturgis did not think Bates would be surprised by that "after the conversation we had about S. G. P." He thought the colonel's firm might lose forty or fifty thousand in brother Sam's failure. Perit & Cabot and Cabot & Co. had also failed, as well as several other respected local firms. Not that these failures would affect the Perkins concern. Sturgis esteemed them richer than generally estimated, and some facts he had recently learned confirmed him in that opinion. "If the Col. went off to day," he confided to Bates, "he would leave *more* than a million of Dollars." Cushing, though not as well off as the colonel, was "likewise very rich."[4]

As late as November, Cushing had dallied with the idea of continuing without the Perkins group. He in Boston and Forbes in Canton could "carry on the business in our own way," perhaps cutting Bryant & Sturgis in on some of their ventures. But by the end of the year he had decided it would be well to discontinue when "the operations that are now in train are concluded." Cushing's evaluation of the colonel had something to do with his decision to quit. He had already warned Forbes that the colonel "is rather forgetful and sometimes recommends what at other times he condemns." In his letter of December 26, when he let Forbes know his decision, he again mentioned that the colonel was getting "too advanced in years to attend to business." The whole burden of "the Hong" would fall on Cushing's shoulders, which because of his present indisposition, were rather frail at the moment.[5]

It was not until three weeks later that he broke the news, "candidly," to the colonel. It would be "impossible" for him to engage in business here, "it being totally different from what I have been accustomed." This, he wanted the colonel to understand "explicitly," was his main reason for not becoming "Head of our Hong." He also disliked the idea of putting himself into a situation where he could not contribute a full share of attention and labor to the task. But he would be glad to advise the group and enter into specific operations with them from time to time. All this, with "the warmest thanks for the offer." A couple of weeks later he sent a copy of the letter to Tom Forbes. With Forbes he was a little more "candid." He wanted to feel free to quit when he pleased. "I cannot by being a member of the House here feel the independence that I wish to after 25 years of fagging." His plans were to operate on his own account or with Bryant & Sturgis "when there is a prospect of doing anything to advantage."[6]

So there was the handwriting on the wall for the colonel. Old and forgetful as he might be, he knew that any future the concern had, would not be with his son or his son-in-law. It was his nephew or no one, and when Cushing declined to carry on, it was the finish of the "Hong." J. & T. H. Perkins had come to the end of a long and very profitable road. All that really remained now was to wind up the activities of the far-flung trading enterprise. This was not easily done. John Forbes, writing to his brother in Canton that spring, remarked that "Mr. Cabot talks a great deal about giving up trade and winding up the concern. James Perkins* says he means to wind up the concern

* SGP's youngest son and a fellow apprentice of John M. Forbes.

as he would a clock, 'to make it go the longer.'" Young apprentices always know so much more than their masters![7]

Although there was no pressing business in the store that winter, there was always employment for these flip fellows in making copies of invoices. Young Forbes kept on the fair-weather side of the old colonel "by always knowing how many brigs and ships are coming up, and which way the wind is." They had even given Forbes a "pretty good dip into the art of stowing teas" by letting him manage the unloading of those on the *Parthian*. Forbes thought they would sell well too, "though if you believe Mr. Cabot, the times are so bad that it is better to make a bad than a good bargain, from the greater security of getting paid." With this kind of business philosophy, it is not difficult to understand the reluctance of Cushing to enter the American firm.[8]

Apprentice Jim Perkins remembered those days in later years, with "the young Colonel" turning up whenever a ship arrived. He would busy himself with the out-of-door work "which alone was congenial to him." With a fine yacht, good horses, an elegant home in Winthrop Place, he had more interesting things to do than hang around the counting rooms. He was "always kind and hospitable to us Juniors," wrote young Jim, "taking us occasionally to the theater and home to supper after the play." The old colonel only appeared "on great occasions, when the larger voyages and operations of the house were under discussion, and then occupied a separate office." The brunt of the daily work was undertaken by Samuel Cabot.[9]

When not making copies of invoices and the like, these young apprentices found things to do. What was left of a ship's stores, when its cargoes had been unloaded, was packed away for future use in the loft of the counting room. Occasionally this included wines or liquors not consumed on the voyage. When they knew the principals were not coming to the office, the clerks would "test the goodness of these remnants from an East India voyage." One stormy winter afternoon in 1829, the heavy snow and blustery weather seemed to guarantee that Mr. Cabot would not appear. The office crew decided this would be a good time for a bit of "testing," and John Forbes was sent up to the loft after a bottle of whisky. The tin pot used to test teas was filled with water and set to heat on the office fire. Some sugar was brought and the makings of a good toddy were on hand. Suddenly, the sound of the stamping of snowy feet downstairs heralded the arrival of Mr.

Cabot. Jim Perkins seized the fire blower and set it in the fireplace, hiding the boiling teapot, just as Cabot entered the office. Over to his desk marched Cabot and began one of those interminable letters to China which all the clerks dreaded since they had to make several copies to be sent by various ships, a necessary precaution in an age of precarious communication.

As Cabot scratched with his quill, the bookkeeper, Mr. Hayward, sitting on his high stool, worked on the account books, occasionally glancing at young Forbes and Perkins and then at the fireplace. The two clerks were busy thinking up excuses why they had water on the fire. The fire roared up the chimney, driven by the air from the blower. Hotter and hotter got the room and the inhabitants until finally Cabot noticed it too.

"What on earth have you got such a fire for; take off that blower!"

Jim Perkins ran to do his bidding. The blower by now had gotten red hot from the fire and he had to take a set of fire tongs in order to remove it. What would happen when the removal of the blower revealed the teapot to Cabot? Both clerks were wildly trying to invent some plausible explanation for the pot. To their great relief, the intense heat of the fire had vaporized all the water and completely melted the tin pot. No explanations needed![10]

The colonel was much like that fire with a perpetual blower in front of him, always thinking up new projects for the concern to attempt, even though he had apparently accepted the fact that they were going to close out the business. Cushing had to write a caution to Forbes at the end of March that they must wind up the old concern before starting the projects Perkins had suggested to Forbes in his last letter. With the colonel, it was always one more venture, then they could close the concern.

As a sort of parting shot, Perkins and Cushing planned a great shipment to Canton for the fall of 1829. The *Bashaw* was to sail in September via England with the largest cargo ever sent east by the Perkins firm. The colonel, even though he pretended to be "quite indifferent on the subject" of speculation, proposed to Cushing that they sail with the *Bashaw* as far as England. Having had his fill of traveling in America, Cushing agreed to go along.

This was all the encouragement the colonel needed, and six weeks later, on July 13, 1829, they were aboard the new ship *Margaret Forbes,* ready to go. By evening Cape Ann glimmered on their starboard side, and then was gone. For the seventh time, the colonel, now age sixty-five, was crossing the Atlantic.

After a rapid journey, during which the sails were never reefed—"rather extraordinary"—they caught sight of England on August 6, 1829. By dawn the next day, Perkins and Cushing had disembarked at the Isle of Wight. A busy two weeks in London followed, with the men spending much time in the company of Joshua Bates. On the twenty-fourth, Perkins and Bates, whose health was also poor, decided to take a jaunt to the Continent. Cushing, who was planning to spend some time in Europe, remained behind in London.[11]

The continental junket lasted three weeks and saw them tearing through France and the Low Countries. In Paris the colonel found his old Monkton associate, Colonel Welles, and dined with him. Other Bostonians and their wives were present—Sears, Codman, and Everett. Then on to Amsterdam, where Perkins was particularly offended at the canals, which he thought filthy, with everything thrown into them.

They took a steamboat from Rotterdam back to England, and by mid-September the colonel was safe in London, with only "the pillage of a part of my box of Segars." Hearing that the *Dover* was sailing from Liverpool to Boston on September 20, with few or no passengers, the colonel decided to try and catch it. Traveling by public coach, he was in Liverpool by the eighteenth, and spent the next day inspecting the great Liverpool and Manchester railway due to open the following year. He was particularly impressed by the great tunnel the railroad went through.[12]

Sunday morning a steamboat towed the *Dover* down the Mersey to the sea. Cushing reported to Cabot a week later that the colonel had sailed, adding that "his health was much improved and there is little doubt it will be quite re-established by the time he reaches home." As usual, Cushing was correct. The trip home was uneventful except for two minor incidents. A careless passenger let the colonel's thermometer fall into the ocean "so that my meterorogical journal is at an end." The other was a dream he had about General Elliot who appeared *"as having grown young, and in the prime and energy of manhood."* If he were inclined to be superstitious, wrote Perkins, he should be uneasy about the general.[13]

A letter to Bates from the colonel when he arrived back in Boston testifies to his restored vigor. After going down the "obituary list,"—Elliot wasn't on it—he says "Of myself I am well—and I give you as evidence of it, that I travelled over the sharp Rocks and Hills at Quincy on Monday, and without inconvenience." Nor had the colonel's enthusiasm for granite suffered a sea change. "Our Quincy stone is quite the thing—Contracts were made in Virginia for stone for the construction of the Norfolk Dock; but it was found it could not be had, and they have made new contracts with the Quincy Granite people."[14]

In fact, Perkins had been quite pleased with the progress of both the granite company and the railway. The railway had been in good order for about a year, and it was moving about 150 tons of stone daily from the quarry to the wharf. But much of the stone was for the railway's private customers, and not for Solomon Willard and the Bunker Hill Monument.

Perkins believed that there would be a great future in Boston for granite. Scarcely a new house or building was being built that did not use their granite "in a greater or less degree": a new hotel in Tremont Street; the front of the new theater built opposite the hotel; a timber shed at the Navy Yard; a dry dock at the Navy Yard that would be capable of "taking in Noahs Ark." "We furnish the Stone for the Dock, which will be finished in 1830—the quantity of Stone we are to supply is about 50,000 tons." Three other docks were contemplated. In addition, many places outside of Boston were buying the Quincy granite for building projects of their own.

The problem, then, was not getting stone out; but getting it to Mr. Willard's monument. Here, Willard's requirements had been imposing delays. He insisted that the stone be sent according to pattern and not weight. In spite of building troubles, Perkins had nothing but praise for the "work as far as it has gone." It was "amongst the most beautiful of the works of art in its way—every course it rises, it is so far finished, in all its parts; and if there is not patriotism to compleat it, in the community, it will be a beautiful object when we leave it."[15]

Willard, however, had no such kind words for the railroad as the colonel had for the monument. It had been "badly managed" he reiterated. "To those who have been eyewitnesses of the management of the company from the beginning, there is nothing which appears mysterious about it—the want of a system, and the proper apparatus for doing the work, is sufficient to account for a part of the unnecessary expenses which has been incurred." But what actually stopped work at the quarry for the monument in January 1829 was not Willard's running feud with Perkins and Bryant, but the association's lack of cash. They had tried hard during the winter of 1828–29 to raise the $50,000 that was estimated would be needed to complete the work on the monument, but depressed commercial conditions prevailing at the time brought their efforts to nothing.[16]

Even the colonel found his interest in the monument weakening. When the annual meeting came round on June 17, 1829, he wrote Dearborn that indisposition—"I have not been on my feet since I had the pleasure to see you"—would keep him from attending. Nor did he wish to stand for re-election, since he had already made plans for his trip to Europe, "to remain there an indefinite period." All of which should have made Willard happy, but did not. For Willard had a new cause for complaint. The monument, what there was of it, that "most beautiful of the works of art," had to be cleaned frequently. It was being used by some of the irreverent inhabitants of the city as a "necessary." A far cry from Everett's oratorical picture of the shaft as an "honor due to the illustrious dead!"[17]

If the monument had proved to be something of a disappointment to all parties, Perkins at least had other projects stemming from the granite quarry. And one of them was the new hotel being built in Boston—the Tremont House. Though not a prime mover in the idea of a luxury hotel for the city, Perkins's Nahant Hotel had been influential. And he had taken, together with his nephew, a large financial interest.

Boston needed a good hotel. The city had more than doubled in population since 1800 and contained about 60,000 inhabitants, compared with Baltimore's 80,000 and New York's 200,000. There was no satisfactory place for the hospitality of the increasing number of travelers who flocked to the metropolis. William Eliot, the colonel's neighbor in Nahant and active in the hotel there, hoped to remedy this with his Tremont House.

One hundred thousand dollars was needed. The city council refused to grant a modest subsidy, so 113 merchants came up with the money. The colonel and James Perkins, Jr., had been two of the five major investors. When it came to an architect, the job went to Isaiah Rogers, another eminent builder. He departed from the traditional idea of a coaching inn, where the attention was focused on the care of the traveler's horse and little on the traveler himself. Instead, he planned a great granite pile with a pillared portico entrance directly from the street, as in other public buildings. Of course the granite came from the Granite Railway Company.[18]

The grand opening dinner was held on October 16, 1829, while Perkins was still on his way home from Europe. It was in honor of the merchants of Boston. During the toastmaking, the absent Perkins was remembered. Daniel Sargent proposed him as "A gentleman whose heart and purse are always open for the public good." Everett, who was the principle speaker of the evening, remarked that he had intended to propose a similar toast. "I could do so with propriety, for he has been my friend ever since I have been old enough to have a friend—the patron of my youth and the benefactor of my poverty." Typical after-dinner persiflage, for all present knew that Everett's benefactor was his father-in-law, Peter C. Brooks, said to be the richest man in New England.[19]

Cushing, who one day would come very near claiming Brooks's title for his own, had gone over to Paris and become violently ill. For the last six weeks, he wrote Cabot in mid-November, he had been unable to sit at his desk without great suffering, and even after that felt not much better. In spite of this, by December he had organized the cargo of the *Bashaw*. The Smyrna agent had purchased 830 chests of opium, and together with the British goods, the ship's cargo would be worth something like $600,000. Cushing expected a profit "under ordinary circumstances" of $150,000 to $250,000. Perkins & Co. was certain to end in a blaze of glory.[20]

That is, if the colonel would only let it end. While still in England with Cushing, he had become very excited about the prospect of shipping teas to France and Holland. Cushing was not taken with the idea and made sure nothing was done about it in England. He advised Cabot, in a private letter not meant for the colonel's eyes, "If you can succeed in keeping him quiet at home I think there is a fair prospect of our bringing our concern to a close in the course of the ensuing 6 months." But Perkins was like an old hunting dog always scenting a new fox on the wind and baying to be off in pursuit.[21]

It seemed as if his outside activities should have kept him fully occupied. In 1830 he was elected president of the Boston Athenaeum, and he served three years, until December 1832, when he declined re-election. Because of his pioneering work with the Granite Railway, he was drawn into some of the many schemes burgeoning in the state for the construction of railroads west, south, and north. As a trustee for his late brother's estate, he was involved in constant real estate transactions to improve that trust for the benefit of the heirs.

All this and the gout too, ought to have kept his mind and body busy, but they did not. Although he claimed to desire that "old dependencies should be closed," he added the significant line, "future adventures will be made on specific accounts." He had a kind of genius for discovering "specific accounts." Sometimes too, the "specific accounts" through strange circumstances "discovered" him. So it proved with the Dutch and French ventures that he had proposed to Cushing the previous fall, and which Cushing tried to discourage. By April, Cushing too saw the possibility of realizing "a cool $100 M" on this venture. But it took a tragedy to open his eyes.[22]

One day in the middle of February 1830, the ship *Tobacco Plant* arrived in Boston with letters for the firm from Russell & Co. in Canton. Samuel Cabot had not come down to the counting room that day so young John Forbes was sent with the unopened letters to Cabot's house. Forbes was in a happy mood, having been to a lively party the previous evening. The news in the letters would change all that.

The previous August, said the letters, shortly after Cushing and the colonel had reached England, Thomas Forbes had received word that the ship *Mentor* from Boston had anchored at Lintin Island with letters from home. The news reached him in Macao and he was anxious to read those letters. The future of the firm was, as far as he knew it, very much up in the air. He was aware that Cushing intended to withdraw, but what the rest of the family had decided was not certain. Against the better judgment of his friends, Forbes set out in his yacht, the *Haidee,* with two Lascars for a crew and accompanied by Mr. Monson, chief clerk of the counting house. The night was hot and sultry, with every indication of a storm. But Lintin was only eighteen miles away and Forbes felt sure he could reach it in two hours.

About seven miles from Macao the wind died down and the boat was becalmed. Forbes anchored and waited for a wind. When it came towards midnight, it blew in fitful gusts that everyone in those parts knew to be the harbinger of a monsoon gale. Since the wind was against him, Forbes decided to return to Macao. The strong winds quickly pushed them back to that town. Mr. Monson, however, became seasick and took to his bunk below. Rather than disturb him by landing that night, Forbes made a fatal decision to anchor under the lee of the town and wait for daylight.

By dawn the wind had reached hurricane force. The sea was so rough it was impossible to make shore. Forbes dropped both anchors, hoping they would hold. But as the wind increased, the strain on the chains became obvious. In preparation for the worst, Forbes stripped off his clothes. One violent gust of the wind, and the first chain snapped. The full weight of the boat rested for a moment on the other anchor; that quickly parted and the boat was rapidly blasted seaward by the gale.

Now at the mercy of the storm, Forbes hoisted a bit of sail to try and keep the boat headed into the wind. They sped by several rocky inlets, but Forbes could see no hope of landing there. Soon, through the driving rain, he could make out a small beach ahead, and he headed the boat for it. Only too late did he see the shallows that changed the waves into breakers. One of them smashed over the boat and nearly swamped it. At that instant, the rudder gave way, and Forbes lost control of the boat. A tremendous wave broke over them and drove the boat sideways into the breakers. The surf began to smash the craft. One of the native crew pushed the skylight to Forbes as a support, but he refused it and grabbed the main shroud instead. For a bit he clung to this and then disappeared under the waves. The Lascars struggled to shore, completely exhausted, and later brought the sad news back to Macao. After the storm, search boats were sent out in hopes that somehow the two men had survived. All they brought back to Macao were the bodies for burial in the English cemetery there.[23]

Cabot had to break the melancholy news to young Forbes and then inform the rest of the family. A letter was rushed off to Cushing, now returned to London, for, distressing as the news was, immediate steps had to be taken to protect the huge investment in the *Bashaw,* whose sailing was imminent. Forbes had left general instructions that if anything happened to him, the activities of his firm were to be taken over by Russell & Co., another New England firm opened in Canton in 1824. Cushing was friendly with Samuel Russell, the principal, and had frequently turned over commission work to his house.

When Cushing learned of Forbes's death, he recommended that Bennet Forbes, who had returned to Boston the previous October, be sent back to Canton to represent their interests in Mr. Russell's house. "I should have every confidence in Bennet by himself," wrote Cushing, "but it would be very desirable to have the benefit of Mr. Russell's experience."[24]

Then Cushing heard that it was quite possible that Russell would be leaving China. Under those circumstances, he thought it worth his going to China, and he embarked on April 15, 1830. The decision to return to China was not taken reluctantly, he assured his friend Sturgis. Both the chance to make that "cool" $100,000 by an expedition to France and Holland (since he would be in Canton himself, he could see the value of the venture) and "not caring much about being amongst the good people of this hemisphere" were the reasons he gave. He confessed to "not caring a pin about Europe." As for Boston, he didn't feel he could "settle myself down and conform to the habits and customs of the good people" of that town. He had tried to feel and think like the people he had to be with "in this hemisphere," but he still felt as much a stranger as when he "first marched home."[25]

Bennet Forbes was approached about taking over the China business, but he shied away from the idea. There was his health, his duty to his mother and family, and the fact that he had been brought up a sailor and not a merchant. He would not want to learn his duty from strangers or crowd into an office "from mere influence of friends when I should be considered one too much." A thousand and one reasons why he should not do it occurred to him. Besides, he had a scheme of his own that he wanted to try out, provided he could persuade his uncle, the colonel, to go along with it. He wanted to take over the Lintin station ship, a floating warehouse for opium awaiting sale. At the same time, its skipper did a fine business selling provisions to ships that passed.

To further his scheme, Forbes went to New York to look over an old Perkins ship, the *Milo,* intending to buy it if he could gain approval for his plans. On his way back to Boston on April 24, 1830, he recognized Colonel Perkins and William Sturgis in two coaches driving past him in the opposite direction. At the next post stop, Forbes left his coach, hired a chaise, and set out in pursuit of them. At the Dedham post stop, he learned that the passengers were planning to spend the night at the halfway house of Mr. Fuller at Walpole. Off to Walpole he raced. Walpole then was a small village dominated by the two inns that stood opposite each other on the main street. The public coaches stopped for dinner at Fuller's in one direction and at Polley's across the street when coming the other way.

Forbes arrived just as the Perkins party, in which there were several young ladies, pulled up at Mr. Fuller's. Bennet took lodgings across the street at Polley's. Realizing the importance of the coming interview he went to the hairdresser's, had a wash, bought a new collar, and then set out to accost his uncle. Perkins and his party were just about to dine. They invited Forbes to join them. After dinner he took Mr. Sturgis to one side and broached the subject of the Lintin station. At the moment it was manned by a Sturgis ship commanded by a Sturgis nephew. Yet Sturgis was sympathetic to Forbes's idea and gave his assent.

Later in the evening, Forbes tackled his uncle. The colonel was agreeable, but raised the difficulty of Sturgis's operation of the station. "If he consents, I shall interpose no objection." Informed of Sturgis' prior approval, Perkins went further and advised his nephew not to buy an old ship but advanced him enough money to buy a new one. The next morning, having dreamed all night of his forthcoming prosperity, Forbes headed for Boston to buy himself a ship.[26]

By the end of May, he could report to Cushing that "I have bought through Mr. Sturgis a new ship." He expected to be in Canton by the first part of November. He would stay at Lintin station for two or three years and, "all parties here are agreed to aid me through ships and influence." Gone were his earlier objections to a long absence from his family and relying on the help of friends, for now it was a project that *he* wanted and not one planned for him by others.[27]

Forbes and his new ship, the *Lintin,* left Boston on July 7, 1830, along with his brother John. Another passenger who was to become a famous name in the China trade was Augustine Heard, going out to represent the Perkins firm in the new establishment of Russell & Co. The arrangements for John Forbes to enter the China house, once he had served his apprenticeship, were made by Cushing, who was already on his way to Canton with the *Bashaw.*

When Cushing arrived in Canton, his hopes for a great profit collapsed. The East India Company ships had been late in reaching Canton, and consequently the market was oversupplied with English goods. Because of a good crop of Malvic opium in India, that drug was abundant. Turkish opium, which had been $870, had fallen to $700. With about 1,000 chests in the *Bashaw*'s hold, that difference represented a huge loss. Even at $700, only small quantities could be sold.

In one sense, Cushing discovered that his trip to China was a needless one. Russell had stayed in Canton, and intended to remain there until some one replaced him. In fact, the day after Cushing had sailed in the *Bashaw,* a letter arrived in London for him from Russell advising him of this. Still, "I do not regret having come out as I have derived much pleasure and satisfaction in seeing my friends in this quarter."[28]

The cargo of the *Bashaw* was another matter, however. By the middle of October its British goods had all been sold at a profit of more than 15 percent. The opium did not sell, and the opinion was it would not until the supplies brought in by the British had been used up. That would probably not be until the end of the year. The trouble was that the Chinese just did not smoke the drug fast enough.

The Perkins & Co. second establishment, meanwhile had been wound up with a profit to the partners of $1,127,432.49. It was still too early to determine what the third establishment would bring since too many accounts remained unsettled. But Cushing made an estimate of his wealth in July 1830 that showed his personal worth at more than $700,000. China, and opium, had been good to him. There was no need for a fourth establishment since Heard was joining the Russell house and "will hereafter attend to our business." Cushing had the "highest opinion" of him. John Forbes had also joined it as an assistant and would become a partner "when duly qualified." Thus, "those who are coming forward" would be taken care of "quite as good as if a new establishment were founded." He did not want Perkins to get any wild ideas![29]

By the end of 1830 only a small amount of the *Bashaw's* opium had been sold, so Cushing decided to transfer the lot to the *Lintin.* This freed the *Bashaw* to be loaded with teas for a homeward cargo. By February 17, Cushing wrote Boston that he intended leaving for home early in March, "though with a heavy heart." He knew that he would never come back to Canton again, yet he kept hoping something would turn up to make it necessary for him to remain, "as I feel better satisfied here than I ever expect to anywhere else." Nothing did turn up, and on March 5, 1831, he bade farewell to "the Celestial

Empire," leaving behind him one of his interminably long letters of instruction to Russell & Co. about their future relations, and what to do about the opium sitting unsold at Lintin. Love and epilepsy were waiting for him in Boston.

Heavy as was Cushing's heart, there were equally heavy hearts in Boston. The annual meeting of the Granite Railway Company was held on March 18 at the new railway hotel that Perkins had built to take advantage of the stream of tourists who came out to see the railroad. The stockholders had to face up to some unpleasant facts and some hard decisions. Just the year before, the stock had been reorganized to reflect the money invested. In five years, $155,000 had been spent, and of this sum, the colonel was in for $132,000. The other four investors had each put up about $6,000 a piece. The results of the 1830 season were not happy reading. The company had sold $64,794.80 worth of granite, but the costs of operation were $61,200.55. The profit was $3,594.25 or about 5 percent of the money invested. Not at all like Lowell! A committee composed of the colonel, William Sullivan, and P. T. Jackson was to study the future of the company.

The committee reported that whether the business was worth pursuing depended on too many contingencies for them to determine at the moment. They would watch matters closely during the year 1831 and then decide whether to continue the business or "to fill out and close the Concern" or to lease the business to some "Association of Persons" on the best terms they could get.[30]

Though the granite market might not be very brisk, everything else was prosperous. The colonel wrote Cushing a happy letter on May 10, 1831 telling of the "fine hit" they had made with the teas shipped by the *Alert*. These had cost 14 cents a pound in Canton. They had to pay 40 cents a pound duty on them in Boston, and they got 86 cents a pound for them at auction. "46 for 14—a pretty fair mercantile profit in these piping times of peace." The killing the Perkinses had made on the *Alert*'s teas, "has set every one, who ever heard of China at work to send an adventure there," Perkins crowed to Cushing. From Philadelphia, thirteen vessels were going or had gone, and perhaps thirty from the country altogether. "I shall not be surprised to find from day to day, new expeditions to China—one or two were mentioned yesterday." The times were so prosperous that the manufacturers were making more money "than the Owners even could wish."[31]

Although Perkins had wanted to spend that summer in Europe, circumstances dictated otherwise. Instead, he went "wandering about thro' our back Country, and amongst the Eastern Rivers, the object rather to keep health, than to get it; in which I have succeeded very well." Cushing returned in August 1831, with a rich cargo in the *Bashaw,* and Perkins could report to Joshua Bates in October that "our voyages from China as far as they have been brought to a close, have terminated famously."[32]

In spite of his dubious attitude towards the Bostonians, Cushing had bought an estate on Summer Street for $55,000, "considered reasonable," Perkins noted. More than one matron had her eye on the rich bachelor, seeing him as ideally suited for whatever stray daughter she had left on her hands. Other Bostonians gaped at the house which began to take on a semi-Oriental aspect. With the Chinese servants that Cushing employed, it brought an exotic quality to staid Summer Street.

And was the colonel settling down too? Going on sixty-seven years of age, was he following the prescription he had long ago set out for himself and his brother: that having improved the heyday of life, they retire from the bustle of the world and enjoy the fruits of their labor? It might seem so. In that October letter to Bates, he wrote that "After an active Mercantile life of nearly half a Century, it is not surprising that I should incline to retire altogether from business concerns—and indeed this is my feeling." Yet his very next words showed what were his truer sentiments: from "a desire to give continuance and support to my Sons in Law Mr. Cabot and Mr. T. G. Cary, I have consented to remain a Partner with them under the same firm."

The young colonel was retiring from the House, nothing hesitant about him! But Cabot and Cary "think the name of the House worth something and they want a portion of my Capital to work with." So they were going to do commission business, with an occasional flier in the China trade in association with Cushing and Bryant & Sturgis. It is doubtful if there was a question in anyone's mind who the principal partner was going to be in the new firm. Retiring from the bustle? Not as long as Bostonians would drink tea and the Chinese would smoke opium!

I see not how men absorbed in business can accomplish the great end of life. That end is to strengthen, to extend and keep in invigorating action the principles of love to God and to our fellow creatures.

William Ellery Channing,
July 3, 1834

---

# 31

# This Class of the Human Family

For over thirty years, Colonel Perkins lived on one side or the other of Pearl Street. It was a highly convenient situation. Just a few blocks walk to the east brought him to his counting room. The same distance north and he was on State Street, where he could share in the gossip and schemes of the merchants on 'Change. Beautiful shade trees and lovely gardens gave the street a delightful rural aspect. At the end of the street, across High Street, was the shore. A short after-dinner stroll would bring the colonel up on Fort Hill, from whose height he could scan the harbor for late-arriving ships and enjoy the scenic view of Boston Bay. A few doors away from his house was his late brother's mansion, now housing the library and art gallery of the Athenaeum.

But time was bringing changes to this pleasant area. Commercial Boston was spreading out in every direction from State Street. Gradually Pearl Street was being engulfed. Houses were even being built on Fort Hill. Boston's expanding overseas trade, to which the colonel himself had contributed in no small measure, required warehouses and these were pushing in from the waterfront. The emigration of the Irish from the poverty and oppression of their homeland had begun. Its effect on Boston was the development of slum areas that were expanding towards the colonel's quiet residential neighborhood. For the first time in its history, a cancerous poverty was taking root in Boston.

As the slums moved towards Pearl Street, as the commercial growth encroached upon it, the colonel began to get restless and started looking for a better place to live. Besides, he was ready to build a new house. The fashionable center of town was now around the Common. Fine mansions and elegant row houses (some by Bulfinch) had set the tone for the section. There was only one open area left, the Washington Gardens, a commercial entertainment park, adjacent to St. Paul's Church, which fronted on the Common.

Access to the Gardens was through a gate in the brick wall surrounding it, or down a deadend alley named appropriately Turnagain Alley. At that period it did not connect with Washington Street, indeed was some feet above it. On the corner of this alley and Common Street (now Tremont), the Masons had built their temple after they were burned out of the old Exchange Coffee House. Early in March 1831, Henry Lee's brother Thomas bought the Gardens as a real estate speculation for nearly $16,000. He laid out twenty house lots on Turnagain Alley and upgraded its name to Temple Place in honor of the Masonic building on the corner. A month after he bought the Gardens, he sold one lot to P. T. Jackson for just under $3,600. When Perkins bought this lot from Jackson a year later on April 21, 1832, it cost him $13,000. That summer he began construction of a large brick mansion.

A true patriarch, Perkins wanted the rest of his family around him on Temple Place too. Samuel Cabot bought the lot across the street, and Perkins bought the lots on either side of his own and started houses for his two daughters and their families, Mary Ann Cary and Caroline Gardiner. T. G. Cary had been given the chance to leave a not-too-successful career in New York and take the place in the firm that Tom, Jr., was vacating. In the fall of 1832, he returned to Boston for good. Daughter Sally, who never married, and son George, whose brain injury necessitated repeated temporary residence in the McLean Asylum, both lived at home. Just by themselves, and not counting their servants, the clan brought a large population to the new street. The Cabots had eight children by that summer, the Cary's and the Gardiner's five each. Tom, Jr. and his wife, with their five living children, passed up this opportunity to move from their comfortable house on Winthrop Place and become a satellite to the patriarch.

What was to be done with the house on Pearl Street? Five years earlier, Perkins had attended a meeting at the Exchange Coffee House called by a Dr. John Fisher. This young Bostonian had recently completed his medical studies in Paris. While there, he had become interested in the work of the Royal Institute for the Young Blind, one of only three or four such institutions then in existence. At this period, little educational work had been done with children handicapped by being deaf, dumb, or blind.

Fisher determined that there ought to be an American counterpart of the Royal Institute. When he returned home in 1826, he began to circulate the idea in Boston. His friends suggested he call a public meeting to see if backing could be secured.

To Fisher's surprise, a large group of men showed up at a meeting held in February 1829. The General Court was in session, and there were many present from the legislature. Fisher explained what was being done elsewhere for the blind, exhibited books he had obtained abroad, which the blind could be taught to read by touch, and suggested that an effort should be made to establish such a school for the blind in Boston.

The audience was receptive. A committee of gentlemen was formed to study the matter, and a week later they sponsored a public meeting in the Representatives' Chamber of the State House. The efforts of the Deaf and Dumb School at Hartford, Conn. were discussed, and sufficient support for the idea of a blind school was indicated so that another committee was appointed to form such an institution. Thirteen prominent individuals were on this committee, though not the colonel. They applied to the legislature for a charter, which was granted without debate.

A charter is not a functioning school. What the group needed more than enthusiasm was a leader—some man who had been trained in teaching the handicapped, who was a good administrator, and also happened to be a first-class fund raiser. A difficult combination, and not to be plucked out of thin air. When the director of the Hartford Deaf and Dumb School resigned in the spring of 1830, it seemed they might get him for Boston's venture, but though he was interviewed by the committee, he finally turned them down.

It was another year before a suitable prospect appeared. This candidate returned to Boston aboard a Perkins vessel, thanks to the generosity of the colonel. When Samuel Gridley Howe arrived home in July 1831, he had no job, nor did he know where he would find one. He was not worried though. His efforts on behalf of the Greeks in their rebellion against Turkish rule had been given wide publicity and he was something of a celebrity. Something would turn up. In August he visited his friend John Fisher, and something did. Fisher realized that Howe had all the qualifications needed to direct a school for the blind, including lack of employment, and he offered him the post.

Howe accepted, and shortly headed back to Europe to study the work going on there with the blind. No sooner had he arrived in Europe, however, before he was charging off to aid another worthy cause: refugees of the unsuccessful Polish revolution. All he got for his pains were five months in a Berlin prison as a suspected revolutionary. When the American consul finally heard of it, Howe was given a nonstop ride to the French border with strict warnings never to set foot in the German states again.

By the end of August 1832, Howe was back in Boston ready to tackle his work with the blind. With him came two European teachers who were themselves blind. Howe scoured the Boston byways, found himself six blind children, brought them back to his father's house on Pleasant Street, and the New-England Institution for the Education of the Blind was on its way. He had two sources of money to draw on: the public, and the legislature. Having already received such wide support from the politicians, the trustees of the institution did not hesitate to submit a petition for a grant of financial aid. The petition was read on January 14, 1833, a day when the governor and legislature also watched an exhibition of the work of eight pupils from the Hartford School. This was so successful that the trustees of the new institution decided to present a similar exhibition by their pupils.

The elite of Boston and the legislature gathered in the chamber of the House of Representatives on Tuesday afternoon, January 29, 1833 for the demonstration. The colonel attended and agreed with the other spectators that in five short months, Howe's pupils had made remarkable progress. First Howe introduced the pupils to the assembly; they ranged in age from six to twenty years old. The program began with the pupils singing a hymn. Next they demonstrated reading from books with raised type using their fingers. (This was not the Braille system, although that had already been invented.) Using special relief maps they answered questions on geography. One little girl showed her ability to knit, another sat sewing in her special darkness, while a boy demonstrated making a basket.

Howe then asked for support of the school. They could all see for themselves what could be done. Unfortunately finances were limited and now almost gone. Unless further help was forthcoming, and soon, the effort would have to be abandoned. The vivid salesmanship worked. The state agreed to underwrite the education of twenty blind students, which amounted to a grant of $6,000 per year.

Next, Howe went after the general public. To an overflow crowd at the Masonic Temple on a Tuesday evening in March, he repeated the demonstration by his blind students. "A large portion of the learning, taste, and fashion of the city" were present, and $708 was collected. The ladies of Salem held a three-day fair early in April and turned over nearly $3,000 to the treasurer of the institution. Not to be outdone, the Boston ladies planned an elaborate fair for May Day, 1833. On the eve of the fair, the public was thrilled to hear that a "Munificent Donation" had been made to the institution which assured its future.

No one can say when the thought first came into the colonel's head to give his house on Pearl Street, valued at $25,000, to the institution. Certainly his brother James's gift of his property to the Athenaeum had been suggestive. Perkins was proud of his house, which had been built from the fruits of his industry. Perhaps by turning it over to an institution, the commercial penetration of the area could be resisted and the dignified character of the street preserved. He may have thought of the Female Asylum, which his mother had so diligently supported, and which was still thriving. And he had been touched by that January demonstration of the blind children.

On April 19 he sat down and wrote a long letter to his friend, Judge William Prescott, father of the historian, one of the trustees of the New-England Institution. "It is desirable," he wrote, "that the fate of this class of the human family should have something to look to. With this in mind I am induced to give the house in which I reside as a permanent asylum for the blind." The gift was conditioned with the customary Perkins self-multiplying feature, a technique that would become common a century later in foundation and government grants. In order to acquire the house, the trustees of the institution had to raise $50,000 as an endowment by public subscription before the end of May. Should the building cease to be used as an asylum for the blind, it would revert to Perkins or his heirs. The letter to Judge Prescott and the trustees acceptance of the offer and challenge were given wide publicity. They were printed in full in the *Daily Advertiser* for April 26 under the heading "Munificent Donation." The very next day the trustees announced that Jonathan Phillips had subscribed $5,000 to help meet the colonel's condition.

The news of the colonel's proposed gift gave a great boost to the ladies fair. All the prominent dames of the city were busy making extraneous items to be sold at exorbitant prices to soft-hearted patrons who would not have the slightest idea what to do with their purchases. Shopkeepers had been so badgered into giving merchandise to the fair that it was rumored some shut their doors when they saw the ladies of the fair committee headed their way. On the day before the fair, Faneuil Hall was open so that the public could inspect the treasures to be offered them on the morrow. Anna, one of the writing Quincy sisters, went and thought the hall "looked very handsome, decorated with evergreens and flowers and surrounded by the tables covered with every description of 'articles.' " The mayor's wife, Mrs. Harrison Gray Otis, was in her glory running the show.

On Wednesday May 1, the Quincy ladies were off early to the big event. The mob—"for I can call it nothing else"—at the door and on the stairs was crushing. The hall itself was so crowded that the Quincys escaped to the gallery. This haven cost an additional dollar, so the crowd there was considerably less. From the gallery, "lifted up above all the disquietudes of the world below," they could watch the amusing scene, the changing crowd, the variety of dresses, "the flowers, the dolls, the gay colours, and buzz of a thousand voices." A dozen cages of canary birds added their trills and cadenzas to the general cackle. "Mrs. Otis' voice," wrote Miss Quincy, "was heard above all the rest, talking, laughing and selling."

The most striking group in this throng were the blind children present, several of whom were with the ladies manning the booths. "How strangely," reflected Anna Quincy, "all these sounds must have seemed to them." It was truly benevolent, she thought, "to throw some light on the darkness that must ever surround them." However, she bought nothing, and took home only some flowers that a gentleman gave her. The contributions of others made the fair a huge success. Mrs. Alexander Everett's table alone, on which the Misses Perkins assisted, earned $2,000. The whole fair brought in the princely sum of $11,400, which, by agreement, could be counted towards the $50,000 that had to be raised that month in order to secure the Perkins mansion.[1]

The ladies were hardly done counting up their receipts before a new excitement gripped the community. Some anonymous person wrote a little fourteen-page pamphlet called "Scenes At the Fair," in which under easily penetrated aliases—"Mr. Houqua" was J. P. Cushing, for example—many prominent Bostonians were satirized. Martha Ward, daughter of Thomas Wren Ward who was the Baring agent in Boston, wrote her father that the trouble with the sketch was that "their peculiarities are too accurately noted and the touches of satire come too near home to be relished by all." Sternly she predicted that whoever wrote it would lose "all reputation for propriety and good taste. Such things will not be tolerated in a sensible and enlightened community."[2]

Perhaps not tolerated, but certainly enjoyed. The sketch opens with "Mrs. Harrowby Grey" (Mrs. H. G. Otis, Jr.) saying: "Most extraordinary and provoking thing I ever knew! Mr. Houqua not yet arrived! and here am I surrounded by millions of men—not a single article purchased!—everybody making love to me, as if this was the moment. Hundreds of proposals before ten o'clock this morning."

But at last the great moment arrived. As the stage directions put it: "(Enter Mr. Houqua. Line formed to let him pass. He advances slowly and stops opposite to Mrs. Neverton's table. He takes up a small painting.)"

Mrs. Neverton [Mrs. Alexander Everett]
Fifty Dollars, Mr. Houqua.
(Mr. Houqua bows and takes out his purse, lays it on the table and moves on.)
Mrs. Neverton, (opening the purse.)
A thousand dollar note!
Many Voices
A thousand dollar note!
Mr. Kirchspiel [Mr. George Parish]
Houqua forever!
Mr. Sago [Henry Rice]
Well, ladies and gentlemen, I think I may say, that upon the whole, this

*was really* a very prudent, that is generous, that is handsome, piece of attention on the part of Mr. Houqua. I suppose however that his fortune is pretty, I may say, very considerable.
There are very few private persons in our country who have a larger, I may almost say, so large a fortune as Mr. Houqua."[3]

While this merry little mischief had been going on, others had been busy scratching up the balance of the $50,000. William H. Prescott, one of the trustees, wrote a friend shortly after the fair that for the last ten days he had been "spinning round like a tee-totum" trying to help raise the money. Such was the spirit of the town that "in little more than a week we have raised within $5–6000 of the whole amount." Nobody but Boston could have done it, wrote Prescott proudly, particularly with the unfinished Bunker Hill monument "on our backs which must be provided for within this month."[4]

Bunker Hill being on their "backs" meant that after five years of no action, the Suffolk Bank called for repayment of the loan they had made to the association. This came at the same time that people were being solicited for the Institution for the Blind. Sourly commenting on this was an anonymous article in the *Daily Advertiser* for May 3, contrasting the generosity of "one citizen" who was building "a glorious monument to himself" with the help of the "joint contributions" of others, and the unfinished state of the monument to the fallen patriots. Even the very battleground itself, "which drank the blood of better men than fell at Thermopylae," he wrote, "must be sold to pay the debts of the Corporation."

The monument in truth had reached less than a fifth of its intended height since its glorious beginnings in 1825. Work had ceased entirely in 1829, and during the interim the directors made every effort to stir up fresh enthusiasm to complete the project, all without avail. Five days after Perkins had written his letter offering his house for the blind, Amos Lawrence had sent a last-ditch appeal to the Massachusetts Charitable Mechanics Association asking their help for the obelisk. The Monument Association was $28,000 in debt and it was estimated they needed another $32,000 to complete the granite shaft. Lawrence offered to give $5,000 if the Mechanics would raise $50,000 in three months. As a further inducement, he offered to contribute a like amount toward the purchase or erection of a headquarters for the Mechanics Association. Despite his preoccupation with the Institution for the Blind, Colonel

Perkins offered to give the Mechanics $2,000 toward their goal of $50,000.

When the Charitable Mechanics finally made their drive, all they could raise was a bit over $19,000. This financed another year and a half of work on the monument under Willard's direction, during which it rose to a height of eighty-two feet. This time Willard avoided difficulties with the railroad by transporting his stone all the way by ox-cart.

By early June, the trustees of the Institution for the Blind could report to Perkins that his conditions had been more than met. The sum of $51,117 was in hand. Perkins replied that he had been so confident they would succeed that he had already deeded the property over to them in May. But while the house on Pearl Street was adequate, more land was needed for a playground. The lot behind the colonel's was owned by Dr. Rand, and while the May fair was going on, Perkins bought this parcel for the school, paying $16,000 for it. When he transferred it to the school, he accepted only $14,000 for it, thus making them another $2000 gift.

Not all his neighbors were overjoyed to see a school for the blind coming into their midst. A story that certainly sounds apocryphal made the rounds, that a Josiah Bradlee, whose land adjoined Perkins's, protested vigorously:

"Colonel, you propose doing an act which will greatly damage my estate."

"How so, Mr. Bradlee?" inquired the colonel.

"Because you are going to let in a lot of blind fellows to overlook my premises. I don't like that prospect."[5]

During the summer, Perkins moved to Brookline as usual and the Pearl Street house was revamped for the new tenants. The brick stable in the courtyard beside the house was converted into schoolrooms and workshops. By September, the changes had been completed and the students, who now numbered about twenty, were moved from Howe's father's house. The first basket woven by the children in the new school was sent to the colonel as a token of thanks from those who were directly benefiting from his "munificent donation."

The last Saturday in September, Perkins picked up his Brookline pastor, Dr. Pierce, drove him into Boston to inspect his new house on Temple Place, then took him to Corinthian Hall to see the statuary, and before they went to the Athenaeum, they visited the new institution for the blind. Pierce noted that the buildings on the Rand place had been removed, the ground leveled and sodded, gravel walks put in, and a substantial fence put round it. "This makes a fine & spacious playground for the pupils, the number of whom is already 27."[6]

By the annual meeting in 1834, the trustees were beginning to complain that the Pearl Street building was too small. Pupils came in so rapidly that they now numbered forty. Two years later the problem had become so acute that something had to be done. Howe designed an addition, which was constructed, even though there was criticism that the Pearl Street place should be sold and a more commodious building purchased in the suburbs where property values were lower.

The main block to selling the Pearl Street house was the clause of reversion that Perkins had attached to his gift. The trustees in their annual report for 1836 explained that this condition was not dictated by any ostentation on the part of the "munificent donor" but by "the forecast of a head as clear as his heart is warm." Since he had "lavished" treasure in the erection of this "noble monument of beneficence," they felt that that monument "should be seen of men," and they wished the most crowded streets of the city "had each such an one." Passers-by would be thus silently reminded of their duty to the unfortunate and be admonished to "go thou and do likewise."

The problem dragged on for two more years. Could Perkins be persuaded to change his mind? Otis was asked to sound him out on the possibilities. Tied with it was another proposition calculated to flatter anyone's vanity.

The colonel, who was on his way to White Sulphur Springs in Virginia, had stopped off in Washington where he was enjoying a pleasant round of dinners with dignitaries like Clay and Webster. His traveling companion was Colonel Washington, and one night he was invited to dine at the White House with President Martin Van Buren. Otis wrote him a letter outlining the situation, sending it by George Perkins who—as Otis wrote joshingly to Howe—"is going to Washington in search of (what might puzzle wiser men) his own father."[7] Otis told Perkins of the great opportunity that had come in the way of the institution. The Mount Washington House in South Boston had to be sold "at a very great sacrifice." A huge building on a handsome site looking over towards Boston, it would prove ideal for the school. Otis had been asked to find out from Perkins "confidentially" how he would "entertain a proposition" of selling Pearl Street and using the money to buy the Washington Hotel. Coupled with this, was another question "if you should think proper to listen to it," and which Otis said he thought was proper "whether you think it or not." This was to change the name of the institution to either the Perkins Asylum or the Perkins Institution for the Blind.

Perkins answered promptly that in "giving the Pearl St. house to the Blind my sole object, if I know anything of my own motives, was to do my share towards relieving in some measure the misfortune to which they had been subjected by nature." He confessed that he did not remember the exact conditions of his gift, though doubtless there had been a reversion clause to his family or some other charitable institution if the Asylum project were to be abandoned. However, if the directors felt the proposed location was more suitable, he would make no objection. Adding only a proper precaution that if the asylum defaulted, then the proportion of their assets represented by his property should become part of the funds of the Massachusetts General Hospital. As to the sweetener, the change of title of the institution, "that I leave to others." Doubtless, he wrote, it would be "grateful to those who follow me, to see my name connected with this charity and," he added cryptically, "it may possibly be useful in another way." Otis and son-in-law Gardiner could settle the matter between them.[8]

In the school's annual report for 1840, in which the story of the removal from Pearl Street is recounted, the trustees announced that wishing to connect the name of the "munificent individual who must ever be considered especially as its patron and who had literally given to it 'a local habitation and a name,'" they felt the removal was a proper occasion to change the name. Henceforth it would be known by the unwieldy title—to be shortened later—of "the Perkins Institution and Massachusetts Asylum for the Blind."

Shortly after the Perkins Institution moved to its new and spacious quarters in South Boston, Howe caught the public attention with the pitiful story of Laura Bridgman. It showed dramatically the extraordinary results of Howe's patient, self-sacrificing care, but even more the beneficial possibilities of the young institution. What Helen Keller was to be to a later generation, Laura Bridgman was to the middle of the nineteenth century. Indeed, her story was to serve as an inspiration for the young Helen Keller.

Laura Bridgman was born in 1829 in Hanover, New Hampshire. An attack of scarlet fever when she was two, left her deaf and blind. Growing up in this terrible soundless darkness, she had become by eight years of age almost unmanageable except through brute force. Howe went to Hanover to see her, and in October of 1837 she was entered into the institution on Pearl Street. Howe quickly began to try to enter that darkness through the only route left him—the sense of touch. Using common objects such as knives, forks, spoons, keys, and such, he pasted labels on them bearing in raised letters the name of each object. Once she had made the correct association, he went on to teach her the individual letters, then the alphabet, and finally her numbers. At first, said Howe, it was like teaching a clever dog to do tricks. Once it dawned on her what was happening, "it was no longer a dog, or parrot,—it was an immortal spirit, eagerly seizing upon a new link of union with other spirits!"

When Charles Dickens on his American tour went to South Boston one fine winter morning in January 1842, he was greatly affected by his visit with the pretty young twelve-year-old girl. Her face radiated intelligence and pleasure. She had braided her own hair, was neatly dressed, knitted, kept a daily journal. "Like other inmates of that house," Dickens reported in his *American Notes,* "she had a green ribbon bound round her eyelids." This was Howe's device to call to the attention of the sighted that they were in the presence of a blind person. A doll that Laura had dressed lay near her upon the ground. "I took it up, and saw that she had made a green fillet such as she wore herself, and fastened it about its mimic eyes."[9]

Howe, with Perkins strengthening his hands, had made a start in loosening the ribbon binding the eyes of the sighted—their indifference to the needs and possibilities of the blind; "this class of the human family."

That each should in his house abide
Therefore was the world so wide.

Ralph Waldo Emerson

# 32

# I Try To Be Contented with What I Have

After a tour of Colonel Perkins's new mansion on Temple Place Parson Pierce inscribed in his diary a remark of Samuel Johnson's that kept recurring to his mind: "Ah! these are the things, that make us unwilling to die!" Indeed, the colonel's "exceedingly elegant and convenient edifice," as Pierce described what he saw, was furnished with the best and latest that money could buy and ingenuity could construct. There were twenty-three fireplaces in the four-story building, and "many curious devices" for heating the whole mansion. One of the early furnaces for central heating—by wood and coal—had been installed in the building. Among the other curious devices shown the parson were those for "bathing" and for supplying every part of the house with water.

The rooms impressed Pierce too, finished as they were in great elegance—the word was never far from his tongue when describing the Perkins mansion. He marveled at the handsome Italian marble mantles over the fireplaces, and at the decorations in each room. "A back chamber in the IIId Story had the walls covered with elegant prints, copies from the finest specimens of painting, ancient & modern." The cost of some of them amazed him too, ten guineas for instance for a print that was only "a little more than 2 feet square." While he would not quarrel with his parishioner's taste, he noted that among them were "too many naked beauties for the contemplation of the young." Certainly, mature individuals like himself, sixty years old, and the sixty-nine-year-old colonel, could contemplate them with equanimity.

On the fourth floor was the colonel's billard table. "Around this room are also prints of great variety & beauty." Whether the young should contemplate these or not, the reverend gentleman did not state. Anyway, he was more interested in the roof. This was covered with thick lead. Girdling the roof was a strong, high iron balustrade, giving fine views of the harbor, islands, and "surrounding circle." No need now for the colonel to stroll up on Fort Hill. He had build his own Fort Hill promenade. "For more than 3/4 of a circle you have a complete view of the sensible horizon." Enchanting also were the skylights that, with their colored glass, gave interesting effects inside and out.

The elegance even extended into the backyard, "finished in a neat style." Flat stones had been laid for the carriages to travel on, and there was a convenient "avenue" into Winter Street, which backed on the colonel's property. "His very stables," exclaimed Pierce, "are handsome." Such elegance and luxury would have made many an American of 1833 "unwilling to die."

Thinking over the day he had spent, and contemplating the colonel's new house in Boston and "his buildings, gardens, & grounds in the country," Johnson's remark again came into his mind. Beneath the parson's stout Puritan exterior beat a strong materialistic heart.[1]

Pierce had frequent opportunities to savor this materialism, since he was often a guest of the colonel's. The previous year when Audubon was a fellow guest at Brookline, Pierce had made one of the party. Perkins had subscribed, at $1,000 each, to two sets of the "Birds," one for himself and one for the Athenaeum. Cushing also purchased a set. Audubon came to Boston that August of 1832, partly to get more subscribers, but principally as a stopover on the first leg of a summer tour of the Bay of Fundy area to sketch birds. He stayed at Joshua Davis's rooming house on Pearl Street and was armed with letters of introduction to his Boston patrons. Perkins he found "an amiable, liberal, and efficient patron." When that patron invited him to dine in Brookline on August 8, 1832, he was quick to accept.*[2]

The day, a Wednesday, being warm and pleasant, Audubon decided to walk out to Brookline from Pearl Street companioned by a fellow dinner-guest, Thomas Nuttall, curator of the Botanical Garden at Harvard College. It was still possible in those days to see birds in Boston other than the present ubiquitous pigeons, sparrows, and starlings. Nuttall testified that even in the "most populous and noisy streets" the red-eyed vireo could commonly be heard from the tall elms. Why should these two ride out in a carriage and miss the chance of a little bird-watching?[3]

Audubon was conspicuous in any group, particularly striding through Boston that August day. Forty-eight years old, he was a rugged outdoors type, with his hair worn long on his shoulders in the virile frontier style of the West. Walking along in their shirtsleeves, conversing about matters ornithological, suddenly they heard the song of an olive-sided flycatcher. This was one of the two birds in New England, Audubon later told Pierce, with which he was not acquainted. While Audubon kept the bird in sight, Nuttall went off in search of a gun. He came back with a large old-fashioned musket, a cow's horn filled with powder, and a handful of shot about the size of peas. When Audubon went to charge the ancient piece, he discovered it was flintless. Finally, they secured a proper gun, and Audubon brought down the flycatcher near Samuel Perkins's barn. He was still excited about his new trophy when they reached the colonel's.†

The Perkins estate in Brookline was three decades old by then. Caroline Gardiner, a grand-daughter, recalled the "dignified white house with a piazza along the front and white columns supporting a piazza above on which my grandfather and grandmother's rooms opened." The real front door was on the side "carefully hidden away in a group of pines." The house had been artificially elevated about six or eight feet by an embankment that sloped away from the piazza. This gave it a good view of Boston. Eliza Cabot remembered being shown from its windows where it was planned to locate the Mill Dam when the project to enclose

* Oddly enough, Audubon had been born in Santo Domingo in 1785 when James Perkins was working there and THP was planning to join him.

† A new species of the flycatcher family, Audubon named it *Nuttallornis* after his walking companion.

the Back Bay was first proposed. The parlor and dining room opened on to the piazza side of the house and were connected by large folding doors. A Chinese wallpaper alive with birds and trees, and furniture largely of bamboo, reminded visitors of the colonel's association with the China trade. The dining room had handsome heavy furniture of mahogany, comfortable sofas, and "Mrs. Perkins's rocking chair, where she used to sit in hot weather with cap strings thrown back and sleeves turned up."

Upstairs on the front were the bedrooms of the colonel and his wife, comfortable and spacious "where they lived chiefly and received their intimate friends," much in the habit of European nobility. "Aunt Sally's room" was on the back of the main house, and looked out onto the treetops. It was a cozy, delightful room and was "the resort of grandchildren of all ages." Made out of the old nursery, it had been built rather oddly, "half a story lower than grandmother's room, with a little staircase leading from one to the other."[4]

"Aunt Sally was much cumbered with flesh." One night some little niece sleeping with her, woke up suddenly from a dream of struggling to climb over a "big rock" to find that she was trying to scale her aunt's mountainous back. Sally's bulk figured in another Brookline story. Bradley, the town constable, came to arrest the cook who allegedly owed the village druggist money. Aunt Sally "came upon him as he was flourishing about and the cook remonstrating and vowing she owed the man no money. It was in the passageway that led across the head of the stair-way going down to the cellar kitchen, and Aunt Sally in her wrath came afoul of him with such momentum that she knocked him downstairs into the kitchen below. He rose vowing vengeance and went and got out a warrant against her. Grandfather had to buy him off."[5]

Using a great deal more of the same money that had quieted the constable, Perkins had gradually turned his Brookline estate into a showplace that drew many of the distinguished visitors to Boston. From the very beginning he spent lavishly on what at first was called simply the "Brooklyne Farm." In this first period of the estate, at the beginning of the century, it was a working farm with cows, chickens, barn, ice house, stone walls, and an orchard and garden. One of the new "Rumford Kitchens" had been installed, which certainly few average farmhouses of the day could boast.

Brookline estate of T. H. Perkins, Heath and Warren Streets, 1800–1865.

By 1818 Perkins was developing Brookline on a much more extensive scale. Returning on the *Galen* from England, he brought a large assortment of trees with him. The next year more trees were sent over from England, and three hundred tiles from Canton, which were to be used in a colorful wall in the gardens. By the 1820's, when Lafayette visited the estate, Perkins was gardening in a concentrated fashion. Some time in the middle of that decade he had a three hundred foot vinery built, where his gardener cultivated a great variety of grapes, as well as peaches and nectarines. As with everything he did, his gardening was done on a munificent scale. He became, as it were, a patron of husbandry long before he became a patron of the blind.

Experiments were made to advance the culture of choice fruits. Encouragement was given to ornamental gardening, with an eye to the art of landscaping. Through his worldwide commercial ties, he collected rare and valuable trees and plants which he freely distributed throughout the country to other interested horticulturists. He had set up his brother Sam in a Brookline estate midway between brother James at Pine Bank in Roxbury and his own place. Sam had taken to gardening and soon was competing earnestly with Perkins and his staff of gardeners, chief of whom for many years was William H. Cowan.

In the summer of 1831, the colonel had a second greenhouse built which, like the first, was nearly 300 feet long. Both were built against a brick wall facing south. The center section, which was the greenhouse proper, was about 60 feet long, 20 feet wide, and rising to 20 feet high. The wings were each about 120 feet long, fifteen feet wide and rising to 17 feet high. A three foot brick wall made the front wall of these houses and the glazed sashes rose above that. Each of the wings were divided into two sixty foot rooms, one for grapes and one for peaches.

Heating these greenhouses through the rugged New England winters was a problem at that stage of the art of indoor heating. Flues were commonly used, or complicated steam apparatus. Perkins experimented with a newly developed hot water heating method and described the results in a letter in the November 30, 1831 issue of the *New England Farmer:*

> With hot water not above 190 deg. of Fah. left by the gardener at 8 o'clock in the evening, heated by Anthracite Coal and with the dampers nearly closed, the state of the house if ordinarily tight, will be found in

the morning within a very few degrees of the state in which it was left twelve hours before.

For its time and period, this was considered amazing.

From 1829 on, for several years, the colonel regularly sent displays to the annual exhibits of the Massachusetts Horticultural Society. Visitors to the gardens, who came in increasing numbers in the thirties and forties, like Audubon and Nuttall, found much to delight them at almost any season. The prize specimens were the camellias. These shrubs, with their handsome white or rose-colored flowers, were all the rage, and there was much genteel competition among the local fanciers, who included nephew Cushing. By the end of the decade, Cowan developed a new camellia seedling which he named after himself, the *Cowanii*. "Very desirable," said the experts, but it is seldom grown today.

Brother Sam did much of his garden work without the aid of gardeners, and perhaps it was his personal attention which made his garden succeed a little better than his brother's. He was fond of his little triumphs over brother Tom, and would often ride over to display his latest success. One day he sauntered casually in with a basket crammed with beautiful grapes, peaches, and apricots. Presenting it to Tom, he said, "Brother Tom, I know you love fine fruit, and fearing you do not often get it, I have brought you something."

"Thank you, Brother Sam," replied the Colonel, manners equally impeccable. "I try to be contented with what I have, and certainly should be, if you were not always bursting in and giving me something that makes me envy you."[6]

Down the middle of the colonel's flower garden went a long trellised walk, hung thick with outdoor grapes each September. North of the first greenhouse wall was the long path one took to the billiard room. Perkins had been a devotee of this game since at least 1809 when he had a billiard room installed in his first Pearl Street residence. The billiard room at Brookline, however, was unique. It was a small building that looked like a New England version of a Grecian temple. Put a steeple on it and it could have been called a chapel. Sometimes the grandsons would be allowed to come along and watch the old gentlemen play, and perhaps even be permitted to fetch the joss stick and light their cigars for them.

Another curiosity of the billiard room was that it too was "entirely papered with pictures." Pictures, engravings, mezzotints—all were placed "as close together as stripes of wallpaper would be." Cushing noted in his diary for August 3, 1836 of driving over to the colonel's to take him "some Chinese paintings & French engravings for his billiard room." The billiard room at Temple Place and the spare room there were also decorated in the same manner. "It must have been," thought Caroline Gardiner, " a great fad with my grandfather to collect them."[7]

The Samuel Cabot family missed the opportunity to see Audubon, having gone to Europe that summer of 1832. Cabot had at last—according to William Sturgis—"mustered up sufficient resolution to undertake" the voyage. "His health is not good but he sometimes fancies himself more indisposed than others think him to be." Eliza, his little daughters, and his oldest son, Thomas Handasyd Cabot, eighteen years old and already a promising artist, went with him. Perkins had thought of going with them, but was "rather too much engaged with his new green house," wrote Cabot, "and a speculation in coal land in Pennsylvania." He had promised to join them in the fall.

Perhaps Cabot would bring home the items Perkins had asked Joshua Bates that spring to purchase for him. "Three pairs Spectacles set in Tortoise with double joint, for a person of a *nameless age,* presumed to be short of a Century—Memo: I want them for myself—I also want two eye glasses in Pearl to suspend from the Neck." Then he added a footnote to this, "to fold in the Center to use to read your prayers if you have not them by heart!"[8]

After a successful expedition to Maine, Audubon returned to Boston for the winter, planning a sketching trip to Labrador for the summer of 1833. During the spring, he was called to New York and Philadelphia, but he was back in Boston early in May. Invited to dine with the colonel and Fanny Kemble and her father Charles, Audubon regretfully had to decline. His chartered vessel was to sail that afternoon for the North. The dinner party went off as scheduled without Audubon, who might just as well have attended, for his boat ran aground in the harbor and was stuck until 9 o'clock that evening.

At twenty-four, Fanny Kemble was the darling of the English stage. Audubon had called on her that Saturday morning and thought her "not handsome, I guess, but appears quite amiable and without humbug." Her American tour was a spectacular success. New York, Philadelphia, Baltimore, Washington, had been applauding her for eight months. Finally, in April, she arrived in Boston, and opened to a full house at the Tremont Theater on the sixteenth. At first, Boston was more critical and she was not welcomed quite as rapturously as elsewhere. Martha Ward laid it to her being "apparently tired and not too amiable." Nor did it help that her father was now quite lame and the effect of some of the plays were "much lessened by his limping about." But soon Fanny won the hearts of the Bostonians and was setting the fashion. She popularized "riding on horseback" for sporty young women. "All our young ladies," Martha wrote her father, "are having their dresses, habits & hats arranged à la Kemble."[9]

Perkins had a regular box at the Tremont, the first on the left side of the stage. Ben Forbes described Perkins as being so tenderhearted that he would burst into tears at the mimic tragedies of the theater. Fanny gave him much to cry about. His young grandson, J. Elliot Cabot responded appropriately too, joining the crowds of young men who swarmed about her, hanging on every word and gesture of this famous belle.

Fanny stayed in the luxurious new Tremont House, where the thoughtfulness of the management provided each room with one permanent toothbrush for the use of all guests. From her windows she could see the crowds clamoring for tickets which were being auctioned off at highly inflated prices, such was the rage now "to see Fanny." Fanny was eager to see everything herself and toured Boston, Harvard, and the surrounding towns. She was even driven out to see that local marvel, the Granite Railway, although for some reason, she was not escorted by Perkins.

Perkins continued as president of the Granite Railway until 1834 when he turned over the chore to his son-in-law T. G. Cary, who held the position until 1854. But long before then, "real" railroads, using steam locomotives, had spread their tracks far and wide across the American landscape. Perkins had been drawn into some of the many schemes for the construction of railroads. He served on various committees, giving advice, and when the mill owners at Lowell proposed a railroad there to accomodate the mills, he became active in that project, since he was a proprietor of the holding organization, the renowned Locks and Canal Company.

This organization was the plum of the Merrimac development. When it appeared that the Lowell mills would be a profitable enterprise, the proprietors set up a single company into which they put the title to the land, water powers, and the patent rights to manufacture the textile machinery. Any further development of the industrial complex at Lowell was channeled through this holding group. One of the conditions Perkins had cannily set upon his entrance into the charmed circle of heavy profits at Lowell in 1828, was that he be allowed to become a proprietor of the Locks and Canal Company.* Thus he was present at a meeting at Patrick Tracy Jackson's house on January 27, 1830 when that group was considering building a railroad to Lowell if the state could be persuaded to finance it. He was put on a committee to survey the costs of such an enterprise.

The legislature approved three private railway companies, one to Vermont, one to Providence, Rhode Island, and one to the Hudson River, but the Boston & Lowell Railroad Co. was not approved. The textile group had blatantly demanded too much monopoly protection and so was turned down. By the spring session of the General Court, however, they had swung their political cohorts into line, and the monopoly powers they wanted were granted them. These hard-headed businessmen were not about to pioneer any project unless they were assured they would reap the full fruits of their pioneering.

Shortly after the Boston & Lowell line project was begun, the Boston & Worcester Railroad was organized. Perkins subscribed for shares of this project too. Unlike the B & L, the B & W began operations as soon as the track reached Newton on April 16, 1834. On July 4 of the following year, trackage to Worcester was completed and full service began. Almost at the same time, service opened on the Boston & Lowell line and the Boston & Providence Railroad. The Railroad Age had begun.

Several of the younger men connected with the Perkins firm had come of age with the railroads and launched their own ventures into an uncertain future by committing marriage. John Perkins Cushing was the first of these, and about time too, for he was nearly forty-six years old. On June 5, 1833, he married the beautiful and epileptic Mary Louisa Gardiner, some years younger than he, and by 1834 he had

* Perkins had gone heavily into the new mills. He took $50,000 worth of stock in the Appleton Mill and $30,000 in the Lowell Mill. He was elected titular president of the Appleton Company.

a young son, John Gardiner Cushing, and a new country estate which he called "Belmont" in a rural section of Watertown.*

Robert Bennet Forbes was married in January 1834 and his young brother John Murray was married in February. Although John was only twenty-one, his baldness which was almost complete, and his maturity, made people think him in his thirties. After a short courtship, he married Sarah Hathaway. Then after a shorter honeymoon of less than a month, he left his wife in Boston and sailed back to China to spend three years in pursuit of a fortune, not the beginning for a marriage that most young men or their wives would choose. Organizing boat races and teaching the local English how to play baseball must have seemed a poor substitute for the joys of matrimony. In December 1836, he concluded his active partnership, took his share of the profits, gave a fancy dress ball, and left for the United States and his waiting bride. A quick run of 120 days brought him to New York, and "the next forenoon found me snugly harbored at my aunt James Perkins's in Pearl Street, where my wife, perhaps by accident, met me after an absence of a little over three years."[10]

James Handasyd Perkins, Samuel's talented son, married a Sarah Elliott in December of that year. James wrote his intended that the colonel "highly approves my engaging myself." He wanted his fiancée to meet his uncle who was "a gentleman of the old school, and looks and talks and acts like the Duke of some European principality." With the condescension of the young, he added, "but you need not fear him, for his nature is kind and simple; his situation has taught him restraint." James thought that the "possession of considerable wealth, in his, as in all cases, has tended to narrow and harden his mind, but he is still princely in his feelings, and willing to aid any good cause with his influence, his purse, and, as far as they go, his talents."[11]

The old colonel had a first-hand experience of the younger generation in the spring and summer of 1835. Seventy years old, he set out on his eighth trip to Europe accompanied by his thirty-eight-year-old son and namesake, and the young colonel's eleven and a half year old son, Thomas Handasyd Perkins, III. The three generations embarked on March 1 from New York on the ship *Canada,* and twenty-one days later landed at Dartmouth, England.

* When this district later separated from Watertown and incorporated itself as a town, it took its name from Cushing's estate.

Perkins called on Audubon in London, who was planning to spend the summer in Scotland, return for the winter, and then sail to America the following spring. "Mrs. Audubon is with him and remains to have an eye to the work in Progress." A visit to a leading nursery impressed the colonel with a new push-button method of "raining" on the plants. "With the weight of the finger you throw a Shower of water on the plants from one end of the house to the other." A steam gun firing 1,050 rounds a minute, a microscope that magnified so much that Perkins was horrified at the "warfare" in a drop of water—all made the Colonel exclaim that one would need a busy year in London to see everything.[12]

They spent scarcely two weeks there, and then moved on to Paris. The city held as many wonders as London. There were quite a few Bostonians in town, and pleasant dinners at Colonel Welles's brought them all together for news of home. Pictures of Revolutionary events reminded him of his first visit to Paris in 1795, now forty years in the past. Perkins was amazed at the change in attitudes from his visit of just six years before. Then Napoleon was never mentioned, now he was everywhere honored. Four or five hours vanished as Perkins wandered about the Louvre alone looking at pictures. Then he was off to Lyons and Italy "with Mr. T. H. Junior and Tertius."

Perkins delighted to visit art galleries when abroad. He usually went alone on such excursions since his son and grandson did not share his interest in art. In Italy, Perkins was left in a "sort of amaze" by the pictures: "It was too much for my head." For his offspring, it was a bore. Typically, they preferred sleep to a tour of the Coliseum in Rome, and they would not walk an eighth of a mile to see a spectacular view in Florence.

Perkins knew most of the American artists of his day, enjoyed a friendship with many of them, and what is infinitely more important to the artist, often bought their paintings. Washington Allston he had known in Boston from 1808 to 1811, when Allston first returned from England. After his second and final return from England in 1818, the colonel saw him on numerous occasions, in connection with the design of the Bunker Hill monument, as an occasional dinner guest at the Perkins table, and in reference to the various exhibits sponsored by the Athenaeum. Perkins made up one of a number of wealthy men who contributed to the Allston Trust. This was an agreement in 1827 by ten men each to contribute a thousand dollars towards the purchase of Allston's "masterpiece-in-progress," the famous *Belshazzar's Feast.* Allston was to draw on this fund as he chose, and thus freed from financial worries, it was hoped he would speedily finish what was everywhere proclaimed his masterpiece. Although he had worked on this picture since the spring of 1817, it was still unfinished at his death in 1843.

Perkins patronized other American artists in various ways. From Alvan Fisher, he purchased at least six paintings, and probably more. He had bought paintings from Thomas Sully as early as 1818, family portraits from Gilbert Stuart, and between 1828 and 1831 he purchased six paintings by Robert Salmon.

A story had come down that when the sculptor Horatio Greenough was about twelve years old, Perkins saw him "copying in chalk a bust of John Adams," and took him to the Athenaeum and asked William Shaw to let the lad copy whatever he wanted to there. Whether this has any basis in fact, it is true that in May 1828, Perkins gave Greenough free passage on one of his ships to Europe, so that he could study and work there. Greenough was still there on Perkins's 1835 trip. While visiting Florence, Perkins spent much of his time at Greenough's studio where he admired the head of Sears that Greenough was sculpting. He studied Greenough's figure of Washington in a toga, commenting that "there is nothing to alarm the most fastidious, in those parts of the figure left bare." Greenough dined with Perkins, his son, and grandson, and escorted them about the city. Through his influence, Perkins was allowed to see corridors in the Pitti Palace not open to the general tourist. "Even with my little knowledge of paintings, I could visit those I have seen every day for a month and think the time too short."[13]

Characteristically, Perkins took an active role in the effort to establish an art gallery in Boston. As early as 1823, the proprietors of the Athenaeum voted to add an exhibition room to their newly acquired property. Perkins subscribed $300 to the project and was immediately added to the building committee. Three years later he was made chairman of the committee, and the project vastly expanded from merely adding on a room to building a large addition on the ground of the Athenaeum that would become an Academy of Fine Arts. Perkins offered to contribute $8,000 to the project if a like sum were subscribed outside his family circle. James Perkins, Jr., gave an additional $8,000 similarly conditioned, and the trustees quickly got busy and raised an additional $16,000.

The next May, the opening show in the new gallery, organized by the enthusiastic Perkins as chairman of the fine arts committee, was a huge success. They had obtained the loan of 317 paintings and miniatures and sold 2,000 season tickets of admission at 50 cents each, plus many single admissions. The practice was to buy pictures for the permanent collection out of the "gate" receipts. The report of Chairman Perkins for the 1829 exhibit is typical: receipts were $3,900 and expenses, which included the purchase of two pictures, only $1,600. The balance of $2,300 went to the treasurer, but the purchase of two additional pictures was recommended, a Waldo and an Allston. A list of other paintings that had been purchased through the year was included. Boston's present prestigious Museum of Fine Arts is an outgrowth of the old Athenaeum Gallery.

During this decade of the thirties, Perkins's business instincts continued to function strongly. Although his old firms were being closed in the first half of the decade, he still had some adventures going overseas from time to time. And the colonel continued to give his sons-in-law the benefit of his advice in their new commission business. Cabot and Cary, acting for Perkins & Co. and joined by the Forbes brothers, Robert Bennet and John Murray, had purchased Samuel Russell's interest in Russell & Co. in Canton for $25,000. Under another name then, the Perkins business in Canton was continuing. Half of the purchase was for Perkins & Co., and half for the Forbes brothers. This purchase was to be made in view of a co-partnership in Boston to begin on January 1, 1835.

Innumerable real estate transactions required his attention. One was rather significant. During the same period when he was building his Temple Place mansion and giving his Pearl Street house to the blind, he helped organize the Winnisimmet Company. This was incorporated on March 27, 1833 and included, besides Perkins, Francis B. Fay, Washington P. Gragg, and son-in-law Gardiner. The purpose of the new company was to develop the area which is now the city of Chelsea.

One of the group's principal acquisitions was the old Ferry Farm, so-called because the Boston ferry docked there. This property they developed as a watering place. The Watts-William homestead was rebuilt into a spacious, two-story hotel, with a wide balcony running the entire length of the first floor. It sat near the summit of a gentle hill with a pleasing view of the creek and river on either side, East Boston across the way, and Boston and Charlestown in the near distance. The place boasted a handsome garden, a well said to give the coolest of waters, and one further attraction which perhaps showed the colonel's hand. This was a circular railroad for children. About thirty feet in diameter, the cars were drawn by flying horses (with the actual motive power coming from a hand crank.) It was claimed that after the Granite Railway, this was the first in the country, though such claims are really rather special.

Yet with all this, Bostonians somehow could not visualize Chelsea as a "watering place." By 1850, not only the house but also the hill was gone and the land had been cut up into house lots, eventually to be jammed with solid blocks of tenements. The company was more successful in developing their other real estate properties in Chelsea. Alonzo Lewis drew up the street plans, and parcels were steadily sold off bringing a fair profit to the proprietors of the company. But this was not really the colonel's cup of tea, and his active direction of the company, not at all clear in any case, seems to have dissipated in a few years. Cary, and later his other son-in-law, William Gardiner stepped in to represent the colonel's interests, which was fitting since Chelsea was Cary's birthplace.

Because of his connection with the Winnisimmet Company, Perkins and his associates regretfully decided not to take part in the group developing Noddle's Island, renamed East Boston, during this same period. The East Boston group even suggested a merger with the Winnisimmet Company, but this was declined and each went its own independent way. Yet it would seem as if Perkins later developed some tie with this group, for when the Maverick House was opened on May 27, 1835 in the center of East Boston, Perkins, who was in Europe, was remembered in the toasting. General Sumner, one of the developers, responded by saying that he would give the colonel the ancient privilege of an ancestor, John Perkins, that of "catching fowle in nets on Noddle's Island." Never mind that the general's genealogy was awry, and that *this* Perkins wasn't related to *that* Perkins as far as is known. Nobody anyway expected to see the old colonel actually casting nets in East Boston.[14]

Perkins was more apt to be off traveling. In the summer of 1837 with his twenty-two-year-old grandson Samuel Cabot, he left for a lengthy trip that included a June visit to several of the mineral springs in Virginia. His visit to the various springs prompted him to pay for the reprinting of a small forty-page pamphlet by Dr. Henry Huntt extolling the benefits of the waters of the Red Sulfur Springs. Perkins went so far as to write a preface for the pamphlet. Since New England was subject to more complaints of the lungs than other places, and the waters of the Red Sulfur were held to be beneficial for this, he thought it valuable to make the information available to "the medical gentlemen of my native state; as well as to present a copy to each of the clergy."[15]

No indication is given of why Perkins visited these springs in 1837. Did some particular complaint draw him there? If there was one, it was no hindrance to the rugged tour he and Dr. Cabot went on after they left the springs. Traveling through the Midwest in that period was scarcely a picnic for a man of seventy-three. Sailboat, steamboat, and stage were the conveyances. In one place they bribed men to use a stage instead of an open wagon since Perkins was not feeling well. Perkins was greatly impressed by the rich farmlands he saw and the abundant harvests. The newness of it all was astonishing. A twenty-four-year-old man in Chicago was one of the first settlers. The large size of Detroit surprised him. At Mackinaw Island, they saw Indians meeting in council, and Perkins talked with Louis Schoolcraft.

During the trip Perkins and Samuel Cabot visited eighteen of the twenty-six states, all the great lakes except Superior, travelled 5,000 miles without accident, and arrived home "highly gratified." They had been gone 110 days, of which 60 had been spent in Virginia, so they certainly did not dawdle.

If Perkins had been tempted to invest in a hotel in Virginia at one of the springs, he resisted the urge. He had his hands well filled with hotels as it was. Besides the house in Chelsea, the Railway Hotel, Tremont House, and perhaps a possible connection with the Maverick House, the one closest to his heart was still the Nahant Hotel. After four seasons of operation that hotel had been sold to Dr. Edward Robbins. The first summer under Robbins's direction was successful, with more than six hundred people crowding the peninsular to celebrate the national holiday on July 4, 1827. The steamboat *Housatonick* was used to transport people back and forth quickly from Boston. Carrying up to two hundred people at a time, it made the hotel accessible and inexpensive to reach.

Robbins, who was also a woolen manufacturer, was badly hurt in the depression of 1829. In June of that year, Perkins paid him $5,000 for a half interest in the hotel, subject to the mortgage that was still unpaid. Two months later he picked up the other half from the trustees to whom the doctor had assigned the property for the benefit of his creditors. Three years later the colonel leased the hotel to R. W. Holman who was a first class hotelier, the best that the colonel could find. Soon the hotel was enlarged by building on an east wing, in which the new dining room was located.

Robbins, who had recovered from his financial losses, and was in one of the up periods of his many ups and downs, was brought back into association with Perkins in running the hotel, perhaps not to its benefit. When Thomas Grattan arrived in Boston in 1839 to take over as the new British consul, he went out to Nahant with his family at the end of July. Looking down his Irish Protestant nose at the place, he was not impressed by anything he saw. The hotel struck him as large and uncomfortable, nothing more than "a huge pigeon-house" to stow away as many lodgers as possible. He hated dining publicly, summoned by an "infernal gong" to the table at ridiculous hours. Then the meals were eaten too fast, it was a mere "matter of business."

One of the popular sports at Nahant, he discovered, was looking for the sea serpent. "For twenty successive years, numbers of persons of respectability and good sense, credible witnesses as to any fact made various depositions as to the time, place, and circumstance of their seeing" this monster of the deep. In fact, almost on schedule, one Sunday afternoon in the middle of August, he himself with hundreds of others had a distant view of "this celebrated nondescript." Although he had been inclined to scoff before, he was now convinced that "the thing was a reality." When his wife got a closeup view of it the next day and estimated it at ninety feet in length, his last doubts vanished. It is a brave husband who doubts his wife's sea serpents.

The most surprising thing about the Nahant Hotel for Grattan was the desolation that struck the place when the easterly storms came at the end of August. In a twinkling, everyone fled the hotel back to the city, and the place closed up. Grattan was "driven"—as he put it—back to unwholesome lodgings in the city. He remonstrated with the "keeper" of the hotel about closing up while a few people wanted to remain.

"I should like very well to keep the house open a month longer," said the hotelkeeper, "but the Colonel and the Doctor positively say it must close."

"Who are they? What have they to do with it?" asked Grattan.

"Why, Sir, don't you know that Dr. R[obbins] and Colonel P[erkins] own the hotel, and that I only work it under their directions?"

A little inquiry revealed to Grattan that "the Colonel and the Doctor" actually interferred so much in the running of the hotel "as to fix the tariff for the prices of the most minute articles furnished at the public table, and reduced every purchase to so mean a minimum, as to afford a perfect excuse to their *locum tenens* for the bad living to which he proverbially confined his guests." Today this would be called "cost control."

Grattan's verdict was that the partners who had undertaken this speculation, "having no taste for the liberal management" of such an establishment, which he thought would have been valuable if made attractive, instead carried it on with the "narrowest possible scale of expense" and thus doomed it to failure. After trying it a few more summers, he gave it up and took a cottage "in the village."[16]

Perhaps this was an insular British view of things. Phillip Hone, a successful commission merchant who had served as mayor of New York, was much more impressed by the colonel's personal taste and munificence. On a visit to Boston, November 16, 1838, he called with Daniel Webster at the colonel's "exceedingly elegant edifice," only to find that "worthy old Don" laid up with the gout. Perkins sent him a note asking him to call again, so the next day, it being a fine cold day, he decided to "see the Boston lions, and make some visits, among the rest to Col. Perkins, who lives *en prince,* and has a fine collection of pictures to which he made many valuable additions during his last visit to Europe."[17]

More than likely Perkins showed Hone the chair that Pierce sat in a month later. Invited to dine with the colonel, Pierce saw the chair "last used by Napoleon Bonparte on the island of St. Helena." Napoleon had taken it with him into exile from France. "It was a plain Roundabout, stuffed, so as to be easy. The probability however is that it was the seat to its occupant of many sad reflections, of many bitter regrets, and of many uncomfortable anticipations." Perkins had secured it "by means of his nephew," Stephen Perkins Higginson. That individual, coming home from Canton in disgrace because of gambling debts, had stopped off at St. Helena when there happened to be an auction of Bonaparte's effects. He purchased the chair and gave it to his uncle, and perhaps escaped some of the censure rightfully due him.[18]

So the grandson of a hatter born in a remote outpost of the British empire in 1764 lived to own the chair of a Corsican lad born five years later, who became the emperor of all the French. It must have given Perkins more than a sense of history whenever he sat in the emperor's seat. Among his reflections may have been one that the merchant business was certainly less risky and more rewarding than the king business.

When I came to Beacon Street that fine elm was a sapling. I have seen it grow, and it has seen me decline. It will be beautiful and stretch its branches over thousands long after I am forgotten.

Harrison Grey Otis

# 33

# A Flicker in the Dying Flame

"We had a fire the other night," wrote a Cabot granddaughter of the colonel's in January 1841, "Quite near us, down among the wooden buildings at the end of the court." If there had been any wind, the fine residences on Temple Place would have been in danger, but fortunately the night was calm. "They had a fine view from Grandfather's, and his only regret was that there was no wind!" This sense of daring the elements, of tempting fate, prompted the seventy-six-year-old colonel to join Bennet Forbes on a trip to Europe the next month. "You will be somewhat astonished to hear of your grandfather in London," Samuel Cabot wrote his son Elliot, who was studying in Heidelberg, Germany. It was a "sudden movement," and would "get rid of a couple of unpleasant months here."[1]

The colonel and his nephew embarked in the Cunard steamer *Columbia,* and had a pleasant trip across. "We talk French together nearly all the time," Forbes wrote to Tom Cary, "intending to make ourselves familiar with the language before we go to Paris, Petersburgh, Moscow, etc.—perhaps we shall visit China—!!!" They were living "in clover," he wrote his wife, eating as sumptuously as if dining at the Tremont House. "Wines and soda water included in the Bill!" What they missed most was a hot bath, "the coal smoke and particles make us all rather sooty."

The ship smoked briskly along, making never less than two hundred miles each day. Forbes found his spyglass useful in deciphering the names of passing ships. The colonel was "remarkably frisky and pleasant," perhaps made talkative by the sea air. "He has told me what disposition he has made of his property," always an interesting bit of information when confided by a rich man. Alas, however, Forbes wrote his wife, "he did not tell me that he had left you any thing!"

At the supper table one night, they were all required to sing a song. Forbes begged off by telling a story instead. The colonel was more canny. When it came his turn to sing, he struck up "God Save the Queen" and the whole group joined in to waft Victoria's praises over the Atlantic waves and drown out the colonel's vocal efforts.

They reached Victoria's realm Tuesday night, March 16, landing the next morning. On their ride to London, Perkins told "many a good story." One was of his first visit to Shakespeare's birthplace some twenty years before. On that occasion he had carried an album with him for people to put their names in, which he said had not been done there before. His was the first name signed, he told Forbes, and since then "dozen of Books have been filled."[2]

In London they lodged in Hanover Square, met local lions like Sir Charles Forbes and the Rothschilds, and of course the Barings and the Bateses. Shortly they headed for Holland and Paris. Forbes claimed that in the latter place he probably "went over more ground and saw less than any American of the day." They soon came back to England and Liverpool. Perkins noted in his diary a visit to Earl Derby's to inspect his collection of birds and quadrupeds. The air of commerce in Liverpool stirred the dormant merchant in his blood, and he noted with interest the improvements made to the docks.[3]

They sailed for home on April 27. An honor awaited Perkins. In Boston, a magnificent new merchant's exchange had been planned. On July 23, Perkins was invited by the directors of the project to lay the cornerstone, because he had "long and honorably sustained the position of *head* of the mercantile community of Boston." Saturday, August 2, was the day set for the event. Items had been carefully gathered for the leaden box to be put in the cornerstone. A silver plate with an inscription appropriate to the occasion, samples of current American coins, plus an historic "Pine Tree shilling" dated 1652, newspapers of the day, and such mementos made up its contents. Perkins wrote out his speech and then "from inadvertance" left it behind him in Brookline, so, as he told the committee a few days later, he had to give a shorter speech than he had planned. Being, as he began his talk, "almost an Octogenaire," he reminisced about State Street as it was "60 years since." The new Exchange was being built almost opposite where his grandfather Peck and he had lived seventy years before. His thoughts went back to the days when the street was his playground, and he and other children had spun tops and played marbles on the lower floor of the Old State House. The building then, he remarked, was "more frequented by little urchins than their seniors."

Rambling on about the people and places of those far-off days, he recalled vividly the Royal Exchange Tavern, "having been taken there, when a child, to see the Corpse of one of the persons killed at the Massacre in 1770." To the young men in his audience, this must have made him seem as old as the pyramids. Talking about the wharfs and merchants of former years, the public buildings, the one hospital (and that just for smallpox), the poor transportation, the inefficient fire protection, the slow ships, he was in a sense reliving his own life and accomplishments. With the manuscript reposing serenely in Brookline, he finally ran out of ramble, and concluded with a proper Bostonian reminder to the deity which had kindly watched over the city in time of adversity and prosperity, to continue "to smile upon us."[4]

The year 1841 drew to a close on a sad note, with the funeral of his brother's widow, Mrs. James Perkins, on November 24, nineteen years after she had buried her husband. What else is so surely on the horizon of an "octogenaire" but a succession of such conclusions? If it is not the death of relatives it is the death of friends. In the fall of the next year, his Boston minister for some three decades, the celebrated Unitarian divine, William Ellery Channing, died. His body was brought back to Boston in a plain pine box stained mahogany. The funeral was held in his Federal Street Church from whose pulpit he had so often eloquently held forth. His associate, Dr. Gannet, was the one to wax eloquent on this occasion. He preached for 175 minutes, said Dr. Pierce, who timed everybody.

The church quickly appointed a committee to memorialize their late pastor and Perkins was on it. They decided on a monument to be placed on his grave at Mount Auburn Cemetery in Cambridge, where the "best" people were now being buried. Washington Allston was asked to design it. George Ticknor prepared the inscription, and Perkins and 111 other members of the congregation gave the $1,780 it cost to have Alpheus Cary cut the design in fine Italian marble. Fortunately, Allston worked faster on this assignment than on *Belshazzar's Feast,* for by the next July Perkins was head of a committee to erect a monument to the recently deceased artist.

For the octogenaire, 1842 had mostly been a good year. He and Cabot smoked their cigars as they played their afternoon game of billiards. Even Mrs. Perkins was more venturesome than usual. One of Elliot's cousins wrote him that "Grandmother has been passing a fortnight with Aunt Nancy—an almost unparalleled instance of her remaining content so long at once, on Nahant." The colonel had brought Dr. Pierce down to Nahant and Mary Cary thought it seemed quite like old times. They tried to get him a tautog, but could not. "We always used to have one for him if possible."[5]

Just before Thanksgiving, however, Perkins fell down on his front steps and hurt his leg. He spent the holiday in bed, his family gathered below for the customary feasting. "Uncle George" was having one of his periodic fits and he too stayed upstairs with "Aunt Sally" to watch over him. After dinner the feasters all went over to the Cary's "so as not to disturb Grandfather."[6]

One by one the lights were going down. Houqua died in September 1843 and five months later they heard of it in America. He had been almost a partner to the men in Perkins & Co. Forbes could truly say that during the many years of business between the two principals, when very large transactions were constantly being made, no writing passed between the two firms, each entering their own figures on their own books, and relying on their mutual trust and good faith to harmonize their accounts.

There was the satisfaction, however, of seeing certain things concluded. On Friday, June 16, 1843, President John Tyler with his entire cabinet and assorted suite arrived in Boston to take part in the ceremonies dedicating the completed monument on Bunker Hill. The third try at finishing this monument had succeeded, although Solomon Willard, his feelings appropriately wounded, was not the man in charge this last time. Tyler, however, was not particularly popular with the conservative Bostonians, and the warmth of the welcome to Lafayette was missing on this occasion. "The honors," noted Pierce, "were conferred rather on the office than on the man who wears it." Still the crowd, the beautiful day, the "universal joyousness" made George Bancroft, the historian, judge it "one of the most sublime and most agreeable spectacles I have ever witnessed."[7]

Webster, in at the beginning, was in at the finish too. He spoke for nearly two hours and was said to have been heard clearly by at least 24,000 people. Bancroft thought he was "heavy" but that the audience "befriended" him. Webster paid tribute to the dignitaries present and to the promoters of the project, living and dead, but the cheers of the crowd were most enthusiastic for the thirteen survivors of the great battle who were present some sixty-eight years later for the completion of the monument to that event.

Two years later, with Bennet Forbes and his sister Emma, Perkins again took off for England on the *Massachusetts,* in which Forbes was a part owner. It was the first American-owned auxiliary steam vessel to cross the Atlantic. This was the colonel's tenth and last trip to Europe, and was almost like a reflexive action—as if he had always to be on the move, no matter the direction. They left New York on September 15, 1845, arrived in Liverpool on October 3, and on the nineteenth of the same month—after only sixteen days in England—he took a Cunard steamer home. He had looked around London, visited Bates at his estate, named "Shane," looked at the moon through Gambadella's telescope, and was restless and ready to depart.

During these later years, Saratoga was his usual refuge from the heat and boredom of a Boston summer,* Perkins went more for the company than for the waters. The fashionable people from the twenty-nine states of the Union came to this "plain country village" to meet their counterparts, to talk and gossip and flirt, to pursue the illusion of well being, to gamble on horses and cards, and either to pursue money or to show

* In the summer of 1846, while at Saratoga, he began an autobiographical notebook titled "To My Children." After rambling on about his early days for some sixty pages of the small notebook, he suddenly breaks off in midsentence, and never finished the reminiscences. We learn nothing after his 1789 trip to Canton, and there are a number of inaccuracies.

they did not need to pursue it. In a sense, it was nineteenth-century America's Las Vegas.

The colonel enjoyed it all immensely, and if he flirted a bit, why at his age it was certainly safe. One of the Cary girls writing to her mother remarked that "every now and then I meet some pretty woman who wants to know how my 'dear grandfather' is, and seems to have a very tender affection for him." This remark was prompted by meeting "a bright, talkative little woman" who had known the colonel at Saratoga and "eaten grapes at his cottage." "He's been," clucked his granddaughter, "a terrible flirt."[8]

His wife never went to Saratoga as far as is known. The furthest trip ever recorded for her was a visit to New York when two of her daughters were living there after their marriages. The colonel's usual stay at Saratoga was about three weeks. The diversions included watching trotting matches between noted horses, the balloon ascension in 1848, and conversation. Richard Henry Dana, Jr., describes "a very pleasant circle, of Col. Perkins, the Forbes, Slidells, etc." after breakfast one July morning. "Col. Perkins gives interesting anecdotes of the early trade to North West Coast, Sandwich Islands, & China, from '83 to 1800."[9]

Many a friend and relative, these latter years, were taking up "a different residence." Elegant and eloquent Harrison Gray Otis died in 1848, leaving a smaller fortune than expected, and distributing it by an "extraordinary & unjust will," that caused much dissension. His wife, it was whispered, was left only a pair of silver wine coolers, which so enraged her that she made a present of them to the keeper of the hotel into which she had moved. Otis's estate, which had been thought to be more than a million, was about $600,000. Eliza Cabot recalled that once at a dinner party at the colonel's, they had been discussing—rich men's conversation!—how many men in Boston were worth a hundred thousand dollars. Otis asserted he did not have so much. The colonel promptly offered him more than a hundred thousand dollars for all his property. Cornered, Otis agreed. But the next day he came round and told the colonel that his wife would not agree to it. She might just as well have, since so little of it went to her.

Two years later, on January 16, 1850, the young colonel succumbed to cancer. He was just three months and eight days past his fifty-third birthday. His latter years had been spent, no longer pursuing women, but health. Asked, a few days before his death, if he was worried where he was going, he replied philosophically that he was about as good as Gus Thorndike, Jim Otis, or Charlie Hammond, and almost as good as Frank Codman. "I shall go where they go, and that is where I wish to be." With a dry eye, the colonel attended the service. But following his son's body into the vault afterwards, he wept his loss in private.[10]

All was change and decay. On the last day of September, of that year, at two o'clock in the afternoon, a fire broke out in Perkins's Brookline mansion. There was only one fire engine in Brookline, which was kept in the village, about two miles distant from the colonel's residence. By the time they arrived, the fire had made considerable headway burning the kitchen area and some of the roof before it was put out. There was much damage from water inside the house, but the building had been saved. Later, Perkins sent the fire company "a substantial present" for their good work.

By this time, almost all of the colonel's brothers and sisters were gone. James and his wife, Sam and his, both the girls who had married the Sturgis brothers and their husbands, and, for a long time, the senior Cushings. Mary Abbott's husband, the preceptor of Exeter, had died, as well as Margaret Forbes's husband. Those two sisters, the colonel and his wife, were all that remained of that generation.

After her son's death, however, the colonel's lady became mentally disturbed. By the summer of 1851, it was felt best to send her to McLean Hospital in Charlestown where son George resided whenever his attacks were too severe to be dealt with at home. Cushing more than once sent his barouche over to McLean and, with a matron accompanying her, Mrs. Perkins was permitted to spend the day at Cushing's estate. But she was not to recover. By February 25, 1852, she was dead at the age of eighty-five.

The Cabots were traveling in Italy when the letters, delayed in transit, arrived giving Eliza the news of her mother's death. It was most "unexpected" wrote Cabot to his son, and "most afflicting to your Mother, on your Grandfather's account. She suffers much from the idea that she had not been there to do what she could towards sustaining and consoling him in this great trial." Judging, however, from the letters, the colonel "has borne it with a noble Fortitude—like himself." Cabot suggested that the children spend as much time as possible in Brookline with Perkins "and supply in a measure at least your mother's place." She, at first, had wanted to rush home immediately, but realized the impracticality of this. Cabot added a word for his son the doctor: "It must have been a satisfaction to Sam to have your grandmother's last expression one of pleasure for good offices to her."[11]

The curtain was slowly coming down. Just five years before, it had gone up in the same room in Temple Place where Mrs. Perkins' funeral was held. Those who mourned, had then been in jovial spirits, anticipating an evening's merriment. For the "Temple Place Players" were about to perform those three sure-fire hits: "Good Night's Rest," "Damon and Pythias," and "Bombastes Furioso."

A few weeks before the performance, some of the colonel's grandchildren and their friends had taken the plunge of home theatricals in the back parlor of Sam Cabot. These amateurs had been hailed by an audience of their family and friends "with shouts of applause," and gales of laughter. "Grandfather," wrote Tom Cary Jr. in a jocular journal he kept of that theatrical enterprise, "was so much pleased—he said we played too well for gentlemen and ladies—that he expressed a wish that we would perform at his house." A Command Performance!

The young thespians were delighted. Elliot Cabot and Tom Cary decided here was the chance to put on a more elaborate production by tapping grandfather's bankroll. "If he wished for music he must pay the piper." Tom persuaded his mother to "attack" the unwitting theatrical "angel." She set the figure too low and got only $50. However, when Tom made an appropriate thanks for the sum, he cleverly induced his grandfather to double the amount.

First they needed a proscenium stage. They built this themselves so that it would stand alone; then they equipped it with a curtain. Next they needed scenery, which they also constructed, sizing and stretching the canvas, with Elliot and Ed Cabot painting the flats, since they were the most capable in that line. Finally, after a great deal of such busy, pleasant trouble, they brought the whole paraphenalia to Temple Place and set the structure up in the Colonel's front parlor where it reached nearly to the ceiling.

Thursday, Feb. 11, 1847, they made their first appearance in their new "theater." All went off well and the hit of the evening was the third play, "Bombastes Furioso."

Encouraged by the audience's reception, they quickly began work on a new production, this time "The Waterman" with Lizzie Cary, the future founder of Radcliffe College, and Mary Gardiner making their stage debuts.

After several other productions came the sad business of tearing down the make-believe world. Tom, assisted by Charley Gardiner and Gus Perkins, rolled up the scenery piece by piece. As the settings came down, their conversation began to peter out. "When the frame was left bare and the light of heaven again shone in, where the footlights and side burners had lately held their sway, we as with one accord, silently and in sorrow pulled down the frame" and stored it away. "The scenes, skies, hangings, wings, baize floor cloth, window, and spare rollers, together with all the weights for wings and loose articles," went into the upper story of the mansion near the billiard room. "The throne, proscenium, and heavy carpet and foot lights were put in the stable."

Going back into the empty parlor for some things, Cary hardly recognized the room. "I felt as in a dream." Even he and Frank seemed changed, for Frank had shaved off his moustache and beard. There were no more rehearsals to look forward to. The room was back to normal, "no scenes, no green benches, and no old candle ends lying on the floor." He stared out the window "and felt as if the world had been to the barber's and had had its hair cut too short, and I wondered if I should ever get used to it."[12]

Tis sweet to know that stocks will stand
When we with Daisies lie—
That Commerce will continue—
And Trades as briskly fly—
It makes the parting tranquil
And keeps the soul serene—
That gentlemen so sprightly
Conduct the pleasing scene.

Emily Dickinson

# 34

# Unveil Thy Bosom, Faithful Tomb

Some summers before he died, into the Colonel's cottage at Saratoga bounded young William Boott. He had just received news of the death of a life-long friend of the Colonel's and hastened to tell him of it. The Colonel listened to the report, said nothing for a moment, then, glancing up at Boott, commented, "William, do you know, it makes my mouth water."

By the fall of 1853, Perkins himself was perceptibly failing. "Grandpa is still suffering with his eyes," wrote Elizabeth Cary Agassiz to her mother. "I think the great trial of blindness is truly commencing upon him. I am very glad Aunt Eliza is there. She must be a comfort and pleasure to him."

Comfort and pleasure were needed, for that winter was face-freezing, nose-nipping, bone-biting cold, even for Boston. A late December storm caught the new steamer *San Francisco* outward bound from Boston for that golden land of sunshine with more than a thousand troops and their families aboard her. Dismasted in a gale, its engines soon broke down, and the vessel drifted helplessly toward Bermuda in the heavy seas. A massive wave on the evening of the twenty-fifth took away much of the superstructure and washed overboard large numbers of the passengers.

The storm reached Boston on Wednesday night the twenty-eighth. It whipped through town all the next day, subsiding by Friday. A few trains worked their way through the drifts by Saturday and reached the city.

The new year itself began with snow, lasting until Sunday noon. Sometime over this weekend of storm and drift robbers with false keys entered the Mercantile Library. They rifled a tin box holding contributions for the building of the Washington Monument.* Penitently they left a note of their deep regret at robbing this sacred repository, but that as no other money was accessible they felt compelled to resort to such a dastardly deed.

By Monday, January 2, Boston was covered by eighteen inches of snow. Yet proper Bostonians pushed on. The annual meeting of the Boston Athenaeum was held that day despite the drifts. A tall, spare gentleman of elderly years, Thomas G. Cary, was elected president of the private library, a position once held by his father-in-law, the colonel. Mr. William H. Gardiner reported for the committee that was raising $120,000 for the library that they were $9,000 over their goal.

By Tuesday, the life of the city was nearing normal. Warm weather succeeded the storm on Wednesday, the fourth of January—"true spring weather," wrote Ellen Dwight. A fine group of the Independent Corps of Cadets, ninety men in the ranks, paraded as escort to the civil authorities. Friday, things were bad all over. There was trouble in Santa Domingo. The war in Turkey, not yet called "The Crimean War," was discussed forwards and backwards. The city election was on Monday, the ninth, a frosty nippy day.

Most of that election Monday the colonel spent settling his bills and papers in his usual manner. That afternoon he had an operation for a slight surgical obstruction on his eye which was performed by his

* In 1848, the colonel learned that the building of the Washington Monument in the nation's capital was being delayed through lack of funds. He suggested putting boxes in various stores and public places throughout Boston and the Commonwealth, where patriotic citizens could contribute coins to the cause. He even wrote the little message attached to these boxes encouraging donations. Sparked by this idea, the lagging cause revived and went on to success.

grandson, Dr. Samuel Cabot, his fellow traveler to St. Louis and the Midwest nearly two decades before. Perkins went to bed after the operation, with his grandson's caution that he not get up the next morning, but remain completely quiet.

The colonel passed a good night. He refused to have an attendant stay in the bedroom with him, and, feeling in good spirits when he awoke Tuesday, he determined to rise despite his doctor's instructions to the contrary. "His *indomitable* will," commented Ellen Dwight, "made him constantly attempt to do what was quite impossible for him and he has had three or four bad falls lately because he *would* try to get about alone." Up he got and partly dressed, felt faint, and lay down on his sofa. The exertion had been too much for him. Hour by hour his condition grew worse. The family summoned the doctors.[1]

Tuesday night brought a thick fog. Inspecting the trees in Concord on Wednesday morning, Henry Thoreau found them hoary white "just as the frost forms on a man's beard or about a horse's mouth." Going about, he saw where a squirrel, "probably a red one had apparently brought up to the mouth of his hole quite a quantity of walnuts and eaten them." This fog had given even "the humblest weed" a coating of "purest white and richest form."[2]

And during that night when the frost was coating weeds, shortly after midnight, without pain or distress, twenty-seven days past his eighty-ninth birthday, the colonel died. "This throws another large family into black," wrote Ellen Dwight, shortly to join that family by marrying into the Cabot branch of it.[3]

The colonel's children had beget with Cabot, Dumeresque, Gardiner, and the brothers Cary. The children resulting had beget with Lee and Hemenway, Hunt and Chadwick, Curtis and Parkman, Felton and Agassiz, Dwight and Pell, Davis and Kuhn, Mifflin and de Lingneur. The colonel's brothers and sisters had established links with almost every prominent Bostonian family. The family tree bore such sturdy branches as Sturgis, Cushing, Paine, Elliot, Higginson, and Forbes. The line stretched out from Abbott to Wheelwright, taking in impartially Callahans and Channings, Searles and Sullivans on the way.

All the papers dutifully carried respectful obituaries. Homage was paid to his many benefactions ("munificent" was the word most favored). All named the Perkins Institution for the Blind. Then they diverged, some emphasizing his gifts to the Mercantile Library Association, others speaking of the Boston Athenaeum, the Bunker Hill Monument, or the recent impetus he had given to the drive to finish the Washington Monument. Bursting into poetry, the *Transcript* exclaimed:

> For his bounty
> There is no winter in't; an autumn 'tis
> That grows the more by reaping.

Privately, like Ellen Dwight, they speculated on who got what. "I have heard nothing as yet," she wrote to a friend, "of the disposition of the property except that young Tom Perkins is left residuary legatee, which I am rather glad of. The will is said to be 60 pages long so that I hope each of the grandchildren are provided for, some of them seem to need so much."

Friday, January 13, was the day before the funeral. The *Transcript* wondered editorially who would take the place of Faneuil, McLean, Perkins, Parkman, Lowell, Elliot, Shaw, Lawrence, Lyman, and Appleton, in generosity to Boston? At one o'clock, some of those named or their descendants and other prominent Boston merchants met at the Merchant's Exchange "to take proper measures respecting the death of Hon. Thomas H. Perkins."

The funeral was Saturday. Both branches of the Massachusetts legislature adjourned early to give members an opportunity to attend the funeral. It was scheduled for noon at the Federal Street Church where the colonel had long worshipped. Promptly at noon the city bells began to toll, continuing till one in honor of the deceased. Stores and warehouses generally were closed for the service. The marine telegraph and the harbor shipping displayed their flags at half mast in honor of the merchant prince.

The "train of mourners" left the colonel's brick house in Temple Place at 11:30 and proceeded churchward. Reaching the church, the coffin was borne up the broad aisle, the organ pealing out a solemn dirge and the congregation standing until, as one paper phrased it, "the honorable load" was put down in front of the pulpit. For the simple service, the choir had been augmented by pupils from the school for the blind, and their youthful voices rang out in Watts's hymn:

> Unveil thy bosom, faithful tomb!
> Take this new treasure to thy trust,
> And give these sacred relics room,
> To seek a slumber in thy dust.

At the end of the service, the attendants were invited to view the face of the departed. This was a novelty, for embalming was still new and expensive. The colonel, having enjoyed the best in life, was launched out on eternity by his family with the best money could buy. A great number of people had gone to the house that morning to see this new thing. Now nearly all present "availed themselves of the invitation." Up the aisle went Governor Washburn and his lieutenant-governor; Otis P. Lord, Abbott Lawrence, Robert C. Winthrop, and the members of the Great and General Court. Merchants galore, officers of the Athenaeum, Dr. Howe of the Perkins Institute for the Blind—"a most striking collection of men—the intellectual and the wealthy of the city—convened in the Temple of God to perform the last sad office to departed worth." And what was his worth? In dollars and cents—how much? And who would get it? There were many guesses among the mourners.[4]

A week later the question was answered: one million, six hundred thousand dollars was what the colonel was "worth." His six surviving children were each to get $100,000. To the heirs of a deceased son went another $100,000. That left $900,000. Mary Abbott and Margaret Forbes, the only sisters then living, each got an annuity of $600 a year. The daughters divided the furniture, paintings, statuary, engravings, plate, and other chattels "as they may agree." George, the mentally unstable son, got all the property at the colonel's cottage at the U.S. Hotel at Saratoga Springs. Three nieces were remembered with bequests, while a fourth, Miss Lydia E. E. Greene, who had cared for Gen. Simon Elliot in his last years was granted $200 a year. The four married children, Eliza, Mary, Caroline, and Nancy, and the grandson, THP Tertius, were left the residuary legatees.

The terms of the bequest to George were very carefully drawn and took up several pages in the will specifying various conditions. All this was made necessary, the will explained, "in consequence of an injury sustained in his youth" which had "repeatedly deprived" him "for seasons of greater or less duration of his natural capacity for the prudent management of property." Since such "seasons" might return if George was "exposed to causes of undue excitement," the colonel was afraid he might go through his inheritance and tied it up so George was protected against himself, and against a possible future wife. Here, though the will did not state it in so many words, was the crux of the matter. George's relapses had each been brought on by his falling passionately in love with some girl whom the family considered unsuitable for him. The colonel was afraid that with his paternal supervision gone, "gold-diggers" would swarm over George and pick him clean. He was taking no chances that his money would be dispersed in this fashion.[5]

Nothing was left by name to any public institution. The newspapers state, though it was not in the will, that the colonel during his lifetime had made all the donations he intended for public groups and causes. However, a half million dollars was given to the executors of the will (who were Samuel Cabot, Thomas and William Cary, William Gardiner, and T. H. Perkins, III). They were instructed to dispose of this as directed by a letter left to them, but not made part of the will. They were not to be accountable to anybody for their disposition of this money, which was not then or even now, a token sum. To this day, nothing is known of where this money went or how it was spent.

Some treasures do not get mentioned in wills. Some time after the colonel's death, Eliza Cabot was clearing out his desk. She was surprised to find in one drawer a little bag of seashells. This was carefully marked with the name of one of his great-grandchildren, "From Bessie Lee." There was also a drawing the child had made which he had considered quite wonderful and had saved.

How can a soul be a merchant? What relation to an immortal being have the price of linseed, the fall of butter, the tare on tallow, or the brokerage on hemp? Can an undying creature debit petty expenses and charge for carriage paid? The soul ties its shoes; the mind washes its hands in a basin. All is incongruous.

Walter Bagehot

# 35

# The Gentleman on the Wall

The year after Perkins died, the new president of the Athenaeum, Thomas G. Cary, wrote a biography of his father-in-law for *Hunt's Merchants Magazine*. The next year, bowing to "popular demand," Cary expanded this into a full-length book, issued in two editions, a quality edition and a cheap stereotype reprint. This work, while giving the essential outline of the colonel's life, was composed extensively of quotes from his travel journals, particularly his trip to the East Indies and China in 1789, and his first European journey in 1795. An appendix printed a number of business letters from a letterbook now missing. The focus was more on his travels to remote places than on the man.

Following the instructions of the will, the daughters divided among themselves the personal effects and chattels of their father, with no more than the usual family squabbling in such matters. There is some hint that Nancy Cary was the most difficult to satisfy. With each subsequent death, these possessions became more and more widely dispersed among the descendants. Today in the home of one there may be only a fan; in the house of another, two Gilbert Stuart portraits and some of the colonel's heavy, handsome silverware. Some of the portraits went west and have disappeared from sight. The Audubon folio that Perkins bought, he himself presented to the Boston Society of Natural History in February 1840. There it remained for more than one hundred years. When that society became the Museum of Science and reorganized its library in 1947, the Audubon folio was sold to the Hancock Library of Biology and Oceanography of the University of Southern California, where it now reposes.

The shipping activities of the colonel and his brother have suffered a "sea change." When Perkins died, Boston temporarily seemed supreme on the ocean due to Donald McKaye's clipper ships. Steam did away with this advantage. Boston's leadership was soon overtaken and lost to other ports. Today, Boston as a shipping terminal is insignificant. In any case, trade with the West Indies has become minimal for United States firms. Wealth lies elsewhere in the world market, particularly where there is oil. Slavery, at best a small part of the Perkins enterprise, is now forbidden under that name. Boston is no longer the tea-drinking city it once was, and what tea there is, comes from India not China. The opium traffic, another prop of the colonel's wealth, has come under the general anathema applied to all such debilitating drugs, old or new. If the colonel attempted to engage in such trade today, he would be heavily fined and imprisoned, such is the change in attitudes towards this line of endeavor. Perkins & Co., which became Russell & Co., has since become part of J. M. Forbes & Co. This firm still does business today from offices on State Street in Boston, though no longer with China.

The sea otters, once hunted nearly to extinction (only an estimated five hundred were alive when Japan, Russia, Canada, and the United States agreed in the Fur Seal Treaty of 1911 to protect them) have made a comeback, and are now being carefully "harvested." In 1968, pelts brought from $1,800 to $2,700 each.

Of all of the colonel's shore activities only one lasted into modern times, and now even that is silent. The Monkton Iron Company in Vergennes was finally sold in the early part of 1831 to John D. Ward from Canada. He operated the company successfully for several decades, until the ore beds of the Midwest put all such marginal industries in the East out of business. The area in Vergennes where the foundries were located has been altered, some of the river being filled in. The Northampton lead mine was operated by David Hinckley for thirteen years. About 1823 he contracted a fever, from the foul air of the mine it was said, and died. With his passing, the working of that mine came to an end.

The Elliot Manufacturing Company had a somewhat longer run. Otis Pettee operated the mill for the Perkinses interests until 1831. That year he left to open a textile machinery company, which many years later became part of the well-known Saco-Lowell shops. Perkins and his associates lent Pettee the money to get started on his own. The depression of 1836 reduced the sales of the Elliot Manufacturing Company to a low level, which was not helped by the fluctuations in the price of cotton. Stockholder disagreements finally led to the liquidation of the enterprise, and Pettee bought the property from the Perkins interests for $46,000.

Although the Tremont House was not so completely a Perkins enterprise as some of the others he engaged in, he was nevertheless heavily invested in it. As the first modern hotel in the world, it was soon eclipsed by John Jacob Astor's Astor Hotel in New York; in some respects a larger version of the Tremont House. Other similar enterprises copied these pioneers. The Tremont House served the traveling public until it was torn down in 1895. When the cornerstone was recovered by the wreckers and the lead box, put there with such ceremony sixty-seven years before, was opened, it was found that someone had forgotten to seal the glass tube in which the parchment scroll had been placed. All the names of the illustrious bond-holders had crumbled into dust.

The colonel and Dr. Robbins ran the Nahant Hotel until 1842, when they sold it for $25,000. Under new management the hotel limped on until October 1, 1859, when it was closed for the last time. During the summer of 1861, a great auction sale was held to dispose of the furnishings. Shortly afterwards, on September 12, the empty building burned flat. Sitting conspicuously as it did on the promontory, the fire was visible for miles along the coast. It was rumored that the fire had a suspicious origin. For many years afterwards, the ruins remained, until the property was taken over for a summer residence by Henry Cabot Lodge, the first senator of that name for the Commonwealth. After his family's ownership ceased, the federal government maintained fortifications on the point. When the government closed these down after the Second World War, the property stood idle until it was given by the government to Northeastern University, which now maintains it as a marine biological station.

Of the shore enterprises Perkins began, only the Granite Railway Company continued in existence almost to the present day. This was because the railway became absorbed into the quarries. Although Perkins relinquished the presidency of the company in 1834, he remained actively interested in the business, continuing to run it through the new president, who was his omnipresent son-in-law, T. G. Cary. In 1846 they were empowered by the legislature to connect onto the Old Colony Railroad line running out of Boston to Plymouth and the Cape. The next year they sold the company to the Quincy Branch Railroad Company, which worked it "with great energy and profit" until 1864, when it was sold to the last group of owners. They and their successors continued to work the quarry until 1942, when after several years of losses, operations were suspended. The hole in the ground had grown so deep that the effort and cost of extracting the stone became unprofitable. But during the period of 1890–1920, there were more than 120 firms employing 5,000 men quarrying granite in Quincy.

The railroad right of way was taken over by the Old Colony Company in 1870, and the Granite Branch Line continued to serve the quarry even after the Old Colony was leased in 1893 to the New York, New Haven and Hartford Railroad. This railroad system became a victim of the motor car. Today a modern highway, the Southeast Expressway, runs over part of the roadbed of what was a marvel of modern progress in 1826. Part of the ancient roadbed was exposed when they were digging for the new highway in 1957. This led a local Quincy archaeologist, Richard Muzzrole, to spend five years of his spare time, digging up much of the line, particularly in the area of Solomon Willard's finishing and loading site. Recent efforts to make this area a protected historical site have not yet succeeded in the General Court, which chartered the original enterprise in 1826.

Stone from the quarries of the Granite Railway Company is still besting the elements in Boston and other cities today. The Bunker Hill Monument, the base of the Boston Custom House, the old City Hall on School Street, all were constructed of this material. Many of the principal business blocks of Boston were built of this stone, only to have it pulverized by the fierce heat of the great fire of 1872. The New

Hampshire State Hospital, the New Orleans Custom House, the Charter Oak Life Insurance Company of Hartford, Connecticut, and the original Astor House in New York were all made of "railway granite"—as it came to be called—hauled out on the Granite Railway.

The various Perkins residences have all disappeared, except for part of the facade and upper story of the Temple Place mansion. The site of the colonel's first house on Pearl Street is now visible from almost any part of the city for the towering new building of the State Street Bank is on the lot where for more than a decade Perkins lived. His house lot across the street, which became the first home of the Perkins School for the Blind, is now partly covered by the New England Telephone Company's building. The "elegant" mansion on Temple Place was sold soon after Perkins's death to the Provident Institution for Savings, and their main offices are still there today. They completely remodeled and extended the building, however. One can still recognize from the outside the general shape of the old house. The bay window that looked up toward the Common is still there, and one of the Italian marble fireplaces can be seen in the bank president's office. Otherwise, all is change, though traces of the original can be discerned in the cellar and the top floor offices of the mansion.

The house in Brookline was pulled down, not long after the colonel's death. The land it stood on was sold, but a large part of the old estate remained intact and was passed down in one line of descent. The old house he built near him for Eliza Cabot, though much modified, still is lived in. The lovely gardens are kept up as well as can be, but the famous greenhouses have all been taken down due to "old age," the last one in 1967.

The cottage at Nahant had a longer life. The Samuel Cabot's only lived there a few years before they turned it over to the Cary's. The Cary family, which included Louis Agassiz as a son-in-law, became so connected with the house that it was known among the natives of Nahant as the Cary Cottage. It was lived in almost without change, except for the addition of a swimming pool. In recent years it passed into the hands of a man who was later accused of being a leader of the Boston underworld. One night in the 1950's the house, unoccupied at the time, burned to the ground, leaving only a stone shell which was not removed until several years later. Thus vanished the last trace of Perkins from the town of Nahant.

Only the charitable enterprises endure. The Boston Athenaeum continues to serve its distinguished membership, as well as a broader category of the public who are given access to its facilities. Among libraries, it is a unique institution in a timeless, classical building designed by Edward Cabot, one of Perkins's grandsons. The Massachusetts General Hospital has become one of the foremost medical centers in the world. The Boston Female Asylum, which his mother helped to start, and which had Perkins's interest and support all through his lifetime continues today in a new guise. Over a hundred years, it merged with a number of similar welfare organizations, although it kept its corporate name until 1947. In that year it united with the Boston Children's Aid Society, the new group calling itself the Children's Aid Association. A further merger in 1956 brought into being the Boston Children's Service Association, which shares in the Massachusetts Bay United Fund. It continues to care for homeless children and aids the emotionally disturbed and the handicapped.

On a hill in Charlestown, not yet obscured by the high-rise buildings springing up in Boston, stands the 221-foot Bunker Hill monument, a tribute to the patriotic endeavors of Bostonians and New Englanders. More than two hundred thousand people are said to visit this monument each year. Only one in ten, however, pays his token fee and climbs the 294 granite steps to the top. In 1919, the Bunker Hill Monument Association deeded the property over to the Commonwealth to hold and administer. The association continues in existence to this day, keeping an eye on the Commonwealth's discharge of its responsibilities. For ten dollars one can become a life member of this organization of which the colonel was a founder.

Without question, the greatest monument to the colonel's generosity is the Perkins School for the Blind. It has long since left the old hotel in South Boston that it purchased out of the proceeds of the sale of the Pearl Street house. In 1910 it began an extended move to the Stickney estate in Watertown, where it is now located. The school is one of the leading institutions of its kind in the world, and the parent of all such schools in the United States. Under five directors in its almost century and a half of operation, it has pioneered many remarkable programs for the benefit of "this class of the human family." More than three hundred students a year enroll in its courses, but its influence is global. As his ships and schooners carried the Perkins name to Canton and back, so today the work of "Perkins" carries the colonel's name around the world. He has been more than repaid for his generous impulse by this immortality.

Something of the "munificent donor" is still to be seen in Boston today. In the vestibule of the Boston Athenaeum as a visitor enters it, there on the left, the colonel in marble stares sightless at proprietors, ticket holders, and intruders. This version of the colonel as a "noble Roman" was cut by Frazee in 1834. Another bust of the colonel, by William Behnes, done in 1826, suddenly appeared on the Athenaeum lists in 1897 and recently reposed in a dark storeroom. For some time a profile of the colonel, in bas relief, hung near the elevator on the fifth floor. It was picked up by the present librarian in the Mercantile Library rooms. Later, it was "promoted" to the first floor gallery.

For a few years on the second floor bay window wall, a darkened ambrotype of Perkins was hanging. This was a near profile of the *left* side of his face. Perkins is seated at a desk or table. The emaciations of age reveal the nose like some great prow cutting into time. A huge pendulous lobe looms at the bottom of the ear. These features have been softened or obscured in all surviving portraits.

In a quiet alcove of the reading room of the Athenaeum hangs the only full-length portrait of the colonel. The painting is in a gilt frame as enormous and oversized as the colonel's fortune. It is what Thomas Sully, the painter of it, called a "whole length" by which he meant that the feet showed. It measures 58 inches wide and 94 inches high. Sully was forty-eight when he painted it and Perkins was almost sixty-seven. The portrait was begun July 7, 1831 at the second house on Pearl Street. It was one of more than 2,500 pictures Sully painted in his long working span of seventy years. The Athenaeum paid him $600 for it, which was the most he had ever received for a portrait up to that time. On May 18, 1832 the picture was finished, according to the register of his work that Sully meticulously kept.

What did Mr. Sully see? While the couch in the painting could be from the colonel's house, the background of the portrait is quasi-Roman. The high stone arch never was in any Boston living room; the remote blue sky and wispy clouds seem foreign to Boston. There is no salt tang, no smacking smell of fish.

The scene itself is uncertain. The gentleman in the picture sits on a fawn-colored sofa, his left arm casually resting on its back rim. Has he just come in from out-of-doors? He has taken off his hat, gloves, and scarf and thrown them on the sofa. In his hand he holds a letter, the seal apparently just broken open.

The gentleman himself seems somewhat remote from us, like the "Duke of some European principality" as a nephew said. In his black shoes, pants, vest, his brown-red long frock coat with genteel black collar, his white cravat and diamond stickpin, it all speaks quiet, restrained elegance. We see he wears glasses, though he has taken them off and holds them in his right hand, which rests on the bolster. A semi-Oriental feeling is induced by the beige rug with the red center design which echoes the red in the ottoman beside the colonel's right foot. A large-lipped vase with a colorful Chinese scene mostly gives the Chinese quality. His artistic interests are suggested by the large red portfolio for drawings with the drawstrings hanging down undone.

The face is turned toward the right to show the colonel's left side. His right ear is not visible. Yet a bit of his right cheek shows. It is a buoyant beefy red. A casual viewer might think it too much madeira. Very cleverly has the painter told the truth to those who knew, and concealed it from those who did not know and need not know. The forehead is broad, and the hair above it grey-white, with some black still showing. The left cheek is ruddy, and the eyebrows are bushy grey, below which dark blue eyes look off to the right. The face is shaven, the mouth unsmiling.

What is he thinking? This man who was born when King George III had been but four years on his throne, when Massachusetts was one of the king's still-loyal colonies, and who was to die in the administration of Mr. Franklin Pierce, fourteenth president of the United States of America. A man who had been lit to bed by George Washington; who had lived in a house whose heavy front door had been made from the oak of the frigate *Constitution;* who owned a chair of Napoleon's and a diamond of Madame Lafayette's; who had shot snipe in the marshes bordering Charles Street where no tide has come now for more than a century.

There is a limit to what even the most skillful artist can show. The slaves, the opium, the tea, the sea-otter skins, the nights of dread on tumultuous seas, the long slow bumping stage journeys to scrutinize iron works, look at granite quarries, inspect railroads, plan monuments, or attend company meetings—none of this shows.

*The Old Colonel, 1828–1854*

Here the picture hangs, overlooking, in the Old Granary Burying Ground, the illustrious dead of Boston and the graves of the five accidental victims of the Boston Massacre so long ago on a bright March night in 1770. There is nothing to disturb them there, or him, here in this quiet room. Not even the asthmatic cough of an old man sunk in a red leather chair and rustling his way through a newspaper. The old man is searching for—yes, now he finds it—the financial page.

It makes the parting tranquil
And keeps the soul serene—
That gentlemen so sprightly
Conduct the pleasing scene!

Genealogy of the Perkins Family

A List of the Perkins Firms

ANCESTRY OF THOMAS HANDASYD PERKINS AND SARAH ELLIOT

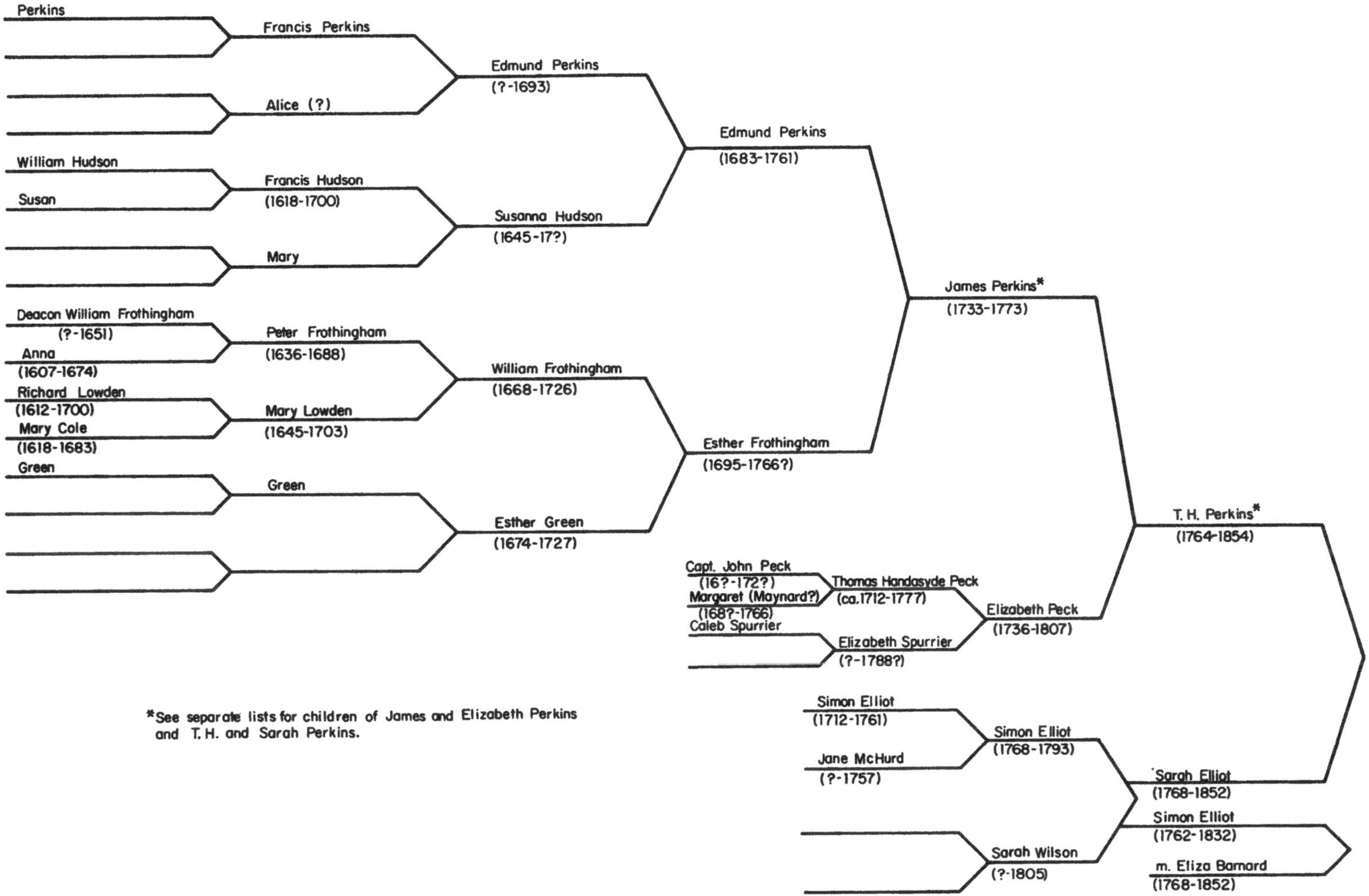


*See separate lists for children of James and Elizabeth Perkins and T. H. and Sarah Perkins.

# The Children of James Perkins and Elizabeth Peck Perkins

Elizabeth:
- b. 1756
- m. 1773 to Russell Sturgis (1750–1826) and had sixteen children
- d. 1843

James:
- b. 1757
- d. in infancy

Anne Maynard (called Nancy):
- b. 1759
- m. Robert Cushing (1755–?) and had two children, Nancy Cushing Higginson (1782–1847) and John Perkins Cushing (1787–1862)
- d. 1793

James:
- b. 1761
- m. 1786 to Sarah Paine (1764?–1841) and had two children, James, Jr. (1791–1828) and Sarah (1789?–1812)
- d. 1822

John Peck:
- b. 1763
- d. in infancy

Thomas Handasyd:
- b. 1764
- d. 1854

Samuel:
- b. 1767*
- m. 1795 to Barbara Cooper Higginson (1774–1843) and had six children
- d. 1847

Mary:
- b. 1769
- m. 1797 to Dr. Benjamin Abbot (1762–1849) as his second wife and had three children
- d. 1863

Esther:
- b. 1771
- m. Thomas Doubleday (1769–1790) and had two sons
- m. 1795 to Josiah Sturgis (1767–1835)
- d. 1810

Margaret Mitchell:
- b. 1773
- m. 1799 to Ralph Bennet Forbes (1773–1824) and had seven children, among them Thomas Tunno (1802–1829), Robert Bennet (1804–1889), John Murray (1813–1898)
- d. 1856

* "A brother between me and Sam as the Great Family Bible shows," wrote T. H. Perkins in 1846.

# The Children of T. H. Perkins and Sarah Elliot Perkins

Sarah Elliot:
- b. December 6, 1788
- d. September 24, 1792

Elizabeth:
- b. March 17, 1791
- m. Samuel Cabot (1784–1863) in 1812 and had eleven children
- d. March 2, 1885

Sarah Elliot:
- b. November 8, 1792
- d. July 8, 1856, unm.

Ann Cushing:
- b. June 25, 1794
- d. February 12, 1799

Thomas Handasyd, Jr.:
- b. October 8, 1796
- m. Jane Frances Dumeresque (1799–1856) in 1820 and had five children including THP III (1823–1900) who had two girls so that no male descendants now bear the name.
- d. January 16, 1850

Mary Ann Cushing:
- b. May 25, 1798
- m. Thomas Graves Cary (1791–1859) in 1820 and had eight children
- d. October 8, 1880

Caroline:
- b. January 4, 1800
- m. William H. Gardiner (1794–1882) in 1823 and had six children
- d. May 24, 1867

Charles Elliot:
- b. October 31, 1801
- d. November 13, 1803

George Cabot:
- b. September 25, 1803
- d. 1868

Ann Cushing (called Nancy):
- b. January 28, 1806
- m. William F. Cary (1795–1881) and had six children
- d. September 16, 1889

James E.:
- b. January 24, 1809
- d. January 24, 1809

# The Perkins Firms

Perkins, Burling & Perkins, May 1, 1786–August 15, 1788, Cape Francis. Partners: James Perkins, Walter Burling, and T. H. Perkins.

Perkins, Burling & Co., August 15, 1788–June 21, 1793, Cape Francis. Partners: James Perkins, Walter Burling, Samuel G. Perkins.

T. H. Perkins & James Magee, August 15, 1788–n.d. Boston. Partners: T. H. Perkins and James Magee.

James and Thomas H. Perkins, September 29, 1792–August 1, 1822, Boston. Partners: James and T. H. Perkins.

E. Bumstead & Co., July 15, 1803–December 5, 1805(?), Canton, China. Partners: Ephraim Bumstead, 25 percent, J. & T. H. Perkins, 75 percent.

Perkins & Co. (first establishment), December 6, 1805–August 1, 1822, Canton, China. Partners: James Perkins, Thomas H. Perkins, John P. Cushing.

S. Cabot Jr., J. & T. H. Perkins, Jrs., January 1, 1817–January 1821(?), Boston. Partners: Samuel Cabot, James Perkins, Jr., T. H. Perkins, Jr.

J. & T. H. Perkins & Sons (first establishment), January 1821–February 20, 1823, Boston. Partners: James Perkins, T. H. Perkins, Samuel Cabot, James Perkins, Jr., T. H. Perkins, Jr.

J. & T. H. Perkins & Sons (second establishment), February 20, 1823–June 22, 1828, Boston. Partners: T. H. Perkins, Sr., and Jr., Samuel Cabot, James Perkins, Jr.

Perkins & Co. (second establishment), February 20, 1823–June 22, 1828, Canton, China. Partners: James Perkins, Jr., T. H. Perkins, John P. Cushing.

J. & T. H. Perkins & Sons (third establishment), June 22, 1828–ca. November 1835, Boston. Partners: Samuel Cabot, Thomas G. Cary, T. H. Perkins.

Perkins & Co. (third establishment), June 22, 1828–ca. November 1835, Boston. Partners: T. H. Perkins, John P. Cushing, Samuel Cabot.

# Sources and Acknowledgments

# Sources

The most valuable source of material on T. H. Perkins exists in the Perkins Collection at the Massachusetts Historical Society. It contains twenty-four volumes of various account books, one letterbook, a nearly complete set of his original diaries of voyages, and an extensive range of his personal and business correspondence and some memorabilia. In addition, material of family members such as the Cabots, Lees, Carys, Curtises, Higginsons, Shattucks, Cushings, Elliots, and Gardiners is also deposited here. Useful secondary deposits are at Baker Library in the Harvard Business School and the Cabot and Cary collections of the Schlesinger Library at Radcliffe.

From 1792 to 1822, the J. and T. H. Perkins partnership kept a complete and elegant set of account books and letterbooks, as did their successor firms. What has survived of these records is indispensable to any account of their business careers. Apparently these many volumes were in the colonel's possession at his death in 1854. If at that time they had been given intact to some repository such as the Massachusetts Historical Society, they would represent a unique record of an important firm for that time and place. Unfortunately, that did not happen.

It is almost impossible to discover what happened to the letterbooks. It would appear that one or more volumes of the letterbooks came into the possession of the Cary family. Excerpts from them were printed in T. G. Cary's biography of the colonel in 1856. Apparently these were never returned to the full set.

## *Sources*

At the turn of the century, James Elliot Cabot, grandson of the colonel and literary executor of Ralph Waldo Emerson, had an extract made from all the letterbooks except the one or more volumes represented in the Cary biography. The earliest letter in his extract is dated June 7, 1786, and the last is March 8, 1841. This was prepared for members of the family who were curious about their noted ancestor. Whether Cabot owned the letterbooks or not is uncertain; he definitely had the use of them. What subsequently happened to the volumes is unknown. During the twenties and thirties the account books started dribbling in to public depositories, nearly all to the Massachusetts Historical Society. Three volumes of account books turned up recently in Baker Library. They had been used as scrapbooks and their pages were covered with clippings from the Civil War period. Only a partial attempt has so far been made to remove these clippings.

Unfortunately, only one of the volumes that came to light is a letterbook: the foreign letterbook of the firm for the period from April 3, 1807 through January 5, 1815, which is now in the Perkins Collection at MHS. It enables a comparison between the original letters and the extracts made from them by J. E. Cabot. It shows clearly the casual, unscholarly nature of his selections.

Cabot's method was to choose a few letters from each month, to ignore most of the business ones, and to pick out items in the letters that seemed interesting to him. A few sentences are copied from these letters, only rarely is an extensive quote given. Sometimes the sentences are copied incorrectly, sometimes they are abbreviated, sometimes words are omitted or rearranged with no indication to the reader that this has been done. Sometimes qualifying phrases are left out. Any reference that might reveal his ancestors or some other people in an unfavorable light is usually screened out of the extracts. Cabot's "Extracts" are indispensible for any study of the life of Perkins, since they give much information available nowhere else. But the comparison with the one existing letterbook shows their fragmentary and unsatisfactory nature, and reveals the great richness that is missing.

All a scholar can do is express regret that family pride would want to hide the remarkable record of a remarkable man. It is to be earnestly hoped that descendants who may have in their possession any other volumes of the firm's letterbooks, will quickly make them available as loans, gifts, or for copying purposes to public repositories.

The following account books are now available to scholars and were used in the preparation of this biography. They are all at the Massachusetts Historical Society unless otherwise indicated.

*J. & T. H. Perkins*

Journal C, 1798–1800
Journal D, 1800–1801
Journal F, 1804–1806
Journal L, 1821–1827
Blotter E, 1797–1798
*Blotter G, 1799–1800
*Blotter L, 1804–1805
Blotter M, 1805–1807
Blotter N, 1807–1810
Blotter R, 1818–1820
Blotter S, 1820–1827
†Ledger F, 1818–1827
Invoices (Inward), 1803–1811
Invoices (Inward), 1820–1832
Invoices (Outward), 1819–1823
Trial Balance, 1820–1825
Current Accounts, 1819–1827
*Ship Book #4, 1804–1815

*J. & T. H. Perkins & Sons*

Journal B, 1825–1827
Journal C, 1827–1835
Ledger B, 1822–1835
Waste B, 1824–1826
Waste C, 1826–1827
Waste A, 1828–1830
Invoices (Outward), 1826–1832
Trial Balance, 1823–1836
Current Accounts, 1821–1835

*Perkins & Co., Canton*

Ephraim Bumstead & Co., 1803–1805
*Perkins & Co., 1820–1823 (vols. 19, 20).
*Private letterbook, J. P. Cushing (1828–1830)
(typescript in Bryant and Sturgis collection)

One of the confusions that can trouble the unwary researcher into the life of Thomas Handasyd Perkins is the existence of a contemporary,

* Baker Library, Harvard Business School, Boston, Mass.
† Dr. George Shattuck

Thomas Perkins, who was active in many of the same pursuits as T. H. Perkins. This plain Thomas Perkins was born in 1763, one year before our Perkins. His father was also James Perkins, and he also had a brother James. This Thomas Perkins married twice, first in 1789 to Charlotte Appleton (1766–1798) and second in 1800 to Anna Dummer Powell (1770–1848). His first father in-law was a Loan Officer in Boston and he succeeded in 1798 to this position. As a merchant he took ventures in ships as did THP, and as a Federalist he was in some of the same organizations as THP. He lived in a Bulfinch mansion on the corner of Mount Vernon and Joy Streets from 1804 until his death in 1836 at the age of seventy-three. Short and rotund (see his picture by Gilbert Stuart), it is said, that he was known as "Short Tom" to distinguish him from T. H. Perkins who was known as "Long Tom." We have seen only two contemporary references to the use of such terms: one is in *How Fortunes Are Made: The Rich Men of Boston* (Boston, 1852), p. 51, and the other in the *Goldthwaite Genealogy* by Charlotte Goldthwaite (Hartford, 1899), p. 352. In a letter of October 1861 by Miss Hannah Goldthwaite Gowen, she remarks that "Katey" Goldthwaite took as her second husband "Mr. William Powell, father to Mrs. Jonathan Mason and Mrs. short Thomas Perkins—he was called short to distinguish him from Thomas Handiside." For this reason, T. H. Perkins always made use of his middle name or initial in one form or another, and for a period during the 1790's was commonly known by his middle name. Once he became the "Colonel," he apparently had no further need to emphasize the middle name. By then, too, he was more active and prominent than his shadow.

During the years of our work on this book we were aided by a great many people. We want first to express our thanks to those who are so seldom thanked, but who perform in anonymity the faithful and daily endeavors that make books like this possible: archivists, catalogers, indexers, typists, librarians, researchers, family descendants, and not least certain scribblers who painfully write their dull books of fact or gossip on obscure subjects that sell five copies and are rare treasures to the historian. To all these collectors and preservers of man's past, so that it may enlighten his future, we are indebted.

Descendants of Colonel Perkins proved most helpful in our research. We are most grateful for the enthusiasms, the constant encouragement, and suggestions of Henry Lee and H. A. Crosby Forbes; for the kindness of Edward Cunningham in providing us with a copy of the "Extracts" and for his helpful letters; and for the delightful visits to Dr. and Mrs.

George C. Shattuck, Mr. and Mrs. William P. Wadsworth, Mrs. Henry Minot, Mrs. Henry Lyman, Mrs. Ralph Bradley, Miss Caroline Cabot, Mr. and Mrs. T. H. P. Whitney, Mr. and Mrs. Geoffrey Whitney, and the late Mr. and Mrs. Samuel Cabot.

It was our good fortune to have excellent facilities with superb resources and dedicated and helpful staffs near at hand. We are much beholden to Walter Muir Whitehill and the staff of the Boston Athenaeum, particularly James Belliveau, Margaret Hackett, Mrs. Phillip Johnson, and the staff of the third floor where we "lived" for a season; to the patient members of the staff, both old and new, at the Massachusetts Historical Society, who cheerfully put up with our constant requests for more documents; to the people at Schlesinger Library, Radcliffe when it was still called the Women's Archives; to the pleasant ladies of the library at the New England Historic and Genealogical Society; to Mrs. Harriet Ropes Cabot and Mrs. Davis G. Maraspin of the Bostonian Society; the State House Archives and Mr. Leo Flaherty; Baker Library and Mr. Robert Lovett; the Essex Institute; the Peabody Museum; the Society for the Preservation of New England Antiquities; the Boston Public Library; the Quincy Historical Society and Mrs. Rudolph Oberg; the Suffolk County Court Archives, Land Office and Probate Registry; and the Museum of the American China Trade, Milton.

We would like to express our thanks also to the directors of Baring Brothers & Co., Ltd., for permission to use documents from their archives, and to their archivist, Mr. T. L. Ingram; the British Museum; the Henry E. Huntington Library; the Vergennes, Vt. Library; the American Antiquarian Society; the Library of Congress; the Vermont Historical Society; the Marine Historical Association; the Middleborough Historical Society; the Sheldon Art Museum and Mrs. Hermon C. Fiske; the Rhode Island Historical Society; the New-York Historical Society; and the New York Public Library.

We received many kindnesses and much assistance from a host of other people and we would like to acknowledge their help with much appreciation: Gershom Bradford, L. Cabot Briggs, Dr. Frank R. Carpenter, Mrs. Elizabeth A. Cobb, Howard G. Cushing, Dr. Jacques M. Downs, Robert M. Faxon, Waldemar H. Fries, Mrs. L. C. Fuller of Lazy Y C Ranch, Miss Ruth E. Gates, John Howe, Dr. George Lawson, Mrs. Nina Fletcher Little, Mrs. H. Gates Lloyd III, Sister Geraldine Mary, O. A. S., Richard Muzzrole, Robert F. Needham, Dow W. Perkins, Rev. Donald F. Robinson, Henry L. Shattuck, Miss Mary Gray Storrow, D. Foster Taylor, and Mrs. Joyce Klain Wilson.

A special word of praise is due our typists, particularly Mrs. Alan Seaburg who triumphed over several versions, and also Mrs. Elaine Johnson Breen, Miss Diane Salerno, Miss Doreen Cootey, and Miss Diane Bernabei.

In conclusion, we would like to congratulate each other for enduring each other during the years of being in "double harness" to Colonel Perkins. Nor would a word of thanks to our families be amiss for putting up with us during the long haul.

Stanley Paterson
Carl Seaburg

*Nahant and Medford, Massachusetts*
*February 1971*

# Notes

# Abbreviations

| | |
|---|---|
| AAS | American Antiquarian Society, Worcester |
| BPL | Boston Public Library, Boston |
| BS | Bostonian Society, Boston |
| CSM | Colonial Society of Massachusetts, Boston |
| HBS | Baker Library, Harvard Business School, Boston |
| MFA | Museum of Fine Arts, Boston |
| NEGHS | New England Historical and Genealogical Society, Boston |
| NYHS | New-York Historical Society, New York City |
| SLR | Schlesinger Library, Radcliffe College, Cambridge (formerly the Women's Archives) |

# Notes

We have provided for the interested reader documentation in these footnotes for all quoted material as well as indications of all our major secondary sources. The scholar who needs more complete references is referred to our original, more extensive manuscript with its fuller documentation, which is on deposit at the Massachusetts Historical Society.

*Chapter 1—Death on the Doorstep*

1. L. Kinvin Wroth and Hiller B. Zobel, eds., *Legal Papers of John Adams* (Cambridge, Mass., Harvard University Press, 1965), III, 170.
2. *Ibid.,* III, 266; *Diary and Autobiography of John Adams,* ed. Lyman H. Butterfield (Cambridge, Mass., Harvard University Press, 1961), III, 291–292.
3. Peck bought this house on May 12, 1767; Suffolk Deeds, vol. 110, p. 160; Wroth and Zobel, *Legal Papers of John Adams,* III, 79.

4. Frederick Kidder, *History of the Boston Massacre . . .* (Albany, Joel Munsell, 1870), p. 151. Unless otherwise noted, Kidder has been relied on for most of the detail in this chapter.
5. *Ibid.*, pp. 60, 67, 74, 134; and Wroth and Zobel, *Legal Papers of John Adams,* III, 111. We have changed one word from its appearance in the nineteenth century records. Instead of "boogers" we have used "buggers," assuming bowdlerization of the improper word. Of course, the depositions might have been attempting to reproduce the contemporary pronounciation of the word.
6. *Boston Daily Times,* January 12, 1854. James Loring reports that Perkins, in a conversation on January 3, 1851, told him he slept through the Massacre. This agrees with every other account Perkins gave of the Massacre.
7. *Diary and Autobiography of John Adams,* p. 291.
8. Hiller B. Zobel, *The Boston Massacre* (New York, W. W. Norton & Co., 1970), p. 192.
9. B. B. Thatcher, *Traits of the Tea Party* (New York, Harper & Brothers, 1835), pp. 102–103.
10. Wroth and Zobel, *Legal Papers of John Adams,* III, pp. 71, 46–47; Albert Matthews, "Captain Preston and the Boston Massacre," *Transactions of the Colonial Society of Massachusetts,* 7 (1905), 2.
11. Thatcher, *Traits of the Tea Party,* pp. 103–104.
12. *Ibid.,* p. 112.
13. Zobel, *The Boston Massacre,* pp. 200–201.
14. Wroth and Zobel, *Legal Papers of John Adams,* III, pp. 79–80.
15. *Diary and Autobiography of John Adams,* III, p. 291.
16. Joseph Belknap, deposition, MHS.
17. T. H. Perkins, "For My Children" (1846), Perkins Papers, MHS. Unless otherwise noted, all Perkins material referred to is part of the Perkins Papers at the MHS.

*Chapter 2—There Is Two Iron Guns In My Store*

1. Thomas H. Peck, letterbook, 1766–1776, MHS.
2. Clifford K. Shipton, *Sibley's Harvard Graduates* (Boston, MHS, 1951), VIII, 386–407; Andrew Crosswell, *A Narrative of the Founding* (Boston, Rogers & Fowle, 1749), p. 6, in the Congregational Library, Boston.
3. John Rowe, diary, August 14, 1769, MHS; "An Alphabetical List of the Sons of Liberty who dined at Liberty Tree, Dorchester, August 14, 1773," *Proceedings of the MHS,* 11 (1869–1870), 140–142.
4. John E. Alden, "John Mein: Scourge of Patriots," *Transactions of the Colonial Society of Mass.,* 34 (1937–1942), 571–599.
5. *Boston Gazette,* September 11, 1769.
6. Peck, letterbook, MHS, June 7, 1774.
7. *Ibid.,* March 1, 1775.
8. Thomas H. Peck to General Gage, April 24, 1775, Gage Papers, American Ser. 128, at Clements Library, Ann Arbor, Mich.
9. Andrew Eliot, in *The Life of Jeremy Belknap,* ed. by his granddaughter (New York, Harper & Brothers, 1847), p. 99.

*Chapter 3—The Drums Beat and Away*

1. C. F. Swift, ed., *Genealogical Notes of Barnstable Families* (Barnstable, F. B. & F. P. Goss, 1888), I, 27; petition in Donald G. Traysee, *Barnstable:*

*Three Centuries of a Cape Cod Town* (Hyannis, Mass., F. B. & F. P. Goss, 1939), p. 128.

2. Reverend John Pierce, "Memoirs," IX, 282, MHS.
3. Shipton, *Sibley's Harvard Graduates,* X, 471–478; *Book of the First Church of Christ in Middleboro,* p. 39.
4. Thomas Weston, *History of the Town of Middleboro, Massachusetts* (Boston, Houghton Mifflin Company, 1906), pp. 314–316, 447–449, 575.
5. Robert F. Seybolt, "Schoolmasters of Colonial Boston," *Transactions of the Colonial Society of Mass.,* 27 (1927–1930), 152–156.
6. Samuel Eliot Morison, *Harrison Gray Otis (1765–1848): The Urbane Federalist* (Boston, Houghton Mifflin Company, 1969), p. 14.
7. Rowe, diary, March, 1776, MHS.
8. Henry Sewall, diary, March 17, 1776, MHS.
9. Thomas G. Cary, *Memoir of Thomas Handasyd Perkins* (Boston, Little, Brown & Company, 1856), p. 8.
10. A. T. Perkins, *Memorial Biographies,* I, 146–148.
11. Samuel Shaw to General Knox, Feb. 14, 1781, in Knox Papers, vol. 5, p. 139, MHS. Year an error for 1782; see Ebenezer Parker, diary, February 9, 1782, MHS.
12. "Memoir of James Perkins," *Proceedings of the MHS,* 1 (1791–1835), 353–368.
13. Elizabeth P. Cabot, "Reminiscences of Eliza Cabot," Schlesinger Library, Radcliffe College (cited hereafter as SLR).
14. T. G. Cary, *Memoir of T. H. Perkins,* p. 9.

*Chapter 4—Puritan in Paradise*

1. General information on Santo Domingo from T. Lothrop Stoddard, *The French Revolution in San Domingo* (Boston, Houghton Mifflin Company, 1914); and Francis Alexander Stanislaus, *A Voyage to Saint Domingue in the Years 1788, 1789, & 1790,* trans. J. Wright (London, 1817), pp. 249, 263, 277.
2. T. G. Cary, *Memoir of T. H. Perkins,* pp. 9–10; [Alicia H. Middleton], *Life in Carolina & New England* (Bristol, R. I., privately printed, 1929), p. 185.
3. *Massachusetts Centinel,* October 1, 1785.
4. "Extracts," July 24, 1786; July 27, 1786.
5. "Extracts," July 24, 1786; September 7, 1786; June 24, 1790.
6. "Extracts," April 1, 1788; August 25, 1786; December 15, 1787.
7. Marriage document owned by the late Samuel Cabot, Jamaica Plain, Massachusetts.
8. Reverend John Pierce, "Memoirs," III, 145, MHS.
9. T. H. Perkins to M. M. Hays, March 27, 1788.
10. E. P. Cabot, "Reminiscences," SLR.
11. *Massachusetts Centinel,* November 26, 1788.
12. E. H. Derby to James Magee, July 15, 1788, Derby letterbook, p. 234, Essex Institute, Salem, Massachusetts.
13. James Bowdoin to E. Dowse, February 3, 1789, Bowdoin letterbook, pp. 277–278, MHS.
14. E. H. Derby, "Memorandum of Agreement with T. H. Perkins, February 14, 1789"; Magee to Derby, November 5, 1788, Derby Papers, Essex Institute.
15. T. H. Perkins, journal, 1789, is the source for the voyage.

*Chapter 5—Into the Bosome of the Ocean*

1. T. G. Cary, *Memoir of T. H. Perkins,* pp. 14–15.
2. *Ibid.,* pp. 15–16.
3. *Ibid.,* pp. 19–20.
4. T. H. Perkins, journal, July 29, 1789.
5. William Hickey, *The Prodigal Rake,* ed. Peter Quennell (New York, E. P. Dutton & Co., 1962), p. 132. We have assumed that this incident reported by Hickey was typical for most ships arriving in Macao from overseas, although there is no reference as such to it in Perkins's Journal.
6. *Ibid.*
7. For the China Trade see Samuel Eliot Morison, *The Maritime History of Massachusetts* (Boston, Houghton Mifflin Company, 1921), chaps. 4, 6; and Foster R. Dulles, *The Old China Trade* (Boston, Houghton Mifflin Company, 1930).
8. William Chalmers to T. H. Perkins, September 25, 1789, Perkins Papers, MHS.
9. For the trip of the *Astrea* see Edwin B. Hewes, "Thomas Handasyd Perkins, Supercargo of the Astrea of Salem," Essex Institute *Historical Collections,* 71 (1935), 203–215; and its manifest in 60 (1924), 194–196.
10. Frederick W. Howay, ed., *Voyages of the "Columbia,"* MHS *Collections,* 79 (1941), 129.
11. J. Elliot Cabot, *Autobiographical Sketch: Family Reminiscences* (Boston, privately printed, 1904), p. 118.
12. *Columbian Centinel,* June 12, 1790.
13. *Ibid.,* July 31; August 4, 1790; and below.
14. "Extracts," September 14, 1790.
15. Joseph Ingraham, "Journal of the Voyage of the Brigantine 'Hope' From Boston to the North-West Coast of America 1790 to 1792," entry for September 16, 1790, Library of Congress.

*Chapter 6—Hence I Hauled My Wind to the North*

1. Ingraham, "Journal of the 'Hope' " is the source for most of the quoted material in this chapter, unless otherwise noted.
2. "Extracts," November 5, 1790.
3. "Extracts," May 27, 1789.
4. "Extracts," October 21, 1789; February 8, 1790.
5. "Extracts," August, 1790.
6. "Extracts," January 23, 1791.

*Chapter 7—On the Edge of Vesuvius*

1. Stoddard, *The French Revolution in San Domingo,* pp. 124–127.
2. *Ibid.,* p. 126.
3. "Extracts," July 9, 1791.
4. Ingraham's journal remains the source for the voyage of the *Hope.*
5. Samuel G. Perkins, "Insurrection in St. Domingo," *Proceedings of the MHS,* 22 (1885–1886), 305–390.
6. Stoddard, *The French Revolution in San Domingo,* pp. 131–132.

*Chapter 8—A Connection Between Brothers*

1. Nathaniel Cutting to John B. Cutting, August 10, 1793, Nathaniel Cutting Papers, MHS.
2. "Extracts from the Diary of Nathaniel Cutting," *Proceedings of the MHS,* 12 (1871–1873), 60–61.
3. Nathaniel Cutting, journal, March 14, 1790, MHS.
4. "Extracts," June 24, 1790.
5. Cutting, journal, May 23, 1790; Cutting to Andrew Hall, March 22, 1791, Cutting Papers, MHS.
6. Cutting to John B. Cutting, February 28, 1791, MHS.
7. Cutting, journal, November 4; November 21, 1791, MHS.
8. *Ibid.,* January 8, 1792.
9. "Extracts," December 13, 1791.
10. "Extracts," March 29, 1792.
11. Cutting, journal, April 6, 1792, MHS.
12. *Ibid.,* May 20, 1792.
13. Frederick W. Howay, ed. *Voyages of the "Columbia," MHS Collections,* 79 (1941), 129.
14. Henry Knox Papers, Vol. 29, p. 109, MHS.
15. Ingraham, "Journal of the 'Hope,'" November 30, 1791; January 22, 1792.
16. "Extracts," July 14, 1792.

*Chapter 9—The Gentlemen Drink Brandy Punch*

1. Cutting, journal, September 4, 1792, MHS.
2. *The Diary of William Bentley, D. D.* (Salem, Mass., Essex Institute, 1905), I, 395.
3. Samuel West, "Family Anecdotes & Memoirs," pp. 172–175, AAS.
4. Eliza Cabot, "Reminiscences," SLR. She writes "Uncle Sam," but he was in the islands; only James was in Boston at this time.
5. Cutting, journal, September 28, 1792, MHS.
6. *Ibid.,* November 15, 1792; Eliza Cabot, "Reminiscences," SLR.
7. S. G. Perkins, "Insurrection in St. Domingo," *Proceedings of the MHS,* 22 (1885–1886), 340–353.
8. Journal and Notebook of William Fitz Paine, Paine Family Papers, AAS; Howard Corning, ed., "Letters of Sullivan Dorr," *Proceedings of the MHS,* 67 (1941–1944), 179.
9. Corning, "Letters of Sullivan Dorr," p. 210.
10. *MHS Collections,* vol. 79, p. 490; Corning, "Letters of Sullivan Dorr," p. 231.
11. As near as can be determined, Ingraham sold the *Hope* and came home on the *Grand Turk,* arriving in Salem on June 12, 1793. See Robert Haswell, log of the *Columbia* (1792–1793), March 3, 1793, MHS; Bentley, *Diary,* II, 28–29; T. H. Perkins, "To My Children"; Eliza Cabot, "Reminiscences," SLR.
12. Jeremy Belknap's Map of Boston Fire, 1794, *Proceedings of the MHS,* 47 (1913–1914), 293.
13. The "Proceedings of Committee respecting fire in Boston 1794" are at the MHS, partly in Perkins's handwriting.
14. M. A. Dufort-Lesgane to Perkins, May 27, 1794, Perkins Papers, MHS.

*Chapter 10—The Game Playing in Europe*

1. "Extracts," May 7, 1793.
2. "Extracts," May 11, 1793.
3. T. G. Cary, *Memoir of T. H. Perkins,* provides the information on Perkins's trip to Paris.
4. Henry Lee, "Lafayette's Son Comes to America," *Proceedings of the Bostonian Society* (1964), 12–22; Lafayette to Perkins, May 3, 1798, Pierpoint Morgan Library, New York.
5. Perkins to James Perkins, June 21, 1795.
6. Perkins to Jeremy Belknap, June 20, 1795, Belknap Papers, MHS.
7. Cutting, journal, written July 2, 1795, MHS.
8. Bryant Lillywhite, *London Coffee Houses* (London, George Allen & Unwin, 1963), pp. 339–340.
9. Thomas Crafts to Perkins, February 16, 1796, Perkins Papers, MHS.

*Chapter 11—Firmly in Federal Paths*

1. William Priest, *Travels in the United States of America* (London, J. Johnson, 1802), p. 157.
2. Cutting, journal, December 5, 1792, MHS; *Columbian Centinel,* December 8, 1792. Many accounts erroneously state that the play was Shakespeare's "Richard the Third." Such contemporary accounts as above cited prove it was Sheridan's "School for Scandal." See also E. M. and S. B. Puknat, "An American Critic and a German Vogue," *Transactions of the CSM,* 43 (1956–1963), 205.
3. Proprietors' Records, Boston Theater, II, April 9, 1793, BPL.
4. For a plan of the Tontine Crescent see "The First 'Row Houses' in Boston" by Frank Choteau Brown in *Old-Time New England,* 37, (1946–1947) 64–65. The Perkins brothers owned apartment number 3. Brother Samuel shared ownership of number 5 with the Reverend John Murray, although Murray lived in it.
5. John Alden, "A Season in Federal Street," *Proceedings of the AAS,* 65 (1955), 9–74.
6. Eliza Cabot, "Reminiscences," SLR. For his own personal protection, Perkins was a member of the Assistant Fire Society. See their records at MHS.
7. See David H. Fischer, *The Revolution of American Conservatism* (New York, Harper & Row, 1965).
8. See *Columbian Centinel* for April 30, May 4, 7, 11, 14, and 18, 1796; and *Independent Chronicle* for May 9, 12, 16, and 19, 1796.
9. Joseph Dennie Jr. to Jeremiah Mason, August 6, 1797, in *Proceedings of the MHS,* 17 (1879–1880), 363.
10. Joseph Sewall to his wife, August 15, 1797, MHS.
11. Joseph Sewall to his wife, August 25, 1797, *Proceedings of the MHS* 17 (1879–1880), 364.
12. Fisher Ames, *Works, with a Selection from His Speeches and Correspondence,* ed. Seth Ames (Boston, Little, Brown & Company, 1854), I, 245–246.
13. Perkins to Harrison G. Otis, April 21, 1798, Otis Papers, MHS.
14. James Perkins to T. H. Perkins, May 23, 1798.
15. Eliza Susan Quincy, ed., *Memoir of the Life of Eliza S. M. Quincy* (Boston,

John Wilson & Son, 1861), p. 77; *Columbian Centinel,* July 7, 1798; *Independent Chronicle,* July 5, 1798.

16. Page Smith, *John Adams* (New York, Doubleday & Company, 1962), II, 1022; *Columbian Centinel,* January 4, 11, 1800.

*Chapter 12—See How We Grovel Here Below*

1. The trip is recorded in Perkins's "Journel to Saratoga Springs" (1800), MHS.
2. *Columbian Centinel,* October 22, 1800.
3. Eliza Cabot, "Reminiscences," SLR. These "Reminiscences," recorded late in life, have to be used with caution. For example, her sketch of Madame Perkins's property does not agree with that the surveyor made when it was purchased on November 5, 1793. See Suffolk Deeds, vol. 177, p. 156.
4. The Perkins family Bible, owned by Mr. and Mrs. Henry Minot, Brookline, Mass., contains a complete record of the eleven children of Thomas and Sally Perkins. Perkins kept the record at least as late as 1850, or over sixty years.
5. Lucius Manley Sargent, *Dealings With the Dead* (Boston, Dutton & Wentworth, and Ticknor & Fields, 1855), I, 172.
6. Items found in the firm's account books at MHS. Family expenses for both brothers as well as their mother were regularly mixed in with business entries in these early years of the firm.
7. One still exists, that of Thomas C. Amory, signed November 4, 1797 by Russell Sturgis and T. H. Perkins. See Misc. Bound, MHS.

*Chapter 13—A Solemn Protest Against the Ice, Winds, Tides, and Rocks*

1. "Extracts," August 28, 1793.
2. Henry G. Pickering, *Nathaniel Goddard* (Cambridge, Mass., Riverside Press, 1906), p. 101.
3. "Extracts," March 29, 1792; October 6, 1792.
4. *Acts and Resolves of Mass.* (*1786–1787*), Boston, Adams and Nourse, 1787; reprinted 1893, Wright and Potter), pp. 615–617.
5. *Report of the Committee of the House of Representatives of Massachusetts . . .* (Boston, Russell & Cutler, 1813), p. 46.
6. See Journal C of the firm, MHS.
7. William F. Megee to C. Sterey, November 5, 1797, Nightingale and Jenckes Papers, Rhode Island Historical Society, Providence.
8. *Columbian Centinel,* December 13, 1797.
9. *Ibid.,* January 17, 1798; "Extracts," December 10, 1797.
10. *Columbian Centinel,* December 20, 1797.
11. "Public Instrument of Protest," January 27, 1798, Megee Papers, Rhode Island Historical Society.
12. See Blotter E of the firm, entries from December 1797 through April 1798.
13. "Extracts," June 21, 1798.
14. "Extracts," Captain Cunningham's letter of October 6, 1801.

*Chapter 14—The Principal Agent of an Important Establishment*

1. Account Book, E. Bumstead & Co., January 25, 1803, Perkins Papers, MHS.
2. See Henry and Sidney Berry-Hill, *George Chinnery: 1774–1852, Artist of the China Coast* (Leigh-On-Sea, Eng., F. Lewis, 1963), p. 42; Ebenezer Townsend, Jr. Diary: "The Voyage of the Neptune," *New Haven Colony Historical Society*

*Papers,* 4 (1888), 1–115 (especially 97); Sullivan Dorr, "Letters," *Proceedings of the MHS,* 67 (1941–1944), 217–218.

3. Bumstead, account book, entries February through April 1804, MHS.
4. "Extracts," November 19, December 12, 1803; January 29, 1804.
5. "Extracts," December 12, 1803; January 1804; May 1804.
6. "Extracts," October 1804.
7. "Extracts," June 22, 1804.
8. See Journal F, entries for May through September.
9. Journal F, October 11, and 12, 1804.
10. *Columbian Centinel,* June 6, 1804.
11. "Extracts," September 1804. The "Extracts" are the source for the remainder of this chapter, with correspondence from November 1804 to June 1805.

*Chapter 15—Party Provoked To All Its Rage*

1. Charles Warren, *Jacobin and Junto* (Cambridge, Mass., Harvard University Press, 1931), p. 187, n. 1.
2. Eliza Cabot, "Reminiscences," SLR.
3. Bentley, *Diary,* III, 274; H. G. Otis to Woodbury Storer, August 29, 1804, Misc. Bound, vol. 18, MHS.
4. Draft letter, William Shaw to Fisher Ames, April 1805, Shaw Collection, BA.
5. Perkins to Shaw, February 8, 1806, Shaw Collection, BA.
6. *Chronicle,* February 27, 1806; William Minot to Leverett Saltonstall, March 1, 1806, Saltonstall Letters, vol. 3, no. 87, MHS.
7. *Chronicle,* March 3, 1806.
8. *Minutes and Proceedings of a Division Court Martial . . .* (Boston, E. Lincoln, 1806).
9. Walter Austin, *A Forgotten Duel* (Privately printed, 1914).
10. *Trial of T. O. Selfridge* (Boston, Russell and Cutler, 1807), p. 57.
11. *Ibid.,* pp. 7–8.
12. Bentley, *Diary,* III, 270.
13. Edward Warren, *The Life of John Collins Warren* (Boston, Ticknor and Fields, 1859), I, 68.

*Chapter 16—Strong Nerves and Long Purses*

1. "Extracts," May 26, 1806.
2. "Extracts," June 6, 1807; foreign letterbook, June 6, 1807.
3. Foreign letterbook, May 13, 1807.
4. *Ibid.,* May 22, 1807; "Extracts," April 23, 1807.
5. Foreign letterbook, May 13, 1807.
6. Foreign letterbook, May 22, 1807; July 13, 1807.
7. Perkins to William F. Megee, June 17, 1804, Megee Papers, Rhode Island Historical Society.
8. James and T. H. Perkins to Megee, December 27, 1803, Nightingale and Jenckes Papers, Rhode Island Historical Society.
9. Jacques M. Downs, "The Merchant As Gambler: Major William Fairchild Megee (1765–1820)," *Rhode Island History,* 28 (1969), 99–110.
10. F. W. Howay, "A List of Trading Vessels in Maritime Fur Trade, 1785–1825," *Transactions of the Royal Society of Canada,* 24 (1930), 111–134; 25 (1931), 117–149; 26 (1932), 43–86; 27 (1933), 119–149; 28 (1934), 11–49.

11. *Centinel,* September 6, 1806; "Extracts," February 1807.
12. "Extracts," October 29, 1806.
13. *Centinel,* February 7, 1807; "Extracts," February 1807.
14. Foreign letterbook, April 15, 1807.
15. *Ibid.,* July 8, 1807; July 6, 1807.
16. *Ibid.,* November 13, 1807.
17. *Ibid.,* August 1, 1807.
18. "Extracts," July 6, 1807.
19. "Extracts," July 10, 1807.
20. Foreign letterbook, August 1, 1807.
21. *Ibid.*
22. *Ibid.,* August 1, 1807; "Extracts," August 13, 1807.
23. Foreign letterbook, August 1, September 25, October 22, November 11, and November 19, 1807.

*Chapter 17—No Boat, Raft, or Float Can Pass Our Castle*

1. Foreign letterbook, January 2, 1808.
2. *Ibid.,* November 13, 1807.
3. The source for their plan is the foreign letterbook, March 29, 1808.
4. Bentley, *Diary,* III, 350; foreign letterbook, August 8, 1808.
5. Christopher Gore to Rufus King, June 16, 1808, King Papers, New York Historical Society.
6. Foreign letterbook, August 8, 1808.
7. Kenneth Wiggins Porter, *John Jacob Astor* (Cambridge, Mass., Harvard University Press, 1931), I, 145.
8. *Ibid.,* I, 146–149.
9. Foreign letterbook, November 16, 1808.
10. Mary and Catherine Byles, letterbook, February 2, 1809, MHS; Bentley, *Diary,* III, 408.
11. E. Quincy, ed., *Memoir of the Life of Eliza S. M. Quincy,* 113.
12. *Centinel,* January 25, 1809.
13. Theodore Sedgwick to Theodore Sedgwick, Jr., February 7, 1809, Sedgwick Papers, MHS.
14. Circular, March 8, 1809, Sedgwick Papers, MHS.
15. Foreign letterbook, March 21, 1809.
16. *Centinel,* March 29, 1809.
17. Foreign letterbook, December 7, 1809.

*Chapter 18—Short Blast on the Otter*

1. Blotter N, December 9, 1807.
2. "Extracts," December 7, 1807, to Dr. Hayward; December 7, 1807 to Johnson.
3. Monkton Iron Works letterbook, January 15, 1808. Original is at Vergennes Public Library; microfilm copies are at Baker Library, Harvard Business School, and MHS.
4. George Higginson to his wife, May 19, 1808, Higginson Papers, MHS; and May 20 and May 23, 1808.
5. Monkton letterbook, April 5, 1808, Vergennes Public Library.
6. *Ibid.,* July 28, 1808. The source for remainder of chapter is the Monkton letterbook, October 1808—August 1809.
7. *Ibid.,* August 17, 1809; foreign letterbook, October 2, 1809.

*Chapter 19—Far Different From Our Calculations*

1. Harrison G. Otis to Andrew Craigie, [1808] Craigie Papers, AAS.
2. Lucius R. Paige, *History of Cambridge* (Boston, H. O. Houghton and Company, 1877), pp. 204–206.
3. Eliza Cabot, "Reminiscences," SLR.
4. Frank Otto Gatell, *John Gorham Palfrey and the New England Conscience* (Cambridge, Mass., Harvard University Press, 1963), p. 14.
5. Monkton letterbook, October 18, September 29, 1810, Vergennes Public Library.
6. Eliza Cabot, "Reminiscences," SLR.
7. Foreign letterbook, October 2, 1809.
8. Monkton letterbook, December 8, 1809, Vergennes Public Library.
9. *Ibid.*, January 17, 1810.
10. Foreign letterbook, January 8, 9, 1810.
11. Monkton letterbook, March 20, April 28, May 10, 1810, Vergennes Public Library.
12. *Diary and Letters of Sir George Jackson* (London, R. Bentley and Son, 1872), October 7, 1809.
13. Monkton letterbook, July 12, 1810; and below, November 5, November 16, December 26, 1810.

*Chapter 20—With No One To Tell My Cares To*

1. Foreign letterbook, March 22, 1811.
2. *Ibid.*, May 5, March 24, 1811.
3. T. H. Perkins, diary, 1811–1812.
4. Alexander Everett, letterbook, vol. 9, November 8, 1811, MHS.
5. *Letters of James Savage* (Boston, Privately Printed, 1906), p. 4.
6. Perkins to Sarah Perkins, October 7, 1811.
7. *Ibid.*, October 4 and 7, 1811; William Gray to Harrison G. Otis, October 15 [1811], Otis Papers, MHS.
8. Samuel Eliot Morison, "The Henry-Crillon Affair of 1812," *Proceedings of the MHS,* 69 (1947–1950), 208.
9. Perkins to Sarah Perkins, November 3, 1811.
10. Henry Lee letterbook, November 24, 1811, Lee Papers, vol. 31, MHS.
11. Perkins to Sarah Perkins, November 11, 1811.
12. A. Everett letterbook, November 11, 1811, vol. 9, Everett Papers, MHS.
13. Morison, *Life and Letters of Otis,* II, 44.
14. U.S. Congress, Senate, *Report of the Committee on Foreign Relations,* 12th Cong., 1st sess., no. 244, 1812, pp. 555–556; and Henry Dearborn to H. A. S. Dearborn, March 21, 1812, BPL.
15. Perkins to Sarah Perkins, December 28, 1811; January 16, 1812.
16. "Memo at Dravel and at Cherbourgh in 1812," Perkins Papers, MHS.
17. "Notes for the Amusement of my Children," MHS.

*Chapter 21—Sticking by the Stall*

1. Eunice Callendar, diaries, June 24, 1812, SLR.
2. "Extracts," June 6, 1812. See Albert Z. Carr, *The Coming of the War* (New York, Doubleday, 1960), a good summary. Attention should be paid to its

splendid concluding essay which has broader implications than the special subject of the book.

3. Foreign letterbook, passim., and below, throughout late 1812.
4. Sarah Cabot to Samuel Cabot Jr., January 10, 1808, Cabot Papers, MHS.
5. Eliza Cabot, "Reminiscences," SLR.
6. Foreign letterbook, November 29, 1812.
7. *Ibid.,* January 6, 1813.
8. "Extracts," January 1813.
9. *Report of the Committee of the House of Representatives of Mass. on the subject of Impressed Seamen* (Boston, Russell & Cutler, 1813), James Perkins's testimony, p. 45; T. H. Perkins's testimony, p. 46.
10. Foreign letterbook, April 24, 1813; "Extracts," March 14, 1813.
11. "Extracts," April 13, 1813.
12. "Extracts," April 20, 1813
13. Nathaniel Spooner to Nathaniel Spooner Jr., June 2, 1813, *Proceedings of the MHS,* 21 (1884–1885), 374–379; Bentley, *Diary,* II, 172.
14. Foreign letterbook, June 28, 1813.
15. "Extracts," July 20, 1813.
16. Trial references are Tyng: 9 Mass 522 (March 1813 term) and 11 Mass 76 (March 1814 term).
17. "Extracts," September 20, 1813.
18. Foreign letterbook, October 26, 1813.
19. G. B. Sawyer, "Biographical Sketch of H. B. Sawyer," *Vermont Historical Magazine,* 1 (1867), 585. G. B. Sawyer dates the voyage a year later than we do, but on that second voyage T. H. Perkins, Jr., was a supercargo and would not have been swabbing decks.
20. Foreign letterbook, January 5, January 14, March 5, 1814.
21. Perkins to Welles, March 21, 1814, Vergennes Public Library.
22. *Boston Centinel,* April 16, 1814.
23. "Extracts," April 14, 1814.
24. *Boston Gazette,* April 14, 1814.
25. Bentley, *Diary,* IV, 260; *Independent Chronicle,* June 20, 1814.

*Chapter 22—A Great Shaking*

1. Reward poster for George Francis Stuart, Perkins Papers, MHS.
2. "Extracts," June 29, 1814. Most likely an error for the ninth.
3. Foreign letterbook, June 19, 1814.
4. *Boston Patriot,* June 22, 1814.
5. Charles Sandos to James Perkins, July 19, 1814, MHS.
6. Sandos to James Perkins, August 9, 1814, MHS.
7. Nathaniel Bowditch to Elizabeth Clarke, October 14, 1814, Forbes Collection, Museum of the American China Trade, Milton; Bentley, *Diary,* IV, 281.
8. Benjamin Goddard, diary, September 8, 1814, Brookline Public Library. See also Walter K. Watkins, "The Defence of Boston in the War of 1812," *Proceedings of the Bostonian Society* (1899), 35–37.
9. *Centinel,* September 21, 1814; Isaac Winslow to Miss Elizabeth Winslow, September 23, 1814, Winslow Papers, MHS.
10. Pickering Papers, vol. 15, p. 38, MHS.
11. T. H. Perkins to Welles, October 1814, Vergennes Public Library.

12. Pickering Papers, vol. 15, p. 44; vol. 30, p. 292, MHS.
13. *Centinel,* October 8, 1814.
14. Brooks to Pickering, November 26, 1814, Pickering Papers, MHS.
15. *Centinel,* November 9, 1814. The editor was Alexander C. Hansom writing in the *Federal Republican,* November 7, 1814.
16. Henry Adams, *History of the United States 1813–1817* (New York, Antiquarian Press, 1962; Charles Scribner's Sons, 1891–1896), p. 294.
17. Otis to C. Gore, December 3, 1814, Otis Papers, MHS.
18. *Boston Yankee,* February 3, 1815.
19. Otis to Mrs. H. G. Otis, February 5, 1815, Otis Papers, MHS; and below, letter of February 9.
20. Morison, *Harrison Gray Otis,* p. 168.
21. T. G. Cary, *Memoir of T. H. Perkins,* p. 219.
22. Otis Ammidon to Jonathan Russell, February 20, 1815, *Proceedings of the MHS*, 54 (1920–1921), 78; Callendar, diary, February 13, 1815.
23. Otis to Mrs. H. G. Otis, February 20, 1815, MHS; Irving Brant, *James Madison, Commander In Chief* (New York, Bobbs-Merrill Co., 1961), VI, 370.
24. Otis to Mrs. H. G. Otis, February 28, 1815, MHS.
25. Samuel Williams to J. & T. H. Perkins, August 16, 1814.
26. John B. Green to T. H. Perkins, August 22, 1814.
27. T. H. Perkins to Samuel Williams, October 8, 1814.
28. Williams to T. H. Perkins, November 17, 1814.
29. Williams to T. H. Perkins, February 21, 1815.
30. Sandos to James Perkins, February 22, 1815.

*Chapter 23—A Cavalcade of Boston Gentlemen*

1. "Extracts," November 1, 1814.
2. "Extracts," June 19, 1805.
3. "Extracts," November 14, 1815.
4. *Ibid.* See however, T. H. Perkins's important letter to Charles Bulfinch, December 21, 1817, at New-York Historical Society.
5. Augustus T. Perkins, *A Private Proof . . . of the Perkins Family* (Boston, T. R. Marvin & Son, 1890), pp. 38–39.
6. Capt. Samuel Hill, "Autobiography," New York Public Library. See also James W. Snyder, Jr., ed., "Voyage of the *Ophelia* from Boston to Canton (excerpts)," *New England Quarterly,* 10 (1937), 355–386.
7. Snyder, "Voyage of the *Ophelia,*" pp. 361–362.
8. January 19, 1817, Forbes Collection, Harvard Business School; Robert Bennet Forbes, *Personal Reminiscences* (2d ed. revised; Boston, Little, Brown, 1882), p. 30.
9. George Dangerfield, *The Era of Good Feelings* (New York, Harcourt, Brace, 1952), p. 177; "Extracts," March 14, 1814.
10. "Extracts," December 21, 1816.
11. Gore to King, December 25, 1816, Rufus King Papers, NYHS.
12. Aaron White, diary, July 2, 1817, MHS.
13. Callendar, diary, July 2, 1817, MHS.
14. Susan Quincy, diary, July 6, 1817, MHS.

15. *Records of the Governor and Council of the State of Vermont* (Montpelier, Joseph Poland, 1880), VIII, 448.

*Chapter 24—A Plain Unvarnished Tale*

1. Bentley, *Diary,* IV, 539.
2. *Boston Daily Advertiser,* November 25, 1848. Perkins's account of seeing the sea serpent printed here is taken from a letter he wrote to J. P. Cushing on October 13, 1820.
3. Sir Charles Lyell, *A Second Visit to the United States . . .* (New York, Harper & Brothers, 1849), p. 112.
4. *Boston Daily Advertiser,* November 25, 1848.
5. C. G. Cary, ed., *The Cary Letters* (Cambridge, Mass., Riverside Press, 1891), p. 226, and below, passim.
6. Foreign letterbook, March 7, 1814.
7. *Centinel,* January 24, 1818. See also Nathaniel Bowditch, *A History of the Massachusetts General Hospital* (Boston, J. Wilson & Son, 1851).
8. William James Reid, *The Building of the Cape Cod Canal* (Privately printed, 1961), pp. 4–7.
9. *Centinel,* February 14, 1818.
10. "Extracts," March 24, 1818.
11. "Extracts," May 6, 1818.
12. "Extracts," November 8, 1817.
13. *Centinel,* November 28, 1818.
14. "Extracts," December 12, 1817; and below, January–July, 1819, passim.
15. *Centinel,* August 28, 1819.

*Chapter 25—The Late Event in My Family*

1. Eliza Cabot, "Reminiscences," SLR.
2. A. T. Perkins, *A Private Proof,* p. 60.
3. Cabot, "Reminiscences," SLR.
4. Mrs. Samuel Perkins to F. W. Paine, November 9 [1820], Paine Papers, AAS. For the reasons we assigned this letter to 1820 see our extended notes at MHS.
5. "Extracts," November 1819.
6. Cabot, "Reminiscences," SLR.
7. H. G. Otis to T. H. Perkins, April 22, 1820, Otis Papers, MHS.
8. James Perkins to H. G. Otis, April 29, 1820, Otis Papers, MHS.
9. "Extracts," May 27, 1820.
10. George W. Sturgis to Paine, August 8, 1816, Paine Papers, AAS.
11. Paine to Bancroft, October 8, 1819, Bancroft Papers, MHS.
12. R. B. Forbes, *Personal Reminiscences,* p. 58.
13. Perkins & Co., Canton, letterbook, January 23, 1820, Harvard Business School.
14. Paine to Bancroft, August 6, 1820, Bancroft Papers, MHS.
15. T. H. Perkins, 1820 diary, Perkins Papers, MHS.
16. "Extracts," March 24, 1818.
17. Perkins & Co., Canton, letterbook, March 27, 1820, Harvard Business School.
18. *Ibid.,* December 30, 1820.
19. *Ibid.,* April 15, 1821.
20. Paine to Bancroft, June 7, 1820, Bancroft Papers, MHS.
21. "Extracts," January 18, 1821; May 25, 1821.

22. Perkins & Co., Canton, letterbook, November 17, 1821, Harvard Business School.

*Chapter 26—The Consequences of Leaving Off His Flannels*

1. Mabel M. Swan, *The Athenaeum Gallery* (Boston, Boston Athenaeum, 1940), pp. 4–5.
2. Perkins to Quincy, December 16, 1838, Cabot Collection, SLR.
3. James Perkins's will $120^2$–159, inventory $120^2$–381, accounting $121^2$–169, Suffolk County Probate records.
4. Perkins to Timothy Pickering, October 28, 1822, Pickering Papers, vol. 31, p. 407, MHS.
5. *Centinel,* January 11, January 15, 1823.
6. C. G. Cary, ed., *Cary Letters,* p. 299; J. Elliot Cabot, "Reminiscences," typescript at SLR.
7. Perkins & Co., Canton, letterbook, November 7, 1822, Harvard Business School.
8. Perkins to Paine, April 1, 1823, Paine Papers, AAS.
9. This and successive descriptions of the hotel are from the circular on the Nahant Hotel at MHS.
10. Callendar, diary, August 30, 1823, SLR.
11. *Daily Advertiser,* December 23, 1823.
12. Perkins to Cushing, April 28, 1824, Perkins Papers, MHS.
13. Charles Francis Adams, *Diary* (Cambridge, Mass., Harvard University Press, 1964), VI, 232.
14. This and the quotations in the following paragraph from M. A. DeWolfe Howe, ed., *The Articulate Sisters* (Cambridge, Mass., Harvard University Press, 1946), pp. 51–61.
15. R. B. Forbes, *Personal Reminiscences,* p. 80.
16. *Ibid.,* p. 81; Eliza Cabot, "Reminiscences," SLR.
17. R. B. Forbes, *Personal Reminiscences,* pp. 81–82.
18. Thomas Forbes to Perkins, November 1, 1824, MHS.

*Chapter 27—Too Much for Mortal Man To Bear*

1. See George Washington Warren, *The History of the Bunker Hill Monument Association* (Boston, James R. Osgood Co., 1877).
2. See William W. Wheildon, *Memoir of Solomon Willard* (Boston, Bunker Hill Monument Association, 1865).
3. Josiah Quincy, *Figures of the Past,* new ed. (Boston, Little, Brown, 1926), p. 111.
4. Elizabeth Peabody to Maria Chase, September 3, 1824 [error for 1825], in *Essex Institute Historical Collections,* 85 (1949), 363.
5. *Proceedings of the Brookline Historical Society* (1903), p. 17.

*Chapter 28—Great Means, Ardent Public Spirit, and Pertinacious Enterprise*

1. Perkins to Dearborn, October 17, 1825, BPL.
2. Willard to George Ticknor, June 1825, BHMA Papers, MHS.
3. Peter C. Brooks, account books, December 7, 1825, MHS.
4. Bryant & Sturgis to Joshua Bates, December 17, 1825, Bryant & Sturgis letterbook, Harvard Business School.
5. "Extracts," February 2, 1826.
6. Justin Winsor, ed. *The Memorial History of Boston* (Boston, Ticknor & Co., 1881), IV, 227–228.

7. Granite Railway Co., to Milton Selectmen, March 15, 1826, Granite Railway Company records, MHS; and Perkins to William Tudor, October 14, 1826, Perkins Papers, MHS.
8. "Extracts," August 10, 1826.
9. Perkins, 1826 diary.
10. "Extracts," August 10, 1826.
11. *Boston Commercial Gazette,* September 11, 1826.
12. Cushing to Perkins, April 1826; and "Extracts," September 17, 1826.
13. Anon., *History of the Granite Railway Company* (Boston, Alfred Mudge & Son, 1870); Historic American Buildings Survey, No. Mass 150, sheets 1–6; contemporary archaelogical work of Mr. Richard Muzzrole, 1957–1962; and Willard to Warren, July 1826, BHMA Papers, MHS.
14. *American Farmer* (Baltimore), June 22, 1827.
15. Thomas Forbes to Cushing, April 3, 1827, Perkins Papers, MHS.
16. Perkins to Cushing, January 11, 1827.
17. "Extracts," May 18, 1827.
18. Here and below, the letters referred to are part of the BHMA Papers, MHS. May 1827, BHMA Papers, MHS.
19. Perkins to Lawrence, June 28, 1827, Lawrence Papers, MHS.
20. John Quincy Adams, *Memoirs* (Philadelphia, J. B. Lippincott Co., 1874–1877) VII, 322.

*Chapter 29—In the Teeth of Mr. P.*

1. Here and below, the source of the quoted material is John Dodge, *Report of the Case of John Dodge, Executor . . . vs. Thomas H. Perkins* (Boston, F. Ingraham, 1830).
2. J. Q. Adams to Perkins, October 3, 1827, Perkins Papers, MHS.
3. Henry Adams, *Documents Relative to New-England Federalism* (Boston, Little, Brown, 1877), p. 44.
4. J. Q. Adams, *Memoirs,* VIII, 78, 79.
5. Everett to Perkins, December 7, 1828.
6. J. Q. Adams, *Memoirs,* VIII, 87–88.
7. H. Adams, *Documents,* pp. 46–62.
8. Perkins to Sullivan, n.d. [1829], Wendell Family Papers, MHS.
9. J. Q. Adams, *Memoirs,* VIII, 115.
10. *Ibid.,* VIII, 237.

*Chapter 30—Retiring from the Bustle?*

1. Cushing to Forbes, March 31, 1828, Museum of the American China Trade. See also *Business History Review,* 40 (1966), 98–107.
2. Sturgis to Bates, December 31, 1828, Baring Brothers Archives, London, HC5.1.10; and Sarah Forbes Hughes, ed., *Letters and Recollections of John Murray Forbes* (Boston, Houghton Mifflin Company, 1899), I, 57.
3. John P. Cushing, letterbook, December 26, 1828, Harvard Business School.
4. Sturgis to Bates, December 31, 1828, HC5.1.10, Baring Brothers Archives, London.
5. John P. Cushing, letterbook, October 13, 1828; November 23, 1828; December 26, 1828, Harvard Business School.
6. *Ibid.,* January 19, 1829; February 1, 1829.

7. Hughes, *John Murray Forbes,* I, 58–59.
8. *Ibid.*
9. Edith Perkins Cunningham, *Owls Nest* (Cambridge, Mass., Riverside Press, 1907), p. 29.
10. Hughes, *John Murray Forbes,* I, 54–55.
11. T. H. Perkins, 1829 journal.
12. Perkins to Bates, September 15, 1829, HC5.1.10, Baring Brothers Archives, London.
13. John P. Cushing, letterbook, September 26, 1829, Harvard Business School; Perkins, 1829 journal.
14. Perkins to Bates, October 28, 1829, HC5.1.10, Baring Brothers Archives, London.
15. Perkins to Tudor, August 15, 1828.
16. Willard to Warren [1828], BHMA Papers, MHS.
17. Perkins to Dearborn, June 17, 1829, BHMA Papers, MHS; and Willard to Dearborn, September 2, 1829, BPL.
18. Henry Lee, "Boston's Greatest Hotel," *Old-Time New England,* 55 (1965), 97–106.
19. *Daily Advertiser,* October 19, 1829.
20. John P. Cushing, letterbook, November 17, December 10, 1829, Harvard Business School.
21. *Ibid.,* December 10, 1829.
22. "Extracts," January 14, 1830; John P. Cushing, letterbook, April 15, 1830.
23. R. B. Forbes, *Personal Reminiscences,* pp. 128–130.
24. "Extracts," March 27, 1830.
25. John P. Cushing, letterbook, April 17, 1830.
26. R. B. Forbes, *Personal Reminiscences,* pp. 131–133.
27. Forbes to Cushing, May 30, 1830, Museum of the American China Trade, Milton.
28. "Extracts," October 20, 1830.
29. "Extracts," November 18, 1830; and below, February 17, 1831.
30. Granite Railway Company records, March 18, 1831, Harvard Business School.
31. Perkins to Cushing, May 10, 1831.
32. Perkins to Bates, October 10, 1831, HC5.1.10, Baring Brothers Archives, London.

*Chapter 31—This Class of the Human Family*

1. Howe, *Articulate Sisters,* pp. 218–221.
2. Martha Ward to T. W. Ward, May 15, 1833, Ward Papers, MHS.
3. G. Parish, Jr., *Scenes at the Fair* (Boston, James B. Dow, 1833), pp. 1, 8.
4. C. Harvey Gardiner, ed., *The Papers of William H. Prescott* (Urbana, University of Illinois Press, 1964), p. 90.
5. T. W. Tucker, *Bannisters Lane* (Boston, Cheltenham Press, 1899), p. 31.
6. Rev. John Pierce, "Memoirs," VI, 87–88, MHS.
7. Otis to S. G. Howe, May 2, 1838, Records of the Perkins School for the Blind, Watertown, Mass.
8. Perkins to Otis, May 25, 1838, Perkins School for the Blind.
9. Charles Dickens, *American Notes* (London, Chapman & Hall Ltd., n.d.), pp. 44–47.

*Chapter 32—I Try To Be Contented with What I Have*

1. Pierce, "Memoirs," VI, 86–88, MHS.
2. F. H. Herrick, *Audubon the Naturalist* (New York, D. Appleton & Co., 1917), II, 28.
3. J. F. Graustein, *Thomas Nuttall, Naturalist* (Cambridge, Mass., Harvard University Press, 1967), p. 246.
4. C. G. Curtis, *Memories of Fifty Years* (Boston, privately printed, 1947), pp. 33–35.
5. Eliza Cabot, "Reminiscences," SLR.
6. Alice G. B. Lockwood, ed., *Gardens of Colony and State* (New York, Charles Scribner's Sons, 1931), I, 46.
7. Curtis, *Memories of Fifty Years,* p. 35; John P. Cushing, diary, August 3, 1831, Boston Athenaeum.
8. Perkins to Bates, March 12, 1832, Baring Brothers Archives, HC5.1.10.
9. Howard Corning, ed., *Letters of John James Audubon* (Boston, Club of Odd Volumes, 1930), p. 215; M. Ward to T. Ward, April 1833, Ward Papers, MHS; *ibid.*, April 26, 1833.
10. Hughes, *John Murray Forbes,* I, 89.
11. Cunningham, *Owls Nest,* p. 95.
12. Perkins, diary, April 4, 1835.
13. Perkins, diary, May 10, 12, 1835.
14. William H. Sumner, *History of East Boston* (Boston, J. E. Tilton & Co., 1858), p. 496.
15. Henry Huntt, *A Visit to the Red Sulphur Springs of Virginia* (Boston, Dutton & Wentworth, 1839), p. 3.
16. Thomas C. Grattan, *Civilized America* (London, Bradbury & Evans, 1859), pp. 42, 43, 52–53, 91–92.
17. Allan Nevins, ed., *The Diary of Philip Hone* (New York, Dodd Mead & Co., 1927), pp. 358, 359.
18. Pierce, "Memoirs," VII, 478.

*Chapter 33—A Flicker in the Dying Flame*

1. E. Cabot to J. Elliot Cabot, January 29, 30, 1841; and S. Cabot to J. Elliot Cabot, February 25, 1841, Cabot Papers, SLR.
2. R. B. Forbes to Rose Forbes, March 10, March 14, March 21, 1841, Museum of the American China Trade, Milton.
3. R. B. Forbes, "Diary of a Trip to Europe 1841," Museum of the American China Trade, Milton; T. H. Perkins, diary, 1841, MHS.
4. Committee to Perkins, July 23, 1841, Misc. Bound, MHS; T. H. Perkins, manuscript notes for speech, 1841, MHS. Also printed in *Proceedings of the Bostonian Society* (1894), pp. 24–35.
5. M. Cary to J. E. Cabot, August 7, 1842, Cabot Papers, SLR.
6. W. Cabot to J. E. Cabot, November 25, 1842, Cabot Papers, SLR.
7. Pierce, "Memoirs," 1843, pp. 43–49; *Proceedings of the MHS,* 42 (1908–1909), 409.
8. E. C. Agassiz to Mary P. Cary, April [?], 25, 1852, Cary Papers, SLR.
9. Robert F. Lucid, ed., *The Journal of Richard Henry Dana Jr.* (Cambridge, Mass., Harvard University Press, 1968), p. 399.
10. A. T. Perkins, *A Private Proof,* p. 112.

11. S. Cabot to J. E. Cabot, March 27, 1852, Cabot Papers, SLR.
12. Tom Cary Jr., diary (typescript only), Cary Papers, SLR.

*Chapter 34—Unveil Thy Bosom, Faithful Tomb!*

1. Ellen Dwight to Ellen Twisleton, January 16, 1854, Cabot Papers, SLR.
2. Henry D. Thoreau, *Journals,* ed. Bradford Torrey and Francis H. Allen (New York, Dover Publications, 1962), p. 682.
3. E. Dwight to E. Twisleton, January 16, 1854, Cabot Papers, SLR.
4. *Daily Evening Traveller,* January 14, 1854.
5. The will is in Suffolk Probate, vol. 152, pp. 98–108, docket no. 38877.

# Index

# Index

# Index

# Index

# Index

# Index

# Index

# Harvard Studies in Business History

1. JOHN JACOB ASTOR, BUSINESS MAN, by Kenneth Wiggins Porter*
2. JAY COOKE, PRIVATE BANKER, by Henrietta M. Larson*
3. THE JACKSONS AND THE LEES: TWO GENERATIONS OF MASSACHUSETTS MERCHANTS, 1765–1844, by Kenneth Wiggins Porter*
4. THE MASSACHUSSETS–FIRST NATIONAL BANK OF BOSTON, 1784–1934, by N. S. B. Gras*
5. THE HISTORY OF AN ADVERTISING AGENCY: N. W. AYER & SON AT WORK, 1869–1949, revised edition, by Ralph M. Hower*
6. MARKETING LIFE INSURANCE: ITS HISTORY IN AMERICA, by J. Owen Stalson*
7. HISTORY OF MACY'S OF NEW YORK, 1858–1919: CHAPTERS IN THE EVOLUTION OF THE DEPARTMENT STORE, by Ralph M. Hower
8. THE WHITESMITHS OF TAUNTON: A HISTORY OF REED & BARTON, 1824–1943, by George Sweet Gibb*
9. DEVELOPMENT OF TWO BANK GROUPS IN THE CENTRAL NORTHWEST: A STUDY IN BANK POLICY AND ORGANIZATION, by Charles Sterling Popple*
10. THE HOUSE OF HANCOCK: BUSINESS IN BOSTON, 1724–1775, by W. T. Baxter*
11. TIMING A CENTURY: HISTORY OF THE WALTHAM WATCH COMPANY, by C. W. Moore*
12. GUIDE TO BUSINESS HISTORY: MATERIALS FOR THE STUDY OF AMERICAN BUSINESS AND SUGGESTIONS FOR THEIR USE, BY Henrietta M. Larson*
13. PEPPERELL'S PROGRESS: HISTORY OF A COTTON TEXTILE COMPANY, 1844–1945, by Evelyn H. Knowlton*
14. THE HOUSE OF BARING IN AMERICAN TRADE AND FINANCE: ENGLISH MERCHANT BANKERS AT WORK, 1763–1861, by Ralph W. Hidy*
15. THE WHITIN MACHINE WORKS SINCE 1831: A TEXTILE MACHINERY COMPANY IN AN INDUSTRIAL VILLAGE, by Thomas R. Navin*
16. THE SACO-LOWELL SHOPS: TEXTILE MACHINERY BUILDING IN NEW ENGLAND, 1813–1949, by George Sweet Gibb*
17. BROADLOOMS AND BUSINESSMEN: A

*Harvard Studies in Business History*

HISTORY OF THE BIGELOW–SANFORD CARPET COMPANY, 1825–1953, by John S. Ewing and Nancy P. Norton

18. NATHAN TROTTER: PHILADELPHIA MERCHANT, 1787–1853, by Elva Tooker

19. A HISTORY OF THE MASSACHUSETTS HOSPITAL LIFE INSURANCE COMPANY, by Gerald T. White

20. THE CHARLES ILFELD COMPANY: A STUDY OF THE RISE AND DECLINE OF MERCANTILE CAPITALISM IN NEW MEXICO, by William J. Parish

21. THE RISE AND DECLINE OF THE MEDICI BANK, 1397–1494, by Raymond de Roover

22. ISAAC HICKS: NEW YORK MERCHANT AND QUAKER, 1767–1820, by Robert A. Davison

23. BOSTON CAPITALISTS AND WESTERN RAILROADS: A STUDY IN THE NINETEENTH CENTURY RAILROAD INVESTMENT PROCESS, by Arthur M. Johnson and Barry E. Supple

24. PETROLEUM PIPELINES AND PUBLIC POLICY, 1906–1959, by Arthur M. Johnson

25. INVESTMENT BANKING IN AMERICA: A HISTORY, by Vincent P. Carosso

26. MERCHANT PRINCE OF BOSTON: COL. T. H. PERKINS, 1764–1854, by Carl Seaburg and Stanley Paterson

* Out of print

Bei Fragen zur Produktsicherheit wenden Sie sich bitte an:
If you have any questions regarding product safety,
please contact:

Walter de Gruyter GmbH
Genthiner Straße 13
10785 Berlin
productsafety@degruyterbrill.com